THE ASLA REPORT ON INTERLIBRARY COOPERATION 1978

SECOND
EDITION

Compiled and Edited
by the
ASLA Interlibrary Cooperation Committee

Chicago
ASSOCIATION OF STATE LIBRARY AGENCIES
1978

Production Assistance by
Aeonian Press, Mattituck, NY 11952

International Standard Book Number: 0-8389-5539-8
Library of Congress Catalog Card Number: 77-94411

Printed in the United States of America

CONTENTS

CONTENTS

PREFACE

The 1978 ASLA Report on Interlibrary Cooperation, second edition, is a compilation of information on current interlibrary cooperation activities in the United States, as reported by the state and territorial library agencies. The information was collected via a survey designed and conducted by the Subcommittee to Produce the 1978 Report of the Interlibrary Cooperation Committee of the Association of State Library Agencies.

A number of changes were made in the expanded second edition, most of them the results of suggestions of users of the 1976 Report. Each agency was asked to add an overview of statewide interlibrary cooperation activities; to list name, address, administrator, type of library served, and financial support sources for each individual cooperative, whether supported by state or by other sources; and to provide fuller information on the extent of participation in multi-state library networks. A set of appendices and a detailed index have been added to make the Report more useful.

The codes denoting types of libraries served are: "p" for public; "a" for academic; "sp" for special; and "sch" for school. Unless otherwise indicated, the states used fiscal 1977 data throughout their responses. The terms "federal support" means only funds disbursed through the state library agency. Other definitions may be found in the Instructions for Completing the Questionnaire, part of the survey instrument in Appendix I.

The second edition is the only single source now available for such broad coverage on current interlibrary cooperation activities. During this dynamic period when cooperative activities are expanding rapidly it is necessary to record the information herein, for decision and assessment purposes. This record would not have been possible without the cooperation of the respondents, who collected the data requested, converted it to camera-ready format, and submitted it in time for publication. The ASLA Subcommittee appreciates this cooperation by the state and territorial agencies as well as the work of special volunteers who made extraordinary efforts to get the Report produced.

Special thanks are due to Jean Ernst for preparing the index, to Zelda Schiffenbauer for index pagination, to Shelley Hutter for work on the appendices, to Margaret Martin for her re-typing work, and to Sandy Cooper for completing the final proofreading.

The ASLA Subcommittee sincerely hopes its publication will aid in the useful exchange of information about interlibrary cooperation.

The ASLA Subcommittee to Produce the 1978 Report

Richard G. Akeroyd, Jr.
William T. DeJohn
W. Lyle Eberhart
Ruth J. Patrick
Mary R. Power
Donald B. Simpson
Beth A. Hamilton, Chair

ACKNOWLEDGEMENTS

The Board of Directors of the Association of State
Library Agencies and the ASLA Committee on Interlibrary Cooperation acknowledge Beth Hamilton for her
fine contribution to ASLA and the library profession.
Her efforts in coordinating the survey process and edit-
orial work of the Interlibrary Cooperation Subcommittee
have resulted in a greatly expanded and improved edition
of this publication.

1. REPORTING AGENCY

    A.   Alabama Public Library Service*
        6030 Monticello Drive
        Montgomery, Alabama 36130

        * A bill will be filed in the next session of the Ala-
          bama Legislature to change the name of the agency to
          "Alabama State Library".

    B.   Chief Officer: Anthony W. Miele, Director

    C.   Fiscal Year: 1976

2. OVERVIEW

There are ten multi-county regional public library systems
and fourteen single-county regional libraries involving
51 of the 67 counties in Alabama. 89.3% of the population
is served by libraries participating in these systems.

Regional systems may be formed under Section 11-90-4 of the
1975 Revised Code of Alabama. This section enables the
library boards of counties and municipalities to contract
with the library boards of another political unit or
government agency to establish or maintain joint library
services. Independent town libraries in the 15 counties
that are not part of regional systems are required to work
through a county library development committee appointed by
the county commission in order to receive state aid. Alabama may enter into interstate library contracts under
Section 41-8-20 of the 1975 code. Model library legislation
regarding multi-type library systems and improved mechanisms
for interlibrary cooperation will be one product of a major
library systems study being conducted during 1977 for the
Alabama Public Library Service by the Public Administration
Service.

3. NUMBER OF LIBRARIES IN THE STATE

Academic:	56
Public:	176
School:	1605
Public:	1312
Private:	293
Special:	124
Profit:	80 est.
Nonprofit:	44 est.
TOTAL:	1961 est.

4. STATE AGENCY INTERLIBRARY COOPERATION UNIT

> Unit Name: Library Development Division
> Person in Charge: Bob Schremser, Consultant for Networks
>   and Institutional Libraries
> No other units charged with interlibrary cooperation activi-
> ties.

5. OTHER STATE-LEVEL GOVERNMENTAL ILC UNITS

There are none.

6. OTHER STATE-LEVEL NON-GOVERNMENTAL ILC UNITS

There are none.

7. SINGLE-TYPE LIBRARY COOPERATIVES

> A. Receiving Continuing Financial Support from the State Library:
>
> > (1) Name: Autauga-Prattville Public Library
> >   Address: Washington Street
> >   Prattville AL 36067
> >   Telephone: 205-365-3396
> >   Administrator: Mrs. Shirley Laseter
> >   Type of Library Served: p
> >   Federal Support: $44,313 (Includes $36,176 Revenue
> >   State Support: $7,266   Sharing)
> >   Local Support: $50,085
> >   Other Support: $10,076
> >   Total Support: $111,740
> >
> > (2) Name: Baldwin County Library Service
> >   Address: P. O. Box 127
> >   Summerdale AL   36580
> >   Telephone: 205-989-6639
> >   Administrator: Mrs. Nancy Bettencourt
> >   Type of Library Served: p
> >   Federal Support: $65,027 (Includes $46,557 Revenue
> >   State Support: $13,468   Sharing)
> >   Local Support: $115,258
> >   Other Support: $55,394
> >   Total Support: $249,147
> >
> > (3) Name: Birmingham-Jefferson County Library
> >   Address: 2020 7th Avenue, North
> >   Birmingham AL   35203
> >   Telephone: 205-254-2551
> >   Administrator: Mr. George R. Stewart
> >   Type of Library Served: p

(continued)

7. SINGLE-TYPE LIBRARY COOPERATIVES (continued)

    (3) Federal Support: $145,696 (Includes $11,236 Revenue
        State Support: $83,713   Sharing)
        Local Support: $2,908,041
        Other Support: $261,171
        Total Support: $3,398,621

    (4) Name: Cahaba Regional Library
        Address: 100 First Avenue
                          Clanton AL   35045
        Telephone: 205-755-2130
        Administrator: Lester McKiernan
        Type of Library Served: p
        Federal Support: $12,367 (Includes $679 Revenue Sharing)
        State Support: $13,577
        Local Support: $58,900
        Other Support: $6,758
        Total Support: $91,602

    (5) Name: Carl Elliott Regional Library
        Address: 20th E. 18th Street
                          Jasper AL   35501
        Telephone: 205-221-2567
        Administrator: Mrs. Willa Dean Daniel
        Type of Library Served: p
        Federal Support: $23,318 (Includes $7,509 Revenue
        State Support: $17,890   Sharing)
        Local Support: $146,466
        Other Support: $6,044
        Total Support: $193,718

    (6) Name: Cheaha Regional Library
        Address: 108 E. 10th Street
                          Anniston AL   36201
        Telephone: 205-238-1581
        Administrator: Nettie Whitley
        Type of Library Served: p
        Federal Support: $67,621 (Includes $45,472 Revenue
        State Support: $37,905   Sharing)
        Local Support: $486,870
        Other Support: $47,637
        Total Support: $640,033

    (7) Name: Choctawhatchee Regional Library*
        Address: 320 James Street
                          Ozark AL   36360
        Telephone: 205-774-5480
        Administrator: Mrs. Alice Doughtie (Retires Oct. 1,
        Type of Library Served: p   1977)

(continued)

7. SINGLE-TYPE LIBRARY COOPERATIVES (continued)

   (7) Federal Support: $44,282 (Includes $2,188 Revenue
     State Support: $37,324   Sharing)
     Local Support: $176,659
     Other Support: $44,964
     Total Support: $303,229

*This regional library will merge with the Dothan Public Library
on a demonstration basis in 1978. Mr. Frank Walker will be
the Project Director.

   (8) Name: Cross Trails Regional Library
     Address: U. S. Highway 331, N.
             Opp AL   36467
     Telephone: 205-493-6423
     Administrator: Mr. George G. Johnson
     Type of Library Served: p
     Federal Support: $38,284 (Includes $12,395 Revenue
     State Support: $37,422   Sharing)
     Local Support: $169,019
     Other Support: $14,570
     Total Support: $259,295

   (9) Name: Cullman County Library
     Address: 200 Clarke Street, N.E.
             Cullman AL   35055
     Telephone: 205-734-2720
     Administrator: Mrs. Bettina Higdon
     Type of Library Served: p
     Federal Support: $13,927 (Includes $914 Revenue
     State Support: $10,929   Sharing)
     Local Support: $41,909
     Other Support: $18,463
     Total Support: $85,228

   (10) Name: Friedman-Tuscaloosa County Library
     Address: 1305 24th Avenue
             Tuscaloosa AL   35401
     Telephone: 205-759-5141
     Administrator: Mrs. Bessie Sasser
     Type of Library Served: p
     Federal Support: $31,987 (Includes $2,021 Revenue
     State Support: $19,863   Sharing)
     Local Support: $233,750
     Other Support: $40,016
     Total Support: $325,616

   (11) Name: George S. Houston-Dothan Public
                      Library

(continued)

7.   SINGLE-TYPE LIBRARY COOPERATIVES (continued)

     (11)   Address: 212 W. Burdeshaw Street
                                 Dothan AL 36301
            Telephone: 205-792-3164
            Administrator: Mr. Wayne Love
            Type of Library Served: p
            Federal Support: $41,266 (Includes $23,486 Revenue
            State Support: $11,121   Sharing)
            Local Support: $214,289
            Other Support: $40,016
            Total Support: $306,692

     (12)   Name: H. Grady Bradshaw-Chambers County
            Address: Highway 29   Library
                                 Shawmut AL 36876
            Telephone: 205-768-3150
            Administrator: Ms. Jane Alston
            Type of Library Served: p
            Federal Support: $17,661 (Includes $2,663 Revenue
            State Support: $8,708   Sharing)
            Local Support: $39,274
            Other Support: $18,049
            Total Support: $83,692

     (13)   Name: Horseshoe Bend Regional Library
            Address: 203 West Street
                                 Dadeville AL 36853
            Telephone: 205-825-9232
            Administrator: Mrs. Myretta Holden
            Type of Library Served: p
            Federal Support: $63,461 (Includes $33,207 Revenue
            State Support: $34,491   Sharing)
            Local Support: $158,228
            Other Support: $22,271
            Total Support: $278,451

     (14)   Name: Macon County-Tuskegee Library
            Address: 118 Eastside
                                 Tuskegee AL 36083
            Telephone: 205-727-5192
            Administrator: Ms. Miriam Martin
            Type of Library Service: p
            Federal Support: $5,650 (Includes $433 Revenue
            State Support: $7,346   Sharing)
            Local Support: $58,532
            Other Support: $5
            Total Support: $71,533

(continued)

7. SINGLE-TYPE LIBRARY COOPERATIVES (continued)

    (15) Name: Mobile City-County Library
          Address: 701 Government Street
                                Mobile AL   36602

- **Name:** Mobile City-County Library
- **Address:** 701 Government Street, Mobile AL 36602
- **Telephone:** 205-433-0483
- **Administrator:** Mr. Dallas Baillio
- **Type of Library Served:** p
- **Federal Support:** $266,711 (Includes $149,277 Revenue Sharing)
- **State Support:** $44,139
- **Local Support:** $1,378,707
- **Other Support:** $92,170
- **Total Support:** $1,781,727

(16)
- **Name:** Montgomery City-County Library
- **Address:** 445 S. Lawrence Street, Montgomery AL 36104
- **Telephone:** 205-263-4735
- **Administrator:** Mr. F. Gillis Doughtie
- **Type of Library Served:** p
- **Federal Support:** $57,308 (Includes $2,923 Revenue Sharing)
- **State Support:** $25,067
- **Local Support:** $597,870
- **Other Support:** $47,365
- **Total Support:** $727,610

(17)
- **Name:** Muscle Shoals Regional Library
- **Address:** 218 N. Wood Avenue, Florence AL 35630
- **Telephone:** 205-764-6563
- **Administrator:** Mrs. Betty Warren
- **Type of Library Served:** p
- **Federal Support:** $114,277 (Includes $86,551 Revenue Sharing)
- **State Support:** $23,016
- **Local Support:** $146,330
- **Other Support:** $59,354
- **Total Support:** $342,977

(18)
- **Name:** North Alabama Cooperative Library System
- **Address:** 108 Fountain Circle, Huntsville AL 35804
- **Telephone:** 205-534-0735
- **Administrator:** Elbert Watson, Director; Helen Moore, Coordinator
- **Type of Library Served:** p
- **Federal Support:** $192,746 (Includes $12,408 Revenue Sharing)
- **State Support:** $48,683
- **Local Support:** $640,394
- **Other Support:** $104,733
- **Total Support:** $986,556

(continued)

7. SINGLE-TYPE LIBRARY COOPERATIVES (continued)

    (19) Name: Northwest Regional Library
         Address: 130 North 1st Street
                            Winfield AL 35594
         Telephone: 205-487-2330
         Administrator: Mrs. Rebecca Adkins
         Type of Library Served: p
         Federal Support: $54,785 (Includes $41,753 Revenue
         State Support: $20,812   Sharing)
         Local Support: $47,769
         Other Support: $8,376
         Total Support: $131,742

    (20) Name: Phenix City-Russell County Library
         Address: 500 14th Street
                            Phenix City AL 36867
         Telephone: 205-297-1139
          Administrator: Mrs. Irma M. Duke
         Type of Library Served: p
         Federal Support: $10,462 (Includes $791 Revenue
         State Support: $9,866   Sharing)
         Local Support: $57,342
         Other Support: $27,232
         Total Support: $104,902

    (21) Name: Public Library of Selma and Dallas
         Address: 1113 Selma Avenue   County
                            Selma AL 36701
         Telephone: 205-875-3535
          Administrator: Mrs. Patricia Blalock
         Type of Library Served: p
         Federal Support: $41,800 (Includes $963 Revenue
         State Support: $11,768   Sharing)
         Local Support: $73,654
         Other Support: $80,850
         Total Support: $208,072

    (22) Name: St. Clair County Library
         Address: 1921 First Avenue N
                            Pell City AL 35125
         Telephone: 205-594-2141
          Administrator: Ms. Beverly Barber
         Type of Library Served: p
         Federal Support: $10,108 (Includes $487 Revenue
         State Support: $7,773   Sharing)
         Local Support: $62,702
         Other Support: $209
         Total Support: $80,792

(continued)

7. SINGLE-TYPE LIBRARY COOPERATIVES (continued)

    (23) Name: Shelby County Library
          Address: P. O. Box 858
                              Columbiana AL 35051

(23) Name:	Shelby County Library
Address:	P. O. Box 858
	Columbiana AL 35051
Telephone:	205-669-7851
Administrator:	Mr. Bill Summers
Type of Library Served: p	
Federal Support:	$33,754 (Includes $25,766 Revenue
State Support:	$9,314 Sharing)
Local Support:	$53,778
Other Support:	$4,138
Total Support:	$100,984

(24) Name:	Wheeler Basin Regional Library
Address:	504 Cherry St., N.E.
	Decatur AL 35601
Telephone:	205-353-2993
Administrator:	Mrs. Nancy Agnew
Type of Library Served: p	
Federal Support:	$28,328 (Includes $2,073 Revenue
State Support:	$22,886 Sharing)
Local Support:	$202,917
Other Support:	$55,647
Total Support:	$309,778

8. MULTI-TYPE LIBRARY COOPERATIVES

   A. Receiving Continuing Financial Support from the State Library:
       There are none.

   B. Receiving No Continuing Financial Support from the State Library:

Name:	Birmingham Resource Center
Address:	Birmingham Public Library
	2020 7th Avenue, North
	Birmingham AL 35203
Telephone:	205-254-2551
Administrator:	George Stewart
Activities:	The Birmingham Resource Center provides interlibrary loan and reference service to all libraries in the state. During 1978 the card catalog of the Birmingham Public Library will be converted to machine readable form as the basis for a COM state-wide union catalog. The Resource Center and part of the development of the COM catalog are funded with LSCA grants.

9. INTERLIBRARY COOPERATION FUNCTIONS *

A.

	State Support	Federal Support Title I	Federal Support Title III	Other Support	Total Support
Interlibrary Loan			41,269		41,269
Continuing Education	7,000	5,000			12,000
Cooperative Acquisitions					
Cooperative Cataloging		103,000		30,720	133,720
Cooperative Delivery					
Cooperative Processing					
Cooperative Reference					
Cooperative Storage					
Legislative Assistance					
Planning/Development	2,000	$50,000	$4,000		$56,000
Union Lists of Serials					
Other (please specify)					
Cooperative Film Service		29,900			29,900
Total Support	9,000	187,900	45,269	30,720	272,889-est.

B. NON-FINANCIAL SUPPORT ROLE OF THE STATE LIBRARY

Through its Division of Library Development, this agency
provides support for these functions with demonstration
activities, continuing education and in-service training
programs, consulting services, planning and technical
assistance. Most notable in 1977 is the initiation of a
Library Systems Study for Alabama conducted by the
Public Administration Service.

10. ILC COMMUNICATION DEVICES / SERVICE NETWORKS

A.

Device/Service	Support ($)	Equipment (#)	Participants
IN-WATS Telephone line	$10,000 est.	1	APLS & all Libraries
SOLINET Terminal	10,000 est.	1	APLS

B. NON-FINANCIAL SUPPORT ROLE OF THE STATE LIBRARY

The state library is providing leadership in library automation through its State Advisory Committee's Library
Automation Subcommittee. Also, APLS is partially funding
the conversion of the card catalog at the Birmingham
Public Library to machine-readable form from which a COM
catalog will be produced. It will be used as a basis for
a statewide union catalog involving also the academic
libraries of the state.

* Estimate from Fiscal Year 1977 LSCA Annual Program Budget.

11.   MACHINE-READABLE DATA BASE REFERENCE SEARCHING SERVICES

There are none.

12.   INTERLIBRARY SERVICES TO SPECIAL GROUPS

Services to the blind and physically handicapped as of October 1,
1977 will be shifted from the Talladega School for the Blind to
APLS.   A new building to house this new function at APLS is
scheduled for completion for Spring 1978.   APLS will provide a
director for Blind and Physically Handicapped Library who will
coordinate services through six subregional libraries in the
State.

Service to the institutionalized (including both mental health
and correctional facilities) is provided through cooperative
arrangements with public libraries located near various institutions.   They are:

(1) Horseshoe Bend Regional Library-Draper, Tutwiler and Frank
      Lee Youth Correctional
(2) Friedman Library of Tuscaloosa-Partlow and Bryce's Mental
      Hospitals
(3) Choctawhatchee Regional Library-Eufaula Youth Adjustment
      Center
(4) Mobile Public Library-Searcy Mental Hospital

In 1977 created a position for a Consultant for Institutional
Libraries.

13.   PARTICIPATION IN MULTI-STATE LIBRARY NETWORKS

Network: Southeastern Library Network (SOLINET)
Financial Support: not reported
Participation: Full voting member
Services Used: On-Line cataloging

14.   LEGAL BASES FOR MULTI-TYPE LIBRARY COOPERATION

There is no enabling legislation.   (Library Systems Study will
recommend model legislation for multi-type library cooperation.)

15.   LEGAL BARRIERS AGAINST PARTICIPATION IN MULTI-TYPE LIBRARY
        COOPERATION

There are no legal barriers.

1. REPORTING AGENCY

    A.   Alaska State Library
        Pouch G
        Juneau, Alaska 99811
        (907) 465-2910

    B.   Chief Officer: Richard B. Engen, Director

    C.   Fiscal Year: 1978

2. OVERVIEW

The Alaska Library Network, an outgrowth of the mandate in AS 14.56.030, has no formal organization except mutual agreement, though involving libraries statewide. Interlibrary loan is regionalized, with centers at the State Library in Juneau, Anchorage Municipal Libraries, and Fairbanks North Star Borough Library. Mail Services (direct service to rural patrons) is partially regionalized. Grants from state and federal aid appropriations are utilized to support these programs. For several libraries in the state, the Processing Center provides centralized purchasing and processing of library materials, cataloging, and catalog card production.

In cooperation with the University of Alaska, the Network is preparing a union list of serials. Other cooperative activities of the Network include systematic referral of information requests, central audiovisual staff and resources (Film Centers in Juneau and in Anchorage), communications forum, photographic and micrographic reproduction of research materials, regional bibliographic center, cooperative development of library automation, and continuing education of library personnel.

3. NUMBER OF LIBRARIES IN THE STATE

Academic:	13	
Public:	85	
School:	157	
Public:	149	
Private:	8	
Special:	38	
Profit:	5	
Non-profit:	33	(includes 9 military)
TOTAL:	293	

4. STATE AGENCY INTERLIBRARY COOPERATION UNIT

    A.   Unit Name: There is no existing unit nor plans to create
                    one.
    B.   Unit Name: Readers Services

(continued)

Title of supervisor: Librarian, Documents

Unit Name: Readers Services, ILL
Title of supervisor: Librarian, Interlibrary loan

Unit Name: Special Services, Paperbacks by mail
Title of supervisor: Librarian, Special Services

Unit Name: Special Services, Film distribution
Title of supervisor: Librarian, Special Services

Unit Name: Special Services, Audio-cassette duplication
Title of supervisor: Librarian, Special Services

Unit Name: Special Services, Blind & Physically Handicapped
Title of supervisor: Librarian, Special Services

Unit Name: Technical Services, Processing Center
Title of supervisor: Librarian, Technical Services

Unit Name: Technical Services, Microfilming
Title of supervisor: Librarian, Technical Services

Unit Name: Technical Services, Newspaper Indexing
Title of Supervisor: Librarian, Technical Services

5. OTHER STATE-LEVEL GOVERNMENTAL ILC UNITS

Unit Name: Governor's Advisory Council on Libraries
Address: Pouch G, Juneau, Alaska 99811 Phone: (907)465-2910
Chairperson: John Carlson (Fairbanks)
Activity: Planning, Evaluating, Advising

6. OTHER STATE-LEVEL NON-GOVERNMENTAL ILC UNITS

Unit Name: Alaska Library Association
Address: c/o E. E. Rasmuson Library
             University of Alaska
             Fairbanks, Alaska 99701
Activity: Cooperates in most of the activities mentioned
             in the overview of the state library agency

7. SINGLE-TYPE LIBRARY COOPERATIVES

A. Receiving Continuing Financial Support from the State
     Library:
          There are none.

B. Receiving No Continuing Financial Support from the State
     Library:
          There are none.

C. Other:
There are none.

8. MULTI-TYPE LIBRARY COOPERATIVES

A. Receiving Continuing Financial Support from the State Library:
There are none.

B. Receiving No Continuing Financial Support from the State
Library:
There are none.

C. Other:
There are none.

9. INTERLIBRARY COOPERATION FUNCTIONS

A. Receiving Continuing Financial Support from the State Library:

	State Support	Federal Support Title I	Title III	Other Support	Total Support
Interlibrary Loan					
Continuing Education					
Cooperative Acquisitions					
Cooperative Cataloging	All of these are part of the continuing				
Cooperative Delivery	program of the Alaska Library Network and				
Cooperative Processing	are so interlaced that breakouts of specific				
Cooperative Reference	funds would, at best, be estimates. Some				
Cooperative Storage	functions are performed for the Network by				
Legislative Assistance	only one library, others by several libraries.				
Planning/Development	These are, in some cases, carried out with-				
Union Lists of Serials	out additional funding and in others, be-				
Other (please specify)	cause of funding.				
Total Support					

B. Non-Financial Support Role of the State Library:
Same as above.

10. ILC COMMUNICATION DEVICES / SERVICE NETWORKS

A. State library agency financial support of cooperative use:

Device/Service	Support ($)	Equipment (#)	Participants
TELEX	Varying	Varying	Statewide

B. Non-Financial Support Role of the State Library:
All State communications such as TELEX and TWX are available
to libraries for interlibrary loan use. University of Alaska
computer network will be used in a similar fashion.

13

11. MACHINE-READABLE DATA BASE REFERENCE SEARCHING SERVICES

   State library agency financially-supported cooperative use of
   machine readable information data bases:

Data Base / Vendor	Support ($)	Terminals (#)	Participants
Medlars	Varying	1	Statewide
DIALOG / Lockheed	Varying	1	Statewide
ORBIT / SDC	Varying	1	Statewide
COSMOS / SMERC	Varying	1	Statewide

12. INTERLIBRARY SERVICES TO SPECIAL GROUPS

   A. Services to special user groups:
      See INTERLIBRARY COOPERATION FUNCTIONS above.

   B. Non-financial support role of the State Library in services to
      special user groups:
      See INTERLIBRARY COOPERATION FUNCTIONS above.

13. PARTICIPATION IN MULTI-STATE LIBRARY NETWORKS

   A. State Library agency memberships in interstate library networks:

      Network: Pacific Northwest Bibliographic Center
      Financial Support: Alaska is a full-member state. State
                          Library pays share for statewide use,
                          based on use.
      Participation: Alaska is a full-member state.
      Services Used: Interlibrary loan, occasional reference queries.

      Network: Washington Library Network
      Financial Support: State Library will pay share for statewide
                          use, based on actual use.
      Participation: Alaska in process of becoming full-member state.
      Services Used: Various uses anticipated, including cataloging
                      information, ILL, subject searches, etc.

      Network: Western Council of State Libraries
      Financial Support: Flat membership fee
      Participation: State Library, in cooperation with other Alaska
                      libraries, participates in meetings and planning.
      Services Used: Continuing education, resource sharing, policy
                      development.

   B. Non-financial support role of the State Library:
      See "A." above.

14. LEGAL BASES FOR MULTI-TYPE LIBRARY COOPERATION

   Alaska Statutes 14.56.030 directs the Department of Education to

(continued)

14. LEGAL BASES FOR MULTI-TYPE LIBRARY COOPERATION (continued)

undertake State Library functions which will benefit the state and its citizens, specifying that it shall "coordinate library service of the state with other educational services and agencies to increase effectiveness and eliminate duplication...". The statute further provides that the agency "apply for, receive, and spend federal, state, or private funds available for library purposes." The general power of state, set forth in Article 12, Section 8 of the Alaska Constitution, provides the authority enabling interstate library compacts.

15. LEGAL BARRIERS AGAINST PARTICIPATION IN MULTI-TYPE LIBRARY COOPERATION

There are no legal barriers.

ARIZONA

1. REPORTING AGENCY

    a. Department of Library, Archives and Public Records
        3rd Floor, Capitol
        Phoenix, Arizona 85007
        (602) 271-3701

    b. Chief Officer: Mrs. Marguerite B. Cooley, Director

    c. Fiscal Year: 1977/78

2. OVERVIEW

    There are six regional library systems in Arizona which include
    all of the state's fourteen counties. All libraries that re-
    ceive state or federal funds are required to participate in
    these systems and the participation of all types of libraries
    is encouraged. A statewide library network is being planned,
    with implementation expected in late 1978.

    The regional systems were funded in accordance with the regu-
    lations of the State Department of Library, Archives and Public
    Records. Article Three, Section 11-951-11954, of the Arizona
    Revised Statutes permits joint ventures between different types
    of public agencies.

3. NUMBER OF LIBRARIES IN THE STATE

    Academic: 22
    Public: 131
    School: 736
        Public   650
        Private   86
    Special: 147
        Profit: 134
        Nonprofit: 13
    TOTAL   1,036

4. STATE AGENCY INTERLIBRARY COOPERATION UNIT

    A. Plans to create a unit specifically responsible for inter-
        library cooperation activities where no such unit now exists.

    B. Other state agency office charged with ILC activities:

        Unit name: Library Extension Service
                     2219 S. 48th Street, Suite D
                     Tempe, AZ 85282
                     (602) 271-5841

        Person in   Edith M. Hart
        charge: Extension Librarian

16

5. OTHER STATE-LEVEL GOVERNMENT ILC UNITS

    Unit name: Northern Arizona University Library
                     Flagstaff, AZ 86001
    Cooperative activity: Courier service

    Unit name: Arizona State University
                     Tempe, AZ 85281
    Cooperative activity: Courier service

6. OTHER STATE-LEVEL NON-GOVERNMENTAL ILC UNITS

    There are none.

7. SINGLE-TYPE LIBRARY COOPERATIVES

    A. Receiving Continuing Financial Support from the State Library:

    <u>Public Library Systems, multi-jurisdictional</u>:

        Name: Apache County Library System
        State Support: $12,274
        Federal Support: $12,650
        Other Support: not reported
        Total Support: $38,061

        Name: Cochise County Library System
        State Support: $14,425
        Federal Support: $ 7,060
        Other Support: not reported
        Total Support: $97,355

        Name: Coconino County Library System
        State Support: $19,325
        Federal Support: $74,151
        Other Support: not reported
        Total Support: $310,753

        Name: Gila County Library System
        State Support: $15,800
        Federal Support: $16,750
        Other Support: not reported
        Total Support: $55,624

        Name: Graham County Library System
        State Support: $13,875
        Federal Support: $ 4,800
        Other Support: not reported
        Total Support: $40,656

        Name: Greenlee County Library System
        State Support: $10,000
        Federal Support: $20,000
        Other Support: not reported
        Total Support: $45,830   (continued)

7. SINGLE-TYPE LIBRARY COOPERATIVES (continued)
    A. Receiving Continuing Financial Support from the State Library:

        Name: Maricopa County Library System
        State Support: $16,125
        Federal Support: 18,000
        Other Support: not reported
        Total Support: $263,368

        Name: Mohave County Library System
        State Support: $16,000
        Federal Support: 0
        Other Support: not reported
        Total Support: $136,255

        Name: Navajo County Library System
        State Support: $16,000
        Federal Support: 23,650
        Other Support: not reported
        Total Support: $83,550

        Name: Pinal County Library System
        State Support: $15,325
        Federal Support: 11,785
        Other Support: not reported
        Total Support: $93,674

        Name: Santa Cruz County Library System
        State Support: $10,000
        Federal Support: 20,000
        Other Support: not reported
        Total Support: $90,379

        Name: Yavapai County Library System
        State Support: $16,610
        Federal Support: 14,725
        Other Support: not reported
        Total Support: $229,097

        Name: Yuma County Library System
        State Support: $16,440
        Federal Support: 0
        Other Support: not reported
        Total Support: $486,834

    B. Receiving No Continuing Support from the State Library:

        Name: Maricopa Community College District
                         2325 East McDowell Road
                         Phoenix, AZ   85006
        Type of library served: a
        Sponsoring body: not reported
        Cooperative activity: technical processing

8. MULTI-TYPE LIBRARY COOPERATIVES

    A. Receiving Continuing Financial Support from the State Library:

Name:	Channeled Arizona Information Network
Address:	not reported
Types of libraries served:	a, p, sch, sp
State Support:	$20,000
Federal Support:	$59,000
Total Support:	$79,000

    B. Receiving No Continuing Financial Support from the State Library:

    There are none.

9. INTERLIBRARY COOPERATION FUNCTIONS

    A. Receiving Continuing Financial Support from the State Library:

	State Support	Federal Support Title I	Title III	Other Support	Total Support
Interlibrary Loan	$22,000	62,350	28,974		n.a.
Cont. Education	10,000	49,050	3,050		n.a.
Cooperative Delivery			20,223		n.a.
Cooperative Reference*					n.a.
Planning/Development					n.a.
Other: Books by Mail		8,600			8,600

    *Reference reported in Interlibrary loan

    B. Non-Financial Support Role of the State Library:

    None reported.

10. ILC COMMUNICATION DEVICES/SERVICE NETWORKS

    A.
Device/Service	Support	Equipment	Participants
TWX	$12,000	12	12
BALLOTS	$12,000	1	1

    B. Non-Financial Support Role of the State Library:

    There is none.

11. MACHINE-READABLE BASE REFERENCE SEARCHING SERVICES

    There are none.

12. INTERLIBRARY SERVICES TO SPECIAL GROUPS

    A. There are no services provided through cooperative arrangements to special groups.

(continued)

12. INTERLIBRARY SERVICES TO SPECIAL GROUPS (continued)

   B. Non-Financial Support Role of the State Library:

   Coordinates service to state agencies and Legislature.

13. PARTICIPATION IN MULTI-STATE LIBRARY NETWORKS

   There is none.

14. LEGAL BASES FOR MULTI-TYPE LIBRARY COOPERATION

   State legislation enabling multi-type library cooperative
   development: Allows Library Extension Service to give advise and
   assistance to "joint ventures" of different types of libraries
   (Arizona Revised Statutes: 41-798.A.4).

   State legislation enabling interstate compact: Two or more public
   agencies may contract for services or jointly exercise common
   powers (Arizona Revised Statutes 11-951-11-954).

   State provided statutory funding for multi-type library cooperative
   development: There is none.

15. LEGAL BARRIERS AGAINST PARTICIPATION IN MULTI-TYPE LIBRARY
   COOPERATION.

   There are no barriers.

1. REPORTING AGENCY

    A. Arkansas Library Commission
       506½ Center Street
       Little Rock, AR 72201
       (501) 371-1524

    B. Chief Officer: Frances Neal, Librarian/Director

    C. Fiscal Year: FY 1978 (July 1 - June 30)

2. OVERVIEW

    The Arkansas Library Commission administers the state aid appro-
    priation for public library service. The formula for distribu-
    tion encourages interlibrary cooperation. Acts of Arkansas 244
    (1927), 177 (1931), 139 (1935), and 742 (1977) permit municipali-
    ties, counties, and the state library agency to enter into agree-
    ments and contracts for joint or cooperative library services.
    Fifteen multi-county units provide public library service for
    citizens of fifty-four of the state's seventy-five counties.

    The Commission fosters interlibrary cooperation among all types
    of libraries. The size of the state makes informal multi-type
    library cooperation easy. The Arkansas Library Commission and
    the Arkansas Library Association promote cooperation through
    workshops, exhibits, conferences, and statewide efforts.

3. NUMBER OF LIBRARIES IN THE STATE

Academic:	35
Public:	40
School:	825
Public:	included above
Private:	included above
Special:	35 est.
Profit:	included above
Nonprofit:	included above
TOTAL:	935 est.

4. STATE AGENCY INTERLIBRARY COOPERATION

    A. Unit Name: Library Development
       Person in Charge: Frances Nix, Associate Director for
                         Library Development

    B. Unit Name: Information Resources
       Person in Charge: Cynthia Pitts, Deputy Director for
                         Information Resources

5. OTHER STATE-LEVEL GOVERNMENTAL ILC UNITS

   Agency: University of Arkansas Medical Sciences Library
   Address: 4301 West Markham Street
         Little Rock, AR 72201
   Activity: Cooperative network coordinating Medical Sciences
         Library with Allied Health Education Center Libraries
         across the state

6. OTHER STATE-LEVEL NON-GOVERNMENTAL ILC UNITS

   Unit Name: Arkansas Library Association
   Address: 701 North McAdoo
           Little Rock, Arkansas 72201
   Telephone: (501) 372-1424
   Administrator: Mrs. Katherine Stanick, Executive Secretary
   Activities: Interlibrary Cooperation Committee

7. SINGLE-TYPE LIBRARY COOPERATIVES

   A. Receiving Continuing Financial Support from the State
     Library:

     Name: Arkansas Library Commission System of
               County and Multi-County Libraries
     Address: 506½ Center Street
               Little Rock, AR 72201
     Administrator: Frances Neal
     Type of
     Library Served: p
     Federal Support: $353,482
     State Support: $793,818

     Name: Central Arkansas Library System
     Address: 700 Louisiana Street
               Little Rock, AR 72201
     Administrator: Alice Gray
     Type of
     Library Served: p
     Federal Support: $24,103 (TQ & FY 1977)
     State Support: $94,054

     Name: Ozarks Regional Library
     Address: 217 E. Dickson Street
               Fayetteville, AR 72701
     Administrator: Carol Wright
     Type of
     Library Served: p
     Federal Support: $16,125
     State Support: $42,847

(continued)

7. SINGLE-TYPE LIBRARY COOPERATIVES (continued)

A. Receiving Continuing Financial Support from the State
    Library:

Name: The Public Library of Pine Bluff and
                    Jefferson County
Address: 200 East Eighth Avenue
                    Pine Bluff, AR 71601
Administrator: Cora Dorsett
Type of
Library Served: p
Federal Support: 0
State Support: $19,195

Name: Southwest Arkansas Regional Library
Address: Hope, AR 71801

Administrator: Hazel Prichard
Type of
Library Served: p
Federal Support: 0
State Support: $58,600

Name: Arkansas River Valley Regional Library
Address: Dardanelle, AR 72834
Administrator: Katharine Keathley
Type of
Library Served: p
Federal Support $51,609 (TQ & FY 1977)
State Support: $59,097

Name: Tri Lakes Regional Library
Address: 200 Woodbine
                    Hot Springs, AR 71901
Administrator: Jean Ledwidge
Type of
Library Served: p
Federal Support: $46,056 (TQ & FY 1977)
State Support: $32,527

Name: Crowley Ridge Regional Library
Address: 315 W. Oak Avenue
                    Jonesboro, AR 72401
Administrator: Ottoleine Echols
Type of
Library Served: p
Federal Support: $25,170 (TQ & FY 1977)
State Support: $24,031

Name: North Arkansas Regional Library
Address: Harrison, AR 72601
Administrator: William L. Larson   (continued)

23

7. SINGLE-TYPE LIBRARY COOPERATIVES (continued)

    A. Receiving Continuing Financial Support from the State
       Library:

       Type of
       Library Served: p
       Federal Support: $31,800
       State Support: $69,185

       Name: Phillips-Lee-Monroe Regional Library
       Address: 623 Pecan Street
                      Helena, AR 72342
       Administrator: Wynelle Williams
       Type of
       Library Served: p
       Federal Support: 0
       State Support: $34,364

       Name: C L O C Regional Library
       Address: 220 East Main Street
                      Magnolia, AR 71753
       Administrator: Florene Bradley
       Type of
       Library Served: p
       Federal Support: 0
       State Support: $58,462

       Name: Mid-Arkansas Regional Library
       Address: 224 West South
                      Benton, AR 72015
       Administrator: Leroy Gattin
       Type of
       Library Served: p
       Federal Support: $44,200 (TQ & FY 1977)
       State Support: $36,270

       Name: White River Regional Library
       Address: 110 Broad Street
                      Batesville, AR 72501
       Administrator: Debra Allen
       Type of
       Library Served: p
       Federal Support: 0
       State Support: $64,004

       Name: Northeast Arkansas Regional Library
       Address: 120 North Twelfth Street
                      Paragould, AR 72450
       Administrator: Kathleen Sharp
       Type of
       Library Served: p

(continued)

7. SINGLE-TYPE LIBRARY COOPERATIVES (continued)

    A. Receiving Continuing Financial Support from the State
       Library:

       Federal Support: $14,747
       State Support: $35,447

       Name: Southeast Arkansas Regional Library
       Address: Monticello, AR 71655
       Administrator: Sharon Gouy
       Type of
       Library Served: p
       Federal Support: 0
       State Support: $13,400

       Name: Faulkner-Van Buren Regional Library
       Address: Conway, AR 72032
       Administrator: Dula Reid
       Type of
       Library Served: p
       Federal Support: 0
       State Support: $18,357

       Name: Scott-Sebastian Regional Library
       Address: Greenwood, AR 72936
       Administrator: Judy Beth Clevenger
       Type of
       Library Served: p
       Federal Support: 0
       State Support: $16,994

    B. Receiving No Continuing Financial Support from the State
       Library:

       Name: Arkansas Foundation of Associated Colleges,
                      Committee of Librarians
       Address: 209 West Capitol
                      Hall Building, Room 214
                      Little Rock AR 72201
       Administrator: Max Jones
       Type of
       Library Served: a - small, private
       Total Support: not available

       Name: Henderson State University--Ouachita
                      Baptist University Consortium
       Address: H.S.U. Box 632
                      Arkadelphia, AR 71923
       Administrator: Edward Coulter
       Type of
       Library Served: a - public/private
       Total Support: not available   (continued)

8. MULTI-TYPE LIBRARY COOPERATIVES (continued)

A. Receiving Continuing Financial Support from the State Library:

Name:	Arkansas Members of AMIGOS
Address:	506½ Center Street
	Little Rock, AR 72201
Telephone:	501-371-1524
Administrator:	Frances Nix
Types of Libs. Served:	a, p, state
Federal Support:	$25,300

B. Receiving No Continuing Support from the State Library: There are none.

9. INTERLIBRARY COOPERATION FUNCTIONS

A. ILC functions available throughout the state which are receiving continuing financial support from the state library:

	State Support	Federal Support Title I	Federal Support Title III	Other Support	Total Support
Continuing Education			3,700		3,700
Cooperative Acquisitions)					
Cooperative Cataloging)	61,942	55,585			117,527
Cooperative Delivery)					
Cooperative Processing)					
Interlibrary Loan					
& Cooperative Reference	39,368	28,015			67,383
Cooperative Storage					
Legislative Assistance					
Planning/Development					
Union Lists of Serials					
Other (please specify)					
Total Support	101,310	83,600	3,700		188,610

B. The Arkansas Library Commission promotes statewide planning and development in all the activities listed above through professional assistance and communication. The Materials Selection Center serves all types of libraries interested in specialized selection.

10. ILC COMMUNICATION DEVICES/SERVICE NETWORKS

A. | Device/Service | Support ($) | Equipment (#) | Participants |
|---|---|---|---|
| WATS | $1,867 | Telephone Service | 85 |

(continued)

10. ILC COMMUNICATION DEVICES/SERVICE NETWORKS (continued)

B. The Arkansas Library Commission initiated efforts to have OCLC data available to Arkansas libraries. Recently a microfiche catalog of 202,000 entries generated by Arkansas libraries in the data base was produced and distributed. In addition to the ten on-line members of AMIGOS, the fiche catalogs were made available to six regional libraries for public service demonstrations.

11. MACHINE-READABLE DATA BASE REFERENCE SEARCHING SERVICES

There are none.

12. INTERLIBRARY SERVICES TO SPECIAL GROUPS

A. State library agency financially-supported cooperative arrangements and/or use of special services to special user groups:

SERVICES	STATE	FEDERAL	TOTAL
Physically Handicapped, including the Blind	$ 79,283	$ 70,175	$149,458
State Institutions	62,818	24,003	86,821
Outreach to Serve the Disadvantaged	278,738	292,973	571,711

B. State library agency non-financial support and role in the cooperative arrangements and/or use of special services to special user groups:

None.

13. PARTICIPATION IN MULTI-STATE LIBRARY NETWORKS

A. Network: AMIGOS/OCLC
Financial Support: Contracted Services
Participation: 11 a; 1 p; state agency
Services Used: Cataloging, professional, advisory

Network: CLENE
Financial Support: $1,500
Participation: Statewide
Services Used: Continuing Education

Network: SLICE/CELS
Financial Support: $2,200
Participation: Statewide
Services Used: Continuing Education

B. Multi-state networks headquartered in the state:

None.

14. LEGAL BASES FOR MULTI-TYPE LIBRARY COOPERATION

Act 139, 1935, amended by Act 464, 1971, creating the Arkansas
Library Commission, charges the Commission with statewide
library development. Act 177, 1931, permits municipalities
to contract for library services. Act 419, 1967, provides
enabling legislation for interstate library cooperation.
Act 742, 1977, permits counties to make interlocal agreements
or contracts with other libraries, agencies, or institutions.

15. LEGAL BARRIERS AGAINST PARTICIPATION IN MULTI-TYPE LIBRARY
     COOPERATION

There are no legal barriers.

1. REPORTING AGENCY

    a. California State Library
        Library & Courts Building
        9th and N Streets
        (P. O. Box 2037)
        Sacramento, CA 95809
        (916) 445-2585
        TWX 910-367-3553

    b. Chief Officer: Ethel S. Crockett, California State Librarian

    c. Fiscal Year: 1976

2. OVERVIEW

    All areas of the state are served by public library systems, and
    many by multi-type library networks and regional reference
    centers. Twenty public library systems, 15 cooperative and five
    single-jurisdiction, are established by the Public Library
    Services Act, (Education Code Sections 18700-18772). Networks and
    reference centers are organized under the Joint Exercise of Powers,
    (Government Code Section 6500 et. seq.), as demonstrations of
    service supported by the federal Library Services and Construction
    Act, or by local agreement. CLASS (California Library Authority
    for Systems and Services), a public agency established in 1976,
    will offer a variety of cooperative services to members at cost,
    beginning in 1978.

3. NUMBER OF LIBRARIES IN THE STATE

    Academic: 161
    Public: 175
    School: 4,300 est.
       Public: 4,000 est.
       Private: 300 est.
    Special: 475 est.
       Profit: 400 est.
       Nonprofit: 75 est.

    TOTAL: 5,111 est.

4. STATE AGENCY INTERLIBRARY COOPERATION UNIT

    A. There is no existing unit nor plans to create one.

    B. Person charged with interlibrary cooperation activities

        Cy H. Silver, Chief,
        Library Development Services Bureau,
        California State Library,
        (address as above)
        Tel. (916) 445-4730.

5. OTHER STATE–LEVEL GOVERNMENT ILC UNITS

    There are none.

6. OTHER STATE–LEVEL NON–GOVERNMENTAL ILC UNITS

    Unit Name: California Library Association
    Address: 717 K Street, Suite 300, Sacramento, CA 95814
    Telephone: (916) 447-8541
    Administrator: Stefan B. Moses, Executive Director
    Activities: Promotes the development of library service of
                    the highest quality and maximum availability for
                    all residents of California.

    Unit Name: California Library Authority for Systems and
                    Services (CLASS)
    Address: 1415 Koll Circle, Suite 101
                    San Jose, CA 95112
    Telephone: (408) 289-1756
    Administrator: Ron Miller, Executive Director
    Activities: Expects to establish a computerized listing of
                    publications in libraries throughout the state
                    for cataloging, interlibrary loan and reference
                    use, and to provide such other services as
                    desired by members.

7. SINGLE–TYPE LIBRARY COOPERATIVES
    A. Receiving Continuing Financial Support from the State Library:
    Name: Berkeley-Oakland Service System
    Address: Oakland Public Library
                    124 14th Street
                    Oakland CA 94612
    Telephone: 415-273-3281
    Administrator: Lelia White, Fiscal Agent
    Type of Library Served: p
    Federal Support: 49,641
    State Support: 18,011
    Local Support: 52,876
    Total Support: 120,528

    Name: Black Gold Cooperative Library System
    Address: San Luis Obispo City-County Library
                    P.O. Box X
                    San Luis Obispo CA 93401
    Telephone: 805-543-1730
    Administrator: Dale W. Perkins, Fiscal Agent
    Type of Library Served: p
    Federal Support: 127,450
    State Support: 39,992
    Local Support: 263,871
    Total Support: 431,313

(continued)

7. SINGLE-TYPE LIBRARY COOPERATIVES (continued)

Name: East Bay Cooperative Library System
Address: Alameda County Library
                   224 W. Winton Avenue
                   Hayward CA 94544
Telephone: 415-881-6337
Administrator: Barbara Boyd, Fiscal Agent
Type of Library Served: p
Federal Support: 102,000
State Support: 35,290
Local Support: 35,816
Total Support: 173,106

Name: 49-99 Cooperative Library System
Address: Stockton-San Joaquin County Public Library
                   605 North El Dorado Street
                   Stockton CA 95202
Telephone: 209-944-8364
Administrator: Geraldine Shelley, Director
Type of Library Served: p
Federal Support: 241,379
State Support: 36,816
Local Support: 11,091
Total Support: 289,286

Name: Inland Library System
Address: 404 North Sierra Way
                   San Bernardino CA 92415
Telephone: 714-383-3907
Administrator: George Elser, Coordinator
Type of Library Served: p
Federal Support: 140,181
State Support: 65,310
Local Support: 1,886
Total Support: 207,377

Name: Kern County Library System
Address: Kern County Library
                   1315 Truxton Avenue
                   Bakersfield CA 93301
Telephone: 805-861-2130
Administrator: Jean Pretorius, Fiscal Agent
Type of Library Served: p
Federal Support: 34,710
State Support: 12,165
Local Support: 2,272,567
Total Support: 2,319,442

(continued)

7.   SINGLE-TYPE LIBRARY COOPERATIVES (continued)

Name: Long Beach Public Library System
Address: Long Beach Public Library
                 101 Pacific Avenue
                 Long Beach CA 90802
Telephone: 213-436-9225
Administrator: Frances Henselman, Fiscal Agent
Type of Library Served: p
Federal Support: 100,010
State Support: 12,835
Local Support: 0
Total Support: 112,845

Name: Los Angeles County Public Library System
Address: Los Angeles County Public Library
                 P.O. Box 111
                 Los Angeles CA 90053
Telephone: 213-974-6501
Administrator: Carol E. Moss, Fiscal Agent
Type of Library Served: p
Federal Support: 135,513
State Support: 117,196
Local Support: 20,605,481
Total Support: 20,858,190

Name: Los Angeles Public Library System
Address: Los Angeles Public Library
                 630 West Fifth Street
                 Los Angeles CA 90071
Telephone: 213-626-7555
Administrator: Wyman H. Jones, Fiscal Agent
Type of Library Served: p
Federal Support: 611,331
State Support: 220,548
Local Support: 15,833,127
Total Support: 16,665,006

Name: Metropolitan Cooperative Library System
Address: City of Pasadena Public Library
                 285 East Walnut Street
                 Pasadena CA 91101
Telephone: 213-577-4081
Administrator: Jan Galbavy, Coordinator
Type of Library Served: p
Federal Support: 231,698
State Support: 49,171
Local Support: 44,756
Total Support: 325,625

(continued)

7.   SINGLE-TYPE LIBRARY COOPERATIVES (continued)

Name: Monterey Bay Area Cooperative Library System
Address: 344 Salinas Street, Suite 107
                   Salinas CA 93901
Telephone: 408-758-9818
Administrator: Helen Gottlober, Coordinator
Type of Library Served: p
Federal Support: 117,675
State Support: 17,641
Local Support: 0
Total Support: 135,316

Name: Mountain Valley Library System
Address: Sacramento Public Library
                   828 I Street
                   Sacramento CA 95814
Telephone: 916-444-0926
Administrator: Virginia Short, Director
Type of Library Served: p
Federal Support   154,174
State Support: 64,515
Local Support: 36,896
Total Support: 255,585

Name: North Bay Cooperative Library System
Address: Sonoma County Library
                   Third & E Streets
                   Santa Rosa CA 95404
Telephone: 707-545-0831 ext. 61
Administrator: David Sabsay, Fiscal Agent
Type of Library Served: p
Federal Support: 55,787
State Support: 37,400
Local Support: 187,751
Total Support: 280,938

Name: North State Cooperative Library System
Address: 257 N. Villa Avenue
                   Willows CA 95988
Telephone: 916-934-2173
Administrator: James H. Kirks, Jr., Coordinator
Type of Library Served: p
Federal Support: 162,806
State Support: 16,659
Local Support: 0
Total Support: 179,465

(continued)

7. SINGLE-TYPE LIBRARY COOPERATIVES (continued)

        Name: Peninsula Library System
        Address: Daly City Public Library
                         40 Wembley Drive
                         Daly City CA 94015
        Telephone: 415-878-5577
        Administrator: James Henson, Coordinator
        Type of Library Served: p
        Federal Support: 174,962
        State Support: 28,990
        Local Support: 14,400
        Total Support: 218,352

        Name: San Francisco Public Library System
        Address: Civic Center
                         San Francisco CA 94102
        Telephone: 415-558-4235
        Administrator: John C. Frantz, Fiscal Agent
        Type of Library Served: p
        Federal Support: 850,000
        State Support: 21,554
        Local Support: 6,118,315
        Total Support: 6,989,869

        Name: San Joaquin Valley Library System
        Address: Fresno County Library
                         2420 Mariposa Street
                         Fresno CA 93721
        Telephone: 209-488-3185
        Administrator: John Kallenberg, Fiscal Agent
        Type of Library Served: p
        Federal Support: 190,215
        State Support: 56,495
        Local Support: 53,439
        Total Support: 300,149

        Name: Santiago Library System
        Address: Orange County Public Library
                         431 City Drive South
                         Orange CA 92668
        Telephone: 714-634-7137
        Administrator: Susan Gilroy, Coordinator
        Type of Library Served: p
        Federal Support: 198,284
        State Support: 67,417
        Local Support: 16,558
        Total Support: 282,259

(continued)

7.   SINGLE-TYPE LIBRARY COOPERATIVES (continued)

       Name: Serra Library System
       Address: San Diego County Public Library
                        5555 Overland Avenue
                        San Diego CA 92101
       Telephone: 714-278-8090 or 278-9710
       Administrator: Sandra Smith, Acting Coordinator
       Type of Library Served: p
       Federal Support: 329,059
       State Support: 75,415
       Local Support: 23,934
       Total Support: 428,408

       Name: South Bay Cooperative Library System
       Address: Santa Clara Public Library
                        2635 Homestead Road
                        Santa Clara CA 95051
       Telephone: 408-243-0560
       Administrator: Donald F. Fuller, Fiscal Agent
       Type of Library Served: p
       Federal Support: 0
       State Support: 74,447
       Local Support: 0
       Total Support: 74,447

8.   MULTI-TYPE LIBRARY COOPERATIVES

       Name: AWLNET (Area-Wide Library Network)
       Address: Fresno County Library
                        2420 Mariposa Street
                        Fresno CA 93721
       Telephone: 209-488-3229
       Administrator: Sharon Vandercook, Reference Coordinator
       Type of Libraries Served: a, p, sch, sp.
       Financial Support: n.a.

       Name: BARC (Bay Area Reference Center)
       Address: San Francisco Public Library
                        Civic Center
                        San Francisco CA 94102
       Telephone: 415-558-2941
       Administrator: Gil McNamee, Director
       Type of Libraries Served: a, p, sch, sp.
       Financial Support: n.a.

(continued)

8. MULTI-TYPE LIBRARY COOPERATIVES (continued)

        Name: CAL (Central Association of Libraries)
        Address: Stockton-San Joaquin County Library
                           605 N. El Dorado Street
                           Stockton CA 95202
        Telephone: 209-944-8257
        Administrator: Geraldine Shelley, Director
        Type of Libraries Served: a, p, sch, sp.
        Financial Support: n.a.

        Name: CIN (Cooperative Information Network)
        Address: Stanford University Libraries
                           Main Library, Rm. 205
                           Stanford CA 94305
        Telephone: 415-329-8287
        Administrator: Ronny Markoe, Coordinator
        Type of Libraries Served: a, p, sch, sp.
        Financial Support: n.a.

        Name: East Bay Information Service
        Address: Oakland Public Library
                           125 14th Street
                           Oakland CA 94612
        Telephone: 415-273-3511
        Administrator: Linda Knudson, Coordinator
        Type of Libraries Served: a, p.
        Financial Support: n.a.

        Name: LOCNET (Libraries of Orange County Network)
        Address: Santa Ana Public Library
                           26 Civic Center Plaza
                           Santa Ana CA 92701
        Telephone: 714-834-6225
        Administrator: Joy Hastings, Reference Network Supervisor
        Type of Libraries Served: a, p, sch, sp.
        Financial Support: n.a.

        Name: San Diego Greater Metropolitan Area Library &
                           Information Agency Council
        Address: University of California, San Diego
                           Central University Library
                           P.O. Box 2367
                           La Jolla CA 92093
        Telephone: 714-452-3958
        Administrator: Mandy Paulson, Reference Librarian
        Type of Libraries Served: a, p, sch, sp.
        Financial Support: n.a.

(continued)

8.   MULTI-TYPE LIBRARY COOPERATIVES (continued)

Name: SCAN (Southern California Answering Network)
Address: Los Angeles Public Library
                     630 W. Fifth Street
                     Los Angeles CA 90071
Telephone: 213-626-7555
Administrator: Evelyn Greenwald, Director
Type of Libraries Served: a, p, sch, sp.
Financial Support: n.a.

Name: SCILL (Southern California Interlibrary Loan
                     Project)
Address: Los Angeles Public Library
                     630 W. Fifth Street
                     Los Angeles CA 90071
Telephone: 213-624-5869
Administrator: Richard Partlow, Coordinator
Type of Libraries Served: a, p, sch, sp.
Financial Support: n.a.

Name: SIRCULS (San Bernardino-Inyo-Riverside Counties
                     United Library Service)
Address: 404 North Sierra Way
                     San Bernardino CA 92415
Telephone: 714-383-3907
Administrator: Patricia Laudisio, Coordinating Librarian
Type of Libraries Served: a, p, sch, sp.
Financial Support: n.a.

Name: TIE (Total Interlibrary Exchange)
Address: Santa Barbara Public Library
                     P.O. Box 1019
                     Santa Barbara CA 93102
Telephone: 805-962-0311
Administrator: Nadine Greenup, Coordinator
Type of Libraries Served: a, p, sch, sp.
Financial Support: n.a.

9. INTERLIBRARY COOPERATION FUNCTIONS

   A. Matrix for ILC functions.

	State Support	Title I	Title III	Other Support
Interlibrary Loan				
Interlibrary Loan	X			
Continuing Education			X	
Cooperative Acquisitions	X			
Cooperative Cataloging	X			
Cooperative Delivery	X			
Cooperative Processing	X			
Cooperative Reference	X	X		
Cooperative Storage				
Legislative Assistance				
Planning/Development	X	X		
Union Lists of Serials		X		
Other				

   B. Non-financial support role of the State Library: Consultant assistance, information sharing, program monitoring.

10. ILC COMMUNICATION DEVICES / SERVICE NETWORKS

   A. No financial support provided.

   B. Non-financial support role of the State Library: Consultant assistance, information sharing.

11. MACHINE-READABLE DATA BASE REFERENCE SEARCHING SERVICES

   There are none.

12. INTERLIBRARY SERVICES TO SPECIAL GROUPS

   A. Services are provided to special user groups through the Public Library Services Act systems, inter-type library networks, and the State Library. Examples are: services to institutions and the physically handicapped, the economically disadvantaged and persons of limited English-speaking ability. Such services are financed by a combination of local, state and federal, (primarily LSCA), funds.

   B. Non-financial support role of the State Library: Consultant assistance, information sharing, program monitoring.

13. PARTICIPATION IN MULTI-STATE LIBRARY NETWORKS

    A. There are none.

    B. BALLOTS
        Willow Trailer - SCIP
        Stanford University
        Stanford, CA 94305

14. LEGAL BASES FOR MULTI-TYPE LIBRARY COOPERATION

    There is no state legislation to enable multi-type library
    cooperative development, except a Joint Exercise of Powers
    Authority. Public library systems are organized under California
    Education Code Sections 18700-18772, Public Library Services Act.
    Most multi-type library cooperation in the state is carried out
    through grants from the federal Library Services and Construction
    Act, administered by the State Library.

15. LEGAL BARRIERS AGAINST PARTICIPATION IN MULTI-TYPE LIBRARY
    COOPERATION

    There are no legal barriers.

1. REPORTING AGENCY

    A.   Colorado State Library
           1362 Lincoln Street
           Denver, CO   80203
           (303) 892-3695

    B.   Chief Officer: Anne Marie Falsone,
                          Assistant Commissioner
                          Office of Library Services

    C.   Fiscal Year: 1978

2. OVERVIEW

Seven regional library service systems cover the state of Colorado. Membership includes 296 state supported libraries made up of: 26 academic, 116 public, 128 school districts, 7 state institutions, 7 BOCES (Boards of Cooperative Services made up of cooperating school districts) and 12 special libraries.

Regional library service systems may be formed under C.R.S. 1973, 24-90-124. "(1) The governing board of any public library may participate in a regional library service system to provide cooperative services under a plan approved by, and operated under an organizational structure approved by, the state board of education. School, academic, and special libraries may elect to participate in such a system. The organizational structure of each regional library service system shall include a governing board."

The multi-type library systems operate under the Colorado State Library Rules for Regional Library Service Systems authorization C.R.S. 1973, 24-90-108 (1)(b). Recent documents which study and support multi-type library development includes: Colorado Library Network Plan, March 1977, prepared by Virginia Boucher, the Regional Library Service Systems Needs Assessment Reports, Volumes 1-8, November 1976, prepared by Dr. Ruth Katz, and Libraries Colorado; a Plan for Development, February 1976, prepared by the Task Force for Revision of the Long-Range Plan sponsored by the Colorado Council for Library Development.

3. NUMBER OF LIBRARIES IN THE STATE

    Academic: 48
    Public: 113
    School:
        Public: 181   17 Boards of Cooperative Services
        Private: not available
    Special: 185 est.   (continued)

3. NUMBER OF LIBRARIES IN THE STATE (continued)

        Profit: not available
        Nonprofit: not available

    TOTAL: 527 est.

4. STATE AGENCY INTERLIBRARY COOPERATION UNIT

        Unit Name: Library Development Services
        Person in Charge: There is none.

        Unit Name: Reference and Information Services
        Person in Charge: Judy Houk (acting)

5. OTHER STATE-LEVEL GOVERNMENT ILC UNITS

        There are none.

6. OTHER STATE-LEVEL NON-GOVERNMENTAL ILC UNITS

        Unit Name: Bibliographical Center for Research
                         Rocky Mountain Region, Inc. (BCR)
        Address: 245 Columbine
                         Denver, CO   80203
        Telephone: (303) 534-6623
        Administrator: Donald B. Simpson
        Activities: BCR, a utility broker for services provides:
                         INTERLOAN, location and specialized services
                         for interlibrary loan, BIBLIO, automated
                         technical services, OCLC, and BALLOTS, METRO,
                         computerized reference service, SDC, Lock-
                         heed, and BRS. BCR is currently administer-
                         ing a COLONET/ICN program funded under an
                         LSCA Title I grant which places TI 733 ter-
                         minals for ILL and data base searching acti-
                         vities, continuing education training, and
                         marketing promotion of the program in the
                         seven Regional Library Service Systems.

        Unit Name: Western Council for State Libraries
        Address: Colorado State Library
        Telephone: (303) 892-3695
        Administrator: Anne Marie Falsone
        Activities: Coordinating library services among state
                         library agencies in the Western region.

                         The purpose of the Western Council is to im-
                         prove library services in the West through
                         providing a means for enunciating a position
                         of Western state librarians on national and
                         regional matters of common concern, providing
                         a forum for resource sharing development,
                                                            (continued)

6. OTHER STATE-LEVEL NON-GOVERNMENTAL ILC UNITS (continued)

                    and providing opportunities for staff de-
                    velopment in each state library agency.

7. SINGLE-TYPE LIBRARY COOPERATIVES

    A. Receiving Continuing Financial Support from the State
        Library:

        There are none.

    B. Receiving No Continuing Financial Support from the State
        Library:

        There are none.

    C. Other:

        There are none.

8. MULTI-TYPE LIBRARY COOPERATIVES

    A. Receiving Continuing Financial Support from the State
        Library:

        Name: Arkansas Valley Regional Library
                                        Service System
        Address: 635 West Corona, Suite 215
                                        Pueblo, CO   81004
        Telephone: (303) 542-2156
        Administrator: Maria Mata
        Types of Libraries Served: a, p, sch, sp
        Federal Support: $ 11,000
        State Support: 80,696
        Local Support: 21,679
        Other Support: -0-
        Total Support: $113,375

        Name: Central Colorado Regional Library
                                        Service System
        Address: 11111 E. Mississippi Avenue
                                        Aurora, CO   80012
        Telephone: (303) 344-1871
        Administrator: Ed Sayre
        Types of Libraries Served: a, p, sch, sp
        Federal Support: $ 11,000
        State Support: 149,681
        Local Support: 67,746
        Other Support: -0-   (continued)

42

8.   MULTI-TYPE LIBRARY COOPERATIVES (continued)

Total Support: $228,427

Name: High Plains Regional Library
                                    Service System
Address: Box 1918
                                    Greeley, CO   80631
Telephone: (303) 356-4000 Ext. 221
Administrator: Ron Stump
Types of Libraries Served: a, p, sch, sp
Federal Support: $ 11,000
State Support: 87,093
Local Support: 9,167
Other Support: -0-
Total Support: $107,260

Name: Pathfinder Regional Library
                                    Service System
Address: S. 1st & Uncompahgre
                                    Montrose, CO   81401
Telephone: (303) 249-9656
Administrator: Norman Sams
Types of Libraries Served: a, p, sch, sp
Federal Support: $ 11,000
State Support: 57,636
Local Support: 10,302
Other Support: -0-
Total Support: $ 78,938

Name: Plains & Peaks Regional Library
                                    Service System
Address: Janitell 1, Rm. 315
                                    Garden Valley Center
                                    Colorado Springs, CO   80906
Telephone: (303) 576-0363
Administrator: Jeanne Owen
Types of Libraries Served: a, p, sch, sp
Federal Support: $ 11,000
State Support: 93,016
Local Support: 49,445
Other Support: 3,000
Total Support: $156,461

Name: Southwest Regional Library
                                    Service System
Address: Box 411
                                    Durango, CO   81301
Telephone: (303) 247-4782
Administrator: Jan Beck
Types of Libraries Served: a, p, sch, sp
                                                      (continued)

8.   MULTI-TYPE LIBRARY COOPERATIVES (continued)

            Federal Support: $ 11,706
            State Support: 69,690
            Local Support: 11,859
            Other Support: -0-
            Total Support: $ 93,255

            Name: Three Rivers Regional Library
                                          Service System
            Address: P.O. Box 396
                                          New Castle, CO   81647
            Telephone: (303) 984-2887
            Administrator: Position open
            Types of Libraries Served: a, p, sch, sp
            Federal Support: $ 11,000
            State Support: 62,188
            Local Support: 3,700
            Other Support: -0-
            Total Support: $ 76,888

    B.   Receiving No Continuing Financial Support from the State
         Library:

         There are none.

    C.   Other (Receiving Occasional Support from the State Library,
         etc.):
         There are none.

9.   INTERLIBRARY COOPERATION FUNCTIONS

    A.   Receiving Continuing Financial Support from the State
         Library:

	State Support	Federal Support			Total Support
		LSCA I	LSCA III	Other	
Interlibrary Loan	$114,000				114,000
Continuing Education			$ 5,954		5,954
Cooperative Acquisitions					
Cooperative Cataloging					
Cooperative Delivery					
Cooperative Processing					
Cooperative Reference					
Cooperative Storage					
Legislative Assistance					
Planning/Development					
Union Lists of Serials					
Other: State Publications Index			$ 54,951		54,951
Total Support	$114,000		$ 60,905		$174,905

                                                            (continued)

44

9. INTERLIBRARY COOPERATION FUNCTIONS (continued)

    B. NON-FINANCIAL SUPPORT ROLE OF THE STATE LIBRARY

       Coordinator of state networking activities.

10. ILC COMMUNICATION DEVICES/SERVICE NETWORKS

    A. There are none.

    B. NON-FINANCIAL SUPPORT ROLE OF THE STATE LIBRARY

Device/Service	LSCA Support	Equipment (#)	Participants
TI 733 terminals	$20,340	9	Regional Library Service Systems
IN-WATS	$15,000	6	Regional Library Service Systems

11. MACHINE-READABLE DATA BASE REFERENCE SEARCHING SERVICES

Data Base/Vendor	LSCA Support ($)	Terminals (#)	Participants
Information Bank BSR, SDC, Lockheed	$10,900	9	Regional Library Service Systems

12. INTERLIBRARY SERVICES TO SPECIAL GROUPS

    A. The Colorado State Library - Services for the Blind and Physically Handicapped functions as a Regional Library in the national network of library service to the blind and physically handicapped, coordinated by the Library of Congress. In providing this service the State Library relies on the assistance of local libraries (public libraries in particular) to insure that the equipment, reading materials, and other information provided are appropriate to individual reading needs.

    Many public libraries are involved in this service as part of their outreach or homebound services. These outreach services include: delivery of record or cassette players (extra needed), loan from a deposit collection of recorded books, delivery of large print books, provision of reader advisory service for talking books, provision of information regarding library service for the handicapped, certification of eligibility for talking books, and communication of complaints regarding talking book service.

    All of the above activities carried out on the local level help to individualize the talking book services provided by the Colorado State Library.

(continued)

12. INTERLIBRARY SERVICES TO SPECIAL GROUPS (continued)

   B. NON-FINANCIAL SUPPORT ROLE OF THE STATE LIBRARY.

   There is none.

13. PARTICIPATION IN MULTI-STATE NETWORKS

   A. Network: Bibliographical Center for Research,
                            Rocky Mountain Region, Inc. (BCR)
      Financial Support: $7,200 access fee
      Participation: Statewide access
      Services Used: INTERLOAN, BIBLIO, METRO

   B. Multi-state Networks which are headquartered in Colorado in
      which the state library agency has no involvement:

   There are none.

14. LEGAL BASES FOR MULTI-TYPE LIBRARY COOPERATION

   Colorado State Library Rules for Regional Library Service Systems
   authorization C.R.S. 1973, 24-90-108 (1) (b) (See Overview in this
   entry).

15. LEGAL BARRIERS AGAINST PARTICIPATION IN MULTI-TYPE LIBRARY
    COOPERATION

   There are no legal barriers.

CONNECTICUT

1. REPORTING AGENCY

    A. Connecticut State Library
        231 Capitol Avenue
        Hartford, Connecticut 06115
        (203) 566-4192

    B. Chief Officer: Charles E. Funk, Jr., State Librarian

    C. Fiscal Year: July 1, 1976 to June 30, 1977

2. OVERVIEW

    Major cooperative activity in Connecticut has centered around
    the Cooperating Library Service Unit Review Board (CLSURB),
    which was established in 1975 by authority of Public Act 75-363,
    An Act Concerning Cooperating Library Service Units. The board
    consists of 15 members representing special, school, academic
    and public libraries and existing regional cooperatives. The
    legislative charge to the board is to "establish criteria for,
    and encourage the formation of, a system of cooperating library
    service units." A cooperating library service unit (CLSU) is
    defined as an association of library service units organized for
    the purpose of improving library service through cooperation.
    Under provisions set forth in the act, the state has been di-
    vided into six regions. Each region will be represented by one
    CLSU. Existing regional cooperatives will be incorporated into
    the CLSU. According to developed guidelines, each CLSU shall be
    incorporated as a non-profit corporation and act as a policy
    making body. Each CLSU will also be required to provide to the
    CLSURB a written statement for its initial phase of development,
    including goals and objectives, with plans and timetable for ad-
    ministration and implementation, documentation of needs, budget
    proposal, and plan for evaluation. A projected "plan of devel-
    opment" will also be required of each CLSU in order to qualify
    for on-going funding. During Fiscal Year 1977 the CLSURB re-
    ceived a $300,000 LSCA grant to provide funds for initial CLSU
    development. State funds will be sought in Fiscal Year 1978 to
    support on-going development of CLSUs.

3. NUMBER OF LIBRARIES IN THE STATE

    Academic: 53
    Public: 204
    School: 968 (estimated)
       Public: 850 (estimated)
       Private: 118 (estimated)
    Special: 350 (estimated)
       Profit: Not available
       Non-Profit: Not available
    Total: 1575 (estimated)

4. STATE AGENCY INTERLIBRARY COOPERATION UNIT.

    A.   There is no existing unit nor plans to create one.

    B.   Unit Name: Interlibrary Loan Center
        Person in Charge: Leon Shatkin, Director

        Unit Name: CONNECTICARD, Reciprocal Borrowing Program.
        Person in Charge: Leon Shatkin, Director, Interlibrary Loan Center

        Unit Name: CONNECTICAR, Library Delivery Service
        Person in Charge: Marjorie Hernandez, Associate State Librarian, Division of Readers' Services

        Unit Name: Library Line, Telephone Reference Service
        Person in Charge: Janet Axman, Director

        Unit Name: Cooperating Library Service Unit Review Board
        Person in Charge: Vincent Juliano, Acting Executive Coordinator

5. OTHER STATE-LEVEL GOVERNMENTAL ILC UNITS

    There are none.

6. OTHER STATE-LEVEL NON-GOVERNMENTAL ILC UNITS

    There are none.

7. SINGLE-TYPE LIBRARY COOPERATIVES

    A.   Receiving Continuing Financial Support from the State Library:

        There are none.

    B.   Receiving No Continuing Financial Support from the State Library:

        Name: CTUW Project
        Address: Interlibrary Loan Office
                                  Yale University
                                  New Haven, CT 06520
        Telephone: (203) 436-1972
        Administrator: Karen Banta
        Type of Library Served: a
        Sponsoring Body: None
        Source of Support: Membership dues   (continued)

7. SINGLE-TYPE LIBRARY COOPERATIVES (continued)

   B. Receiving No Continuing Financial Support from the State
      Library: (continued)

      Name: Capitol Area Health Consortium
                                     Libraries
      Address: Hartford Hospital Library, CCU3
                                     80 Seymour Street
                                     Hartford, CT 06115
      Telephone: (203) 524-2971
      Administrator: Gertrude Lamb
      Type of Library Served: sp
      Sponsoring Body: None
      Source of Support: None

      Name: Connecticut Association of Health
                                     Science Libraries
      Address: Middlesex Memorial Hospital Library
                                     28 Crescent Street
                                     Middletown, CT 06457
      Telephone: (203) 347-9471 x 387
      Administrator: Patricia Earley
      Type of Library Served: sp
      Sponsoring Body: None
      Source of Support: Membership dues

      Name: Connecticut Film Circuit
      Address: Russell Library
                                     119 Broad Street
                                     Middletown, CT 06457
      Telephone: (203) 347-2528
      Administrator: Linda Rusczek
      Type of Library Served: p
      Sponsoring Body: None
      Source of Support: Membership dues

      Name: Eastern Connecticut Film Circuit
      Address: Waterford Public Library
                                     Rope Ferry Road
                                     Waterford, CT 06385
      Telephone: (203) 443-0224
      Administrator: Patricia Holloway
      Type of Library Served: p
      Sponsoring Body: None
      Source of Support: Membership dues

(continued)

7. SINGLE-TYPE LIBRARY COOPERATIVES (continued)

    B. Receiving No Continuing Financial Support from the State
        Library: (continued)

Name:	Film Coop of Connecticut
Address:	Seymour Public Library
	Seymour, CT 06483
Telephone:	(203) 888-3903
Administrator:	Janet Gluz
Type of Library Served:	p
Sponsoring Body:	None
Source of Support:	Membership dues

Name:	Greater Hartford Consortium for Higher Education
Address:	201 Bloomfield Avenue
	West Hartford, CT 06117
Telephone:	(203) 233-1553
Administrator:	Robert M. Vogel
Type of Library Served:	a
Sponsoring Body:	None
Source of Support:	Membership dues

Name:	Higher Education Center for Urban Studies Libraries
Address:	328 Park Avenue
	Bridgeport, CT 06602
Telephone:	(203) 334-9348
Administrator:	A. Matzek
Type of Library Served:	a
Sponsoring Body:	None
Source of Support:	Membership dues

Name:	Librarians' Conference of the Connecticut Community Colleges
Address:	Asnuntuck Community College
	Box 68
	Enfield, CT 06082
Telephone:	(203) 745-1603
Administrator:	Michael Moran
Type of Library Served:	a
Sponsoring Body:	None
Source of Support:	Membership dues

(continued)

7. SINGLE-TYPE LIBRARY COOPERATIVES (continued)

    B. Receiving No Continuing Financial Support from the State
        Library: (continued)

Name:	Northwestern Connecticut Health Science Library Consortium
Address:	Danbury Hospital
	24 Hospital Avenue
	Danbury, CT 06810
Telephone:	(203) 744-2300 x 279
Administrator:	Maryanne Witters
Type of Library Served:	sp
Sponsoring Body:	None
Source of Support:	Membership dues

Name:	Southwestern Health Science Library Consortium
Address:	Stamford Hospital
	Shelburne Road & West Broad Street
	Stamford, CT 06902
Telephone:	(203) 327-1234
Administrator:	Charlotte Kirkpatrick
Type of Library Served:	sp
Source of Support:	Membership dues.

8. MULTI-TYPE LIBRARY COOPERATIVES

    A. Receiving Continuing Financial Support from the State
        Library:

    There are none.

    B. Receiving No Continuing Financial Support from the State
        Library:

Name:	Capitol Region Library Council
Address:	275 Windsor Street
	Hartford, CT 06120
Telephone:	(203) 549-0404
Administrator:	Dency Sargent
Types of Libraries Served:	a, p, sch, sp
Sponsoring Body:	None
Sources of Support:	Membership dues, grants

(continued)

8. MULTI-TYPE LIBRARY COOPERATIVES (continued)

    B. Receiving No Continuing Financial Support from the State
       Library: (continued)

Name:	Cooperative Libraries in Central Connecticut
Address:	Council of Governments 20 East Main Street Waterbury, CT 06702
Telephone:	(203) 274-6720
Administrator:	Joan Rintelman
Types of Libraries Served:	a, p, sch, sp
Sponsoring Body:	Council of Governments
Sources of Support:	Membership dues

Name:	Eastern Connecticut Library Association
Address:	Thompson Public Library P. O. Box 188 Thompson, CT 06277
Telephone:	(203) 923-9779
Administrator:	Mariellen Baxter
Types of Libraries Served:	a, p, sch
Sponsoring Body:	None
Sources of Support:	Membership dues, grants

Name:	Library Group of Southwestern Connecticut
Address:	Nyselius Library Fairfield University Fairfield, CT 06430
Telephone:	(203) 255-5411 x 451
Administrator:	Dorothy Kijanka
Types of Libraries Served:	a, p, sch, sp
Sponsoring Body:	None
Sources of Support:	Membership dues

Name:	Region One Cooperative Library Service Unit
Address:	Watertown Library 470 Main Street Watertown, CT 06795
Telephone:	(203) 274-6720
Administrator:	Joan Rintelman
Types of Libraries Served:	a, p, sch, sp
Sponsoring Body:	None
Source of Support:	Membership dues, grants

(continued)

8. MULTI-TYPE LIBRARY COOPERATIVES (continued)

    B. Receiving No Continuing Financial Support from the State
        Library: (continued)

        Name: Southeastern Connecticut Library
                                     Association
        Address: Groton Public Library
                                     Groton, CT 06340
        Telephone: (203) 448-0528
        Administrator: Gretchen Hammerstein
        Types of Libraries
        Served: a, p, sch, sp.
        Sponsoring Body: None
        Sources of Support: Membership dues, grants

        Name: Southern Connecticut Library
                                     Council
        Address   Middletown Library Service Center
                                     786 South Main Street
                                     Middletown, CT 06457
        Telephone: (203) 347-2528
        Administrator: Arlene Bielefield
        Types of Libraries
        Served: a, p, sch, sp
        Sponsoring Body: None
        Sources of Support: Membership dues, grants

        Name: Southwestern Connecticut Library
                                     Council
        Address: Bridgeport Public Library
                                     925 Broad Street
                                     Bridgeport, CT 06603
        Telephone: (203) 367-6439
        Administrator: Ann Neary
        Types of Libraries
        Served: a, p, sch, sp
        Sponsoring Body: None
        Sources of Support: Membership dues, grants

        Name: Town and Gown Film Circuit
        Address: Village Library
                                     Farmington, CT 06032
        Telephone: (203) 677-1529
        Administrator: Barbara Gibson
        Types of Libraries
        Served: p, sch
        Sponsoring Body: None
        Sources of Support: Membership dues

9. INTERLIBRARY COOPERATION FUNCTIONS

A. Receiving Continuing Financial Support from the State Library:

	State Support	Federal* Support	Total Support
Interlibrary Loan	$ 35,517	$264,244	$ 299,761
Cooperative Acquisition	None	None	None
Cooperative Cataloging	None	None	None
Cooperative Processing	None	None	None
Cooperative Delivery	64,916	None	64,916
Cooperative Reference	86,067	None	86,067
Union Lists of Serials	23,145	None	23,145
Cooperative Storage	None	1,689	1,689
Continuing Education	None	8,000	8,000
Planning/Development	336,494	23,806	360,300
Legislative Assistance	None	None	None
Audiovisual Services	25,000	27,461	52,461
Reciprocal Borrowing	300,000	None	300,000
TOTAL SUPPORT	871,139	325,200	1,196,339

* Includes LSCA Title I and III combined

B. NON-FINANCIAL SUPPORT ROLE OF THE STATE LIBRARY:

Through its Division of Library Development and its Department of
Planning and Research, the State Library provides non-financial
support for these functions with demonstration activities, continuing
services, planning, and technical assistance.

10. ILC COMMUNICATION DEVICES/SERVICE NETWORKS

A.

Device/Service	Support	Equipment	Participants
Telephone (WATS)	$ 19,477	10	2
Teletype	10,403	13	11
On-line Computer Terminals (OCLC)	108,654	2	2

B.
NON-FINANCIAL SUPPORT ROLE OF THE STATE LIBRARY:

Through its Division of Library Development and its Department of
Planning and Research, the State Library provides non-financial
support for these functions with demonstration activities, continuing
education and in-service training programs, consulting services,
planning, and technical assistance.

11. MACHINE-READABLE DATA BASE REFERENCE SEARCHING SERVICES

Data Base/Vendor	Support	Number of Terminals	Participants
New York Times Information Bank	$17,709	1	1

12. INTERLIBRARY SERVICES TO SPECIAL GROUPS

A.

Services	State Support	Federal	Total Support
Blind and Physically Handicapped	$87,483	$47,505	$134,988
Institutionalized	75,262	63,529	138,791

With the exception of the two programs indicated above, our services to special groups are not categorized into separate programs,but rather are provided through a combination of our general consulting activities, special project grants, and as components of our overall statewide service programs.

B.
NON-FINANCIAL SUPPORT ROLE OF THE STATE LIBRARY

Through its Division of Library Development, Department of Planning and Research, Library for the Blind and Physically Handicapped, and its Department of Services to State Agencies and Institutions,the State Library provides non-financial support for these functions with demonstration activities, continuing education and in-service training programs, consulting services, planning,and technical assistance.

13. PARTICIPATION IN MULTI-STATE LIBRARY NETWORKS

A.
Network: New England Library Board (NELB)
Financial Support: $34,434
Participation: State Librarian serves as an officer of the Board
Services Used: Cooperative serials service, regional legislative network, materials conservation

Network: New England Library Information Network (NELINET)
Financial Support: $108,654 (for OCLC costs)
Participation: Library staff serve on study committees
Services Used: OCLC

B.
Network: Research Libraries Group
                          45 South Main Street
                          Branford, CT 06405

14. LEGAL BASES FOR MULTI-TYPE LIBRARY COOPERATION

Connecticut General Statutes (Revised, 1977) Sec. 11-1c.

Provides for the establishment of an interagency library planning committee to aid the State Library Board in planning for statewide library services, except for school libraries. The committee may be composed of from 15 to 25 members, of whom 20% are to be library users, and 80% representatives (continued)

14. LEGAL BASES FOR MULTI-TYPE LIBRARY COOPERATION (continued)

of "established agencies or associations concerned with the provision of, or planning for, library services on a regional or statewide basis."

Connecticut General Statutes (Revised, 1977) Sec. 11-9a, 9b.

Provides for the establishment of the CLSU Review Board described in the overview statement above.

American Library Laws. 4th ed. Chicago: American Library
   Assoc., 1973, p. 423-428.

Provides for the establishment of interstate library cooperation among the six New England states, and provides the authority for the New England Library Board as the governing body for the compact.

15. LEGAL BARRIERS AGAINST PARTICIPATION IN MULTI-TYPE LIBRARY COOPERATION

Connecticut General Statutes (Revised, 1977) Sec., 11-1c.

This section defines the duties and responsibilities of the State Library Board. In so doing it specifically prohibits school libraries from an otherwise broad statement of authority to engage in planning for statewide library services among all types of libraries.

1. REPORTING AGENCY

    A. Delaware Division of Libraries
       630 State College Road
       Dover, Delaware 19901
       (302) 678-4748

    B. Chief Officer: Sylvia Short, State Librarian

    C. Fiscal Year: 1978

2. OVERVIEW

Delaware has had since 1968 an interlibrary loan network known as DRILL (Delaware Rapid Interlibrary Loan). This arrangement with the University of Delaware and the Wilmington Institute libraries permits public libraries throughout the state to borrow fiction and non-fiction materials not available in their own collections. Totally funded with Library Services Construction Act Title III monies, there is no state statute which requires or enables such an organization.

3. NUMBER OF LIBRARIES IN THE STATE

Academic:	11
Public:	24
School:	
Public:	
Private:	
Special:	32
Profit:	
Non-profit	
Total:	67 est.

4. STATE AGENCY INTERLIBRARY COOPERATION UNIT

    A. Specific   Delaware Rapid Interlibrary Loan and Reference
       Unit Name: Service

    Person in Charge: Ulysses L. Steele
                        Reference Librarian

    B. There are no other state agency units for ILC activities.

5. OTHER STATE-LEVEL GOVERNMENT ILC UNITS

    There are none.

6.   OTHER STATE-LEVEL NON-GOVERNMENTAL ILC UNITS

        Unit Name: Medical Library Resource Improvement
                            Consortium (MEDICKS)
        Address: Delaware State College Library
                            State College Road
                            Dover, Delaware   19901
        Telephone: (302) 678-5111
        Administrator: Daniel Coons, (Librarian of Delaware State College)
                            Dover, Delaware   19901
        Activities: MEDICKS' goal is to promote the sharing of medical
                            information in those areas of the State outside the
                            metropolitan area.

        Unit Name: Delaware Library Association
        Address: State College Road, Dover, Delaware   19901
        Telephone: (302) 678-5111
        Administrator: Daniel Coons, President
        Activities: Library Development Committee

7.   SINGLE-TYPE LIBRARY COOPERATIVES

A. Receiving Continuing Financial Support from the State Library:
There are none.

B. Receiving No Continuing Financial Support from the State Library:
There are none.

C. Receiving Occasional Financial Support from the State Library:
There are none.

8.   MULTI-TYPE LIBRARY COOPERATIVES

   A.   Name: DRILL
         Address: 630 State College Road, Dover, Delaware   19901
         Telephone: (302) 678-4748
         Administrator: Sylvia Short, State Librarian
         Types of Libraries Served: p, a, sp
         State Support: None
         Local Support: None

9.   INTERLIBRARY COOPERATION FUNCTIONS

   A.   Interlibrary Loan – Federal Support under Title III
         Union List of Serials – Federal Support under Title III
         Cooperative Delivery – Federal Support under Title III

(continued)

9. INTERLIBRARY COOPERATION FUNCTIONS (continued)

    B. NON-FINANCIAL SUPPORT ROLE OF THE STATE LIBRARY
        There is none.

10. ILC COMMUNICATION DEVICES/SERVICE NETWORKS

    A.
Device/Service	Support	Equipment (#)	Participants
Enterprise telephone line	All state	2	Statewide

    B. There is no non-financial support role for these services.

11. MACHINE-READABLE DATA BASE REFERENCE SEARCHING SERVICES
        There are none.

12. INTERLIBRARY SERVICES TO SPECIAL GROUPS

    A. Through cooperative service arrangements within the state,
        special services are supplied to the blind and visually handi-
        capped, to the physically handicapped, and to the institution-
        alized.

    B. There are none.

13. PARTICIPATION IN MULTI-STATE LIBRARY NETWORKS

    A. There is none.

    B. There are no multi-state networks headquartered in Delaware.

14. LEGAL BASES FOR MULTI-TYPE LIBRARY COOPERATION
        There is no enabling legislation.

15. LEGAL BARRIERS AGAINST PARTICIPATION IN MULTI-TYPE LIBRARY
    COOPERATION
        There are no legal barriers.

1. REPORTING AGENCY

    A. The State Library of Florida
       R. A. Gray Building
       Tallahassee, FL 32304
       (904) 487-2651

    B. Chief Officer: Barratt Wilkins, State Librarian

    C. Fiscal Year: 1977 (Note: FY 1976 data used for Item 7.)

2. OVERVIEW

    The basic unit of library development in Florida is the county-wide library system. Forty-nine of Florida's counties comprising eighty percent of the state's population are served by countywide library systems. Twenty-nine of the forty-nine counties are organized into nine regional or multi-county library systems.

    The establishment of regional or multi-county systems is permissive under Chapter 125.01(1)(f)(p), Florida Statutes, where counties may enter into agreements with other governmental agencies within or outside the boundaries for joint performance, or performance by one unit on behalf of the other, of any of either agency's authorized functions. Municipalities have similar power under Chapter 166.021, Florida Statutes. Florida may enter into interstate library compacts under Chapter 257.28-33, Florida Statutes.

    Chapter 257.17-19 provides for operating, establishment, and equalization grants from state general revenue appropriations for countywide library services.

3. NUMBER OF LIBRARIES IN THE STATE

    Academic: 112
    Public: 149 (administrative units; 315 including branches)
    School: 3,132
       Public: 1,982
       Private: 1,150
    Special: 193
       Profit: 41
       Nonprofit: 152

    TOTAL: 3,586

4. STATE AGENCY INTERLIBRARY COOPERATION UNIT

    A. Unit Name: Bureau of Library Development
       Person in Charge: Mrs. Virginia C. Grigg, Chief of
                         Library Deveopment

(continued)

4. STATE AGENCY INTERLIBRARY COOPERATION UNIT (continued)

        Unit Name   Bureau of Library Services
        Person in Charge: Mr. Ronald A. Kanen, Chief of Library
                                Services

Task force approach is utilized to discuss and plan for state library direction in interlibrary cooperation activities. The composition of task force is derived from appropriate units of state library agency and from other state and local governmental agencies or units.

5. OTHER STATE-LEVEL GOVERNMENTAL ILC UNITS

    There are none.

6. OTHER STATE LEVEL NON-GOVERNMENTAL ILC UNITS

    Unit Name: Florida Library Association
    Address: 3705 Mockingbird Drive
                      Tallahassee, FL 32303
    Telephone: (904) 385-5468
    Administrator: Mrs. Mary Ann Rutledge
    Activities: Interlibrary Cooperation Committee

7. SINGLE-TYPE LIBRARY COOPERATIVES

    A. Receiving Continuing Financial Support from the State
        Library (FY 1976 financial data):

        Name: Central Florida Regional Library System
        Address: 15 Southeast Osceola Avenue
                        Ocala, FL 32670
        Telephone: (904) 629-8551
        Administrator: Thomas Scott
        Type of Library Served: p
        Federal Support: $ 27,971
        State Support: $ 31,410
        Local Support: $307,778
        Other Support $ 25,613
        Total Support: $392,772

        Name: Charlotte-Glades County Library System
        Address: 801 Northwest Aaron Street
                        Port Charlotte, FL 33952
        Telephone   (813) 629-1715, 625-6470
        Administrator: Mary Ellen Fuller
        Type of Library Served: p
        Federal Support: $ 46,915
        State Support: $ 11,919
        Local Support: $170,452
        Other Support: $ 4,307
        Total Support: $233,593   (continued)

7. SINGLE-TYPE LIBRARY COOPERATIVES (continued)

Name: Jacksonville Public Library System
Address: 122 North Ocean Street
                        Jacksonville, FL 32202
Telephone: (904) 633-6870
Administrator: Harry Brinton
Type of Library Served: p
Federal Support $ 377,673
State Support $ 145,251
Local Support: $1,756,319
Other Support: $ 63,168
Total Support: $2,342,411

Name: Leon-Jefferson Library System
Address: 127 North Monroe Street
                        Tallahassee, FL 32301
Telephone: (904) 487-2665
Administrator: Paul T. Donovan
Type of Library Served: p
Federal Support: $ 62,522
State Support: $ 30,049
Local Support: $ 448,481
Other Support: $ 500
Total Support: $ 541,552

Name: Northwest Regional Library System
Address: 25 West Government Street
                        Panama City, FL 32401
Telephone: (904) 785-3457
Administrator: Jane Patton
Type of Library Served: p
Federal Support: $ 57,400
State Support: $ 35,979
Local Support: $ 319,162
Other Support: $ 25,395
Total Support: $ 437,936

Name: Orlando Public Library
Address: Ten North Rosalind Street
                        Orlando, FL 32801
Telephone: (305) 425-4694
Administrator: Glenn Miller
Type of Library Served: p
Federal Support: $ 133,950
State Support: $ 146,311
Local Support: $2,867,881
Other Support: 215,037
Total Support: $3,363,179

Name: St. Lucie-Okeechobee Regional Library
Address: 124 North Indian River Drive
                        Fort Pierce, FL 33450   (continued)

62

7. SINGLE-TYPE LIBRARY COOPERATIVES (continued)

          Telephone: (305) 468-5708
          Administrator: A. D. Henehan, Jr.
          Type of Library Served: p
          Federal Support: $ -0-
          State Support: $ 17,477
          Local Support: $192,413
          Other Support: $ 12,588
          Total Support: $222,478

          Name: Suwannee River Regional Library
          Address: Pine Avenue
                            Live Oak, FL 32060
          Telephone: (904) 362-2317
          Administrator: John D. Hales, Jr.
          Type of Library Served: p
          Federal Support: $ 22,751
          State Support: $ 28,483
          Local Support: $111,183
          Other Support: -0-
          Total Support: $162,417

          Name: West Florida Regional Library
          Address: 200 West Gregory Street
                            Pensacola, FL 32501
          Telephone: (904) 438-5479
          Administrator: Nellie Sanders
          Type of Library Served: p
          Federal Support: $ 20,476
          State Support: $ 33,055
          Local Support: $517,259
          Other Support: $ 1,500
          Total Support: $572,290

    B. Receiving No Continuing Financial Support from the State
        Library:

        There are none.

    C. Other:

        There are none.

8. MULTI-TYPE LIBRARY COOPERATIVES

    A. Receiving Continuing Financial Support from the State Library:

          Name: Florida COMCAT
          Address: c/o Orlando Public Library
                            Ten North Rosalind Street
                            Orlando, FL 32801
          Telephone: (305) 425-4694   (continued)

63

8. MULTI-TYPE LIBRARY COOPERATIVES (continued)

> Administrator: John Claytor
> Types of Libraries Served: p, a
> Federal Support: $ 30,000
> State Support: $ -0-
> Local Support: $ -0-
> Other Support: $ -0-
> Total Support: $ 30,000

> Name: Florida Library Information Network
> Address: c/o State Library of Florida
>   R. A. Gray Building
>   Tallahassee, FL 32304
> Telephone: (904) 487-2651
> Administrator: Jeanne Henning
> Types of Libraries Served: p,a, sch, sp
> Federal Support: $ 34,570
> State Support: $107,711
> Local Support: $ -0-
> Other Support: $ -0-
> Total Support: $142,281

B. Receiving No Continuing Financial Support from the State Library:

There are none.

C. Other:

> Name: Florida Union List of Serials
> Address: University of Florida Libraries
>   Library West
>   Gainesville, FL 32611
> Telephone: (904) 392-0341
> Administrator: Dr. G. A. Harrer
> Types of Libraries Served: p, a, sp
> Sponsoring Body: State Library of Florida
> Source(s) of Support: State Funds

9. INTERLIBRARY COOPERATION FUNCTIONS

A. Receiving Continuing Financial Support from the State Library:

	State Support	Federal Support		Other Support	Total Support
		Title I	Title III		
Interlibrary Loan	107,711		34,570		142,281
Continuing Education		38,812			38,812
Cooperative Acquisitions					
Cooperative Cataloging					
Cooperative Delivery					
Cooperative Processing					
Cooperative Reference					
Cooperative Storage					

(continued)

9. INTERLIBRARY COOPERATION FUNCTIONS (continued)

	State Support	Federal Support Title I	Federal Support Title III	Other Support	Total Support
Legislative Assistance	825				825
Planning/Development			46,920		46,920
Union List of Serials					
Other					
Total Support	108,536	38,812	81,490		228,838

B. Non-financial Support Role of the State Library:

There is no non-financial support role.

10. ILC COMMUNICATION DEVISES/SERVICE NETWORKS

A.
Device/Service	Support	Equipment	Participants
Teletype Communications	7,752	5-28KSB Teletype	5
TWX Communications	20,446	11-#33 TWX	11
On-line computer terminal	25,000	5-OCOC Mod. 100	5

B. Non-financial Support Role of the State Library:

There is no non-financial support role for these services.

11. MACHINE-READABLE DATA BASE REFERENCE SEARCHING SERVICES

There are none.

12. INTERLIBRARY SERVICES TO SPECIAL GROUPS

A.
Services	State Support	Federal Support	Local Support	Total Support
Service to Blind & Physically Handicapped	611,822	221,502	54,056	887,380
Service to Institutionalized	211,827	166,000		377,827
Service to Aged		65,050	32,520	97,570
Service to Economically Disadvantaged		317,239	195,387	512,627
Service to Bi-Lingual		160,416	80,000	240,416

B. Non-financial Support Role of the State Library:

There is none.

13. PARTICIPATION IN MULTI-STATE LIBRARY NETWORKS

A. Network: Southeastern Library Network (SOLINET)
Financial Support: $85,000
Participation: State Library is a charter member of
SOLINET, the regional network providing
OCLC services. State library agency has
(continued)

13. PARTICIPATION IN MULTI-STATE LIBRARY NEWTORKS (continued)

| | seven (7) on-line terminals and four (4) printing units |
| Services Used: | OCLA services |

Network:	Continuing Library Education Network and Exchange (CLENE)
Financial Support:	$ 2,812
Participation:	State Library is one of agencies providng funding
Services Used:	Publications

B. Multi-state Library Networks Headquarters in State in Which State Library has no involvement:

There are none.

14. LEGAL BASES FOR MULTI-TYPE LIBRARY COOPERATION

There is no enabling legislation.

15. LEGAL BARRIERS AGAINST PARTICIPATION IN MULTI-TYPE LIBRARY COOPERATION

There are no legal barriers.

1. REPORTING AGENCY

    A. Division of Public Library Services
        Georgia Department of Education
        156 Trinity Avenue, S.W.
        Atlanta, Georgia   30303

    B. Chief Officer: Carlton J. Thaxton, Director

    C. Fiscal year: 1976-77

2. OVERVIEW

    Thirty-six multi-county regional library systems and twelve
    single-city/county systems serve the people of all 159 Georgia
    counties. Public libraries, including multi-county regional
    systems, may be formed and funded under the Code of Georgia 1975,
    s.32-2701 to 32-2708. Additional funding is available from the
    State Board of Education Code of Georgia 1975, s.32-2604 to 32-
    2607; 32-626a. Georgia libraries are permitted to enter into
    interstate compacts under Code of Georgia 1975, s.32-27a.

    Forty-six public library systems, forty-one academic libraries,
    and twenty-six special libraries participate in the Georgia
    Library Information Network (GLIN), which serves as an inter-
    library loan locator service. GLIN is funded through LSCA Title
    III and is not a separate legal entity. It is administered
    through the Division of Public Library Services.

3. NUMBER OF LIBRARIES IN THE STATE

        Academic: 82
        Public: 309
        School: Not available
           Public: 1,767
           Private: Not available
        Special: 143 est.
           Profit: 54 est.
           Non-Profit 89 est.

    TOTAL: 2,301 est.

4. STATE AGENCY INTERLIBRARY COOPERATION UNIT

    A. There is no existing unit nor plans to create one.
    B. Unit Name: Readers Services
        Person in charge: Lucia Patrick, Consultant
        Unit Name: Library for the Blind and Physically
                            Handicapped
        Person in charge: James R. DeJarnatt

5. OTHER STATE-LEVEL GOVERNMENTAL ILC UNITS

     There are none.

6. OTHER STATE-LEVEL NON-GOVERNMENTAL ILC UNITS

    Name: Georgia Library Association (GLA)
    Address: P.O. Box 833
                     Tucker, Georgia   30084
    Telephone: (404) 934-7118
    Administrator: Anne W. Morton, Executive Secretary
    Activities: Supports and encourages development of coopera-
                  tive library activities in all types of librar-
                  ies; adopted Georgia Interlibrary Loan Code in
                  1975.

7. SINGLE-TYPE LIBRARY COOPERATIVES
A. Receiving Continuing Financial Support from the State Library:

Name: Albany-Dougherty Public
Address: 2215 Barnsdale Way
         Albany, Ga.   31707
Telephone: (912) 435-2104
Administrator: Harold W. Todd, Director
Type of Library Served: p
Federal Support: 64,828
State Support: 99,129
Local Support: 324,035
Other Support: Included above
Total Support: 487,992

Name: Athens Regional
Address: 120 W. Dougherty Street
         Athens, Ga.   30601
Telephone: (404) 543-5538
Adminstrator: Miss Roxanna Austin, Director
Type of Library Served: p
Federal Support: 35,514
State Support: 156,601
Local Support: 209,764
Other Support:
Total Support: 401,879

Name: Atlanta Public
Address: 10 Pryor Street, S.W.
         Atlanta, Ga.   30303
Telephone: (404) 688-4636
Administrator: Mrs. Ella Yates, Director
Type of Library Served: p
Federal Support: 219,501
State Support: 384,937
Other Support:
Local Support: 23,033,689

(continued)

7. SINGLE-TYPE COOPERATIVES (continued)

Other Support:
Total Support: 23,638,127

Name: Augusta Regional
Address: 902 Greene Street
          Augusta, Ga.   30902
Telephone: (404) 724-1871
Administrator: Miss Wanda Calhoun, Director
Type of Library Served: p
Federal Support: 52,875
State Support: 239,735
Local Support: 654,336
Other Support:
Total Support: $946,946

Name: Bartram Trail Regional
Address: P.O. Box 430 Liberty and Jefferson Streets
          Washington, Ga.   30673
Telephone: (404) 678-7736
Administrator: Mrs. Marjorie Morrow, Director
Type of Library Served: p
Federal Support: 16,143
State Support: 186,638
Local Support: 154,906
Other Support:
Total Support: 357,687

Name: Ben Hill County
Address: Fitzgerald Carnegie Library
          118 S. Lee Street
          Fitzgerald, Ga.   31750
Telephone: (912) 423-3642
Administrator: Mrs. Rose Turner, Librarian
Type of Library Served: p
Federal Support: 6,457
State Support: 20,661
Local Support: 38,463
Other Support:
Total Support: 65,581

Name: Brunswick-Glynn County
Address: 208 Gloucester Street
          Brunswick, Ga.   31520
Telephone: (912) 264-7360
Administrator: Miss Lila Rice, Director
Type of Library Served: p
Federal Support: 20,155
State Support: 392,410
Local Support: 1,005,493
Other Support:
Total Support: 1,418,058

(continued)

7. SINGLE-TYPE COOPERATIVES (continued)

Name: Chattahoochee Valley Regional
Address: Bradley Drive
        Columbus, Ga.   31906
Telephone: (404) 327-0211
Administrator: Mrs. Sandra Ott., Acting Director
Type of Library Served: p
Federal Support: 48,646
State Support: 236,281
Local Support: 547,451
Other Support:
Total Support: 832,378

Name: Chatham-Effingham-Liberty Regional
Address: 2002 Bull Street
        Savannah, Ga.   31401
Telephone: (912) 234-5127
Administrator: Jerry Brownlee, Director
Type of Library Served: p
Federal Support: 42,377
State Support: 209,791
Local Support: 820,763
Other Support:
Total Support: 1,072,931

Name: Cherokee Regional
Address: P.O. Box 707 - 305 S. Duke Street
        LaFayette, Ga.   30728
Telephone: (404) 638-2992
Administrator: Mrs. Margaret W. Browne, Director
Type of Library Served: p
Federal Support: 35,121
State Support: 114,149
Local Support: 161,656
Other Support:
Total Support: 310,926

Name: Chestatee Regional
Address: 127 N. Main Street
        Gainesville, Ga.   30501
Telephone: (404) 532-3311
Administrator: Miss Dorothy Dickinson, Director
Type of Library Served: p
Federal Support: 20,986
State Support: 90,617
Local Support: 200,083
Other Support:
Total Support: 311,686

Name: Coastal Plain Regional
Address: ABAC Station
        Tifton, Ga.   31794

(continued)

7. SINGLE-TYPE LIBRARY COOPERATIVES (continued)

    Telephone: (912) 386-3400
    Administrator: Walter T. Johnston, Director
    Type of Library Served: p
    Federal Support: 30,672
    State Support: 108,281
    Local Support: 140,624
    Other Support:
    Total Support: 279,577

    Name: Cobb County Library System
    Address: 30 Atlanta Street, S.E.
              Marietta, Ga.   30060
    Telephone: (404) 427-2462
    Administrator: Miss Mary Louise Rheay, Director
    Type of Library Served: p
    Federal Support: 18,744
    State Support: 134,575
    Local Support: 773,021
    Other Support:
    Total Support: 926,340

    Name: Colquitt-Thomas Regional
    Address: 204 Fifth Street, S.E., Moultrie, GA   31768
    Telephone: (912) 985-6540
    Administrator: Miss Melody Stinson, Director
    Type of Library Served: p
    Federal Support: 32,001
    State Support: 64,579
    Local Support: 192,819
    Other Support:
    Total Support: 289,399

    Name: Dalton Regional
    Address: P.O. Box 1567 - 101 S. Selvidge Street
              Dalton, Ga.   30720
    Telephone: (404) 278-4507
    Administrator: Lee S. Trimble, Jr., Director
    Type of Library Served: p
    Federal Support: 32,286
    State Support: 127,605
    Local Support: 161,005
    Other Support:
    Total Support: 320,896

    Name: DeKalb Library System
    Address: 215 Sycamore Street
              Decatur, Ga.   30030
    Telephone: (404) 378-7569
    Administrator: Miss Louise Trotti, Director
    Type of Library Served: p   (continued)
    Federal Support: 74,257

7. SINGLE-TYPE LIBRARY COOPERATIVES   (continued)

    State Support: 341,198
    Local Support: 1,131,269
    Other Support:
    Total Support: 1,546,724

    Name: DeSoto Trail Regional
    Address: 145 E. Broad Street
               Camilla, Ga.   31730
    Telephone: (912) 336-8372
    Administrator: George R. Mitchell, Director
    Type of Library Served: p
    Federal Support: 27,443
    State Support: 96,526
    Local Support: 72,994
    Other Support:
    Total Support: 196,963

    Name: Elbert County Library
    Address: 345 Heard Street
               Elberton, Ga.   30635
    Telephone: (404) 283-5375
    Administrator: Mrs. Paula F. Suddeth, Acting Director
    Type of Library Served: p
    Federal Support: 23,778
    State Support: 21,219
    Local Support: 20,516
    Other Support:
    Total Support: 65,513

    Name: Flint River Regional
    Address: 800 Memorial Drive
               Griffin, Ga.   30223
    Telephone: (404) 227-2756
    Administrator: Walter H. Murphy, Director
    Type of Library Served: p
    Federal Support: 58,114
    State Support: 245,806
    Local Support: 599,760
    Other Support:
    Total Support: 903,680

    Name: Hart County Library
    Address: Benson Street
               Hartwell, Ga.   30643
    Telephone: (404) 376-4655
    Administrator: William W. Johnson, III, Acting Director
    Type of Library Served: p
    Federal Support: 11,762
    State Support: 18,509
    Local Support: 28,641
    Other Support:
    Total Support: 58,912

(continued)

7. SINGLE-TYPE LIBRARY COOPERATIVES (continued)

Name: Houston County Public Library System
Address: 1201 Washington Avenue
         Perry, Ga.   31069
Telephone: (912) 987-3050
Administrator: Mrs. Judith Golden, Director
Type of Library Served: p
Federal Support: 53,540
State Support: 72,200
Local Support: 412,811
Other Support:
Total Support: $538,551

Name: Jefferson County
Address: 138 E. Broad Street
         Louisville, Ga.   30434
Telephone: (912) 625-3751
Administrator: Mrs. Barbara W. Prescott, Director
Type of Library Served: p
Federal Support: 6,457
State Support: 22,279
Local Support: 45,795
Other Support:
Total Support: 74,531

Name: Kinchafoonee Regional
Address: Main Street
         Dawson, Ga.   31742
Telephone: (912) 995-2902
Administrator: Mrs. Dorris Wightman, Director
Type of Library Served: p
Federal Support: 27,964
State Support: 119,476
Local Support: 106,553
Other Support:
Total Support: 253,993

Name: Lake Blackshear Regional
Address: 307 East Lamar Street
         Americus, Ga.   31709
Telephone: (912) 924-8091
Administrator: Mrs. Juanita Brightwell, Director
Type of Library Served: p
Federal Support: 74,390
State Support: 102,593
Local Support: 189,618
Other Support:
Total Support: 366,601

Name: Lake Lanier Regional
Address: 275 Perry Street, Lawrenceville, GA   30245
Telephone: (404) 963-5231

(continued)

7. SINGLE-TYPE LIBRARY COOPERATIVES (continued)

    Administrator: Mrs. Marcia LeRoux, Director
    Type of Library Served: p
    Federal Support: 56,045
    State Support: 106,700
    Local Support: 299,699
    Other Support:
    Total Support: 462,444

    Name: Middle Georgia Regional
    Address: 911 First Street
          Macon, Ga. 31201
    Telephone: (912) 745-5813
    Administrator: Charles J. Schmidt, Director
    Type of Library Served: p
    Federal Support: 54,886
    State Support: 265,342
    Local Support: 687,942
    Other Support:
    Total Support: 1,008,170

    Name: Mountain Regional
    Address: Box 157
          Young Harris, Ga. 30582
    Telephone: (404) 379-3732
    Administrator: Mrs. Hellen H. Kimsey, Director
    Type of Library Served: p
    Federal Support: 12,914
    State Support: 57,713
    Local Support: 38,026
    Other Support:
    Total Support: 108,653

    Name: Northeast Georgia Regional
    Address: Jefferson Street
          Clarkesville, Ga. 30523
    Telephone: (404) 754-4413
    Administrator: Mrs. Emily H. Anthony, Director
    Type of Library Served: p
    Federal Support: 21,590
    State Support: 89,790
    Local Support: 132,836
    Other Support:
    Total Support: 244,216

    Name: Ocmulgee Regional
    Address: 207 Fifth Avenue, N.E.
          Eastman, Ga. 31023
    Telephone: (912) 374-4711
    Administrator: Guy D. Chappell, II, Director
    Type of Library Served: p
    Federal Support: 30,672

(continued)

7. SINGLE-TYPE LIBRARY COOPERATIVES (continued)

    State Support: 99,017
    Local Support: 73,961
    Other Support:
    Total Support: 203,650

    Name: Oconee Regional
    Address: 801 Bellevue Avenue
          Dublin, Ga. 31201
    Telephone: (912) 272-5710
    Administrator: Mrs. Elizabeth D. Moore, Director
    Type of Library Served: p
    Federal Support: 30,672
    State Support: 148,784
    Local Support: 170,416
    Other Support:
    Total Support: 299,872

    Name: Ohoopee Regional
    Adress: 606 Jackson Street
          Vidalia, Ga. 30474
    Telephone: (912) 537-9283
    Administrator: Ed McCabe, Director
    Type of Library Served: p
    Federal Support: 12,914
    State Support: 68,576
    Local Support: 66,345
    Other Support:
    Total Support: 147,835

    Name: Okefenokee Regional
    Address: P.O. Box 1669 - 401 Lee Avenue
          Waycross, Ga. 31501
    Telephone: (912) 283-3126
    Administrator: Mrs. Martha P. Donaldson, Director
    Type of Library Served: p
    Federal Support: 39,874
    State Support: 117,484
    Local Support: 120,598
    Other Support:
    Total Support: 277,956

    Name: Piedmont Regional
    Address: Midland Avenue
          Winder, Ga. 30680
    Telephone: (404) 867-2762
    Administrator: T. E. Roberts, Director
    Type of Library Served: p
    Federal Support: 27,443
    State Support: 103,960
    Local Support: 122,965
    Other Support:
    Total Support: 254,368

(continued)

7. SINGLE-TYPE LIBRARY COOPERATIVES   (continued)

Name: Pine Mountain Regional
Address: 218 Perry Street, N.W. - P.O. Box 508
           Manchester, Ga.   31816
Telephone: (404) 846-2186
Administrator: Mrs. Marjorie McKenzie, Director
Type of Library Served: p
Federal Support: 27,443
State Support: 90,547
Local Support: 106,406
Other Support:
Total Support: 224,396

Name: Roddenbery Memorial
Address: North Broad Street
           Cairo, Ga.   31728
Telephone: (912) 377-3632
Administrator: Miss Wessie Connell, Director
Type of Library Served: p
Federal Support: 12,785
State Support: 43,335
Local Support: 110,580
Other Support:
Total Support: 166,700

Name: Satilla Regional
Address: 617 E. Ward Street
           Douglas, Ga.   31533
Telephone: (912) 384-4667
Administrator: Mrs. Patricia Nazworth, Director
Type of Library Served: p
Federal Support: 12,914
State Support: 66,829
Local Support: 126,135
Other Support:
Total Support: 205,878

Name: Screven-Jenkins Regional
Address: 302 E. Ogeechee Street
           Sylvania, Ga.   30467
Telephone: (912) 564-7526
Administrator: Miss Clare Mincey, Director
Type of Library Served: p
Federal Support: 9,686
State Support: 41,580
Local Support: 46,424
Other Support:
Total Support: 97,690

Name: Sequoyah Regional
Address: 400 Main Street
          Canton, Ga.   30114
Telephone: (404) 479-3090

(continued)

7. SINGLE-TYPE LIBRARY COOPERATIVES (continued)

Administrator: Mrs. Dorothy G. Hales, Director
Type of Library Served: p
Federal Support: 12,914
State Support: 64,945
Local Support: 91,975
Other Support:
Total Support: 169,834

Name: South Georgia Regional
Address: 300 Woodrow Wilson Way
          Valdosta, Ga.   31601
Telephone: (912) 247-3405
Administrator: Mrs. Roddelle B. Folsom, Director
Type of Library Served: p
Federal Support: 36,971
State Support: 108,652
Local Support: 108,277
Other Support:
Total Support: 253,900

Name: Southwest Georgia Regional
Address: Corner of Shotwell and Monroe Streets
          Bainbridge, Ga.   31717
Telephone: (912) 246-3887
Administrator: Mrs. Ruth T. Marshall, Director
Type of Library Served: p
Federal Support: 38,737
State Support: 101,978
Local Support: 67,649
Other Support:
Total Support: 208,364

Name: Statesboro Regional
Address: 124 S. Main Street,
Telephone: (902) 764-7573, Statesboro, GA   30458
Administrator: Miss Isabel Sorrier, Director
Type of Library Served: p
Federal Support: 30,671
State Support: 106,613
Local Support: 153,681
Total Support: 290,965

Name: Thomas Public
Address: 323 Persons Street, Fort Valley, GA   31030
Telephone: (912) 825-8540
Administrator: James H. Smith, Director
Type of Library Served: p
Federal Support: 6,457
State Support: 23,793
Local Support: 46,208
Other Support:
Total Support: 76,458

(continued)

7. SINGLE-TYPE LIBRARY COOPERATIVES (continued)

Name: Tri-County Regional
Address: 606 W. First Street - P.O. Box 277
          Rome, Ga.   30161
Telephone: (404) 291-9360
Administrator: Mrs. Emily C. Payne, Director
Type of Library Served: p
Federal Support: 71,377
State Support: 176,273
Local Support: 382,455
Other Support:
Total Support: 630,105

Name: Troup-Harris-Coweta Regional
Address: 500 Broome Street
          LaGrange, Ga.   30240
Telephone: (404) 882-7784
Administrator: Mrs. Doris Dean, Director
Type of Library Served: p
Federal Support: 24,214
State Support: 111,093
Local Support: 182,079
Other Support:
Total Support: 317,386

Name: Uncle Remus Regional
Address: Route 2, Box 6
          Madison, Ga.   30650
Telephone: (404) 342-1206
Administrator: Mrs. Jane Lake Whetzel, Director
Type of Library Served: p
Federal Support: 16,143
State Support: 67,550
Local Support: 40,614
Other Support:
Total Support: 124,307

Name: West Georgia Regional
Address: Rome Street at Spring
          Carrollton, Ga.   30117
Telephone: (404) 832-2163
Administrator: Leroy Childs, Director
Type of Library Served: p
Federal Support: 35,514
State Support: 149,938
Local Support: 190,866
Other Support:
Total Support: 376,318

Name: University Center in Georgia, Inc.
Address: Room 620 A Main Library Annex
          University of Georgia - Athens, Ga.   30601
Telephone: (404) 542-3715   (continued)

7.   SINGLE-TYPE LIBRARY COOPERATIVES (continued)

     Administrator: Dr. Richard K. Murdoch, Director
     Type of Library Served: a
     Sponsoring body: None
     Source(s) of support: Membership fees, federal funds, state funds

B.   Receiving No Continuing Financial Support from the State Library:

     Name: Atlanta Theological Association
     Address: Columbia Theological Seminary
               701 Columbia Drive - Decatur, Ga.   30031
     Administrator: Dr. Milton Gardiner
     Type of Library Served: a
     Sponsoring body: None
     Source(s) of support: Memberships

     Name: Atlanta University Center, Inc. Council of Librarians
     Address: Trevor Arnett Library
               273 Chestnut Street, S.W. - Atlanta, Ga.   30314
     Telephone: (404) 681-0251 ext. 225
     Administrator: Casper Jordan
     Type of Library Served: a
     Sponsoring body: Member libraries
     Source(s) of support: None

     Name: East Georgia Library Triangle
     Address: Georgia Southern College
               Box 8074-Statesboro, Ga.   30458
     Telephone: (912) 681-5115
     Administrator: Kenneth G. Walter
     Type of Library Served: a
     Sponsoring body: Member libraries
     Source(s) of support: None

8.   MULTI-TYPE LIBRARY COOPERATIVES
A.   Receiving Continuing Financial Support from the State Library:

     Name: Georgia Library Information Network (GLIN)
     Address: 156 Trinity Avenue, S.W.
               Atlanta, Ga.   30303
     Telephone: (404) 656-2461
     Administrator: Carlton J. Thaxton, Director
     Type of Library Served: a, sp, p
     Federal Support: $63,651
     State Support: 40,764
     Local Support:
     Other Support:
     Total Support: $104,415

(continued)

8. MULTI-TYPE LIBRARY COOPERATIVES

    B. Receiving No Continuing Financial Support from the State Library:

Name: Atlanta Health Sciences Libraries Consortium
Address: DeKalb General Hospital Library
          2701 N. Decatur Road - Decatur, Ga.   30033
Telephone: (404) 292-4444 ext. 5083
Administrator: Marilyn Gibbs, chairperson
Type of Library Served: a, sp
Sponsoring body: None
Source(s) of support: Supplies and time donated by member institutions.

Name: Augusta Area Committee for Health Information Resources (AACHIR)
Address: Audiovisual Department
          Medical College of Georgia - 1459 Laney-Walker Blvd.
          Augusta, Ga.   30902
Telephone: (404) 828-2360
Administrator: Sister Elizabeth Langley, Chairperson
Type of Library Served: a, sp
Sponsoring body: None
Source(s) of Support: Time and resources donated by member institutions

Name: Business Information Center
Address: Georgia State University
          University Plaza - Atlanta, Ga.   30303
Telephone: (404) 658-3550
Administrator: Lee Quarterman, Director
Type of Library Served: a, sp, p
Sponsoring body: University System of Georgia
Source   of support: University System of Georgia

Name: Central Georgia Associated Libraries
Address: Augusta Regional Library
          902 Greene Street - Augusta, Ga.   30902
Telephone: (404) 724-1871
Administrator: Wanda Calhoun, Chairperson
Type of Library Served: not reported
Sponsoring Body: None
Sources of Support: Dues from member institutions; Title II funds

Name: Coosa Valley Libraries Association
Address: Shorter College Library
          Shorter Ave., Box 5 - Rome, Ga.   30161
Telephone: (404) 232-2463
Administrator: Mrs. Betty Sumner, Chairperson
Type of Library Served: a, p, sp, sch
Sponsoring body: None
Source(s) of support: Annual dues

8. MULTI-TYPE LIBRARY COOPERATIVES (continued)

B. Receiving No Continuing Financial Support from the State Library:

Name: Health Science Libraries of Central Georgia (HSLCG)
Address: Medical Library, Mercer Univ. Sch. of Medicine, Macon, GA 31207
Telephone: (912) 745-6811 ext. 225
Administrator: Jocelyn Rankin, Secretary
Type of Library Served: a, sp
Sponsoring body: None
Source of support: NLM grant

Name: Information Exchange Center
Address: Price Gilbert Memorial Lib., GA Inst. of Tech., Atlanta 30332
Telephone: (404) 894-4526
Administrator: James B. Dodd
Type of Library Served: a, p, sp
Sponsoring body: University System of Georgia
Source(s) of support: University System of Georgia

Name: LENDS (Library Extends Catalog Access and Delivery Service)
Address: Price Gilbert Memorial Lib., GA Inst. of Tech., Atlanta 30332
Telephone: (404) 894-4511
Administrator: Ruth Hale
Type of Library Served: a, p, sp
Sponsoring body: Georgia Institute of Technology
Sources of support: GA Institute of Technology; fiche catalog sales

Name: Savannah Union Catalog
Address: Armstrong State College Library
          11935 Abercorn St. - Savannah, Ga.   31406
Telephone: (912) 925-4200 ext. 251
Administrator: Ethel Miller, Editor
Type of Library Served: a, p, sp
Sponsoring body: None
Source(s) of support: Materials and time donated by participants.

Name: South Georgia Associated Libraries
Address: Albany-Dougherty Public Library
          2215 Barnsdale Way - Albany, Ga.   31707
Telephone: (912) 435-2104
Administrator: Mike Dugan
Type of Library Served: a, p, sp
Sponsoring body: None
Source(s) of support: Membership fees; federal grant

Name: Union Catalog of the Atlanta-Athens Area
Address: Candler Library Building
          Emory University - Atlanta, Ga.   30322
Telephone: (404) 634-5726
Administrator: Mrs. Marjory Simpkins, Editor
Type of Library Served: a, p, sp
Sponsoring body: University Center in Georgia, Inc.
Sources of support: Univ. Center in GA, federal funds, subscriptions

9. INTERLIBRARY COOPERATION FUNCTIONS

   A. RECEIVING CONTINUING FINANCIAL SUPPORT FROM THE STATE LIBRARY:

	State Support	Federal Support Title I	Title III	Other Support
Interlibrary Loan	40,764	*	67,651	0
Continuing Education	*	0	*	0
Cooperative Acquisitions	0	0	0	0
Cooperative Cataloging	0	0	0	0
Cooperative Delivery	0	0	0	0
Cooperative Processing	0	0	0	0
Cooperative Reference	*	0	*	0
Cooperative Storage	0	0	0	0
Legislative Assistance	0	0	0	0
Planning/Development	*	0	*	0
Union Lists of Serials	0	0	0	0

   * Not available

   Total support figures not available.

   B. NON-FINANCIAL SUPPORT ROLE OF THE STATE LIBRARY:

   Consulting, planning, technical assistance, and coordinative activities.

10. ILC COMMUNICATION DEVICES/SERVICE NETWORKS

A. Device/Service	Support ($)	Equipment (#)	Participants

    WATS Telephone   16,728   7   116 a, p, sp

    B. NON-FINANCIAL SUPPORT ROLE OF THE STATE LIBRARY:

    Consulting, instructional workshops.

11. MACHINE-READABLE DATA BASE REFERENCE SEARCHING SERVICES:

    There are none.

12. INTERLIBRARY SERVICES TO SPECIAL GROUPS

    During FY 1977, there were 47 special programs directed to national and regional priorities: Disadvantaged - 29; Physically handicapped- 2; Early Childhood - 8; Continuing Education - 1; Aging - 2; Right to Read - 3; Other Programs - 2.

    Support for 13 subregional Talking Book Centers under the auspices of the Georgia Library for the Blind and Physically Handicapped is estimated as follows:

Talking Book Ctr. Grants	State Funds	Federal Funds	Local Funds	Total
$160,099	$49,412 est.	$18,724 est.	$84,130 est.	$312,367 est.

13. PARTICIPATION IN MULTI-STATE LIBRARY NETWORKS

   A. NETWORKS IN WHICH THE STATE LIBRARY HOLDS MEMBERSHIPS:

   Network: Southeastern Regional Medical Library Program
   Financial Support: None
   Participation: Informal Cooperation
   Services Used: Interlibrary loan referrals, reference
                         referrals

   Network: Southeastern Library Network, Inc. (SOLINET)
   Financial Support: $8,498.88
   Participation: Member
   Services Used: On-line cataloging and bibliographic search-
                         ing; computer-printed catalog cards

   B. NETWORKS HEADQUARTERED IN THE STATE IN WHICH THE STATE LIBRARY
      HAS NO INVOLVEMENT:

   Network: Cooperative College Library Center, Inc. (CCLC)
   Address: 159 Forrest Avenue, N.E. Suite 602
               Atlanta, GA 30308
   Telephone: (404) 659-6886
   Administrator: Hillis D. Davis

   Network: USDA Regional Document Delivery
   Address: Science Library
               University of Georgia
               Athens, GA 30602
   Telephone: (404) 542-4535
   Administrator: Rita Fisher

14. LEGAL BASES FOR MULTI-TYPE LIBRARY COOPERATION

   There is no enabling legislation.

15. LEGAL BARRIERS AGAINST PARTICIPATION IN MULTI-TYPE LIBRARY
    COOPERATION

   There are no legal barriers.

1. REPORTING AGENCY

    A.   State of Hawaii
         Department of Education
         Office of Public Library Services
         478 So. King Street
         Honolulu, HI 96813
         (808) 548-2431

    B.   Chief Officer: Ruth Itamura, State Librarian/
                        Assistant Superintendent for Library
                        Services

    C.   Fiscal Year: 1976/77

2. OVERVIEW

    The public and school library systems have joined in both
    selection, acquisition, cataloging, and processing. There is
    no statutory enablement or restriction. The coverage includes
    all inhabited islands, since a single State agency, the
    Department of Education, operates both the public and the
    school library systems.

3. NUMBER OF LIBRARIES IN THE STATE

    Academic: 22
    Public: 1 system, 44 branches
    School: 311
       Public: 226
       Private: 85 est.
    Special: 85
       Profit: 8 est.
       Non-profit: 77 est.

    TOTAL: 419

4. STATE AGENCY INTERLIBRARY COOPERATION UNIT

    A.   Unit Name: Research and Evaluation Services
         Person in Charge: Mrs. Masae Gotanda, Head

    B.   There is no other ILC unit in the state library.

5. OTHER STATE-LEVEL GOVERNMENTAL ILC UNITS

    There are none.

6. OTHER STATE-LEVEL NON-GOVERNMENTAL ILC UNITS

    There are none.

7. SINGLE-TYPE LIBRARY COOPERATIVES

   A. Receiving Continuing Financial Support from the State Library:

       Name: Hawaii State Public Library System
       Address: Hawaii State Library
                             478 So. King Street
                             Honolulu, HI 96813
       Telephone: (808) 548-2431
       Administrator: Ruth Itamura
       Type of Library Served: p
       Federal Support: $428,820
       State Support: $7,060,400
       Local Support: -0-
       Other Support: -0-
       Total Support: $7,489,220

   B. Receiving No Continuing Financial Support from the State Library:
       There are none.

   C. Receiving Occasional Financial Support from the State Library:
       There are none.

8. MULTI-TYPE LIBRARY COOPERATIVES

   A. Receiving Continuing Financial Support from the State Library:
       There are none.

   B. Receiving No Continuing Financial Support from the State Library:
       There are none.

   C. Receiving Occasional Financial Support from the State Library:
       There are none.

9. INTERLIBRARY COOPERATION FUNCTIONS

   A. Receiving Continuing Financial Support from the State Library:

	State Support	Federal Support Title I	Federal Support Title III	Other Support	Total Support
Interlibrary Loan	15,000		17,000		32,000
Continuing Education			6,000		6,000
*Cooperative Acquisitions	168,000				168,000
*Cooperative Cataloging					
Cooperative Delivery					
*Cooperative Processing					
Cooperative Reference					
Cooperative Storage					
Legislative Assistance					
Planning/Development	20,000		20,000		40,000
Union Lists of Serials					
Other					

85

(continued)

9. INTERLIBRARY COOPERATION FUNCTIONS (continued)

A. Functions	State Support	Federal Support Title I	Federal Support Title III	Other Support	Total Support
Total for all functions	$203,000		$43,000		$246,000

*For school and public libraries in the State Department of Education.

B. Non-Financial Support Role of the State Library:

There is no non-financial support role.

10. ILC COMMUNICATION DEVICES/SERVICE NETWORKS

A. Device/Service	Support ($)	Equipment (#)	Participants
Datatel	$17,000		1 a, 4p

B. Non-Financial Support Role of the State Library:
There is no non-financial support role for these services.

11. MACHINE-READABLE DATA BASE REFERENCE SEARCHING SERVICES

There are none.

12. INTERLIBRARY SERVICES TO SPECIAL GROUPS

A. Blind and Physically Handicapped
Institutionalized
Outreach

B. Non-Financial Support Role of the State Library:
There is none.

13. PARTICIPATION IN MULTI-STATE LIBRARY NETWORKS

A. There is none.

B. There are no multi-state networks headquartered in Hawaii.

14. LEGAL BASES FOR MULTI-TYPE LIBRARY COOPERATION

HRS 312-1 enables library cooperative development by assigning to
the Department of Education the managerial and fiscal responsibilities of providing library service within reach of all residents
throughout the State and particularly of all public and private
school children.

15. LEGAL BARRIERS AGAINST PARTICIPATION IN MULTI-TYPE LIBRARY
COOPERATION

There are no legal barriers.

1. REPORTING AGENCY

    A. Idaho State Library
        325 W. State St.
        Boise, ID 83702
        208-384-2150

    B. Chief Officer: Helen M. Miller, State Librarian

    C. Fiscal Year: 1977

2. OVERVIEW

    Six Regional Library Systems in Idaho covering all 44 counties of the
    state, rely on state and federal aid for operation, and provide CE,
    interlibrary loan and resource sharing, planning, and coordination of
    library services.

    The Idaho State Library Board, appointed by the State Board of Educa-
    tion, has the power "to contract with other libraries or agencies,
    within or without the state of Idaho, to render library services to
    people of the state of Idaho. The state library board shall have
    authority to reasonably compensate such other library unit or agency
    for the cost of the services it renders under any such contract."
    (Idaho Code Sec. 33-2504, par. 3)
    The Regional Library Systems are defined, organized, financed and
    governed in accordance with the Code Secs. 33-2609 thru 33-2616.
    Interstate Library Compacts authorized in Sec. 33-2505 to 33-2509, and
    interagency contracts sanctioned in Sec. 67-2332.

3. NUMBER OF LIBRARIES IN THE STATE

    Academic: 10
    Public: 120
    School: 403
       Public: 377
       Private: 26
    Special: 12
       Profit: 3
       Non-profit: 9

    TOTAL: 545

4. STATE AGENCY INTERLIBRARY COOPERATION UNIT

    A. There is no existing unit nor plans to create one.

    B. All professional library staff members are involved in the
        promotion of interlibrary cooperation activities.
        Supervisor: Helen M. Miller, State Librarian.

5. OTHER STATE-LEVEL GOVERNMENTAL ILC UNITS

   There are none.

6. OTHER STATE-LEVEL NON-GOVERNMENTAL ILC UNITS

   Unit Name: Idaho Library Association
   Address: 325 W. State St.
                    Boise, ID 83702
                    c/o Idaho State Library
   Telephone: 208-384-2150
   Administrator: President elected annually by general members
   Activities: Library Development Committee & CE Committee
   Types of Libraries: a, p, sch, sp

7. SINGLE-TYPE LIBRARY COOPERATIVES

   A. Receiving Continuing Financial Support from the State Library:

      Name: Health Information Retreival Center (HIRC)
      Address: 130 E. Bannock
                Boise, ID 83702
      Telephone: 208-345-1771 or 800-632-1216
      Administrator: Rita Ryan
      Type of Library Served: sp
      Federal Support: -0-
      State Support: $30,000
      Local Support: -0-
      Other Support: -0-
      Total Support: $30,000

   B. Receiving No Continuing Financial Support from the State Library:

      There are none.

   C. Other: (3 year Federal Grant Project)

      Name: Idaho Health Libraries Network (IDA-HEAL-NET)
      Address: 325 W. State St.
                Boise, ID 83702
      Telephone: 208-384-2150
      Administrator: Helen M. Miller, State Librarian
      Type of Library Served: sp
      Sponsoring Body: Idaho State Library with National Library of
                        Medicine Grant
      Sources of Support: NLM Grant 1st yr. $43,675 + State in-kind
                           NLM Grant 2nd yr. $38,000 + State in-kind
                           NLM Grant 3rd yr. $31,500 + State in-kind

8. MULTI-TYPE LIBRARY COOPERATIVES

    A. Receiving Continuing Financial Support from the State Library:

        Name: Panhandle Regional Library System
        Address: 703 Lakeside
                  Coeur d'Alene, ID 83814
        Telephone: 208-664-3284
        Administrator: William Wilson
        Types of Libraries Served: p, sch, a, community
        Federal Support: $42,319
        State Support: $24,431
        Local Support: -0-
        Other Support: -0-
        Total Support: $66,750

        Name: North Central Regional Library System
        Address: 533 Thain Road
                  Lewiston, ID 83501
        Telephone: 208-743-2561
        Administrator: Edward G. Linkhart
        Types of Libraries Served: p, sch, a, community
        Federal Support: $42,637
        State Support: $24,613
        Local Support: -0-
        Other Support: -0-
        Total Support: $67,250

        Name: Southwestern Idaho Regional Library System
        Address: 715 Capitol Boulevard
                  Boise, ID 83706
        Telephone: 208-384-4269
        Administrator: William F. Hayes
        Types of Libraries Served: p, sch, a, community
        Federal Support: $98,080
        State Support: $56,620
        Local Support: -0-
        Other Support: -0-
        Total Support: $154,700

        Name: Magic Valley Regional Library System
        Address: 434 2nd Street East
                  Twin Falls, ID 83301
        Telephone: 208-733-2964
        Administrator: Arlan Call
        Types of Libraries Served: p, sch, a, community
        Federal Support: $34,743
        State Support: $20,057
        Local Support: -0-
        Other Support: -0-
        Total Support: $54,800

(continued)

8. MULTI-TYPE LIBRARY COOPERATIVES (continued)

> Name: Gateway Regional Library System
> Address: 5210 Stuart
>   Pocatello, ID 83201
> Telephone: 208-237-2192
> Administrator: Anna Green
> Types of Libraries Served: p, sch, a, community
> Federal Support: $50,276
> State Support: $29,024
> Local Support: -0-
> Other Support: -0-
> Total Support: $79,300

> Name: Eastern Idaho Regional Library System
> Address: 457 Broadway
>   Idaho Falls, ID 83401
> Telephone: 208-524-7302
> Administrator: Jeanne Goodrich
> Types of Libraries Served: p, sch, a, community
> Federal Support: $48,945
> State Support: $28,255
> Local Support: -0-
> Other Support: -0-
> Total Support: $77,300

B. Receiving No Continuing Financial Support from the State Library:

There are none.

C. Other:

There are none.

9. INTERLIBRARY COOPERATION FUNCTIONS

A. Receiving Continuing Financial Support from the State Library:

	State Support	Federal Support Title I	Title III	Other	Total
Interlibrary Loan	$183,000	317,000	20,500	-0-	$520,500
Continuing Education	$ 8,436	-0-	-0-	-0-	$ 8,436
Cooperative Storage	maintained at and by State Library $ unavailable				
Planning/Development	$11,427 (establishment grants to new districts)				

B. Non-financial Support Role of the State Library:

State Library budget provides the personnel and materials for
support services in Public Services, Administration & Development,
Consulting, Continuing Education, etc.

10. ILC COMMUNICATION DEVICES / SERVICE NETWORKS

   A. | Device/Service | Support ($) | Equipment (#) | Participants |
      |---|---|---|---|
      | Teletype dataphone | $3,310 | 5 | 5 a |
      | Telephone credit cards | $4,075 | 90 | 90 p, sch, a |

   B. Non-financial Support Role of the State Library:

   Professional staff provide consultations and back-up resources.

11. MACHINE-READABLE DATA BASE REFERENCE SEARCHING SERVICES

Data Base/Vendor	Support ($)	Terminals (#)	Participants
MEDLINE	$30,000	3	37 sp

12. INTERLIBRARY SERVICES TO SPECIAL GROUPS

   A. The State Library provides library services and programs for the
   Blind & Physically Handicapped, Indians, & Disadvantaged. The
   provision of these services is not under contract with any other
   library in the state, however, as part of the regional systems
   the local libraries are involved in providing services to special
   groups.

   B. Non-financial Support Role of the State Library:

   Described above.

13. PARTICIPATION IN MULTI-STATE LIBRARY NETWORKS

   A. Name: Pacific Northwest Bibliographic Center
   Financial Support: $5,627
   Participation: State Library pays membership fee for all libraries
                   in Idaho.
   Services Used: all

   Name: Western Council of State Libraries (formerly WILCO/WICHE)
   Financial Support: $3,000
   Participation: member state
   Services Used: all

   B. There are none.

14. LEGAL BASES FOR MULTI-TYPE LIBRARY COOPERATION

   Power of State Library Board - IDAHO CODE Sec. 33-2504
   Interstate Library Compacts authorized - Sec. 33-2505 to 33-2509
   Interagency contracts authorized - Sec. 67-2332
   Regional Library Systems established - Sec. 33-2609 to 33-2616.

15. LEGAL BARRIERS AGAINST PARTICIPATION IN MULTI-TYPE LIBRARY COOPERATION
   There are no legal barriers.

1. REPORTING AGENCY

    A. The Illinois State Library
        275 Centennial Building
        Springfield, Illinois   62756
        (217) 782-7848

    B. Chief Officer: Kathryn J. Gesterfield, Director

    C. Fiscal Year: 1978

2. OVERVIEW

    There are a variety of organizations involved in interlibrary
    cooperation in Illinois. The State Library is coordinating
    interlibrary cooperation statewide through the network of li-
    brary systems and through the Illinois Library and Information Net-
    work (ILLINET). The systems are charged, by law, with serving public
    libraries. They now accept all other types of libraries as af-
    filiate members. The systems are organized under state statutes,
    funded by the state, and cover the entire state. The State Li-
    brary is funding a cooperation consultant program for the systems
    which provides staff to develop interlibrary cooperation activi-
    ties. The Illinois Regional Library Council provides planning
    in the Chicago area. In addition, the state library is develop-
    ing a bibliographic service, delivery service, and other state-
    wide component services to support the network.

3. NUMBER OF LIBRARIES IN THE STATE

Academic:	141	
Public:	572	
School:		
Public:	4,001	
Private:	?	
Special:	316	
Profit:	122 est.	
Non-profit:	194 est.	
TOTAL:	5,030 est.	

4. STATE AGENCY INTERLIBRARY COOPERATION UNITS

    A. Unit Name: Library Development Group
        Person in Charge: Frank Van Zanten, Associate Director for
                              Library Development

(continued)

4. STATE AGENCY INTERLIBRARY COOPERATION UNITS (continued)

    B. Unit Name: Public Services Department
        Person in Charge: Albert Halcli, Associate Director for
                             Public Services
    C. Unit Name: Circulation and Services Branch
        Person in Charge: Joyce Horney, Head
    D. Unit Name: Legislative and General Reference and
                             Information Branch
        Person in Charge: Mary Redmond, Head
    E. Unit Name: Government Documents Branch
        Person in Charge: Janet Lyons, Head

5. OTHER STATE-LEVEL GOVERNMENTAL ILC UNITS

    Unit Name: Illinois Office of Education
    Address: 100 North First Street
                    Springfield, IL 62777
    Telephone: (217) 782-3810
    Administrator: Marie Sivak, Educational Consultant
    Activities: Work primarily with school libraries/media
                    centers. Cooperates with Illinois State
                    Library and Illinois Library Systems in
                    exchanging information, appearances at
                    meetings, etc. . Serves on Illinois State
                    Library Advisory Committee.

    Unit Name: Illinois Resource and Dissemination Network,
                    State Board of Education
    Address: Illinois Office of Education
                    100 North First Street
                    Springfield, IL 62777
    Telephone: (217) 782-0763
    Administrator: Carol Reisinger, Project Director
    Activities: Designed to assist local educators in a sys-
                    tematic approach to acquire educational know-
                    ledge and to facilitate educational problem
                    solving. Has access to the data bases of the
                    Dialog Information System, the NIMIS file and
                    agency-developed Illinois Resources Files. Has
                    agreed to receive eligible requests from local
                    educators who use local libraries through the
                    Illinois Library and Information Network. IRDN
                    primarily supplies citations to local educa-
                    tors and requests they first try local public
                    and university libraries to obtain hardcopy.

6. OTHER STATE LEVEL NON-GOVERNMENTAL ILC UNITS

    There are none.

7. SINGLE-TYPE LIBRARY COOPERATIVES

    A. Receiving Continuing Financial Support from the State Library:

        There are none.

    B. Receiving no Continuing Financial Support from the State Library:

        Name: Conference of Directors of State University Librarians of Illinois (CODSULI)
        Address: c/o Western Illinois University
                              900 West Adams Street
                              Macomb, Illinois 61455
        Telephone: (309) 298-1845
        Administrator: Pierce S. Grove
        Type of Library Served: a
        Sponsoring Body: There is none.
        Source of Support: Membership dues.

        Name: Chicago Cluster of Theological Schools
        Address: 1100 East 55 Street
                              Chicago, Illinois 60615
        Telephone: (312) 667-3500
        Administrator: Neil Gerdes
        Type of Library Served: a
        Sponsoring Body: Not Available
        Source(s) of Support: Not Available

        Name: Chicago Academic Library Council
        Address: Roosevelt University
                              Murray-Green Library
                              430 South Michigan
                              Chicago, Illinois 60605
        Telephone: (312) 341-3640
        Administrator: Adrian Jones
        Type of Library Served: a
        Sponsoring Body: Not Available
        Source(s) of Support: Not Available

        Name: ILLOWA Higher Education Consortium
        Address: c/o Western Illinois University
                              103 Sherman Hall
                              Macomb, Illinois 61455
        Telephone: (309) 298-1650
        Administrator: Dr. Richard Alter, Coordinator
        Type of Library Served: a
        Sponsoring Body: Not Available
        Source(s) of Support: Not Available

(continued)

7. SINGLE-TYPE LIBRARY COOPERATIVES (continued)

    Name: Lake County Medical Library
                        Services Consortium
    Address   Condell Memorial Hospital
                        Cleveland and Stewart Avenue
                        Libertyville, Illinois 60048
    Telephone: (312) 362-2900
    Administrator: Emily Bergmann
    Type of Library Served: sp
    Sponsoring Body: Not Available
    Source(s) of Support: Not Available

    Name: LIBRAS
    Address: c/o Doris Colby
                        Aurora College
                        Aurora, Illinois 60507
    Telephone: (312) 892-6431, Extension 61
    Administrator: Not Available
    Type of Library Served: a
    Sponsoring Body: Not Available
    Source(s) of Support: Not Available

    Name: West Suburban Intercollegiate Council
    Address: Box 471
                        Lisle, Illinois 60532
    Telephone: (312) 971-0960
    Administrator: Claudette Dwyer
    Type of Library Served: a
    Sponsoring Body: Not Available
    Sources of Support: Not Available

    Name: Sangamon Valley Academic Library Consortium
    Address: c/o Illinois College
                        Schewe Library
                        Jacksonville, Illinois 62650
    Telephone: (217) 245-7126
    Administrator: Richard L. Pratt
    Type of Library Served: a
    Sponsoring Body: Not Available
    Source (s) of Support: Not Available

    Name: Illinois Library Materials Processing Center
    Address: 4036 East State Street
                        Rockford, Illinois 61108
    Telephone: (815) 348-2441
    Administrator: Julian Bruening
    Types of Library served: p
    Federal Support: $180,000
    State Support: There is none.

(continued)

7. SINGLE-TYPE LIBRARY COOPERATIVES (continued)

          Local Support: Not Available
          Other Support: Not Available
          Total Support: Not Available

          Name: Private Academic Library Group of Illinois
          Address: c/o Herb Biblo
                            Illinois Institute of Technology
                            John Crerar Library
                            35 West 33rd Street
                            Chicago, Illinois   60616
          Telephone: (312) 225-2526
          Administrator: Herb Biblo
          Type of Libraries Served: a
          Federal Support: There is none.
          State Support: There is none.
          Local Support: Not Available
          Other Support: Not Available
          Total Support: Not Available

          Name: Metropolitan Consortium
          Address: c/o Illinois Masonic Medical Center
                            Noah Van Cleef Memorial Medical Library
                            836 Wellington Avenue
                            Chicago, Illinois   60657
          Telephone: (312) 525-2300, Extension 328
          Administrator: Harriette M. Cluxton
          Type of Library Served: sp
          Sponsoring Body: Not Available
          Source(s) of Support: Not Available

          Name: Illinois Health Libraries Consortium
          Address: c/o National Dairy Council Library
                            6300 North River Road
                            Rosemont, Illinois   60018
          Telephone: (312) 696-1020, Extension 339
          Administrator: William D. Siarny, Jr.
          Type of Library Served: sp
          Sponsoring Body: Not Available
          Source(s) of Support: Not Available

          Name: Illinois Department of Mental Health &
                               Developmental Disabilities
                            Professional Library Consortium
          Address: c/o Adolf Meyer Center Professional Library
                            2310 Mound Road
                            Decatur, Illinois   62526
          Telephone: (217) 877-3410, Extension 220
          Administrator: Eugene D. Roskin

                                                            (continued)

7. SINGLE-TYPE LIBRARY COOPERATIVES (continued)

>   Type of Library Served: sp
>   Sponsoring Body: Not Available
>   Source (s) of Support: Not Available

>   Name: Areawide Hospital Library Consortium of
>   Southwestern Illinois (AHLC)
>   Address: c/o St. Joseph Hospital
>   915 East Fifth Street
>   Alton, Illinois 62002
>   Telephone: (618) 465-8831
>   Administrator: Judith Messerle
>   Type of Library Served: sp
>   Sponsoring Body: Not Available
>   Source(s) of Support: Not Available

>   Name: Heart of Illinois Library Consortium
>   Address: c/o St. Francis Hospital-Medical Center
>   530 N.E. Glen Oak Avenue
>   Peoria, Illinois 61637
>   Telephone: (309) 672-2210
>   Administrator: Mary Anne Parr
>   Type of Library Served: sp
>   Sponsoring Body: Not Available
>   Source(s) of Support: Not Available

C. Other:

>   There is none.

8. MULTI-TYPE LIBRARY COOPERATIVES

A. Receiving Continuing Financial Support from the State Library:

>   Name: Bur Oak Library System
>   Address: 405 Earl Road
>   Shorewood, Illinois 60436
>   Telephone: (815) 729-3345
>   Administrator: Peter J. McElhinney
>   Types of Libraries Served: a, p, sp
>   Federal Support: $ 90,506.50
>   State Support: 537,635.60
>   Local Support: 0
>   Other Support: 0
>   Total Support: 628,142.10

(continued)

8. MULTI-TYPE LIBRARY COOPERATIVES (continued)

    Name: Chicago Library System
    Address: c/o Chicago Public Library
                       425 North Michigan
                       Chicago, Illinois 60611
    Telephone   (312) 269-2900
    Administrator: David L. Reich
    Types of Libraries Served: a, p, sp
    Federal Support: $ 339,935.90
    State Support: $2,596,316.92
    Local Support: 0
    Other Support: 0
    Total Support: $2,936,252.82

    Name: Corn Belt Library System
    Address: 412 Eldorado Road
                       Bloomington, Illinois 61701
    Telephone: (309) 663-2211
    Administrator: Henry Meisels
    Types of Libraries Served: a, p, sch, sp
    Federal Support: $ 47,438.90
    State Support: $255,412.35
    Local Support: 0
    Other Support: 0
    Total Support: $302,851.25

    Name: Cumberland Trail Library System
    Address: 12th and McCawley Streets
                       Flora, Illinois 62839
    Telephone: (618) 662-2741
    Administrator: Glenn Dockins
    Types of Libraries Served: a, p, sch, sp
    Federal Support: $ 37,479.80
    State Support: $315,801.71
    Local Support: 0
    Other Support: 0
    Total Support: $353,281.51

    Name: DuPage Library System
    Address: 127 South First Street
                       P.O. Box 268
                       Geneva, Illinois 60134
    Telephone: (312) 232-8457
    Administrator: Alice E. McKinley
    Types of Libraries Served: a, p, sch, sp
    Federal Support: $ 83,676.82
    State Support: $524,947.15
    Local Support: 0
    Other Support: 0
    Total Support: $608,623.97

(continued)

8. MULTI-TYPE LIBRARY COOPERATIVES (continued)

          Name: Great River Library System
          Address: 515 York Street
                         Quincy, Illinois   62301
          Telephone: (217) 223-2560
          Administrator: Stillman Taylor
          Types of Libraries Served: a, p, sch, sp
          Federal Support: $ 19,305.00
          State Support: $233,855.07
          Local Support: 0
          Other Support: 0
          Total Support: $253,160.07

          Name: Illinois Valley Library System
          Address: 808 North Glenwood Avenue
                         Peoria, Illinois   61606
          Telephone: (309) 673-3132
          Administrator: Ray Howser
          Types of Libraries Served: a, p, sch, sp
          Federal Support: $ 41,653.40
          State Support: $384,129.87
          Local Support: 0
          Other Support: 0
          Total Support: $425,783.27

          Name: Kaskaskia Library System
          Address: 306 North Main Street
                         Smithton, Illinois   62285
          Telephone: (618) 235-4220
          Administrator: Edgar W. Chamberlin
          Types of Libraries Served: a, p, sch, sp
          Federal Support: $ 34,860.60
          State Support: $289,384.71
          Local Support: 0
          Other Support: 0
          Total Support: $324,245.31

          Name: Lewis & Clark Library System
          Address: P.O. Box 368
                         Edwardsville, Illinois   62025
          Telephone: (618) 656-3216
          Administrator: Neil Flynn
          Types of Libraries Served: a, p, sch, sp
          Federal Support: $ 39,530.10
          State Support: $372,112.11
          Local Support: 0
          Other Support: 0
          Total Support: $411,642.21

(continued)

8. MULTI-TYPE LIBRARY COOPERATIVES (continued)

Name: Lincoln Trail Library System
Address: 1704 West Interstate Drive
                    Box 3471 Country Fair Station
                    Champaign, Illinois 61820
Telephone: (217) 352-0047
Administrator: Elaine Albright
Types of Libraries Served: a, p, sp
Federal Support: $ 72,622.20
State Support: $432,073.47
Local Support: 0
Other Support: 0
Total Support: $504,695.67

Name: North Suburban Library System
Address: 200 West Dundee Road
                    Wheeling, Illinois 60090
Telephone: (312) 459-1300
Administrator: Robert McClarren
Types of Libraries Served: a, p, sch, sp
Federal Support: $ 199,594.00
State Support: $ 916,961.71
Local Support: 0
Other Support: 0
Total Support: $1,116,555.71

Name: Northern Illinois Library System
Address: 4034 East Street
                    Rockford, Illinois 68151
Telephone: (815) 229-0330
Administrator: Lila Brady
Types of Libraries Served: a, p, sch, sp
Federal Support: $ 81,185.80
State Support: $587,413.47
Local Support: 0
Other Support: 0
Total Support: $668,599.27

Name: River Bend Library System
Address: P.O. Box 125
                    Coal Valley, Illinois 61240
Telephone: (309) 799-3131
Administrator: George Curtis
Types of Libraries Served: a, p, sch, sp
Federal Support: $ 51,775.80
State Support: $186,825.35
Local Support: 0
Other Support: 0
Total Support: $238,601.15

(continued)

8. MULTI-TYPE LIBRARY COOPERATIVES (continued)

> Name: Rolling Prairie Libraries
> Address: 345 West Eldorado Street
>   Decatur, Illinois   62522
> Telephone: (217) 429-2586
> Administrator: Ray Ewick
> Types of Libraries Served: a, p, sch, sp
> Federal Support: $ 45,974.30
> State Support: $415,651.00
> Local Support: 0
> Other Support: 0
> Total Support: $461,625.30

> Name: Shawnee Library System
> Address: R.R. 2, Box 136 A
>   Carterville, Illinois   62918
> Telephone: (618) 985-3711
> Administrator: James Ubel
> Types of Libraries Served: a, p, sch
> Federal Support: $ 34,981.90
> State Support: $584,424.08
> Local Support: 0
> Other Support: 0
> Total Support: $619,40 5.98

> Name: Starved Rock Library System
> Address: Hitt and Swanson Streets
>   Ottawa, Illinois   61350
> Telephone: (815) 434-7537
> Administrator: Richard Willson
> Types of Libraries Served: a, p, sch, sp
> Federal Support: $ 18,409.70
> State Support: $205,840.84
> Local Support: 0
> Other Support: 0
> Total Support: $224,250.54

> Name: Suburban Library System
> Address: 125 Tower Drive
>   Burr Ridge, P.O.
>   Hinsdale, Illinois   60521
> Telephone: (312) 325-6640
> Administrator: Lester Stoffel
> Types of Libraries Served: a, p, sp
> Federal Support: $ 165,878.50
> State Support: $1,075,482.28
> Local Support: 0
> Other Support: 0
> Total Support: $1,241,360.78

(continued)

8. MULTI-TYPE LIBRARY COOPERATIVES (continued)

Name: Western Illinois Library System
Address: 58 Public Square
                  Monmouth, Illinois 61462
Telephone: (309) 734-7141
Administrator: Camille Radmacher
Types of Libraries Served: a, p, sch, sp
Federal Support: $ 49,673.60
State Support: $230,139.32
Local Support: 0
Other Support: 0
Total Support: $279,812.92

Name: Illinois Regional Library Council
Address: 425 North Michigan Avenue, Suite 1366
                  Chicago, Illinois 60611
Telephone: (312) 828-0928
Administrator: Beth A. Hamilton, Executive Director
Types of Libraries Served: a, p, sch, sp
Federal Support: $83,747   (Fiscal 1978)
State Support: There is none.
Local Support: $ 7,060
Other Support: $ 5,425
Total Support: $96,232

Name: Illinois Library and Information Network
                    (ILLINET)
Address: c/o Illinois State Library
                  275 Centennial Building
                  Springfield, Illinois 62756
Telephone: (217) 782-2994
Administrator: Kathryn J. Gesterfield
Types of Libraries Served: a, p, sch, sp
Federal Support: Not Available
State Support: Not Available
Local Support: Not Available
Other Support: Not Available
Total Support: Not Available*

*The Illinois Library and Information Network (ILLINET) is a statewide,
multitype cooperative library network of the Illinois Library Systems
and their academic, public, school, and special libraries, the Research and Reference Centers and Special Resource Centers. ILLINET is
coordinated by the Illinois State Library. Library systems and libraries voluntarily have formally agreed to work together to provide services and resources to satisfy the needs of Illinois citizens.

Library systems receive state and federal support as shown on previous
pages. Isolating specific percentages of state and federal

(continued)

8. MULTI-TYPE LIBRARY COOPERATIVES (continued)

support that go into total ILLINET activities is not possible. In addition, the Illinois State Library provides staff services as well as materials, which are supported by state appropriations from the Illinois General Assembly. It is not possible to isolate specific amounts of support for ILLINET and specific amounts for support of state government information functions.

Research and Reference Centers and Special Resource Centers receive state grants for filling interlibrary loan and information requests from local academic, public, school, and special libraries that cannot be filled at the library system level. These centers include the Illinois State Library, University of Illinois/Champaign, Chicago Public Library, Southern Illinois University/Carbondale, John Crerar Library, University of Chicago, and Northwestern University Libraries at Evanston. There is a state appropriation of $670,000 for Fy 1977.

Seventeen Illinois library systems received grants for improving interlibrary cooperation activities by employing an interlibrary cooperation consultant. Following are systems involved in the program:

Name of System		NUMBER OF LIBRARIES JOINING SYSTEM			
		(3) p	(4) a	(4) sp	(4) (5) sch
Bur Oak		20	5	1	0
Chicago[2]	Eva Brown	1	39	135	0
Corn Belt	John Bradbury	21	2	4	11
Cumberland Trail	Vincent Schmidt	17	6	2	29
DuPage	recruiting (1)	26	6	15	14
Great River	Cynthia Altgilbers	22	5	5	34
Illinois Valley	recruiting (1)	34	6	11	5
Kaskaskia	Connie Etter	18	3	4	26
Lewis & Clark	Alexi Fosse	29	6	8	2
Lincoln Trail	Leonard Swift	47	5	6	0
North Suburban	Linda Crowe	35	12	38	61
Northern Illinois	recruiting (1)	59	9		64
River Bend	Mary Root	20	7	6	3
Rolling Prairie	Chuck DeYoung	42	9	12	25
Shawnee	Patsy-Rose Hoshiko	34	4	0	61
Starved Rock	Geri Schmidt	27	1	10	47
Suburban	Robert Drescher	70	12	16	0
Western Illinois	Kathleen Costello	27	4	0	20
	Totals	549	141	273	402

See footnotes on next page

(continued)

8. MULTI-TYPE LIBRARY COOPERATIVES (continued)

(1) October 1, 1977

(2) a library system consisting of a single library serving a city of over 500,000 population

(3) FY 77

(4) October 1, 1977

(5) represents number of school districts/school libraries signing agreements. Districts sign one agreement, but have many school libraries.

   B. Receiving No Continuing Financial Support from the State Library:

      Name: Center for Research Libraries
      Address: 5721 South Cottage Grove Avenue
                         Chicago, Illinois 60637
      Telephone: (312) 955-4545
      Administrator: Gordon Williams
      Types of Libraries Served: a, p, sp
      Sponsoring Body: Not Available
      Source of Support: Membership fees

      Name: Midwest Health Science Library Network
                           (MHSLN)
      Address: 35 West 33rd Street
                         Chicago, Illinois 60616
      Telephone: (312) 225-2526, Extension 78
      Administrator: Chester Pleztke, Coordinator
      Types of Libraries Served: a, p, sp
      Sponsoring Body: Not Available
      Source of Support: National Library of Medicine

   C. Other:

      There are none.

9. INTERLIBRARY COOPERATION FUNCTIONS

A. Receiving Continuing Financial Support from the State
   Library:

	State Support	Federal Support Title I	Federal Support Title II	Other Support	Total [1] Support
Interlibrary Loan	$670,000				
Continuing Education	x				
Cooperative Acquisitions	x	x			
Cooperative Cataloging	x	$180,000			
Cooperative Delivery	x				
Cooperative Processing	x	x			
Cooperative Reference	x				
Cooperative Storage	x				
Legislative Assistance	x				
Planning/Development	x	11,861			
Union Lists of Serials	x				
Interlibrary Cooperation	x	270,000	171,000		
Network Research	x	14,141			

(1) No single dollar amount available. The $670,000.00 for Inter-
library Loan also supports Cooperative Reference Services from
the Research and Reference Centers. The Interlibrary Cooperation amount under Title I also supports interlibrary loan and
reference services in certain library systems. Isolating specific amounts of State support and Federal support that go into
these activities is not possible at this time. Library systems
provide all of activities in column one through use of state
grants made by the State Legislature and coordinated by the
Illinois State Library

B. Non-financial support role of the State Library:

The Illinois State Library is organizationally arranged into
three major sections: Library Administration; Library Operations; and Library Development. Each section contributes to
the functions of interlibrary cooperation through daily operational functions or consulting on a specialist and generalist
basis.

The Illinois Library and Information Network is a total network
which affects each ISL staff member. We have consultants in the
area of continuing education, blind and physically handicapped &
institutional services, manpower, system services, children and
young adult services, and interlibrary cooperation. We also
have specialists in statistics, systems analysis, and public information. Reference librarians in specialized areas, such as

(continued)

9. INTERLIBRARY COOPERATION FUNCTIONS (continued)

legislative research, are also an integral part of our "state library agency non-financial" support. Consultants and specialists, as well as the library operations staff in interlibrary loan, circulation, collection development and processing are all kept informed on ILLINET development such as:

INTERLIBRARY LOAN: Statewide workshops by staffs of Research and Reference Centers to assist System staffs in better utilization of the services from the Centers.

COOPERATIVE ACQUISITION: A statewide committee representative of all types of libraries has developed a plan for cooperative collection development in Illinois among libraries at all levels in ILLINET. Staff from the State Library serve as liaison and members of the Committee.

COOPERATIVE CATALOGING/PROCESSING: See below involvement with OCLC. ISL staff provides staff support for training and administration of statewide OCLC programs.

COOPERATIVE REFERENCE: ILLINET is also an information network. Reference staff from ISL and R & R Centers provide workshops at system level.

CONTINUING EDUCATION: Statewide committee of all types of librarians, trustees, and educators has been appointed to aid the Illinois State Library in planning for the coordination of educational and training activities to meet the needs of the library community in Illinois.

BLIND & PHYSICALLY HANDICAPPED: State Library also provides consultant services in the areas of services to the handicapped.

10. ILC COMMUNICATION DEVICES/SERVICE NETWORKS

A. State Library agency financial support of functional communication devices and service networks among libraries within the state:

DEVICE/SERVICE	SUPPORT	EQUIPMENT	PARTICIPANTS
Teletypewriter (1)		21 units	20 systems
Delivery (2)			R & R Centers

(continued)

10. ILC COMMUNICATION DEVICES/SERVICE NETWORKS (continued)

A.

Device/Service	Support ($)	Equipment (#)	Participants
Ohio College Library Center	120,000	94 terminals	80 academic libs.
	4 telephone circuits plus modems, etc.		
CLSI LIBS 100	100,000	PD5 11/05 CPU 5 special terminals for remote dial up access.	4 systems and the state library

(1) housed in library systems and supported by system budgets which are appropriated by General Assembly. All research and Reference Centers have TWX supported by state grants administered by state library agency for services rendered to library systems. Equipment and participants pertain only to library systems and Research and Reference Centers. Many systems have WATS, Credit cards, etc.

(2) systems support own services and contract with each other for delivery services to libraries. In Chicago Metropolitan area, 5 library systems financially support Northeastern Illinois Delivery Service (NEIDS) coordinated by the Illinois Regional Library Council. NEIDS connects University of Illinois Research and Reference Center in Urbana with Chicago Area libraries.

B. NON-FINANCIAL SUPPORT ROLE OF THE STATE LIBRARY

The State Library administers services available from OCLC to Illinois participants. Staff and operating costs are paid from State funds.

11. MACHINE-READABLE DATA BASE REFERENCE SEARCHING SERVICES

Data Base/Vendor	Support ($)	Terminals (#)	Participants

Illinois Regional Library Council supporting such services through federal support grant and local funds. Contact Council for specifics.

12. INTERLIBRARY SERVICES TO SPECIAL GROUPS

The blind and physically handicapped are served through regular ILLINET service patterns. The public libraries provide basic services as defined in "Implementing Library Services for the Blind and Physically Handicapped: An Implementation Paper to Measures of Quality," Illinois Libraries, 57:7:460-466. Library systems maintain backup resources (materials, equipment, personnel) which provide frequently requested materials, the state/regional library provides consultant and material backup to the systems, and the Library of Congress provides backup support to the state/regional level.

A state appropriation funds the system and state/regional levels of the network. Congress funds the national level; local appropriations fund local services.

B. State library also provides consultant services in the areas of services to the handicapped and institutionalized.

13. PARTICIPATION IN MULTI-STATE LIBRARY NETWORKS

A. Networks: CCLN, CRL, MHSLN, CLENE
   Financial Support: Membership fees
   Participation: not reported

   Services Used: not reported

B. Multi-State Networks Headquartered in state in which state library agency has no involvement

   There are none.

14. LEGAL BASES FOR MULTI-TYPE LIBRARY COOPERATION

State legislation enabling multi-type library cooperative development:

Legislation	Citation to American Library Laws
Illinois State Library Chapter 128: 106; 107; 118	pp. 547-552
Library Systems Act Chapter 81: 111; 117; 122	pp. 552-558
Local Libraries Chapter 81: 1004-11; 4-7; 22	pp. 589-590 pp. 612-613
Corporation Law Chapter 32	

State legislation enabling interstate library compact:

Interstate Library Compact Chapter 81: 101-104	pp. 559-561

State-provided statutory funding for multi-type library cooperative development

Illinois State Library Chapter 128: 106-107; 118	pp. 547-552
Local Libraries Chapter 81: 118	pp. 555-556

15. Legal barriers which prohibit or limit participation in state-wide multi-type library cooperative activities by any libraries within the state:

1) Activity not clearly defined in law though allowable in statutes cited above. No specific overall legislation at this time.

2) From the Illinois State Library's viewpoint, legislation is available to carry out activities; however, this type of legislation (see above) is not represented in state statutes for the Illinois Office of Education (elementary and secondary) and the Illinois Board of Higher Education.

109

1. REPORTING AGENCY

    A. Indiana State Library
        140 North Senate Avenue
        Indianapolis, IN   46204
        (317) 633-5440

    B. Chief Officer: Jean Jose, Acting Director

    C. Fiscal Year:
        For Public Libraries: Year ending December 31, 1976
        For Other Libraries: Year ending June 30, 1976

2. OVERVIEW

    Formalized interlibrary cooperation activities are through the
    Indiana Cooperative Library Services Authority (INCOLSA), eleven
    Area Library Services Authorities (ALSAs), the TWX communica-
    tions network, and access to automated data bases through the
    State Library.   INCOLSA and ALSAs are established and organized
    under the Library Services Authority Act of Indiana (IC 20-13-6),
    and funding for them as well as the TWX network and data base
    access is from LSCA.   All types of libraries compose the member-
    ship of INCOLSA and ALSAs.   INCOLSA is a statewide organization;
    ALSAs are based on fourteen socio-economic areas of the state;
    and the TWX network is statewide with 181 public library
    satellites, thirteen public library centers, four state univer-
    sity centers, one medical library center, and the State Library.
    Principal activities of INCOLSA include development of an
    automated Indiana data base through OCLC, updating and main-
    tenance of the Indiana Union List of Serials, and cataloging and
    processing services for small libraries through a processing
    center.   ALSAs provide interlibrary loan and reference referral
    service, continuing education program, and selected other ser-
    vices to member libraries.   The TWX network is used for inter-
    library loan and reference referral.   Closer integration of these
    activities for the most efficient and cost-effective service will
    be the next development.   Indiana has an Interstate Library
    Compact law (IC 20-13-20), which allows the state to enter into
    agreements with bordering states provided they have a substan-
    tially similar law.

3. NUMBER OF LIBRARIES IN THE STATE

        Academic: 57
        Public: 239
        School: 2,149 (1974 – last year available)
          Public: Not available
          Private: Not available
        Special: 37 (institutional)
                          23 (estimated other)
        Total: 2,505 (estimate)

4. STATE AGENCY INTERLIBRARY COOPERATION UNIT

    A. Unit Name: Indiana State Library
                            Extension Division*
                         *(not the sole responsibility of the
                            Division)
        Person in Charge: Barney McEwen, Division Head

    B. There is none. (ILC is a part of other on-going activities)

5. OTHER STATE-LEVEL GOVERNMENT ILC UNITS.

        There are none.

6. OTHER STATE-LEVEL NON-GOVERNMENTAL ILC UNITS

    Unit Name: Indiana Cooperative Library Services Authority
    Address: 1100 W. 42nd Street
                        Indianapolis, IN 46208
    Telephone: (317)926-3361
    Administrator: Barbara E. Markuson
    Cooperative activity: INCOLSA's goal is to develop a computer-
                        based cooperative bibliographic center to
                        facilitate rapid exchange of bibliographic
                        information among Indiana libraries of all types.

7. SINGLE-TYPE COOPERATIVES

    A. Receiving Continuing Financial Support from the State Library:

        Name: Indiana Library Film Circuit
        Address: 2201 Godman Avenue
                        Muncie, IN 47303
        Telephone: (317) 289-4271
        Administrator: Mrs. Suzanne Kieffer
        Type of Library Served: p
        Local Support: Not known (membership fees)
        State Support: 0
        Federal Support: $37,200 (FY 1977) (for specific project -
                        Festival Film)

    B. Receiving No continuing Financial Support from the State
        Library:

        Name: Library Flicks
        Address: 2201 Godman Avenue
                        Muncie, IN 47303
        Telephone: (317) 289-4271
        Administrator: Mrs. Suzanne Kieffer
        Type of Library Served: p
        Sources of Support: Membership Fees

8.   MULTI-TYPE LIBRARY COOPERATIVES

   A.   Receiving Continuing Financial Support from the State Library:

   Name: Northwest Indiana ALSA
   Address: 200 West Indiana Avenue, P.O. Box 948
                  Chesterton, IN   46304
   Telephone: (219) 926-1146
   Administrator: Mrs. Gail Birdcell
   Types of Libraries Served: a, p, sch, sp, institutional

   State Support: 0
   Federal Support: $76,059.10 (1977)
   Total Support: $76,059.10

   Name: ALSA 2
   Address: 219 West Market Street
                  Nappanee, IN   46550
   Telephone: (219) 773-3641
   Administrator: Margaret McNeill
   Types of Libraries Served: a, p, sch, sp, institutional

   State Support: 0
   Federal Support: $73,940.00 (1977)
   Total Support: $73,940.00

   Name: Wabash Valley ALSA
   Address: 222 South Washington
                  Crawfordsville, IN   47933
   Telephone: (317) 362-4235
   Administrator: Miss Judy Greeson
   Types of Libraries Served: a, p, sch, sp, institutional

   State Support: 0
   Federal Support: $32,845.00 (6/77-5/78)
   Total Support: $32,845.00

   Name: Central Indiana ALSA
   Address: 1100 West 42nd Street
                  Indianapolis, IN   46208
   Telephone: (317) 926-6561
   Administrator: Judy Wegener
   Types of Libraries Served: a, p, sch, sp, institutional

   State Support: 0
   Federal Support: $68,899.45 (8/76-7/77)
   Total Support: $68,899.45

   Name: Whitewater Valley ALSA
   Address: 512½ Central Avenue
                  Connersville, IN   47331
   Telephone: (317) 825-7296

(continued)

8. MULTI-TYPE LIBRARY COOPERATIVES (continued)

A. Receiving Continuing Support from the State Library:

    Administrator: Carl Holland
    Types of Libraries Served: a, p, sch, sp, institutional

    State Support: 0
    Federal Support: $54,177.00 (9/76 - 9/77)
    Total Support: $54,177.00

    Name: Stone Hills ALSA
    Address: 2222 West 8th Street
               Bedford, IN 47421
    Telephone: (812) 279-5182
    Administrator: Polly Coe
    Types of Libraries Served: a, p, sch, sp, institutional

    State Support: 0
    Federal Support: $77,671.00 (1976-1977)
    Total Support: $77,671.00

    Name: Southeastern Indiana ALSA
    Address: 428 North State St., P.O. Box 168
               North Vernon, IN 47265
    Telephone: (812) 346-5521
    Administrator: Mrs. Loraine Mooney
    Types of Libraries Served: a, p, sch, sp, institutional

    State Support: 0
    Federal Support: $66,687.25 (8/76-7/77)
    Total Support: $66,687.25

    Name: Four Rivers ALSA
    Address: 22 South East 5th Street
               Evansville, IN 47708
    Telephone: (812) 425-2621
    Administrator: John Medcraft
    Types of Libraries Served: a, p, sch, sp, institutional

    State Support: 0
    Federal Support: $54,436.00 (1/77 - 1/78)
    Total Support: $54,436.00

    Name: Heritage Hills ALSA
    Address: 102 North Indiana Avenue
               Sellersburg, Indiana 47172
    Telephone: (812) 246-3114
    Administrator: Mrs. Christa Gimbel
    Types of Libraries Served: a, p, sch, sp, institutional

    State Support: 0
    Federal Support: $66,000.00 (1/77-12/77)
    Total Support: $66,000.00   (continued)

8. MULTI-TYPE LIBRARY COOPERATIVES (continued)

A. Receiving Continuing Financial Support from the State Library:

      Name: Area 6 ALSA
      Address: 310 East Charles
                    Muncie, IN 47305
      Telephone: (317) 286-1670
      Administrator: Mrs. Martha E. Catt
      Types of Libraries Served: a, p, sch, sp, institutional

      State Support: 0
      Federal Support: $68,965.00 (7/77 - 7/78)
      Total Support: $68,965.00

B. Receiving No Continuing Financial Support from the State Library:

There are none.

C. Other:

There are none.

9. INTERLIBRARY COOPERATION FUNCTIONS

A. Receiving Continuing Support from the State Library:

	State Support	Federal Support Title I	Federal Support Title III	Other Support	Total Support
Interlibrary Loan	0	$33,710.03	$34,781.18	$6,248.98	$74,740.19
Continuing Education	0	12,774.28	0	0	12,774.28
Cooperative Acquisitions	0	0	0	0	0
Cooperative Cataloging	0	6,510.70	0	0	6,510.70
Cooperative Delivery	0	1,650.00	0	0	1,650.00
Cooperative Processing	(see entry under cooperative cataloging)				
Cooperative Reference	0	42,720.32	34,413.75	0	77,134.07
Cooperative Storage	0	0	0	0	0
Legislative Assistance	0	0	0	0	0
Planning/Development	0	30,787.00	0	0	30,787.00
Union List of Serials	(see entry under Other - Bibliographic Services)				
Other Bibliographic Services	0	169,700.00	0	0	169,700.00
	0	$297,852.33	$69,194.93	$6,248.98	$373,296.24

B. The State Library serves as catalyst, as planning and consultant agent, and as evaluation center for many of the state's interlibrary cooperative functions. It provides technical assistance as required, also legislative reference, and coordination of library activities.

10.   ILC COMMUNICATION DEVICES / SERVICE NETWORKS

    A.   Financial Support Role of the State Library Agency:

Device/Service	Support ($)	Equipment (#)	Participants
Teletypes & Telephones	$ 74,740.19	20 (teletype)	199
INDIRS	77,134.07	13	all citizens of state
OCLC Terminals	169,700.00	68	124

    B.   Non-Financial Role of the State Library Agency:
       The Indiana State Library serves as catalyst, as planning and
       consulting agent, and as evaluation center for library activities.

11.   MACHINE-READABLE DATA BASE REFERENCE SEARCHING SERVICES

Data Base/Vendor	Support ($)	Terminals (#)	Participants
INCOLSA	$169,700.00	68	47 libraries
N.Y. Times Informa- tion Data Bank	27,000.00	1	all citizens of state

12.   INTERLIBRARY SERVICES TO SPECIAL GROUPS
       A. Services provided through cooperative arrangements:
           Blind and physically handicapped - subregional libraries and
             regional library.
           Institutional libraries - consultant service and federal
             financial support.
           Indiana University Medical Center - TWX Center in teletype
             network for hospital and health science personnel.
       B.   Non-Financial Support Role of the State Library:
           The Indiana State Library serves as catalyst, as planning
           and consultant agent as evaluation center for library
           activities

13.   PARTICIPATION IN MULTI-STATE LIBRARY NETWORKS

    A.   Extent of Participation in Multi-State Networks:

       Network: OCLC
       Financial Support: Through INCOLSA Budget
       Participation: not reported
       Services Used: Cataloging

    B.   There are no multi-state networks headquartered in Indiana.

14.   LEGAL BASES FOR MULTI-TYPE LIBRARY COOPERATION

       Library Services Authority Act of 1967. Chapter 47, Acts
       of 1967 (Burns 41-1201-1214) IC 1971, 20-13-6-1 --
       20-13-6-14.

(continued)

14.   LEGAL BASES FOR MULTI-TYPE LIBRARY COOPERATION (continued)

"It is the purpose of this act to encourage the development
and improvement of all types of library service and to
promote the efficient use of finance, personnel, materials,
and properties by enabling government authorities having
library responsibilities to join together in a municipal
corporation called a library service authority, which will
provide such services and facilities as the governing
authorities party to the establishment and support of the
library service authority may determine".

15.   LEGAL BARRIERS AGAINST PARTICIPATION IN MULTI-TYPE LIBRARY COOPERA-
TION.

There are no legal barriers.

1. REPORTING AGENCY

   A. State Library Commission of Iowa
       Historical Building
       Des Moines, IA   50319
       (515) 281-4113

   B. Chief Officer: Barry L. Porter, State Librarian

   C. Fiscal Year: 1977

2. OVERVIEW

   In Iowa, the major intertype library co-operative is I-LITE
   (Iowa Library Information Teletype Exchange). I-LITE, a program of the State Library Commission of Iowa, helps Iowans utilize the resources of twenty-one major Iowa libraries of all
   types through a "dedicated circuit" teletype network. The
   State Library is currently co-ordinating a long-range planning
   effort which would eventually replace I-LITE with a combination
   of compatible automated circulation systems and the OCLC interlibrary loan subsystem.

   Other interlibrary co-operative activities in Iowa include:

       (1) a regional library program, which divides Iowa into
           seven public library regions and is established under
           Chapter 303B of the Iowa Code;
       (2) six academic library consortia;
       (3) four multi-type library cooperatives;
       (4) the Iowa OCLC Council;
       (5) a newly formed (September 1977) Iowa Private Academic
           Library Consortium.

   Chapter 303A.8 of the Iowa Code authorizes the State Library to
   enter into interstate compacts with comparable agencies in
   states bordering Iowa for the purpose of creating and maintaining co-operative projects to improve library service. The Iowa
   Code contains no other statutory provision to either encourage
   or restrict multi-type library cooperative activities.

3. NUMBER OF LIBRARIES IN THE STATE

Academic (post-secondary):	65
Public:	500
School:	2,019 est.
Public	1,794
Private:	225 est.
Special:	68
Profit:	38 est.
Non-profit:	30
Total	2,652 est.

4. STATE AGENCY INTERLIBRARY COOPERATION UNIT

    A.   Name: Office of Interlibrary Cooperation
          Person in Charge: Douglas Baker, Director

    B.   There is no other state library office charged with ILC
       activities.

5. OTHER STATE-LEVEL GOVERNMENTAL INTERLIBRARY COOPERATION UNITS

    A.   Name: Iowa Department of Public Instruction
          Address: Grimes Building
                              Des Moines, IA 50319

          Activity: Resource sharing for school libraries
                              through area media centers.

6. STATE-LEVEL NON-GOVERNMENTAL INTERLIBRARY COOPERATION UNITS

        Name: Iowa OCLC Council

        Activities: 1. to coordinate, advise, and set
                              policy on OCLC-related matters for
                              Council member libraries;
                              2. to provide a forum for discussion
                              of OCLC-related matters;
                              3. to coordinate the working relation-
                              ship between Council member libraries
                              and the OCLC vendor network.
        Membership: Twenty-two private colleges, one
                              private university, three special
                            libraries.
        Address: Douglas Baker, President
                              Iowa OCLC Council
                              State Library Commission of Iowa
                              Historical Building
                              Des Moines, IA 50319

        Name: Iowa Private Academic Library
                              Consortium
        Address: Christopher McKee, Chairperson
                              Burling Library
                              Grinnell College
                              Grinnel, IA 50112
        Activities: Resource sharing
         Membership: Still not confirmed, consortium formed
                            in September 1977.

7. SINGLE-TYPE LIBRARY COOPERATIVES

A. Receiving Continuing Financial Support from the State Library:

```
Name:            Central Regional Library System
Address:         Wakonda Shopping Center
                 4233 Fleur Drive
                 Des Moines, IA    50315
Telephone:       (515) 287-3102
Administrator: Marjorie Humby
Type of Library Served: p
Federal Support:    $ 43,416.00
State Support:       133,892.53
Local Support:        - 0 -
Other Support:         1,029.94
Total Support:      $178,338.47
```

```
Name:            East Central Regional Library System
Address:         1500 2nd Ave, S.E., Suite 203
                 Cedar Rapids, IA   52403
Telephone:       (319) 365-0521
Administrator: Nelle Neafie
Type of Library Served: p
Federal Support:    $ 36,616.00
State Support:       100,583.93
Local Support:        - 0 -
Other Support:        - 0 -
Total Support:      $137,199.93
```

```
Name:            North Central Regional Library System
Address:         P.O. Box 379
                 Mason City, IA   50401
Telephone:       (515) 423-6917
Administrator: Ann Swanson
Type of Library Served:  p
Federal Support:    $ 39,520.00
State Support:        75,559.10
Local Support:        - 0 -
Other Support:         9,281.35 (incl. Non-LSCA Federal Funds)
Total Support:      $124,360.45
```

```
Name:            Northeast Regional Library System
Address:         619 Mulberry Street
                 Waterloo, IA   50703
Telephone:       (319) 233-1200
Administrator: Beverly Lind
Type of Library Served: p
Federal Support:     $36,616.00
State Support:       100,585.93
Local Support:         0
Other Support:         1,276.25
Total Support:      $138,478.18
```

(continued)

7. SINGLE-TYPE LIBRARY COOPERATIVES (continued)

A. Receiving Continuing Financial Support from the State Library:

    Name: Northwest Regional Library System
    Address: Sioux City Public Library
                     Sioux City, IA   51106
    Telephone: (712) 279-6717
    Administrator: John Houlahan
    Type of Library Served: p
    Federal Support: $ 30,024.00
    State Support: 92,592.35
    Local Support: - 0 -
    Other Support: 2,567.62
    Total Support: $125,183.97

    Name: Southeast Regional Library System
    Address: Davenport Public Library, Davenport, IA   52801
    Telephone: (319) 324-0019
    Administrator   Marie Lindquist
    Type of Library Served: p
    Federal Support: $ 34,344.00
    State Support: 105,914.99
    Local Support: - 0 -
    Other Support: 7,838.45
    Total Support: $148,097.44

    Name: Southwest Regional Library System
    Address: P.O. Box 327, Missouri Valley, IA   51555
    Telephone: (712) 642-4131
    Administrator: Lucile Walensky
    Type of Library Served: p
    Federal Support: $ 41,464.00
    State Support: 69,277.73
    Local Support: - 0 -
    Other Support: 1,658.19
    Total Support: $112,399.92

B. Receiving no Continuing Financial Support from the State Library:

    Name: Schools of Theology in Dubuque Library
    Address: Duncan Brocklay
                     2570 Asbury Road
                     Dubuque, IA   52001
    Telephone: (319) 557-2604
    Type of Library Served: a
    Sponsoring Bodies: Aquinas Institute of Technology
                        University of Dubuque Seminary
                        Wartburg Theological Seminary

(continued)

7. SINGLE-TYPE LIBRARY COOPERATIVES (continued)

   B. Receiving No Continuing Financial Support from the State Library:

   Name: Tri-College Cooperative Effort (TCCE)
   Address: c/o Robert Klein
                            Loras College Library
                            Dubuque, IA 52001
   Telephone: (319) 588-7125
   Type of Library Served: a
   Sponsoring Bodies: Loras College
                       Clarke College
                       University of Dubuque

   Name: Librarians of Colleges of Mid-America, Inc.
   Address: c/o Mary Ann Gray
                            Buena Vista College Library
                            Storm Lake, IA 51104
   Telephone: (712) 749-2141
   Type of Library Served: a
   Sponsoring Body: Colleges of Mid-America (CMA)
                       c/o Dr. James Beddow
                       Sioux Falls College
                       1501 South Prairie
                       Sioux Falls, SD 57101

   Name: North East Iowa Academic Libraries (NEIAL)
   Address: c/o Suzanne Reisner
                            Loras College Library
                            Dubuque, IA 52001
   Telelphone: (319) 588-7125
   Type of Library Served: a

   Name: Southeast Iowa Academic Libraries (SIAL),
                            formerly IMI
   Address: c/o David Netz
                            Central College Library
                            Pella, IA 50219
   Telephone: (515)628-4151 ext. 346
   Type of Library Served: a

   Name: Bi-State Academic Libraries (Bi-Sal)
   Address: c/o Sister Joan Sheil
                            Marycrest College Library
                            Davenport, IA 52804
   Telephone: (319) 326-9254
   Type of Library Served: a

8. MULTI-TYPE LIBRARY COOPERATIVES

    A. Receiving Continuing Financial Support from the State Library:

        Name: I-LITE (Iowa Library Information Exchange)
        Address: I-LITE
                               State Library Commission of Iowa
                               Historical Building
                               Des Moines, IA 50319
        Telephone: (515) 281-4407
        Administrator: Douglas Baker
        Types of Libraries Served: a,p, state library
        Federal Support: LSCA I $ 33,469
                               (for State Library
                                staff salaries)
                               LSCA III $ 50,468
                                                     $ 83,937
        State Support: $ 40,000
        Local Support $ 8,100
        Other Support: - 0 -
        Total Support $132,037

    B. Receiving No Continuing State Library Support:

        Name: Dubuque Area Library Consortium
        Address: c/o James Lander
                               Health Science Library
                               Mercy Medical Center
                               Mercy Drive
                               Dubuque, IA 52001
        Telephone   (319) 588-8400
        Types of Libraries Served: a, sp

        Name: Polk County Bio-Medical Consortium
        Address   c/o Patricia Dawson
                               Cowles Library
                               Drake University
                               Des Moines, IA 50311
        Telephone: (515) 271-2113
        Types of Libraries Served: a, sp

        Name: Siouxland Health Science Library Consortium
        Address: c/o Barbara Knight
                               St. Luke's Medical Center Library
                               2720 Stone Street
                               Sioux City, IA 51104
        Telephone: (712) 279-3500
        Types of Libraries Served: a, p, sch, sp

(continued)

8. MULTI-TYPE LIBRARY COOPERATIVES (continued)

>Name: Cedar Rapids Area Library Consortium
>Address: c/o Tom Carney
>   Cedar Rapids Public Library
>   Cedar Rapids, IA   52401
>Telephone: (319) 398-5731
>Types of Libraries Served: a, p, sch, sp

9. INTERLIBRARY COOPERATION FUNCTIONS

A. Receiving Continuing Financial Support from the State Library:

	State Support	Federal Support Title I	Federal Support Title III	Other Support	Total Support
Interlibrary Loan	$40,000	$33,469	$43,006	$8,100	$124,575
Cooperative Cataloging & Processing		$75,000			75,000
Cooperative Reference			$ 7,462		$ 7,462
Total Support	$40,000	$108,469	$50,468	$8,100	$207,037

B. Non-financial support role of the State Library :

The Director of the Office of Interlibrary Cooperation
works in a coordinating role to help organize library groups
interested in interlibrary cooperation. Two notable examples are the Iowa OCLC Council and the Iowa Private
Academic Library Consortium.

10. INTERLIBRARY COOPERATION COMMUNICATIONS DEVICES/SERVICE NETWORKS

I-LITE is a teletype network including 24 teletypes, with
22 participants, costing $64,235 for lines and equipment.

11. MACHINE-READABLE DATA BASE SEARCHING SERVICES

In Fiscal Year 1977, the State Library supported regular searching of the OCLC data base to provide materials locations for
interlibrary loan requests unfilled in Iowa. For Fiscal Year
1978, we are sponsoring an introduction and training for the
METRO Program of the Bibliographical Center for Research (BCR).

12. INTERLIBRARY SERVICES TO SPECIAL GROUPS

In Iowa, these are not handled through Interlibrary Cooperative
agreements, but instead through individual direct project grants
and consultation.

13. PARTICIPATION IN MULTI-STATE LIBRARY NETWORKS

      Network: Bibliographical Center for Research (BCR)
      Financial Support: $9,000
      Participation: Statewide comprehensive membership
      Services Used: BIBLIO (OCLC Broker) and in 1978 METRO
                              (computerized Data Base Broker)

14. LEGAL BASES FOR MULTI-TYPE LIBRARY COOPERATION

    There are none.

15. LEGAL BARRIERS AGAINST PARTICIPATION IN MULTI-TYPE LIBRARY
COOPERATION

    There are none.

1. REPORTING AGENCY

> A. The Kansas State Library
> 4th Floor – 535 Kansas Avenue
> Topeka, Kansas 66603
> (913) 296-3259

> B. Chief Officer: Ernestine Gilliland, State Librarian

> C. Fiscal Year: 1978

2. OVERVIEW

> Kansas is divided into seven regional systems of cooperating
> libraries, as provided by Kansas Statutes Annotated 75-2547.
> The law provides for a half-mill local ad valorem property
> tax to be levied on all property not already taxing a public
> library tax. This tax in addition to approximately $40,000
> in state-federal aid (K.S.A. 75-2553) comprise the seven system
> budgets.

> With the State Librarian acting as coordinator, the Kansas
> Library Service Network provides support to the libraries of
> the State in the following areas:

> > a. Kansas Information Circuit (Interlibrary loan).
> > b. Computer-based reference and information
> >   services.
> > c. Automated technical services system.
> > d. Kansas Union Catalog.
> > e. Human Resource Development.
> > f. Consulting service to Kansas libraries.

> The Kansas Library Service Network is a program designed to
> improve library services for the 2,249,071 people in Kansas
> through statewide networking.

3. NUMBERS OF LIBRARIES IN THE STATE

> Academic: 48
> Public: 304
> School: n.a.
>   Public: 1,600
>   Private: n.a.
> Special: 95 est.
>   Profit: n.a.
>   Nonprofit: n.a.

> TOTAL: 2,047 est.

4.   STATE AGENCY INTERLIBRARY COOPERATION UNIT

      A.   Unit Name: Interlibrary Cooperation, Resource
                                  Sharing and Development Services
                                  Division

      B.   Person in Charge: Charles Bolles, Division Director

5.   OTHER STATE-LEVEL GOVERNMENT ILC UNITS

      There are none.

6.   OTHER STATE-LEVEL NON-GOVERNMENT ILC UNITS

      There are none.

7.   SINGLE-TYPE LIBRARY COOPERATIVES

      There are none.

8.   MULTI-TYPE LIBRARY COOPERATIVES
    1976 budget used for support figures

      A.   Receiving Continuing Financial Support from the State
           Library:

           Name: Central Kansas Library System
           Address: 1409 Williams
                         Great Bend, Kansas 67530
           Telephone: (316) 792-4865
           Administrator: James Swan
           Type of Libraries Served: a, p, sch, sp
           Federal Support: $ 19,500
           State Support: $ 41,602
           Local Support: $305,720
           Other Support: $ 9,476
           Total Support: $376,298

           Name: North Central Kansas Library System
           Address: Juliette & Poyntz
                         Manhattan, Kansas 66502
           Telephone: (913) 776-4741
           Administrator: Margaret Gates
           Type of Libraries Served: a, p, sch, sp
           Federal Support: $ 13,000
           State Support: $ 41,603
           Local Support: $133,046
           Other Support: $ 12,519
           Total Support: $200,168

(continued)

8. MULTI-TYPE LIBRARY COOPERATIVES (continued)

Name: Northeast Kansas Library System
Address: 5121 Cedar - P. O. Box 2901
                        Shawnee Mission, Kansas 66201
Telephone: (913) 831-4993
Administrator: Glen Plaisted
Type of Libraries Served: a, p, sch, sp
Federal Support: $ 62,349
State Support: $ 41,602
Local Support: $188,492
Other Support: $ 22,293
Total Support: $314,736

Name: Northwest Kansas Library System
Address: 408 N. Norton
                        Norton, Kansas 67654
Telephone: (913) 877-5148
Administrator: Ed Nickel
Type of Libraries Served: a, p, sch, sp
Federal Support: $ -0-
State Support: $ 41,603
Local Support: $ 97,788
Other Support: $ 11,978
Total Support: $151,369

Name: South Central Kansas Library System
Address: 901 N. Main
                        Hutchinson, Kansas   67501
Telephone: (316) 663-5441
Administrator: Duane Johnson
Type of Libraries Served: a, p, sch, sp
Federal Support: $ 46,000
State Support: $ 41,602
Local Support: $432,925
Other Support: $ 38,804
Total Support: $559,331

Name: Southeast Kansas Library System
Address: 218 E. Madison
                        Iola, Kansas 66749
Telephone: (316) 365-6976
Administrator: Lucile Wagner
Type of Libraries Served: a, p, sch, sp
Federal Support: $ 4,200
State Support: $ 41,602
Local Support: $210,789
Other Support: $ 15,218
Total Support: $271,809

(continued)

8. MULTI-TYPE LIBRARY COOPERATIVES (continued)

          Name: Southwest Kansas Library System
          Address: 606 1st Avenue
                              Dodge City, Kansas 67801
          Telephone: (316) 225-1231
          Administrator: Joyce Davis
          Type of Libraries Served: a, p, sch, sp
          Federal Support: $ 14,500
          State Support: $ 41,603
          Local Support: $ 64,876
          Other Support: $ 19,221
          Total Support: $140,200

B. Receiving No Continuing Financial Support From The State Library:

          Name: Farrell Library
          Address: Kansas State University
                              Manhattan, Kansas 66506
          Telephone: (913) 532-6516
          Administrator: Dr. G. Jay Rausch
          Type of Libraries Served: a, p, sch, sp
          Sponsoring Body: The State of Kansas
          Sources of Support: State, Private

          Name: Watson Library
          Address: University of Kansas
                            Lawrence, Kansas 66045
          Telephone: (913) 864-3347
          Administrator: Dr. James Ranz
          Type of Libraries Served: a, p, sch, sp
          Sponsoring Body: The State of Kansas
          Source of Support: State, Private

          Name: Washburn University Library
          Address: Topeka, Kansas 66621
          Telephone: (913) 295-6300
          Administrator: Charlene Hurt (acting)
          Type of Libraries Served: a, p, sch, sp
          Sponsoring Body: City of Topeka
          Source of Support: City Funds, Private

C. Other:

          There are none.

9. INTERLIBRARY COOPERATION FUNCTIONS

    A. Because of the financial structure, it is impossible to provide dollar amounts for financial support of these activities.

    B. There is no non-financial support role.

10. ILC COMMUNICATION DEVICES / SERVICE NETWORKS

    A. The State Library agency supports the statewide interlibrary loan network (Kansas Information Circuit) by the installation of on-line computer terminals. The participating library maintains the terminals and pays communication costs.

Device/Network	Support ($)	Equipment (#)	Participants
Texas Instruments 733 - ASR	Not Available	7	3 Regional System Libraries, 3 Public Libraries,
Hazeltine 2000 with TI 743 Printer	Not Available	7	1 State Library, 3 Public Libraries, 4 Academic Libraries.

    B. The State Library compiles and routes lists for the Kansas Information Circuit (KIC), identifies out-of-state locations for materials not owned by Kansas libraries, and provides initial trouble shooting if terminals malfunction.

11. MACHINE-READABLE DATA BASE REFERENCE SEARCHING SERVICES

As part of the State Library agency's support of the Kansas Information Circuit, terminals installed for the communication of interlibrary loan requests can be used for machine-readable reference searching services. See question 10 for specific details. The data bases searched include the Information Bank and those available through SDC and Lockheed.

12. INTERLIBRARY SERVICES TO SPECIAL GROUPS

    A. Regional network of libraries for blind and physically handicapped which distribute talking books, cassette books etc. Library services to the institutionalized are partially supported through the regional library systems.

(continued)

12.   INTERLIBRARY SERVICES TO SPECIAL GROUPS (continued)

> B.   The State Library provides the staff and space for the
> regional library for the blind and physically handicapped
> and monitors the expenditure of LSCA funds for the
> institutionalized.

13.   PARTICIPATION IN MULTI-STATE LIBRARY NETWORKS

> A.

> Network (s):   Bibliographical Center for Research (BCR)
> Financial Support: $7,200 (state membership)
> Participation: State Librarian is a member of executive
> Services Used: BIBLIO, (OCLC, Ballots) METRO   board.
>   (Lockheed Dialog, SDC Orbit, Information
>   Bank) Interloan.

> B.   There are none.

14.   LEGAL BASES FOR MULTI-TYPE LIBRARY COOPERATION

> Regional Library Systems - American Library Laws, 3rd ed.,
> second supplement, 1965-66, p. 141-143.

15.   LEGAL BARRIERS AGAINST PARTICIPATION IN MULTI-TYPE LIBRARY COOPERA-
      TION

> There are no legal barriers.

KENTUCKY

1. REPORTING AGENCY

    A. Kentucky Department of Library & Archives
        Box 537
        Frankfort, KY   40602
        (502) 564-7910

    B. Chief Officer: Mrs. Barbara Williams, State Librarian

    C. Fiscal Year: 1977

2. OVERVIEW

    Kentucky Revised Statutes 171.150 and 171.200 charge the state
    library with authority to plan for suitable cooperative arrange-
    ments between public library, school library, college or uni-
    versity library, and special library systems. KRS 171.221
    empowers the state library to enter into an agreement with any
    state for the purpose of providing cooperative library services.
    The state library currently sponsors an interlibrary coopera-
    tion network based on geographic regions grouped around six
    state-supported universities. The state library has reference
    staff in these six locations. The program is funded from both
    state and federal LSCA Title III funds.

    LSCA Title III funds also provide the Kentucky Union List of
    Serials which is produced annually on COM and distributed to
    88 college, university, special and public libraries.

3. NUMBER OF LIBRARIES IN THE STATE

        Academic: 49
        Public: 112
        School: 1305.6
           Public: 1165.6
           Private: 140
        Special: 76
           Profit: 25
           Nonprofit: 51

        TOTAL: 1542.6

4. STATE AGENCY INTERLIBRARY COOPERATION UNIT

    A. Unit Name: Interlibrary Cooperation
        Person in Charge: Lyn Strange, Librarian
                            Interlibrary Cooperation

    B. There are no other state library offices for ILC activities.

5. OTHER STATE-LEVEL GOVERNMENT ILC UNITS

        There are none.

6. OTHER STATE-LEVEL NON-GOVERNMENTAL ILC UNITS

    There are none.

7. SINGLE-TYPE LIBRARY COOPERATIVES

    A. Receiving Continuing Financial Support from the State Library:

        There are none.

    B. Receiving No Continuing Financial Support from the State Library:

Name:	State-Assisted Academic Library Council of Kentucky
Address:	Northern Kentucky State University 1401 Dixie Highway Highland Heights, KY 41076
Telephone:	(606) 781-2600
Administrator:	Bobby Holloway, Chairperson
Type of Library Served:	a
Sponsoring Body:	Eight state universities
Sources of Support:	Individual library budgets
Name:	Council of Independent Colleges and Universities Libraries
Address:	Bellarmine College Newberg Road Louisville, KY 40205
Telephone:	(502) 452-8411
Administrator:	Sister Betty Pelius
Type of Library Served:	a
Sponsoring Body:	Member colleges and universities
Sources of Support:	Participating libraries' budgets

    C. There are none.

8. MULTI-TYPE LIBRARY COOPERATIVES

    A. Receiving Continuing Financial Support from the State Library:

Name:	Kentucky Cooperative Library Information Project (KENCLIP)
Address:	Box 537 Frankfort, KY 40602
Telephone:	(502) 564-2480
Administrator:	Lyn Strange
Types of Libraries Served:	a,p, and sp
Federal Support:	$ 33,912.00
State Support:	129,988.00
Local Support:	.00
Other Support:	.00
Total Support:	$163,900.00

(continued)

8A. MULTI-TYPE LIBRARY COOPERATIVES (continued)

Name: Kentuckiana Metro University
                                     Library Council
Address: Alta Vista Road
                                   Garden Court
                                   Louisville, KY   40207
Telephone: (502) 897-3374
Administrator: Dr. John Ford
Types of Libraries Served: a, sp, and p
Federal Support: $ .00
State Support: 5,000.00
Local Support: .00
Other Support: .00
Total Support: $5,000.00

Name: Kentucky Union List of Serials
Address: University of Louisville Li-
                                     braries
                                   2301 S. Third Street
                                   Louisville, KY   40208
Telephone: (502) 588-5930
Administrator: Mrs. Betty Herz
Types of Libraries Served: a, sp, and p
Federal Support: $13,500.00
State Support: .00
Local Support: .00
Other Support: .00
Total Support: $13,500.00

B. Receiving No Continuing Financial Support from the State Library:

Name: Kentucky Health Science Libraries
                                     Consortia
Address: St. Joseph's Infirmary
                                   Box 17264
                                   Louisville, KY   40217
Telephone: (502) 636-7011
Administrator: Elizabeth Fischer
Type of Library Served: a, p, sp
Sponsoring Body: None
Source of Support: No formal support.

Name: Southeastern Kentucky Regional
                                     Library Cooperative
Address: Alice Lloyd Junior College
                                   Pippa Passes, KY   41844
Telephone: (606) 368-2101
Administrator: Mrs. Charlotte Madden
Types of Libraries Served: a, p, sch
Sponsoring Body: 0
Sources of Support: 0

(continued)

133

8B. MULTI-TYPE LIBRARY COOPERATIVES (continued)

Name:	Health Info. Lib. Program
Address:	Medical Center Annex #2
	Lexington, KY 40506
Telephone:	(606) 233-5727
Administrator:	Janet Stith
Types of Libraries Served:	p, sp, and a
Sponsoring Body:	University of Kentucky Medical
	Center Library
Source(s) of Support:	$43,394 (National Library of
	Medicine)

    C.   There are none.

9. INTERLIBRARY COOPERATION FUNCTIONS

A.

	State Support	Federal Support Title I	Support Title III	Total Support
Interlibrary Loan	$129,988		$33,912	$163,900
Continuation Education		$15,000		
Cooperative Acquisitions				
Cooperative Cataloging				
Cooperative Delivery				
Cooperative Processing				
Cooperative Reference				
Cooperative Storage				
Legislative Assistance				
Planning/Development				
Union Lists of Serials			$13,500	$13,500
Other (please specify)				

B.   Cooperative Acquisitions - State Library supports 106 p
                                    Libraries
       Cooperative Cataloging - State Library supports 106 p Lib-
                                    raries
       Cooperative Delivery - State Library supports 106 p Librar-
                                    ies
       Cooperative Processing - State Library supports 106 p Lib-
                                    raries
       Cooperative Reference - Toll-free # provided

10. ILC COMMUNICATION DEVICES / SERVICE NETWORKS

A.

Device/Services	Support ($)	Equipment (#)	Participants
Teletype	$46,000	17 machines	Academic - 10
			Public - 7
Credit Card	Included in above total		106 libraries

(continued)

10. ILC COMMUNICATION DEVICES/ SERVICE NETWORKS (continued)

OCLC	---	1 terminal	106 p libr. state government agencies & bureaus

    B. There are none.

11. MACHINE-READABLE DATA BASE REFERENCE SEARCHING SERVICES

Data Base/Vendor		Support ($)	Terminals (#)	Participants
Courier Journal-Louisville Times	Data Courier	$40,000	1	106 p libr. all state agencies & bureaus

12. INTERLIBRARY SERVICES TO SPECIAL GROUPS

    A. A Library for the Blind & Physically Handicapped distributes 30,000 public library titles in various forms to 2,500 blind and physically handicapped citizens of Kentucky.

    Special Services Division provides library services to 10,000 residents of 8 Kentucky institutions such as the School for the Deaf and the Eddyville State Penitentiary. Special Services Division also provides grants for special projects reaching about 43,000 disadvantaged citizens of Kentucky.

    Special Services Division also provides grant money for a special bookmobile project reaching 62,447 senior citizens in Kentucky.

    B. Through the Department's regional library network, regional librarians employed by the state advise county public library boards and librarians on programming of local dollars.

13. PARTICIPATION IN MUTLI-STATE LIBRARY NETWORKS

    A. Network(s): SOLINET
       Financial Support: $150,000 over 2 years
       Participation: Retrospective conversion, update of present acquisitions
       Services used: Bibliographic, cataloging, interlibrary loan

    B. There are none.

(continued)

14. LEGAL BASES FOR MUTLI-TYPE LIBRARY COOPERATION

       Kentucky Revised Statutes 171.150 and 171.200 (see Overview)

15. LEGAL BARRIERS AGAINST PARTICIPATION IN MUTLI-TYPE LIBRARY COOPERA-
     TION

       There are none.

1. REPORTING AGENCY

    A. The Office of the State Library
        P. O. Box 131
        Baton Rouge, LA   70821
        (504) 389-6651

    B. Chief Officer: Thomas F. Jaques, State Librarian

    C. Fiscal Year: 1978

2. OVERVIEW

    Of the 64 parishes (counties) in Louisiana, 36 have libraries
    which have joined together in multi-type cooperatives involving
    36 public, 18 academic and 6 special libraries. 57.8% of the
    total population is served by libraries participating in this
    type of cooperation.

    Parishes (counties) and municipalities were granted the author-
    ity to act jointly in the "Local Services Law," Act. No. 246 of
    1942. This is the basis for multi-type library cooperation.
    Act No. 216 of 1968 provided enabling legislation in the form
    of the Interstate Library Compact.

    There has not been any state-provided statutory funding for
    multi-type cooperative development.

3. NUMBER OF LIBRARIES IN THE STATE

        Academic: 32
        Public: 64
        School: 1,316
           Public: 1,316
           Private: not available
        Special: 65
           Profit: 11
           Nonprofit: 54

        TOTAL   1,477 est.

4. STATE AGENCY INTERLIBRARY COOPERATION UNIT

    A. Unit Name: Library Development Division
        Person in Charge: Miss Vivian Cazayoux, Associate
                                State Librarian for Library
                                Development

    B. Unit Name: Readers' and Technical Services
                                Division
        Cooperative Activity: Processing Center for public and
                                institutional libraries

(continued)

4. STATE AGENCY INTERLIBRARY COOPERATION UNIT (continued)

       Title of Supervisor: Coordinator, Technical Services

       Unit Name: Readers' and Technical Services Division

       Cooperative Activity: Union Catalog of Louisiana Items

       Title of Supervisor: Coordinator, Technical Services

       Unit Name: Readers' and Technical Services Division

       Cooperative Activity: LNR: Numerical Register of Books in Louisiana Libraries

       Title of Supervisor: Coordinator, Technical Services

       Unit Name: Reference Section

       Cooperative Activity: Interlibrary Loan and Referral

       Title of Supervisor: Head, Reference Librarian

5. OTHER STATE-LEVEL GOVERNMENTAL ILC UNITS

    There are none.

6. OTHER STATE-LEVEL NON-GOVERNMENTAL ILC UNITS

      Unit Name: Louisiana Library Association

      Address: P. O. Box 131, Baton Rouge, LA 70821

      Telephone: (504) 389-6651

      Administrator: Mrs. Chris Thomas

      Activities: Louisiana Union Catalog is a union catalog on microfiche of Louisiana items

      Types of Libraries: a, p, sp, and state

      Activities: Louisiana Numerical Register is a computer based union catalog on microfiche based on the LC card number of retrospective and current holdings

      Types of Libraries: a, p, sp, and state

      Activities: Ad Hoc Committee on Interlibrary Loan is compiling for publication (1978) the Louisiana Interlibrary Loan Code and Procedure Manual for use by all types of libraries for interlibrary loan purposes

      Types of libraries: a, p, sp, and state

7. SINGLE-TYPE LIBRARY COOPERATIVES

    A.   Receiving Continuing Financial Support from the State Library:

(continued)

7. SINGLE-TYPE LIBRARY COOPERATIVES (continued)

    There are none.

    B.   Receiving No Continuing Financial Support from the State Library:

Name:	South Central Regional Medical Library Program
Address:	5323 Harry Hines Boulevard, Dallas, TX 75235
Telephone:	(214) 688-2627
Administrator:	Mr. Joe McCord
Type of Library Served:	sp
Sponsoring Body:	University of Texas Health Science Center at Dallas
Source(s) of Support:	Federal Funds

Name:	U.S.D.A. Southwestern Regional Document Delivery System
Address:	Louisiana State University Library, Baton Rouge, LA 70803
Telephone:	(504) 388-2138
Administrator:	National Agricultural Library
Type of Library Served:	a
Sponsoring Body:	National Agricultural Library
Source(s) of Support:	Federal Funds

Name:	LSU SINET (Louisiana State University System Interlibrary Network)
Address:	Louisiana State University Library, Baton Rouge, LA 70803
Telephone:	(504) 388-2217
Administrator:	Mr. George Guidry
Type of Library Served:	a
Sponsoring Body:	Joint sponsorship
Source(s) of Support:	State

Name:	Center for Research Libraries
Address:	Louisiana State University, Baton Rouge, LA 70803
Telephone:	(504) 388-2217
Administrator:	Mr. George Guidry
Type of Library Served:	a
Source of Support:	State

Name:	Louisiana - Mississippi Microform Network
Address:	Louisiana State University Library, Baton Rouge, LA 70803

(continued)

7. SINGLE-TYPE LIBRARY COOPERATIVES (continued)

    B.   Telephone: (504) 388-2217

Telephone:	(504) 388-2217
Administrator:	Mr. George Guidry
Type of Library Served:	a
Sponsoring Body:	Joint sponsorship
Source(s) of Support:	Federal

Name:	Louisiana College Library Interchange
Address:	Louisiana State University Library at Alexandria, Alexandria, LA 71301
Telephone:	(318) 445-3672
Administrator:	Mrs. Ada Jarred
Type of Library Served:	a
Sponsoring Body:	Louisiana College, Pineville, and Louisiana State University, Alexandria
Source(s) of Support:	State and Private

Name:	New Orleans Consortium
Address:	St. Mary's Dominican College Library, P. O. Box 902, New Orleans, LA 70118
Telephone:	(504) 866-4826
Administrator:	Mrs. Mary H. Ellis
Type of Library Served:	a
Sponsoring Body:	Joint sponsorship
Source(s) of Support:	Private

    C.   Other:

    There are none.

8. MULTI-TYPE LIBRARY COOPERATIVES

    A.   Receiving Continuing Financial Support from the State Library:

Name:	Trail Blazer Library System
Address:	1800 Stubbs Avenue, Monroe, LA 71201
Telephone:	(318) 323-8494
Administrator:	Dr. Drucilla Motley
Types of Libraries served:	a, p
Federal Support:	$62,904
State Support:	-0-
Local Support:	-0-
Other Support:	-0-
Total Support:	$62,904
Name:	Green Gold Library System

(continued)

8. MULTI-TYPE LIBRARY COOPERATIVES (continued)

    Address: 400 Edwards Street, Shreveport,
LA 71120
    Administrator: Mr. William O. Drewett, III
    Types of Libraries Served: a, p, sp
    Federal Support: $53,184
    State Support: -0-
    Local Support: -0-
    Other Support: -0-
    Total Support: $53,184

    Name: Bayouland Library System
    Address: 301 West Congress, Lafayette,
LA 70501
    Telephone: (318) 233-7548
    Administrator: Mrs. Carla Klapper
    Types of Libraries Served: a, p
    Federal Support: $62,936
    State Support: -0-
    Local Support: -0-
    Other Support: -0-
    Total Support: $62,936

    Name: Southeast Louisiana Library
Network Cooperative (SEALLINC)
    Address: 219 Loyola Avenue, New Orleans,
LA 70140
    Administrator: Mr. M. E. Wright, Jr.
    Types of Libraries Served: a, p, sp
    Federal Support: $63,102
    State Support: -0-
    Local Support: -0-
    Other Support: -0-
    Total Support: $63,102

    B.   Receiving No Continuing Financial Support from the State
Library:

    Name: Louisiana SOLINET Interlibrary
Loan Project
    Address: Southeastern Louisiana Univer-
sity, Sims Memorial Library,
P. O. Drawer 896, Union Station,
Hammond, LA 70402
    Telephone: (504) 549-2234
    Administrator: Dr. Landon Greaves, Chairman
    Types of Libraries Served: a, p
    Sponsoring Body: Joint sponsorship
    Source(s) of Support: State, Local, and Private

    C.   Other (Receiving Occasional Support from the State Library,
etc.)

(continued)

8. MULTI-TYPE LIBRARY COOPERATIVES (continued)

    There are none.

9. INTERLIBRARY COOPERATION FUNCTIONS

A.

	State Support	Federal Support Title I	Title III	Other Support	Total Support
Interlibrary Loan	$235,000	$477,000			$712,000
Continuing Education	none				
Cooperative Acquisitions		Included in Cooperative Processing			
Cooperative Cataloging		Included in Cooperative Processing			
Cooperative Delivery		Included in Interlibrary Loan			
Cooperative Processing	$ 72,500	$ 72,500		$55,000	$200,000
Cooperative Reference		Included in Interlibrary Loan			
Cooperative Storage	none				
Legislative Assistance		Included in Interlibrary Loan			
Planning/Development	$ 50,000	$ 37,000			$ 87,000
Union Lists of Serials	none				
Other (please specify)					
La Numerical Register			$7,500		$ 7,500
La Union Catalog	$ 11,500	$ 11,500			$ 23,000
TOTAL SUPPORT	$369,000	$598,000	$7,500	$55,000	$1,029,500

B. Non-Financial Support Role of the State Library:

Consultant services for public and institutional libraries promote different types of cooperation statewide;

Publish and distribute to all types of libraries a newsletter and continuing education calendar;

Work closely with local libraries to coordinate services in order to improve the level of service available to all patrons of cooperating agencies;

Serve as a liaison with state computer center in programming and printing with Louisiana Numerical Register.

10. ILC COMMUNICATION DEVICES / SERVICE NETWORKS

A.

Device/Service	Support ($)	Equipment (#)	Participants
Telephone	$12,700	61	61
Teletype	8,200	6	6
Telefacsimile	none		
Computer terminal	none		
Other devices	none		

B. NON-FINANCIAL SUPPORT ROLE OF THE STATE LIBRARY

(continued)

10. ILC COMMUNICATION DEVICES / SERVICE NETWORKS (continued)

There is no non-financial support role for these services.

11. MACHINE-READABLE DATA BASE REFERENCE SEARCHING SERVICES

There are none.

12. INTERLIBRARY SERVICES TO SPECIAL GROUPS

A. Public and institutional libraries identify and refer visually and physically handicapped persons to the state
library agency for service and they also help publicize
this service.

Blind and Physically Handicapped Section of the state
library locates instructional material for persons with
special needs. It also records text material and special-
izes in translating and recording Spanish. It answers
special reference requests about blindness and other hand-
icapping conditions.

State library agency provides interlibrary loan, films,
recordings and free book processing to state health and
correctional libraries.

B. NON-FINANCIAL SUPPORT OF THE STATE LIBRARY

Consult with public and institutional librarians and plan
ways to improve local services to blind and physically
handicapped, elderly and disadvantaged.

13. PARTICIPATION IN MULTI-STATE LIBRARY NETWORKS

A. Network(s):   Southwestern Library Interstate Co-
                         operative Endeavor (SLICE)
    Financial Support: $2,500
    Participation: State librarian on council
    Services Used: Humanities project, continuing educa-
                         tion packages, continuing education
                         calendar

B. There are none.

14. LEGAL BASES FOR MULTI-TYPE LIBRARY COOPERATION

The Local Services Act No. 242 of 1942 is the enabling legislation for multi-type cooperative development in Louisiana. State
legislation which enables interstate agreements is: Interstate
Library Compact Act No. 216 of 1968. There is no state-provided
statutory funding for multi-type library cooperative development.

15. LEGAL BARRIERS AGAINST PARTICIPATION IN MULTI-TYPE LIBRARY COOPERA-
TIVES

There are no legal barriers.

1. REPORTING AGENCY

    A.   The Maine State Library
           Cultural Building
           Augusta, Maine 04333
           (207) 289-3561

    B.   Chief Officer: J. Gary Nichols, State Librarian

    C.   Fiscal Year: 1977

2. OVERVIEW

    The Maine Regional Library System includes three library
    districts, each having a designated area reference and resource
    center (Bangor Public Library, Portland Public Library and the
    Maine State Library) and each having access to consultant ser-
    vices. Resource center services include the following: inter-
    library loan; free access to district residents; inward WATS
    from member libraries; back-up reference; and support of
    district consultant activities. The regional library program
    also includes direct state aid to local library units.
    Statutory basis: Maine Revised Statutes, Title 27, Chapter 626
    (1973), 125 (1977) and 555 (1977).

3. NUMBER OF LIBRARIES IN THE STATE

Academic:	22
Public:	238
School:	353
Public:	
Private:	
Special:	50 est.
Profit:	
Non-profit:	
TOTAL	663 est.

4. STATE AGENCY INTERLIBRARY COOPERATION UNIT

    A.   Unit Name: Library Development Services
           Person in Charge: Carolyn Nolin, Assistant State Librarian

5. OTHER STATE-LEVEL GOVERNMENT ILC UNITS

    There are none.

6. OTHER STATE-LEVEL NON-GOVERNMENTAL ILC UNITS

    There are none.

7. SINGLE-TYPE LIBRARY COOPERATIVES

There are none.

8. MULTI-TYPE LIBRARY COOPERATIVES

A. Receiving Continuing Financial Support from the State Library:

Name: Maine Regional Library System
Address: Maine State Library, Augusta, Maine 04333
Telephone: 289-3328
Administrator: Richard E. Arnold
Types of Libraries Served: p, a, sch, sp
Federal Support: $20,000
State Support: 190,000
Local Support: -
Other Support: -
Total Support: $210,000

B. Receiving No Continuing Financial Support from the State
Library:

There are none.

9. INTERLIBRARY COOPERATION FUNCTIONS

A.

	State Support	Federal Support Title I	Federal Support Title III	Other Support	Total Support
Interlibrary Loan	20,000	20,000			40,000
Continuing Education					
Cooperative Acquisitions					
Cooperative Cataloging					
Cooperative Delivery					
Cooperative Processing					
Cooperative Reference					
Cooperative Storage					
Legislative Assistance					
Planning/Development					
Union Lists of Serials					
Other					
Direct State Aid					
Per Capita	80,000				80,000
District Consultants	60,840				60,840
Audio Visual					
Services	10,000				10,000
Handicapped Services	10,000				10,000
Fiction Resource	1,000				1,000
Library District					
Offices	7,460				7,460
Maine Library					
Commission	700				700
Total Support	190,000	20,000			210,000

(continued)

9. INTERLIBRARY COOPERATION FUNCTIONS (continued)

B. Non-Financial Support Role of the State Library:

The Maine State Library provides the coordination and administrative support services for the Maine Regional Library System.
The State Library also serves as the area reference and resource center for one of the three library districts. This
service includes interlibrary loan, free access, inward WATS
from member libraries, back-up reference and support of
district consultant activities.

10. ILC COMMUNICATION DEVICES / SERVICE NETWORKS

A.

Device/Service	Support ($)	Equipment (#)	Participants
WATS	$ 6,338	–	–
TWX	3,507	9	9
NELINET	27,418	2	3

B. Non-Financial Support Role of the State Library:

There is no non-financial support for these devices/
services.

11. MACHINE-READABLE DATA BASE REFERENCE SEARCHING SERVICES

The ERIC data base searching service is located at the Maine
State Library but is not financially supported by the State
Library. The Maine Department of Educational and Cultural
Services provides the financial support. The Maine State
Library provides staff time needed to organize and instruct in
the use of ERIC.

12. INTERLIBRARY SERVICES TO SPECIAL GROUPS

A. The Maine State Library provides financial support to five subregional libraries which offer special services (talking books)
to residents in their respective areas. Financial support is
also provided to seven institutional libraries.

B. Non-Financial Support Role of the State Library:

The Maine State Library is the regional library for services
to the blind and physically handicapped. The role of the state
library includes coordination and consultant services for the
statewide program. The state library also provides consultant
services to institutional libraries.

13. PARTICIPATION IN MULTI-STATE LIBRARY NETWORKS

A. Network: New England Library Board (NELB)
Financial Support: $8,550

(continued)

13. PARTICIPATION IN MULTI-STATE LIBRARY NETWORKS (continued)

        Participation: Maine, New Hampshire, Vermont, Rhode Island, Massachusetts, and Connecticut
        Services Used: New England Document Conservation Center; New England Serials Service

        Network: North Country Film Cooperative
        Financial Support: $8,300
        Participation: Maine, New Hampshire and Vermont
        Services Used: Cooperatively purchased 16mm films are rotated among the three states

  B. Multi-State Networks Headquartered in Maine

      There are none.

14. LEGAL BASES FOR MULTI-TYPE LIBRARY COOPERATION

The Maine Regional Library System was created in 1973 by Maine Revised Statutes Annotated, Title 27, Sec. 110-118, and amended by Chapter 125 (1977) and Chapter 555 (1977). Maine's participation with the New England Library Board is authorized by Maine Revised Statutes Annotated, Title 27, Section 143.

15. LEGAL BARRIERS AGAINST PARTICIPATION IN MULTI-TYPE LIBRARY COOPERATION

There are no legal barriers.

1. REPORTING AGENCY

   A. Division of Library Development and Services
      Maryland State Department of Education
      P.O. Box 8717, BWI Airport
      Baltimore, Maryland 21240

   B. Chief Officer: Nettie B. Taylor, Assistant State
                     Superintendent for Libraries

   C. Fiscal Year: 1978

2. OVERVIEW

   The State Library Resource Center, designated by law in 1971 as
   the Central Library of the Enoch Pratt Free Library of Baltimore,
   provides reference and interlibrary loan service for all public,
   academic, and special libraries in the state, plus access to its
   full collection and services to any Maryland citizen who chooses
   to use it directly. Support services are provided by the University of Maryland, College Park; Johns Hopkins University; and
   a number of other public and academic libraries. There are three
   Regional Resource Centers providing service to the smaller public
   library systems. Financial support is provided by the State for
   the operation of the entire network.

   Current emphasis has been on the development of union catalogs and
   listings of the monographic and serial holdings of the major
   libraries and securing access to large or specialized library
   collections for the benefit of all network users.

3. NUMBER OF LIBRARIES IN THE STATE

Academic:	48
Public:	24
School:	24
Public:	24
Private:	NA
Special:	265
Profit:	125
Non-profit:	140
Total:	361

4. STATE AGENCY INTERLIBRARY COOPERATION UNIT

   A. Specific ILC Unit: None
   B. Other office: J. Maurice Travillian, Specialist in
                          Networking and Interlibrary Cooperation

5. OTHER STATE-LEVEL GOVERNMENTAL ILC UNITS

   There are none.

6. OTHER STATE-LEVEL NON-GOVERNMENTAL ILC UNITS

    Unit Name: Maryland Library Center for Automated Processing
                   (MALCAP)
    Address: McKeldin Library
                   University of Maryland
                   College Park, Maryland   20742
    Telephone: 301-454-3020
    Administrator: Walter C. Hamner, Chairman
    Activities: MALCAP produces catalog cards from the MARC files
                   of the University of Maryland's data base and pro-
                   vides a linkage to OCLC for its members desiring
                   to use that resource.

7. SINGLE-TYPE LIBRARY COOPERATIVES

    A. Receiving Continuing Financial Support from the State Library:

        Name: Eastern Shore Regional Library
        Address: P.O. Box 950
                       Salisbury, Maryland   21801
        Telephone: 301-742-1537
        Administrator: Mary Harispe, Director
        Type of Library Served: p
        Federal Support: $86,000
        State Support: $219,664
        Local Support: --
        Other Support: --
        Total Support: $305,664

        Name: Southern Maryland Regional Library Association
        Address: La Plata, Maryland   20646
        Telephone: 301-934-9442
        Administrator: Katharine Hurrey, Director
        Type of Library Served: p
        Federal Support: $52,000
        State Support: $103,819
        Local Support: $50,221
        Other Support: --
        Total Support: $206,040

        Name: Western Maryland Regional Library
        Address: 100 S. Potomac Street
                       Hagerstown, Maryland   21740
        Telephone: 301-739-3250
        Administrator: Mary Mallery, Director
        Type of Library Served: p
        Federal Support: $62,000
        State Support: $148,517
        Local Support: --
        Other Support: --
        Total Support: $210,517

(continued)

7. SINGLE-TYPE LIBRARY COOPERATIVES (continued)

    Name: Maryland Materials Center
    Address: 655 S. Salisbury Boulevard
                       Salisbury, Maryland 21801
    Telephone: 301-749-3480
    Administrator: Rosali Meinersmann, Director
    Federal Support: $30,000
    State Support: --
    Local Support: $212,608
    Other Support: --
    Total Support: $242,608

    B.   Receiving No Continuing Financial Support from the State
        Library:

        There are none.

    C.   Other:

        There are none.

8. MULTI-TYPE LIBRARY COOPERATIVES

    A.   Receiving Continuing Financial Support from the State Library:

        Name: State Library Resource Center
        Address: 400 Cathedral Street
                       Baltimore, Maryland 21201
        Telephone: 301-396-5395
        Administrator: Ernest Siegel
        Type of Libraries Served: a, p, sp
        Federal Support: $30,000
        State Support: $1,574,000
        Local Support: --
        Other Support: --
        Total Support: $1,604,000

    B.   Receiving No Continuing Financial Support from the State
        Library:

        There are none.

    C.   Other:

        There are none.

9. INTERLIBRARY COOPERATION FUNCTIONS

A. Receiving Continuing Financial Support from the State Library:

	State Support	Federal Support	Other Support	Total Support
Interlibrary Loan	$584,000	--	$135,000*	$719,000
Continuing Education	63,000	--	--	63,000
Cooperative Acquisitions	425,000	100,000	--	525,000
Cooperative Cataloging	--	15,000	75,000	90,000
Cooperative Delivery	--	17,000	35,000*	52,000
Cooperative Processing	--	15,000	75,000	90,000
Cooperative Reference	60,000*	--	--	60,000
Cooperative Storage	--	--	--	--
Legislative Assistance	--	--	--	--
Planning/Development	8,000	--	--	8,000
Union Lists of Serials	35,000	5,000	11,000*	51,000
Other	--	--	--	--
Total Support	$1,175,000	$152,000	$331,000	$1,658,000

*Estimated

B. Non-Financial Support Role for the State Library:
The Division provides coordination and leadership for
interlibrary cooperation and network development.

10. ILC COMMUNICATION DEVICES / SERVICE NETWORKS

A. Receiving Continuing Financial Support from the State Library:

Device/Service	Support ($)	Equipment (#)	Participants
TWX Teletype	$60,000	32 TWX ASR	27
OCLC	$30,000	2 computer terminals	NA

B. Non-Financial Support Role for the State Library:
The Division provides technical assistance and consultant services regarding communication equipment.

11. MACHINE-READABLE DATA BASE REFERENCE SEARCHING SERVICES

A. Receiving Continuing Financial Support from the State Library:

Data Base/Vendor	Support ($)	Terminals (#)	Participants
Dialog Access	$17,000	1 computer terminal	3

B. Non-Financial Support Role for the State Library:
The Division of Library Development and Services provides
technical assistance and consultant services regarding
searching services.

12. INTERLIBRARY SERVICES TO SPECIAL GROUPS

     A. Public libraries provide access points for the blind and
         physically handicapped to use the collection of the Library
         for the Blind and Physically Handicapped. Service to the
         institutionalized also involves the cooperation of many
         local library systems.

     B. The Division of Library Development and Services provides
         leadership in the development of services to each of these
         special groups and coordinates arrangements among various
         libraries for this purpose.

13. PARTICIPATION IN MULTI-STATE LIBRARY NETWORKS

     There is none.

14. LEGAL BASES FOR MULTI-TYPE LIBRARY COOPERATION

     The Code of Maryland, Article 77, Section 166, provides:

     "Under the general direction of the State Board of Education,
     and subject to its approval, the division of library development
     and services shall have the following powers and duties:
        (1) To provide leadership and guidance for the planning and
     coordinated development of library and information service in
     the State;
        (2) To develop statewide public library and school library
     services, and library networks, resource centers, and other
     arrangements as will meet the library and information needs of
     the State;
        (3) To provide professional and technical advisory services
     to public library and school library officials, to State govern-
     ment agencies, and others for the purpose of improving library
     services in the State;
        (4) To collect library statistics and other data; to identify
     and provide for needed research and studies of library needs; and
     to publish and disseminate findings in these areas;
        (5) To coordinate library services with other information and
     educational services and agencies."

15. LEGAL BARRIERS AGAINST PARTICIPATION IN MULTI-TYPE LIBRARY
     COOPERATION

     There are no legal barriers -- only political and financial ones.

1. REPORTING AGENCY

   A. Massachusetts Bureau of Library Extension
      648 Beacon Street
      Boston, MA 02215
      (617) 267-9400

   B. Chief Officer: Alice Cahill, Acting Director

   C. Fiscal Year: 1977

2. OVERVIEW

   Chapter 760 of the Massachusetts Acts of 1960 authorized the Board of
   Library Commissioners to establish a comprehensive statewide program
   of regional public library service supported by state funds appropriated on a per capita basis. During 1962 through 1967 contracts were
   signed by the Board of Library Commissioners with the Springfield,
   Worcester and Boston Public Libraries establishing the Western,
   Central and Eastern Regions respectively. In addition, contracts were
   signed with selected libraries within the regions establishing subregional centers for services. In 1972, Boston Public Library, as
   Library of Last Recourse, was funded at a level of 2.5 cents per
   capita per annum. Primary services provided by the Regions are interlibrary loan, delivery service, audiovisual services, bookmobile
   and deposit collections, consultant services, centralized purchasing,
   publications, reference and research.

   The Comprehensive Library Media Services Act of 1974 charges the
   Massachusetts Board of Library Commissioners with responsibility for
   the establishment and development of cooperation and coordination
   among "library media centers"; that is, intertype library cooperation.
   Although no state monies have been appropriated specifically for this
   purpose, grant programs for intertype library cooperation are provided
   under Title III of the Library Services and Construction Act. The
   lack of state financial support and the inadequacy of the annual Title
   III appropriation among other factors have inhibited the development
   of a statewide network in Massachusetts for intertype library cooperation. The cooperative groups which have developed are generally
   characterized by the following: geographic proximity; institutional
   subsidies and/or membership fees to provide services; primarily
   academic library membership.

3. NUMBER OF LIBRARIES IN THE STATE

Academic:	116
Public:	384
School:	1882*
Public:	not available
Private:	not available
Special:	350**
Profit:	not available
Non-profit	not available
Total	2732

(continued)

3. NUMBER OF LIBRARIES IN THE STATE (continued)

   *Based on ESEA participation estimated at 95% to 99%. No public-private breakdown available.

   **1977 data. No profit-non-profit breakdown available. Does not include special libraries within academic library systems.

4. STATE AGENCY INTERLIBRARY COOPERATION UNIT

   During FY1977 a federally funded position has been budgeted to provide a senior staff consultant for statewide interlibrary coop-eration, and for supervision of the LSCA Title III program. While this position remains unfilled, work in this area is done by the LSCA Project Director with the assistance of other staff who work under her supervision. Supervision of the Regional Public Library System Programs is the responsibility of that program's coordinator.

   Contact Persons: Mary M. Burgarella, LSCA Project Director
                     Marilyn Curtis, Academic Library Specialist
                     Nancy Johmann, Coordinator of the Regional
                         Public Library Systems

5. OTHER STATE-LEVEL GOVERNMENTAL ILC UNIT

   There are none.

6. OTHER STATE-LEVEL NON-GOVERNMENTAL ILC UNIT

   There are none.

7. SINGLE-TYPE LIBRARY COOPERATIVES

   A. Receiving Continuing Financial Support from the State Library
      Agency:

      Name: State Funded Regional Public Library Systems
      Address: Massachusetts Bureau of Library Extension
                         648 Beacon Street
                         Boston, MA 02215
      Telephone: (617) 267-9400
      Administrator: Nancy Johmann, Coordinator
      Type of Library Served: p
      Federal Support: -0-
      State Support: 2,566,982.00
      Local Support: -0-
      Other Support: -0-
      Total Support: 2,566,982.00

(continued)

7. SINGLE-TYPE LIBRARY COOPERATIVES (continued)

    B. Receiving No Continuing Financial Support from the State Library Agency:

    Name: Boston Theological Institute Library
                                Development Program
    Address: 545 Francis Street
                                Cambridge, MA 02138
    Telephone: (617) 495-5780
    Administrator: Andrew Scrimgeour, Director
    Type of Library Served: a
    Sponsoring Body: Boston Theological Institute
    Source of Support: Information not available.

    Name: Northeast Consortium for Health Information
    Address: Lowell General Hospital
                                295 Varnum Avenue
                                Lowell, MA 01854
    Telephone: (617) 454-0411
    Administrator: Mary Lehtinen, Chairperson
    Type of Library Served: sp
    Sponsoring Body: NA
    Source of Support: Information not available.

    Name: Consortium for Information Resources
    Address: 260 Bear Hill Road
                                Waltham, MA 02154
    Telephone: (617) 890-6550
    Administrator: Jeanette McGhee
    Type of Library Served: sp
    Sponsoring Body: West Suburban Hospital Association
    Source of Support: Information not available.

    Name: Southeastern Massachusetts Health Sciences
                                Libraries
    Address: Cape Cod Hospital
                                27 Park
                                Hyannis, MA 02601
    Telephone: (617) 771-1800
    Administrator: Agnes Kiernan, President
    Type of Library Served: sp
    Sponsoring Body: NA
    Source of Support: Information not available.

8. MULTI-TYPE LIBRARY COOPERATIVES

    A. Receiving Continuing Financial Support from the State Library Agency:

    There are none.

(continued)

8. MULTI-TYPE LIBRARY COOPERATIVES (continued)

B. Receiving No Continuing Financial Support from the State Library
   Agency:

   Name: Consortium of Central Massachusetts Health-
                                  Related Libraries
   Address: Nashoba Community Hospital
                                  200 Groton Road
                                  Ayer, MA 01432
   Telephone: (617) 772-0200
   Administrator: Edythe Salzman
   Types of Libraries Served: a, sp
   Sponsoring Body: NA
   Source of Support: Information not available

   Name: Haverhill Libraries Consortium
   Address: Haverhill Public Library
                                  99 Main Street
                                  Haverhill, MA 01830
   Administrator: Virginia B. Bernard
   Telephone: (617) 373-1586
   Types of Libraries Served: a, p, sch, sp
   Sponsoring Body: NA
   Source of Support: Information not available

C. Other (Past Recipients of State-Administered Federal Aid, but
   not on a continuing basis):

   Name: Boston Library Consortium
   Address: c/o Boston Public Library
                                  Copley Square
                                  Boston, MA 02117
   Telephone: (617) 267-0380
   Administrator: David R. Watkins, President
   Types of Libraries Served: a, p
   Sponsoring Body: NA
   Source of Support: Information not available.

   Name: Community Health Information Network
   Address: Mt. Auburn Hospital
                                  330 Mt. Auburn Street
                                  Cambridge, MA 02138
   Telephone: (617) 492-3500
   Administrator: Wendy Fink
   Types of Libraries Served: sp , a
   Sponsoring Body: NA
   Source of Support: Information not available

   Name: Cooperating Colleges of Greater Springfield:
                                  Librarians' Committee

(continued)

8. MULTI-TYPE LIBRARY COOPERATIVES (continued)

> Address: Springfield College
>   263 Adlen Street
>   Springfield, MA 01109
> Telephone: (413) 787-2341
> Administrator: Gerald F. Davis, Project Chairman
> Types of Libraries Served: a, p
> Sponsoring Body: NA
> Source of Support: Information not available
>
> Name: Essex County Cooperating Libraries
> Address: Peabody Institute Library
>   Peabody, MA 01960
> Telephone: (617) 531-0100
> Administrator: Thomas F. Scully, Chairperson
> Types of Libraries Served: a, p, sp, sch
> Sponsoring Body: NA
> Source of Support: Information not available
>
> Name: Fenway Library Consortium
> Address: Simmons College Library
>   300 The Fenway
>   Boston, MA 02115
> Telephone: (617) 738-2241
> Administrtor: Dorothy C. Senghas
> Types of Libraries Served: a, sp
> Sponsoring Body: NA
> Source of Support: Information not available
>
> Name: Hampshire Interlibrary Center, Inc.
> Address: Amherst College Library
>   Amherst, MA 01002
> Telephone: (413) 549-0135
> Administrator: Gregory Wilson, Director
> Types of Libraries Served: a, p
> Sponsoring Body: Five Colleges, Inc.
> Source of Support: Information not available
>
> Name: Lowell Area Council on Interlibrary Networks
> Address: Northeastern University Library
>   Burlington, MA 01803
> Telephone: (617) 272-5500
> Administrator: Ralph Coffman
> Types of Libraries Served: a, p, sch
> Sponsoring Body: NA
> Source of Support: Information not available
>
> Name: Project MARINE
> Address: Bristol Community College
>   Fall River, MA 02720

(continued)

8. MULTI-TYPE LIBRARY COOPERATIVES (continued)

      Telephone: (617) 678-2811, ext. 115
      Administrator: Richard Sobel
      Types of Libraries Served: a, εch
      Sponsoring Body: NA
      Source of Support: Information not available

      Name: Southeastern Massachusetts Cooperating
                       Libraries
      Address: c/o Wheaton College Library
                       Norton, MA 02766
      Telephone: (617) 285-7722, ext. 354
      Administrator: Sherrie Bergman, Chairperson, SMCL Board of
                       Directors
      Types of Libraries Served: a, p, sp
      Sponsoring Body: NA
      Source of Support: Information not available

      Name: Worcester Area Cooperating Libraries
      Address: Learning Resources Center
                       Worcester State College
                       Worcester, MA 01602
      Telephone: (617) 754-3964
      Administrator: Fay Zipkowitz, Director
      Types of Libraries Served: a, p, sp
      Sponsoring Body: Worcester Consortium for Higher Education,
                       Inc.
      Source of Support: Information not available

9. INTERLIBRARY COOPERATION FUNCTIONS

   A. Receiving Continuing Financial Support from the State Library:

	State Support	Federal Support Title I	Title III	Other Support
Interlibrary Loan				
Continuing Education				
Cooperative Acquisitions				
Cooperative Cataloging				
Cooperative Delivery				
Cooperative Processing				
Cooperative Reference				
Cooperative Storage				
Legislative Assistance				
Planning/Development				
Union Lists of Serials				
Other (please specify)				
Total Support				

State funded Regional Public Library Systems is a program administered by the state agency and funded on a per capita basis. Level of funding for FY77: $2,566,982.00. Major services provided through the Systems are: bookmobile, ILL, reference and research, delivery, lending of films and other AV materials.

(continued)

9. INTERLIBRARY COOPERATION FUNCTIONS (continued)

   B. Non-Financial Support Role of the State Library:

   Planning, evaluation, regulation and supervision of the Regional Public Library Systems.

   Development of minimum standards for personnel, accessibility, appropriateness of services and local budget support for eligibility for state aid under the Comprehensive Library Media Services Act.

   Research and needs assessments relative to implementation of the Comprehensive Library Media Services Act.

   Consulting services to existing cooperating groups and libraries initiating cooperative activities.

10. ILC COMMUNICATION DEVICES/SERVICES NETWORKS

    A. Financial Support Role of the State Library:

Device/Service	($) Support	(#) Equipment	Participants
Telephone Communications*	$39,765		n.a.
Teletype Networks**	15,000	13 units	13 pub. libs.

    *Includes WATS, credit cards and regular phone usage.
    **Federal LSCA support

    B. Non-Financial Support Role of the State Library:

    There is none.

11. MACHINE-READABLE DATA BASE REFERENCE SEARCHING SERVICES

    There are none.

12. INTERLIBRARY SERVICES TO SPECIAL GROUPS

    A. Financial Support Role of the State Library:

SERVICES (to)	STATE	FEDERAL	TOTAL
Blind and visually handicapped			
Physically handicapped			
Persons over 65			
Special language groups	*	$19,312	NA
Disadvantaged			
Institutionalized		$48,526	NA

    *Budgeting procedures in state-supported regional public library systems preclude allocation of program costs in these categories.

    B. Non-Financial Support Role of the State Library Agencies:

    Consultant services to systems and consortia

(continued)

12. INTERLIBRARY SERVICES TO SPECIAL GROUPS (continued)

developing proposals for services to special user groups; i.e.,
handicapped, disadvantaged, linguistic minorities,
institutionalized.

Approval of LSCA special purpose grants and interlibrary
cooperation grants addressed to needs of special user groups.

13. PARTICIPATION IN MULTI-STATE LIBRARY NETWORKS

A. Network: New England Library Board (NELB)
    Financial Support: $13,996 (FY 1977)
    Participation: Member
    Services Used: NA

B. Massachusetts-based Multi-State Library Networks:

Name: New England Library Information Network
                          (NELINET)
Address: 40 Grove Street
                          Wellesley, MA   02181

Name: New England Regional Medical Library
                          Service
Address: Francis A. Countway Library of Medicine
                          10 Shattuck St.
                          Boston, MA   02115

14. LEGAL BASES FOR MULTI-TYPE LIBRARY COOPERATION

State legislation enabling multi-type library cooperative development:
Comprehensive Library Media Services Act (Chapter 78, Section 19E,
General Laws of the Commonwealth of Massachusetts), enacted without
funding in 1974, charges the Massachusetts Board of Library
Commissioners with responsibility for the establishment and develop-
ment of cooperation and coordination among library media centers.
Library media centers are defined to include public libraries, school
libraries, school media centers, academic libraries, state or county
institution libraries and special libraries. The Bureau of Library
Extension is the executive agency of the Massachusetts Board of
Library Commissioners.

15. LEGAL BARRIERS AGAINST PARTICIPATION IN MULTI-TYPE LIBRARY
     COOPERATION

There are no legal barriers.

1. REPORTING AGENCY

    A.   Michigan State Library
           Box 30007
           Lansing, MI 48909
           (517) 373-1580

    B.   Chief Officer: Francis X. Scannell, State Librarian

    C.   Fiscal Year: 1977

2. OVERVIEW

Twenty-four public library systems functioned under Act. No.286 of the Public Acts of 1965. On Aug. 2, 1977, Act No. 89 of the Public Acts of 1977 became effective. P.A. 89 of 1977 repeals P.A. 286 of 1965 and provides for the establishment of cooperative libraries and for the appropriation of State aid to cooperative libraries and to public libraries participating in cooperative libraries. In order to be recognized as a cooperative library and so that the cooperative library and its participating public libraries may receive State aid, each cooperative library board must submit a preliminary cooperative library plan by Feb. 1, 1978. In order to be eligible for membership in a cooperative library a public library must maintain a minimum local support of 3/10 of a mill on State equalized valuation in the fiscal year before Oct. 1 of the year before distribution. Geographically all areas of the State shall be covered by the cooperative libraries but all areas shall not necessarily participate in cooperative libraries.

In 1970 Public Act 55 established the regional educational media centers to serve all school districts, local and intermediate, within the State.

The regional film centers were established in 1975 with LSCA Title I funds and every public library in Michigan is eligible to participate.

The first subregional libraries for the blind and physically handicapped were established 1972 and there are now 9 serving 55 counties. There are plans for bringing 24 unserved counties into the network within the next five to six years.

3. NUMBER OF LIBRARIES IN THE STATE

Academic:	97
Public:	359
School:	3,725 est.
Public:	3,375 est.
Private:	350 est.
Special:	110 est.

(continued)

3. NUMBER OF LIBRARIES IN THE STATE (continued)

> Profit: 64 est.
> Non-profit: 46 est.
> Total: 4,291 est.

4. STATE AGENCY INTERLIBRARY COOPERATION UNIT

> A. Unit Name: College and University Program
>   Person in Charge: Dale H. Pretzer, Program Manager

5. OTHER STATE-LEVEL GOVERNMENTAL ILC UNITS

> There are none.

6. OTHER STATE-LEVEL NON-GOVERNMENTAL UNITS

> Unit Name: Michigan Library Consortium
> Address: G. Flint Purdy Library
>   Wayne State University
>   Detroit, MI 48202
> Telephone: (313) 577-4061
> Administrator: John Aubrey, Director
> Activities: Membership is available to academic,
>   public, school and non-profit special
>   libraries. Through Consortium, members
>   participate in OCLC. Promotes all types
>   of interlibrary cooperation and sponsors
>   training in the use of OCLC, biblio-
>   graphic data bases, interlibrary loan,etc.

> Unit Name: Michigan Library Association
> Address: 226 W. Washtenaw
>   Lansing, MI
> Telephone: (517) 487-1161
> Administrator: Frances Pletz, Executive Secretary
> Activities: Promotes interlibrary cooperation through
>   its conference programs and workshops.

> Unit Name: Access Office
> Address: Michigan State University Library
>   East Lansing, MI 48824
> Telephone: (517) 355-2341
> Administrator: Dr. Richard E. Chapin, Director
> Activities: As one of Michigan's major research li-
>   braries, MSU receives annual LSCA Title III
>   grant to provide interlibrary loan ser-
>   vice to a geographical portion of the
>   State.

> Unit Name: Access Office
> Address: University of Michigan Library
>   Ann Arbor, MI 48104   (continued)

6.   OTHER STATE-LEVEL NON-GOVERNMENTAL UNITS   (continued)

Telephone:	(313) 764-9356
Administrator:	Dr. Frederick Wagman, Director
Activities:	As one of Michigan's major research libraries, UM receives an annual LSCA III grant to provide interlibrary loan services to a geographical portion of the State.

Unit Name:	Access Office - Wayne State University
Address:	G. Flint Purdy Library
	Detroit, MI 48202
Telephone:	(313) 577-4020
Administrator:	Dr. Vern M. Pings, Director
Activities:	As one of Michigan's major research libraries, WSU receives an annual LSCA III grant to provide interlibrary loan services to a geographical portion of the State.

7.   SINGLE-TYPE LIBRARY COOPERATIVES

   A.   Receiving Continuing Financial Support from the State Library:

   PUBLIC LIBRARY SYSTEMS

Name:	Blue Water Library Federation
Address:	210 McMorran Blvd.
	Port Huron, MI 48060
Telephone:	(313) 987-7323
Administrator:	Harry P. Wu, Director
Type of Library Served:	p
Federal Support:	$11,689
State Support:	$27,603
Local Support:	$25,535 (1976)
Other Support:	$ 8,000
Total Support:	$72,827

Name:	Capital Area Library Federation
Address:	401 S. Capitol
	Lansing, MI 48933
Telephone:	(517) 374-4600
Administrator:	Kenneth Browand, Director
Type of Library Served:	p
Federal Support:	$18,833
State Support:	$40,350
Local Support:	$27,292 (1976)
Other Support:	$ 8,000
Total Support:	$94,475

(continued)

7. SINGLE-TYPE LIBRARY COOPERATIVES (continued)

A. Receiving Continuing Financial Support from the State Library:

Name: Central Michigan Library System
Address: 145 W. Ash Street
                       Mason, MI 48854
Telephone: (517) 676-9088
Administrator: J. Edward Smith, Director
Type of Library Served: p
Federal Support: $13,722
State Support: $38,299
Local Support: $21,538 (1976)
Other Support: $ 8,000
Total Support: $81,559

Name: Chippewa Library League
Address: 301 University Avenue
                       Mt. Pleasant, MI 48858
Telephone: (517) 773-3242
Administrator: Evald Kruut, Director
Type of Library Served: p
Federal Support: $10,936
State Support: $23,422
Local Support: $50,204 (1976)
Other Support: $ 8,000
Total Support: $92,562

Name: Detroit Associated Libraries
Address: 5201 Woodward Avenue
                       Detroit, MI 48202
Telephone: (313) 833-1000
Administrator: Mrs. Clara Jones, Director
Type of Library Served: p
Federal Support: $139,456
State Support: $301,043
Local Support: $159,674 (1976)
Other Support: $ 8,000
Total Support: $608,173

Name: Eastern Peninsula Library System
Address: 541 Library Drive
                       Sault Ste. Marie, MI 49783
Telephone: (906) 632-9331
Administrator: Joseph Marconi, Director
Type of Library Served: p
Federal Support: $ 3,830
State Support: $14,881
Local Support: $28,636 (1976)
Other Support: $ 8,000
Total Support: $55,347

(continued)

7. SINGLE-TYPE LIBRARY COOPERATIVES (continued)

    A. Receiving Continuing Financial Support from the State Library:

        Name: Kalamazoo Area Library System
        Address: 315 S. Rose Street
                                  Kalamazoo, MI 49006
        Telephone: (616) 342-9837
        Administrator: Mark Crum, Director
        Type of Library Served: p
        Federal Support: $ 21,812
        State Support: $ 53,069
        Local Support: $ 23,242 (1976)
        Other Support: $ 8,000
        Total Support: $106,123

        Name: Kent County Library System
        Address: 775 Ball, N. E.
                                  Grand Rapids, MI 49503
        Telephone: (616) 774-3261
        Administrator: Miss Joyce Pleune
        Type of Library Served: p
        Federal Support: $19,969
        State Support: $46,521
        Local Support: $24,407 (1976)
        Other Support: $ 8,000
        Total Support: $98,897

        Name: Lakeland Library Federation
        Address: Library Plaza, N. E.
                                  Grand Rapids, MI 49502
        Telephone: (616) 456-4400
        Administrator: Miss Alberta Massingill, Director
        Type of Library Served: p
        Federal Support: $ 32,713
        State Support: $ 86,892
        Local Support: $ 43,436 (1976)
        Other Support: $ 8,000
        Total Support: $171,041

        Name: Library Network of Macomb
        Address: 21930 Dunham Road
                                  Mt. Clemens, MI 48043
        Telephone: (313) 469-5300
        Administrator: Thomas E. Alford, Director
        Type of Library Served: p
        Federal Support: $ 34,485
        State Support: $ 84,968
        Local Support: $ 44,908 (1976)
        Other Support: $ 8,000
        Total Support: $172,361

(continued)

7. SINGLE-TYPE LIBRARY COOPERATIVES (continued)

    A. Receiving Continuing Financial Support from the State Library:

        Name: Library System of SW Michigan
        Address: 213 E. Wall Street
                                Benton Harbor, MI 49022
        Telephone: (616) 926-6741
        Administrator: Vacant
        Type of Library Served: p
        Federal Support: $13,662
        State Support: $30,005
        Local Support: $25,971   (1976)
        Other Support: $ 8,000
        Total Support: $77,638

        Name: Mideastern Michigan Library Cooperative
        Address: 1026 East Kearsley
                                Flint, MI 48502
        Telephone: (313) 232-7119
        Administrator: Ransom L. Richardson, Director
        Type of Library Served: p
        Federal Support: $ 48,232
        State Support: $108,584
        Local Support: $ 86,047 (1976)
        Other Support: $ 8,000
        Total Support: $250,863

        Name: Mid-Michigan Library League
        Address: P. O. Box 700
                                Cadillac, MI 49601
        Telephone: (616) 755-6541
        Administrator: Donald A. Best
        Type of Library Served: p
        Federal Support: $ 14,628
        State Support: $ 37,846
        Local Support: $100,567 (1976)
        Other Support: $ 8,000
        Total Support: $161,041

        Name: Mid-Peninsula Library Federation
        Address: 401 Iron Mountain Street
                                Iron Mountain, MI 49801
        Telephone: (906) 774-3005
        Administrator: Ralph W. Secord, Director
        Type of Library Served: p
        Federal Support: $ 12,421
        State Support: $ 44,913
        Local Support: $ 42,726 (1976)
        Other Support: $ 8,000
        Total Support: $108,060

(continued)

7. SINGLE-TYPE LIBRARY COOPERATIVES (continued)

A. Receiving Continuing Financial Support from the State Library:

Name: Muskegon County Library System
Address: 635 Ottawa Street, County Building
Muskegon, MI 49440
Telephone: (616) 724-6248
Administrator: Warren McFerran, Director
Type of Library Served: p
Federal Support: $ 9,689
State Support: $20,914
Local Support: -0-
Other Support: $ 8,000
Total Support: $38,603

Name: Northland Library System
Address: 303 N. 2nd Street
Alpena, MI 49707
Telephone: (517) 356-1622
Administrator: Roger Mendel, Director
Type of Library Served: p
Federal Support: $ 6,720
State Support: $ 17,390
Local Support: $ 82,347 (1976)
Other Support: $ 8,000
Total Support: $114,457

Name: Raisin Valley Library System
Address: 3700 S. Custer Road
Monroe, MI 48161
Telephone: (313) 241-5277
Administrator: Bernard Margolis, Director
Type of Library Served: p
Federal Support: $ 18,187
State Support: $ 57,659
Local Support: $ 29,678 (1976)
Other Support: $ 8,000
Total Support: $113,524

Name: Superiorland Library System
Address: 213 N. Front Street
Marquette, MI 49855
Telephone: (906) 228-9510
Administrator: Mrs. Ruth Kell
Type of Library Served: p
Federal Support: $ 7,079
State Support: $19,946
Local Support: $12,138 (1976)
Other Support: $ 8,000
Total Support: $47,163

(continued)

7. SINGLE-TYPE LIBRARY COOPERATIVES (continued)

    A. Receiving Continuing Financial Support from the State Library:

        Name: Warren Public Library System
        Address: 5951 Beebe Street
                                 Warren, MI 48092
        Telephone: (313) 264-8720
        Administrator: Lawrence Davenport, Director
        Type of Library Served: p
        Federal Support: $16,134
        State Support: $34,827
        Local Support: $18,000 (1976)
        Other Support: $ 8,000
        Total Support: $76,961

        Name: Wayne County Federated Library System
        Address: 33030 Van Born Road
                                 Warren, MI 48184
        Telephone: (313) 722-8000
        Administrator: Leo Dinnan, Director
        Type of Library Served: p
        Federal Support: $ 175,186
        State Support: $ 382,656
        Local Support: $ 585,827 (1976)
        Other Support: $ 8,000
        Total Support: $1,151,669

        Name: White Pine Library System
        Address: 4570 Lawndale Road
                                 Saginaw, MI 48603
        Telephone: (517) 792-0001
        Administrator: Ms. Susan J. Hill, Director
        Type of Library Served: p
        Federal Support: $ 41,978
        State Support: $ 90,238
        Local Support: $ 50,845 (1976)
        Other Support: $ 8,000
        Total Support: $191,061

        Name: Willard Library System
        Address: 7 W. Van Buren
                                 Battle Creek, MI 49017
        Telephone: (616) 968-8166
        Administrator: Robert Raz, Director
        Type of Library Served: p
        Federal Support: $ 23,051
        State Support: $ 51,375
        Local Support: $ 20,690 (1976)
        Other Support: $ 8,000
        Total Support: $103,116

(continued)

7. SINGLE-TYPE LIBRARY COOPERATIVES (continued)

A. Receiving Continuing Financial Support from the State Library:

PUBLIC LIBRARY REGIONAL FILM CENTERS

Name:	Michigan North Film Region
Address:	411 S. Lake St., P.O. Box 700
	Cadillac, MI 49601
Telephone:	(616) 775-6541
Administrator:	Donald A. Best
Type of Library Served: p	
Federal Support:	$100,000
State Support:	-0-
Local Support:	-0-
Other Support:	-0-
Total Support:	$100,000

Name:	Eastern Michigan Film Region
Address:	1026 E. Kearsley
	Flint, MI 48502
Telephone:	(313) 232-7119
Administrator:	Eugene B. Griffel
Type of Library Served: p	
Federal Support:	$100,000
State Support:	-0-
Local Support:	-0-
Other Support:	-0-
Total Support:	$100,000

Name:	Regional Film Library of Southwest
Address:	315 South Rose Street Michigan
	Kalamazoo, MI 49006
Telephone:	(616) 342-9837
Administrator:	Dr. Mark Crum
Type of Library Served: p	
Federal Support:	$100,000
State Support:	-0-
Local Support:	-0-
Other Support:	-0-
Total Support:	$100,000

Name:	Southeast Michigan Regional Film Library
Address:	3700 South Custer Road
	Monroe, MI 48161
Telephone:	(313) 241-5277
Administrator:	Bernard A. Margolis
Type of Library Served: p	
Federal Support:	$100,000
State Support:	-0-
Local Support:	-0-
Other Support:	-0-
Total Support:	$100,000

(continued)

7.   SINGLE-TYPE LIBRARY COOPERATIVES (continued)

   A.   Receiving Continuing Financial Support from the State Library:

REGIONAL EDUCATIONAL MEDIA CENTERS

        Name: REMC 1 - Cooper Country ISD
        Address: 302 Front Street
                                 Hancock, MI 49930
        Telephone: (906) 482-5250
        Administrator: Jaswant Singh, Director
        Type of Library Served: sch
        Federal Support: $11,313
        State Support: $19,139
        Local Support: $ 6,072 (1976)
        Total Support: $36,524

        Name: REMC 2 - Grand Traverse Bay ISD
        Address: 2325 Garfield
                                 Traverse City, MI 49684
        Telephone: (616) 946-9260
        Administrator: Steve Norvilitis, Director
        Type of Library Served: sch
        Federal Support: $ 44,507
        State Support: $ 31,268
        Local Support: $127,176 (1976)
        Total Support: $202,951

        Name: REMC 3 - Cheboygan-Otsego-Presque Isle
        Address: 6065 Learning Lane   ISD
                                 Indian River, MI 49749
        Telephone: (616) 238-9394
        Administrator: Jack Keck, Director
        Type of Library Served: sch
        Federal Support: $ 23,241
        State Support: $ 23,469
        Local Support: $ 84,260 (1976)
        Total Support: $130,970

        Name: REMC 4 - Muskegon ISD
        Address: 630 Harvey Street
                                 Muskegon, MI 49442
        Telephone: (616) 777-2637
        Administrator: Arnold Fege, Director
        Type of Library Served: sch
        Federal Support: $ 36,972
        State Support: $ 28,462
        Local Support: $108,164 (1976)
        Total Support: $173,598

        Name: REMC 5 - Clare-Gladwin ISD
        Address: 4041 East Mannsiding
                                 Clare, MI 48617   (continued)

7.　SINGLE-TYPE LIBRARY COOPERATIVES (continued)

A.　Receiving Continuing Financial Support from the State Library:

REGIONAL EDUCATIONAL MEDIA CENTERS

```
Telephone:                (517) 386-9927
Administrator:            Richard Zubulake, Director
Type of Library Served:  sch
Federal Support:          $ 30,949
State Support:            $ 26,294
Local Support:            $159,813 (1976)
Total Support:            $217,056


Name:                     REMC 6 - Bay Arenac ISD
Address:                  4228  2 Mile Road
                          Bay City, MI 48706
Telephone:                (517) 686-4410
Administrator:            Robert Hayhurst, Director
Type of Library Served:  sch
Federal Support:          $ 28,250
State Support:            $ 25,334
Local Support:            $ 79,017 (1976)
Total Support:            $132,601


Name:                     REMC 7 - Ottawa ISD
Address:                  101 West 48th Street
                          Holland, MI 49423
Telephone:                (616) 392-2304
Administrator:            Edward Howard, Director
Type of Library Served:  sch
Federal Support:          $ 36,750
State Support:            $ 28,462
Local Support:            $102,555 (1976)
Total Support:            $167,767


Name:                     REMC 8 - Kent ISD
Address:                  2650 E. Beltline, SE
                          Grand Rapids, MI 49507
Telephone:                (616) 949-9270
Administrator:            Russell Hornbaker, Director
Type of Library Served:  sch
Federal Support:          $ 96,534
State Support:            $ 50,062
Local Support:            $213,152 (1976)
Total Support:            $359,748


Name:                     REMC 9 - Saginaw ISD
Address:                  6235 Gratiot Road
                          Saginaw, MI 48603
Telephone:                (517) 793-3760
Administrator:            Ronald Zolton, Director
```

(continued)

7.   SINGLE-TYPE LIBRARY COOPERATIVES (continued)

A.   Receiving Continuing Financial Support from the State Library:

REGIONAL EDUCATIONAL MEDIA CENTERS

        Type of Library Served: sch
        Federal Support: $ 40,132
        State Support: $ 29,674
        Local Support: $125,142 (1976)
        Total Support: $194,948

        Name: REMC 10 - Tuscola ISD
        Address: 6410 Main
                                 Cass City, MI 48726
        Telephone: (517) 872-4212
        Administrator: Don Richards, Director
        Type of Library Served: sch
        Federal Support: $ 24,202
        State Support: $ 23,828
        Local Support: $ 56,659 (1976)
        Total Support: $104,689

        Name: REMC 11 - Berrien ISD
        Address: 711 St. Joseph Avenue
                                 Berrien Springs, MI 49103
        Telephone: (616) 471-7725
        Administrator: Richard Pennington, Director
        Type of Library Served: sch
        Federal Support: $ 48,841
        State Support: $ 32,867
        Local Support: $ 88,055 (1976)
        Total Support: $169,763

        Name: REMC 12 - Kalamazoo Valley ISD
        Address: 1819 East Milham
                                 Kalamazoo, MI 49002
        Telephone: (616) 381-4620
        Administrator: Warren Lawrence, Director
        Type of Library Served: sch
        Federal Support: $ 71,346
        State Support: $ 41,005
        Local Support: $286,472 (1976)
        Total Support: $398,823

        Name: REMC 13 - Ingham ISD
        Address: 2630 W. Howell Rd.
                                 Mason, MI 48854
        Telephone: (517) 676-3222
        Administrator: Robert Townsend, Director
        Type of Library Served: sch
        Federal Support: $ 62,392

(continued)

173

7.   SINGLE-TYPE LIBRARY COOPERATIVES (continued)

A.   Receiving Continuing Financial Support from the State Library:

State Support: $ 37,776
Local Support: $223,603 (1976)
Total Support: $323,771

Name: REMC 14 - Genesee ISD
Address: 2413 West Maple Avenue
                        Flint, MI 48507
Telephone: (313) 767-4310
Administrator: Mr. Vernon Tyree, Director
Type of Library Served: sch
Federal Support: $105,558
State Support: $ 53,511
Local Support: $205,258 (1976)
Total Support: $364,327

Name: REMC 15 - Jackson ISD
Address: 2301 E. Jackson Ave.
                        Jackson, MI 49202
Telephone: (517) 787-2800
Administrator: Gerald Lang, Director
Type of Library Served: sch
Federal Support: $ 29,550
State Support: $ 25,810
Local Support: $162,682 (1976)
Total Support: $218,042

Name: REMC 16 - Washtenaw ISD
Address: 1819 South Wagner
                        Ann Arbor, MI 48103
Telephone: (313) 769-6522
Administrator: Peter Finney, Director
Type of Library Served: sch
Federal Support: $ 45,407
State Support: $ 31,394
Local Support: $ 27,711 (1976)
Total Support: $104,512

Name: REMC 17 - Oakland ISD
Address: 2100 Pontiac Lake Road
                        Pontiac, MI 49054
Telephone: (313) 645-1011
Administrator: Robert Fichtenau, Director
Type of Library Served: sch
Federal Support: $ 162,581
State Support: $ 72,763
Local Support: $ 786,500 (1976)
Total Support: $1,021,844

(continued)

7.   SINGLE-TYPE LIBRARY COOPERATIVES (continued)

   A.   Receiving Continuing Financial Support from the State Library:

      Name: REMC 18 - Macomb ISD
      Address: 44001 Garfield Road
                           Mt. Clemens, MI 48043
      Telephone: (313) 286-8800
      Administrator: Kent Voigt, Director
      Type of Library Served: sch
      Federal Support: $140,963
      State Support: $ 66,511
      Local Support: $240,807 (1976)
      Total Support: $448,281

      Name: REMC 19 - Lenawee ISD
      Address: 2345 North Adrian Hwy.
                           Adrian, MI 49221
      Telephone: (517) 263-2108 X53
      Administrator: Mrs. Diana Raine, Director
      Type of Library Served: sch
      Federal Support: $ 36,625
      State Support: $ 28,349
      Local Support: $101,659 (1976)
      Total Support: $166,633

      Name: REMC 20 - Wayne ISD
      Address: 33500 Van Born Road
                           Wayne, MI 48184
      Telephone: (313) 326-9300 X251
      Administrator: George Grimes, Director
      Type of Library Served: sch
      Federal Support: $379,763
      State Support: $153,377
      Local Support: $381,620 (1976)
      Total Support: $914,760

      Name: REMC 21 Marquette - Alger ISD
      Address: 427 West College Avenue
                           Marquette, MI 49855
      Telephone: (906) 228-9400
      Administrator: Daniel Blomquist, Director
      Type of Library Served: sch
      Federal Support: $29,997
      State Support: $25,974
      Local Support: $16,356 (1976)
      Total Support: $72,327

      Name: REMC 22 - Eastern Upper Peninsula ISD
      Address: Box 883
                           Sault Ste Marie, MI 49783

(continued)

7. SINGLE-TYPE LIBRARY COOPERATIVES (continued)

A. Receiving Continuing Financial Support from the State Library :

    Telephone: (906) 632-3373
    Administrator: Mrs. Betty Patrick, Director
    Type of Library Served: sch
    Federal Support: $ 8,657
    State Support: $18,152
    Local Support: $26,570 (1976)
    Total Support: $53,379

B. Receiving No Continuing Financial Support from the State Library:

    Name: Council of State College & University
                       Library Directors of Michigan
    Address: G. Flint Purdy Library, Wayne State
                                University
                       Detroit, MI 48202
    Telephone: (313) 577-4020
    Administrator: Dr. Vern M. Pings
    Type of Library Served: a
    Sponsoring Body: 13 library directors
    Source of Support: No funding involved

    Name: Extramural Coordinates Program - KOM
    Address: Shiffman Medical Library
                       4325 Brush Street
                     Detroit, MI 48201
    Telephone: (313) 577-1088
    Administrator: James F. Williams II
    Type of Library Served: sp
    Sponsoring Body: National Library of Medicine
    Source of Support: National Institute of Health

    Name: Great Lake's Colleges Association
    Address: 220 Collingwood, Suite 240
                     Ann Arbor, MI 48103

    Telephone: (313) 761-4833
    Administrator: Jon. W. Fuller, President
    Type of Library Served: a
    Sponsoring Body: 12 private colleges in Michigan, Indiana,Ohio
    Source of Support: Dues

    Name: Health Instructional Resources Association
    Address: Shiffman Medical Library
                     4325 Brush Street
                     Detroit, MI 48201
    Telephone: (313) 577-1088
    Administrator: Mollie Lynch

(continued)

7. SINGLE-TYPE LIBRARY COOPERATIVES   (continued)

    B. Receiving No Continuing Financial Support from the State Library:

        Type of Library Served: sp
        Sponsoring Body: Participating libraries
        Source of Support: Dues

        Name: Kentucky - Ohio - Michigan Regional
                                                   Medical Library
        Address: Wayne State University
                                  4325 Brush Street
                                  Detroit, MI 48201
        Telephone: (313) 577-1088
        Administrator: James F. Williams, II
        Type of Library Served: sp
        Sponsoring Body: Participating libraries
        Source of Support: National Library of Medicine

        Name: Metropolitan Detroit Medical Library Group
        Address: Shiffman Medical Library
                                  4325 Brush Street
                                  Detroit, MI 48201
        Telephone: (313) 577-1088
        Administrator: Elizabeth Gabhart
        Type of Library Served: sp
        Sponsoring Body: Personal & Institutional Memberships
        Source of Support: Dues

        Name: Oakland County Library Hotline
        Address: Oakland University Library
                                  Rochester, MI 48063
        Telephone: (313) 377-2473
        Administrator: Elizabeth Titus
        Type of Library Served: p
        Sponsoring Body: Oakland County Library Board
        Source of Support: Local funds

        Name: Project Loex
        Address: Center of Educational Resources
                                  Eastern Michigan University
                                  Ypsilanti, MI 48197
        Telephone: (313) 487-0168
        Administrator: Carolyn Kirkendall, Director
        Type of Library Served: a
        Sponsoring Body: Eastern Michigan University
        Source of Support: Council of Library Resources

(continued)

7. SINGLE-TYPE LIBRARY COOPERATIVES (continued)

    C. Receiving Occasional Support from the State Library:

        Name: Michigan Library Film Circuit
        Address: St. Clair County Library
                                    210 McMorran Blvd.
                                    Port Huron, MI 48060
        Telephone: (313) 987-7323
        Administrator: Harry Wu, President
        Type of Library Served: p
        Sponsoring Body: Membership
        Sources of Support: Dues & occasional LSCA I grant

8. MULTI-TYPE LIBRARY COOPERATIVES

    A. Receiving Continuing Financial Support from the State Library:

        There are none.

    B. Receiving No Continuing Financial Support from the State Library:

        Name: Berrien Library Consortium
        Address: Lake Michigan College
                                    2755 East Napier
                                    Benton Harbor, MI 49022
        Telephone: (616) 927-3571
        Administrator: William Hessel
        Types of Libraries Served: a - p - sp
        Sponsoring Body: Participating libraries
        Source of Support: Dues

        Name: Grand Rapids Area Union List of Serials
        Address: Grand Rapids Junior College Learning
                                    140 Ransom   Center
                                    Grand Rapids, MI 49502

        Telephone: (616) 456-4876
        Administrator: John A. Lally
        Types of Libraries Served: a - p - sp
        Sponsoring Body: 13 member libraries
        Source of Support: Sold union list to recover cost of printing.

        Name: Kalamazoo Area Library Consortium
        Address: Western Michigan University
                                    Dwight B. Waldo Library
                                    Kalamazoo, MI 49001
        Telephone: (616) 383-4961
        Administrator: Carl Sachtleben
        Types of Libraries Served: a - p - sp
        Sponsoring Body: Member libraries
        Source of Support: Members contribute services

(continued)

8. MULTI-TYPE LIBRARY COOPERATIVES (continued)

    B. Receiving No Continuing Financial Support from the State Library:

        Name: Oakland County Union List of Serials
        Address: Oakland University Library
                                  Rochester, MI 48063
        Telephone: (313) 377-2473
        Administrator: Elizabeth Titus
        Types of Libraries Served: a - p - sch - sp
        Sponsoring Body: Oakland County Library Board
        Source of Support: Local funds & sell union list

        Name: Soo Area International Library Association
        Address: Lake Superior State College
                                  Sault Ste. Marie, MI 49783
        Telephone: (906) 632-6841
        Administrator: Charles E. Nairn, Co-Chairperson
        Types of Libraries Served: a - p - sch - sp
        Sponsoring Body: Member libraries
        Source of Support: None at present

9. INTERLIBRARY COOPERATION FUNCTIONS

    A. Receiving Continuing Financial Support from the State Library:

    Interlibrary Loan
    Continuing Education
    Cooperative Acquisitions
    Cooperative Cataloging
    Cooperative Delivery
    Cooperative Processing
    Cooperative Reference   STATISTICS NOT AVAILABLE
    Cooperative Storage
    Legislative Assistance
    Planning/Development
    Union Lists of Serials
    Other (please specify)

    B. Non-Financial Support Role of the State Library:

        Promote and support all of the above ILC functions through pro-
        grams, services, grants, workshops and conferences.

10. ILC COMMUNICATION DEVICES / SERVICE NETWORKS

   A. Receiving Continuing Financial Support from the State Library:

Device/Service	Support ($)	Equipment (#)	Participants
Telefacsimile	$14,250	19	19 public library Systems
Telefacsimile	$16,500	22	22 Regional Educational media centers

   B. Non-Financial Support Role of the State Library:

   There are an increasing number of university and college libraries that are installing telefacsimile communications at their own expense in order to communicate with the State Library and other libraries in the State regarding interlibrary loan and other matters.

11. MACHINE-READABLE DATA BASE REFERENCE SEARCHING SERVICES

Data Base/Vendor	Support	Terminals (#)	Participants
SDC, Lockheed	$5,000	One at State Library	All libraries in the State
OCLC	$1,000	Two at State Library	All libraries in the State

12. INTERLIBRARY SERVICES TO SPECIAL GROUPS

   A. Receiving Continuing Financial Support from the State Library

   Financial Support Role of the State Library:

   A combination of LSCA Title I grants and local funds support the State network of subregional libraries for the blind and physically handicapped. Over the past five years LSCA I grants have been given to public library systems which have enabled them to serve special user groups.

   B. Non-Financial Support Role of the State Library:

   The regional library for the blind and physically handicapped which is located at the State Library maintains a regularly scheduled hotline service to the subregional network. The subregional libraries may also contact the regional library on a State-wide WATS telephone line. The regional library provides the subregional libraries with material and equipment, interloan, consultant, training, reference and information services and also serves as the subregional libraries' link to the

   (continued)

12. INTERLIBRARY SERVICES TO SPECIAL GROUPS

    B. Non-Financial Support Role of the State Library (continued)

        Library of Congress, Division for the Blind & Physically Handi-
        capped. The State Library works with State and local correc-
        tional and mental facilities, the Office of the Aging and the
        Migrant Education Program to provide library service to special
        user groups through public and school libraries.

13. PARTICIPATION IN MULTI-STATE LIBRARY NETWORKS

    A. State library agency holds membership in:

        NETWORK: MIDLNET
        FINANCIAL SUPPORT: $2,500
        PARTICIPATION: Share membership cost with Michigan
                                              Library Consortium
        SERVICES USED: None

    B. There are presently no Multi-State networks headquartered in
        Michigan.

14. LEGAL BASES FOR MULTI-TYPE LIBRARY COOPERATION

    Public Act No. 89 of 1977 permits any type of library to be a member
    of the cooperative area library. However, it provides funding for
    only public libraries. Public Act 371 of 1972 is known as the li-
    brary network act. It states that the State Library shall ad-
    minister the interlibrary loan service for the State and provides
    for the connecting of the largest research libraries (a minimum
    collection of 1,000,000 volumes) in the State so their collections
    may be made available through interlibrary loan.

15. LEGAL BARRIERS AGAINST PARTICIPATION IN MULTI-TYPE LIBRARY
    COOPERATION.

    There are no legal barriers in Michigan.

1. REPORTING AGENCY

    A. Office of Public Libraries and Interlibrary Cooperation
       301 Hanover Building
       480 Cedar Street
       St. Paul, MN 55101
       (612) 296-2821

    B. Chief Officer: William G. Asp, Director

    C. Fiscal Year: 1977

2. OVERVIEW

    Statewide interlibrary cooperation activities include resource
    sharing, development of bibliographic data bases for serials
    and monographs, back-up reference service, and continuing
    education. MINITEX links 146 academic, public, state agency
    and special libraries, and interfaces with a number of spec-
    ialized subject networks and consortia. Public library re-
    quests for monographs are processed first through the St. Paul
    Public Library and the collections of other metropolitan public
    libraries and the Cooperative Libraries in Consortium.

    Thirteen multi-county regional library systems, seven consoli-
    dated and six federated, include 69 counties and 22 cities in
    9 additional counties. 93.5% of the state's population is
    served by libraries participating in regional library systems.
    Systems can be organized under four provisions in Minnesota
    Statutes: (1) 375.335 is the basic regional library law; (2)
    134.12 gives library boards the power to contract; (3) 471.59
    provides for joint exercise of power among governmental units;
    and (4) 317 provides for establishment of nonprofit corpora-
    tions. State appropriations are authorized under Minnesota
    Statutes 134.035 and language accompanying the biennial
    appropriation.

    Numerous networks and consortia facilitate interlibrary coopera-
    tion among libraries of specialized types or libraries in a
    specific geographic area. Many of these are organized infor-
    mally.

3. NUMBER OF LIBRARIES IN THE STATE

    Academic: 71
    Public: 143
    School: 1,984 (estimate)
      Public: 1,509 (estimate)
      Private: 475 (estimate)
    Special: 100 (estimate)
      Profit: 65 (estimate)
      Nonprofit: 35 (estimate)

(continued)

3. NUMBER OF LIBRARIES IN THE STATE (continued)

    TOTAL: 2,298 estimate

4. STATE AGENCY INTERLIBRARY COOPERATION UNIT

    A. Unit Name: Entire agency functions in interlibrary cooperation activities.

5. OTHER STATE-LEVEL GOVERNMENTAL ILC UNITS

    A. Unit Name: Minnesota Higher Education Coordinating Board

        Address: 400 Capitol Square Building
                             550 Cedar Street
                             St. Paul, MN 55101

        Telephone: (612) 296-9672
        Administrator: David B. Laird, Deputy Director
        Activities: The Minnesota Interlibrary Telecommunications Exchange (MINITEX) is a program of HECB under contract with the University of Minnesota. Biennial appropriations to HECB support academic library participation in MINITEX, with public library participation funded through OPLIC.

    B. Unit Name: Educational Media Unit, Minnesota Department of Education

        Address: 6th floor, Capitol Square Building
                             550 Cedar Street
                             St. Paul, MN 55101

        Telephone: (612) 296-2206
        Administrator: Robert Miller, Unit Supervisor
        Activities: Development of school media centers, interlibrary cooperation.

6. OTHER STATE-LEVEL NON-GOVERNMENTAL ILC UNITS

    A. Unit Name: St. Paul Public Library
        Address: 90 West Fourth Street
                     St. Paul, MN 55102
        Telephone: (612) 224-3383
        Administrator: J. Archer Eggen
        Activities: Under an agreement with OPLIC, the St. Paul Public Library provides interlibrary loan of monographs from its collection and from other Twin Cities public library collections to regional public library systems.

    B. Unit Name: Minnesota Library Film Circuit
        Address: 301 Hanover Building   (continued)

6. OTHER STATE-LEVEL NON-GOVERNMENTAL ICL UNITS (continued)

        Address: 480 Cedar Street
                   St. Paul, MN 55101
        Telephone: (612) 296-2821; (612) 784-1100
        Administrator: Jerry Young, President
        Activities: Purchase and sharing of 16mm films.

    C. Unit Name: Minnesota Library Association
        Address: State Organization Service
                   319 15th Avenue S.E.
                   Minneapolis, MN 55455
        Telephone: (612) 938-3531
        Administrator: Mary Heiges, President
        Activities: Long Range Planning and Development
                   Committee.

    D. Unit Name: Minnesota Educational Media Organization
        Address: Southwest Secondary School
                   3414 47th Street
                   Minneapolis, MN
        Telephone: (612) 920-1965
        Administrator: Helen E. Stub, President
        Activities: School Media Center-Public Library
                   Cooperation Committee.

    E. Unit Name: Minnesota Health Science Library Network
        Address: Biomedical Library
                   University of Minnesota
                   Minneapolis, MN 55455
        Telephone: (612) 373-5564
        Administrator: Judith McKloskey, coordinator
        Activities: The Minnesota component of the Midwest
                   Health Science Library Network, Region VII,
                   of the National Library of Medicine bio-
                   medical communications network.

7. SINGLE-TYPE LIBRARY COOPERATIVES

    A. Receiving Continuing Financial Support from the State Library:

    Name: Arrowhead Library System
    Address: 701 11th Street North
                 Virginia, MN 55792
    Telephone: (218) 741-3840
    Administrator: Ken Nielsen, Director
    Type of Library Served: p
    Federal Support: $96,550 (LSCA Title I)
    State Support: $244,018
    Local Support: $2,102,484 (est.)

(continued)

7. SINGLE-TYPE LIBRARY COOPERATIVES (continued)

        Other Support: $287,454
        Total Support: $2,730,506

        Name: Crow River Regional Library
        Address: 410 W. Fifth
                            Willmar, MN 56201
        Telephone: (612) 235-3162
        Administrator: Burton Sundberg, Director
        Type of Library Served: p
        Federal Support: $21,793 (LSCA Title I)
        State Support: $76,216
        Local Support: $239,780
        Other Support: $19,995
        Total Support $357,784

        Name: East Central Regional Library
        Address: 244 S. Birch
                            Cambridge, MN   55008
        Telephone: (612) 689-1901
        Administrator: Vacant
        Type of Library Served: p
        Federal Support: $28,595 (LSCA Title I)
        State Support: $99,986
        Local Support: $186,300
        Other Support: $11,956
        Total Support: $326,837

        Name: Great River Regional Library
        Address: 124 S. Fifth Avenue
                            St. Cloud, MN   56301
        Telephone: (612) 251-7282
        Administrator: Darro Willey, Director
        Type of Library Served: p
        Federal Support: $40,822 (LSCA Title I)
        State Support: $142,709
        Local Support: $540,292 (est.)
        Other Support: $26,508
        Total Support: $750,331

        Name: Kitchigami Regional Library
        Address: Pine River, MN 56474
        Telephone: (218) 587-2171
        Administrator: Marlys O'Brien, Director
        Type of Library Served: p
        Federal Support: $20,819 (LSCA Title I)
        State Support: $73,336
        Local Support: $112,135 (est.)
        Other Support: $12,036
        Total Support: $218,326

(continued)

7. SINGLE-TYPE LIBRARY COOPERATIVES (continued)

```
Name:              Lake Agassiz Regional Library
Address:           Box 699
                   Moorhead, MN  56561
Telephone:         (218) 233-7594
Administrator:     Lon Dickerson, Director
Type of Library Served:  p
Federal Support:   $57,297 (LSCA Title I)
State Support:     $102,208
Local Support:     $377,959
Other Support:      $29,659
Total Support:     $567,123


Name:              Metropolitan Library Service Agency
Address:           S-275 Griggs-Midway Building
                   1821 University Avenue
                   St. Paul, MN  55104
Telephone:         (612) 645-5731
Administrator:     Joel Rosenfeld, Director
Type of Library Served:  p
Federal Support: $253,779 (LSCA Title I)
State Support:     $687,091
Local Support: 17,616,055
Other Support:    $274,863
Total Support: 18,831,788


Name:              Northwest Regional Library
Address:           101 E. First Street
                   Thief River Falls, MN  56701
Telephone:         (218) 681-4325
Administrator:     Dottie Hiebing, Director
Type of Library Served:  p
Federal Support:   $49,207 (LSCA Title I)
State Support:      $63,966
Local Support:    $117,082 (est.)
Other Support:     $10,357
Total Support:    $240,612


Name:              Plum Creek Library System
Address:           P. O. Box 184
                   Worthington, MN  56187
Telephone:         (507) 376-5803
Administrator:     Virgene Anderson, Director
Type of Library Served:  p
Federal Support:   $51,395 (LSCA Title I)
State Support:      $71,016
Local Support:    $430,832
Other Support:     $73,029
Total Support:    $626,272
```

(continued)

7. SINGLE-TYPE LIBRARY COOPERATIVES (continued)

Name: Southeastern Libraries Cooperating
Address: 304 Marquette Bank Building
                      Rochester, MN 55901
Telephone: (507) 288-5513
Administrator: Ray Ogden, Executive Director
Type of Library Served: p
Federal Support: $89,272 (LSCA Title I)
State Support: $177,573
Local Support: $1,770,317 (est.)
Other Support: $82,130
Total Support: $2,119,292

Name: Traverse des Sioux Library System
Address: 100 E. Main
                      Mankato, MN 56001
Telephone: (507) 625-6169
Administrator: John Christenson, Executive Director
Type of Library Served: p
Federal Support: $93,410 (LSCA Title I)
State Support: $118,328
Local Support: $936,277
Other Support: $77,650
Total Support: $1,225,665

Name: Viking Library System
Address: 125 North Union
                      Fergus Falls, MN 56537
Telephone: (218) 739-2896
Administrator: Stephen Von Vogt, Director
Type of Library Served: p
Federal Support: $176,161 (LSCA Title I)
State Support: $89,946
Local Support: $260,605
Other Support: $17,122
Total Support: $543,834

Name: Western Plains Library System
Address: 204 S. First St.
                      Montevideo, MN 56265
Telephone: (612) 269-6501
Administrator: Robert Boese, Director
Type of Library Served: p
Federal Support: $51,120 (est. FY 1978) (LSCA Title I)
                                  (Incl. $45,959 Est. Gr.)
State Support: $17,966 (est. FY 1978)
Local Support: $191,822
Other Support: $4,000
Total Support: $264,908

(continued)

7. SINGLE-TYPE LIBRARY COOPERATIVES (continued)

   B. Receiving No Continuing Financial Support from the State Library:

      Name: Arrowhead Professional Libraries Association
      Address: Miller-Dwan Hospital and Medical Center
                         502 East Second Street
                         Duluth, MN 55805
      Telephone: (218) 727-8762
      Administrator: Faye Krasner
      Type of Library Served: sp
      Sponsoring Body: There is none.
      Source of Support: Membership dues.

      Name: Capitol Area Library Consortium, Inc.
      Address: Department of Transportation Library
                         B-10 Transportation Building
                         St. Paul, MN 55105
      Telephone: (612) 296-2385
      Administrator: Jerry Baldwin, President
      Type of Library Served: sp
      Sponsoring Body: There is none.
      Source of Support: Membership dues.

      Name: Cooperating Libraries in Consortium
      Address: Hill Reference Library
                         4th & Market Streets
                         St. Paul, MN 55102
      Telephone: (612) 227-9531
      Administrator: Virgil Massman
      Type of Library Served: a
      Sponsoring Body: The eight member institutions.
      Source of Support: Member assessments.

      Name: Lake Superior Association of Colleges and
                             Universities
      Address: 505 Alworth Bldg.
                         Duluth, MN 55802
      Telephone: (218) 722-5511
      Administrator: Judith Kotar, Acting Director
      Type of Library Served: a
      Sponsoring Body: There is none.
      Source of Support: Contributions from the institutions.

      Name: Medi-Sota Library Consortium
      Address: Canby Community Hospital
                         Canby, MN 56220
      Telephone: (507) 223-7277
      Administrator: Linda Raiber
      Type of Library Served: sp
      Sponsoring Body: There is none.
      Source of Support: None.   (continued)

7. SINGLE-TYPE LIBRARY COOPERATIVES (continued)

         Name: Minnesota Association of Law Libraries
         Address: Lawyer's Joint Law Library
                            3930 IDS Tower
                            Minneapolis, MN 55402
         Telephone: (612) 338-4320
         Administrator: Maureen Dunnigan, President
         Type of Library Served: sp
         Sponsoring Body: There is none.
         Source of Support: Membership dues.

         Name: Minnesota Department of Public Welfare
                               Library Consortium
         Address: Medical Library
                            Glen Lake State Sanatorium
                            Minnetonka, MN 55343
         Telephone: (612) 938-7621
         Administrator: Sue Ager
         Type of Library Served: sp
         Sponsoring Body: Minnesota Department of Public Welfare
         Source of Support: Minnesota Department of Public Welfare

         Name: Twin Cities Biomedical Consortium
         Address: Abbott-Northwestern Hospital
                            810 East 27th Street
                            Minneapolis, MN 55407
         Telephone: (612) 874-4185
         Administrator: Donna Johnson, President
         Type of Library Served: sp
         Sponsoring Body: There is none.
         Source of Support: Membership dues.

         Name: Valley Medical Network
         Address: St. Lukes Hospital
                            5th and Mills Avenue
                            Fargo, North Dakota 58102
         Telephone: (701) 235-3161
         Administrator: Bob Blackman, President
         Type of Library Served: sp
         Sponsoring Body: There is none.
         Source of Support: Membership dues.

8. MULTI-TYPE LIBRARY COOPERATIVES

    A. Receiving Continuing Financial Support from the State Library:

    Name: Minnesota Interlibrary Telecommunications Exchange
              (MINITEX)
    Address: 30 Wilson Library
                       University of Minnesota

(continued)

8. MULTI-TYPE LIBRARY COOPERATIVES (continued)

                      Minneapolis, MN 55455
```
Telephone:         (612) 376-3925
Administrator:     Alice Wilcox, Director
Types of Libraries Served:  p, a, sp
Federal Support:   $48,664 (LSCA Title III)
State Support:     $421,336
Local Support:        -0-
Other Support:     $102,777
Total Support:     $572,777
```

B. Receiving No Continuing Financial Support from the State Library:

```
Name:              South Central Minnesota Interlibrary Exchange
                      (SMILE)
Address:           University of Minnesota Technical College
                   Waseca, MN  56093
Telephone:         (507) 835-1000
Administrator:     Bill Andrews, President
Types of Libraries Served:  a, p, sp, sch
Sponsoring Body:  There is none.
Sources of Support:  Membership dues, income from services,
                        and grants.
```

```
Name:              Tri-College University Library Consortium
Address:           Moorhead State University
                   Moorhead, MN  56560
Telephone:         (218) 236-2844
Administrator:     Darrel Meinke
Types of Libraries Served:  a, p, sp
Sponsoring Body:  Tri-College University Consortium
Source of Support:  Local institutions and grants.
```

```
Name:              Waseca Interlibrary Resource Exchange (WIRE)
Address:           LeSeuer-Waseca Regional Library
                   408 N. State
                   Waseca, MN  56093
Telephone:         (507) 835-2910
Administrator:     David Hennessey
Types of Libraries Served:  p, a, sch
Sponsoring Body:  There is none.
Source of Support:  Member contributions.
```

C. Other:

    There are none.

9. INTERLIBRARY COOPERATION FUNCTIONS*

A.

	State Support	Federal Support Title I	Federal Support Title III	Other Support	Total Support
Interlibrary Loan	$109,375		$16,625		$126,000
Continuing Education	591		409		1,000
Cooperative Acquisitions					
Cooperative Cataloging					
Cooperative Delivery	2,972		2,028		5,000
Cooperative Processing					
Cooperative Reference	11,890		8,110		20,000
Cooperative Storage					
Legislative Assistance					
Planning/Development					
Union Lists of Serials	14,862		10,138		25,000
Other (please specify)					
Communications	16,646		11,354		28,000
Total Support	$156,336		$48,664		$205,000

*Exclusive of funds for regional public library systems.
All figures are estimates.

B. NON-FINANCIAL SUPPORT ROLE OF THE STATE LIBRARY:

OPLIC staff members consult with librarians and organizations
representing all types of libraries in planning and implementation of cooperative activities and services.

10. ILC COMMUNICATION DEVICES / SERVICE NETWORKS

A. Device/Service   Support ($)   Equipment (#)   Participants
Funded through MINITEX

B. NON-FINANCIAL SUPPORT ROLE OF THE STATE LIBRARY

OPLIC staff members provide consultative assistance on interlibrary
communications and service networks.

11. MACHINE-READABLE DATA BASE REFERENCE SEARCHING SERVICES

Data Base / Vendor   Support ($)   Terminals (#)   Participants
Handled largely through MINITEX

12. INTERLIBRARY SERVICES TO SPECIAL GROUPS

A. Library services for persons in Department of Welfare and
Department of Corrections Institutions.
Library services for the blind and physically handicapped.

B. NON-FINANCIAL SUPPORT ROLE OF THE STATE LIBRARY
OPLIC staff provide consultative assistance.

13. PARTICIPATION IN MULTI-STATE LIBRARY NETWORKS

   A. Network: Midwest Region Library Network
      Financial Support: Initial membership payment of $10,000
      Participation: Member of the board
      Services used: Several libraries in the state are con-
                        tracting for reference data base searching.
                        There is participation in continuing educa-
                        tion activities.

   B. Network: Minnesota Library Telecommunications Exchange
      Financial Support: $120,000 (FY 1977)
      Participation: Funding for public library participation;
                        ex-officio member of advisory committee.
      Services used: Communications system, document delivery,
                        union list of serials, back-up reference
                        service, continuing education.

14. LEGAL BASES FOR MULTI-TYPE LIBRARY COOPERATION

   There is no enabling legislation.

15. LEGAL BARRIERS AGAINST PARTICIPATION IN MULTI-TYPE LIBRARY
    COOPERATION

   Current state grant appropriations to OPLIC only fund aid to
   public libraries or services to public libraries.

1. REPORTING AGENCY

    A. Mississippi Library Commission
        P. O. Box 3260
        Jackson, Mississippi 39207
        (601) 354-6369

    B. Chief Officer: Jack C. Mulkey, Director

    C. Fiscal Year: 1978

2. OVERVIEW

    Sixteen regional or multi-county systems in Mississippi include
    libraries in 56 of the state's 82 counties. Additionally, there
    are 28 county libraries in the state that make possible some form
    of public library service. The 44 administrative units, which
    include the 16 regional and the 28 county libraries, all participate
    in interlibrary cooperation in varying degrees.

    Regional libraries may be formed under Sections 39-3-9 and 39-3-11,
    Mississippi Code 1972. The establishment of county libraries is
    permitted under Section 39-3-5. Contracts between municipalities
    and counties and/or regional libraries are authorized under Section
    39-3-13, Mississippi Code 1972.

3. NUMBER OF LIBRARIES IN THE STATE

Academic:	46
Public:	44
School:	621
Public:	621
Private:	n.a.
Special:	28
Profit:	n.a.
Non-profit:	n.a.
Total:	739 est.

4. STATE AGENCY INTERLIBRARY COOPERATION UNIT

    A. Unit Name: Library Development Division
        Person in Charge: Linda Gates, Assistant Director, Library
                           Development

    B. Unit Name: Library Operation Division
        Person in Charge: Gerald Buchanan, Assistant Director,
                           Library Operation

5. OTHER STATE-LEVEL GOVERNMENTAL ILC UNITS

    There are none.

6. OTHER STATE-LEVEL NON-GOVERNMENTAL ILC UNITS

 Organization: Consortium for Library Automation in Mississippi
       (CLAM)

   Address: P. O. Box 5408
       Mississippi State, MS 39762

  Telephone: (601) 325-4225

   President: Ms. Frances Coleman

   Activity: To investigate, analyze and determine the cooperative
       library automation needs of the Mississippi library
       and information community

7. SINGLE-TYPE LIBRARY COOPERATIVES

 A. Receiving Continuing Financial Support from the State Library:
   (Note: All Financial Support figures are Fiscal 1976)

    Name: Copiah-Jefferson Regional Library
    Address: Box 590
           Hazlehurst, MS 39083
    Telephone: (601) 894-1681
    Administrator: Ms. Kathleen Hutchison
    Type of Library Served: p
    Federal Support: $ 1,702
    State Support: 12,320
    Local Support: 47,197
    Total Support: 61,219

    Name: Dixie Regional Library
    Address: 114 North Main
           Pontotoc, MS 38863
    Telephone: (601) 489-3522
    Administrator: Mr. Elliott Thompson
    Type of Library Served: p
    Federal Support: $ 1,599
    State Support: 12,768
    Local Support: 57,936
    Total Support: 72,303

    Name: East Mississippi Regional Library
    Address: 103 East Church Street
           Quitman, MS 39355
    Telephone: (601) 776-4611
    Administrator: Ms. Louise Evans
    Type of Library Served: p
    Federal Support: $ -0-
    State Support: 18,480
    Local Support: 72,324   (continued)

7. SINGLE-TYPE LIBRARY COOPERATIVES (continued)

    Total Support: $90,804

    Name: First Regional Library
    Address: 59 Commerce Street, N. W.
                            Hernando, MS 38632
    Telephone: (601) 368-4439
    Administrator: James F. Anderson
    Type of Library Served: p
    Federal Support: $ 5,865
    State Support: 71,524
    Local Support: 293,380
    Total Support: 370,769

    Name: Jackson-George Regional Library System
    Address: Box 937
                            Pascagoula, MS 39567
    Telephone: (601) 762-3406
    Administrator: Ms. Kathleen McIllwain
    Type of Library Served: p
    Federal Support: $ 5,022
    State Support: 41,664
    Local Support: 321,459
    Total Support: 368,145

    Name: Jackson Metropolitan Library System
    Address: 301 North State Street
                            Jackson, MS 39201
    Telephone: (601) 352-3677
    Administrator: Harold J. Ard
    Type of Library Served: p
    Federal Support: $ 17,938
    State Support: 197,848
    Local Support: 1,193,440
    Total Support: 1,409,226

    Name: Kemper-Newton Regional Library System
    Address: Union MS 39365
    Telephone: (601) 774-7811
    Administrator: William Majure
    Type of Library Served: p
    Federal Support: $ 1,461
    State Support: 12,880
    Local Support: 68,836
    Total Support: 83,177

    Name: Lee-Itawamba Library System
    Address   319 Madison Street
                            Tupelo, MS 38801
    Telephone: (601) 844-2377
    Administrator: Ms. Betty Kemp
    Type of Library Served: p   (continued)

195

7. SINGLE-TYPE LIBRARY COOPERATIVES (continued)

```
        Federal Support:            $  3,150
        State Support:                38,584
        Local Support:               168,915
        Total Support:               210,649


        Name:                   Lincoln-Lawrence-Franklin Regional Library
        Address:                Box 541
                                Brookhaven, MS  39601
        Telephone:              (601)  833-3369
        Administrator:          Ms. Sharman Smith
        Type of Library Served:        p
        Federal Support:            $  2,267
        State Support:                22,288
        Local Support:               123,022
        Total Support:               147,577


        Name:                   Mid-Mississippi Regional Library
        Address:                201 South Huntington Street
                                Kosciusko, MS  39090
        Telephone:              (601)  289-5146
        Administrator:          Richard Greene
        Type of Library Served:        p
        Federal Support:            $  3,669
        State Support:                47,863
        Local Support:               198,189
        Total Support:               249,721


        Name:                   Northeast Regional Library
        Address:                1023 Fillmore Street
                                Corinth, MS  38834
        Telephone:              (601)  287-2441
        Administrator:          Walter Browne
        Type of Library Served:        p
        Federal Support:            $  4,280
        State Support:                40,880
        Local Support:               146,788
        Total Support:               191,948


        Name:                   Pike-Amite Library System
        Address:                114 State Street
                                McComb, MS  39648
        Telephone:              (601)  684-7034
        Administrator:          Ms. Jane Bryan
        Type of Library Served:        p
        Federal Support:            $  2,276
        State Support:                27,440
        Local Support:               111,699
        Total Support:               141,415
```

(continued)

7. SINGLE-TYPE LIBRARY COOPERATIVES (continued)

Name: Pine Forest Regional Library
Address: P. O. Drawer L
                                      Richton, MS 39476
Telephone: (601) 788-6539
Administrator: Ms. Carrie Widdon
Type of Library Served: p
Federal Support: $ 2,746
State Support: 21,280
Local Support: 112,221
Total Support: 136,247

Name: South Mississippi Regional Library
Address: 900 Broad Street
                                      Columbia, MS 39429
Telephone: (601) 736-5516
Administrator: Wes Stant
Type of Library Served: p
Federal Support: $ 1,790
State Support: 12,320
Local Support: 67,160
Total Support: 81,270

Name: Tombigbee Regional Library
Address: East Broad Street
                                      West Point, MS 39773
Telephone: (601) 494-4872
Administrator: Ms. Esther Pippen
Type of Library Served: p
Federal Support: $ 3,568
State Support: 30,912
Local Support: 132,967
Total Support: 167,447

Name: Yazoo-Sharkey-Issaquena Libraries
Address: 310 Main Street
                                      Yazoo City, MS 39194
Telephone: (601) 746-5557
Administrator: Ms. Jane Smith
Type of Library Served: p
Federal Support: $ 1,949
State Support: 23,520
Local Support: 87,577
Total Support: 113,046

B. Receiving No Continuing Financial Support from the State Library:

    There are none.

C. Other:

    There are none.

8. MULTI-TYPE LIBRARY COOPERATIVES

    A. Receiving Continuing Financial Support from the State Library:

       There are none.

    B. Receiving No Continuing Financial Support from the State Library:

       There are none.

    C. Other:

       There are none.

9. INTERLIBRARY COOPERATION FUNCTIONS

    A. Receiving Continuing Financial Support from the State Library:
       (All financial support figures are fiscal 1976)

	State Support	Federal Support Title I	Federal Support Title III	Other Support	Total Support
Interlibrary Loan	$165,118		40,000	–	$205,118
Cooperative					
Acquisitions)					
Cataloging)	83,316	77,433		–	160,749
Processing)					
Delivery	–		–	–	–
Reference	See Interlibrary Loan above				
Storage	–		–	–	–
Continuing Education	–		–	–	–
Legislative Assistance	–		–	–	–
Planning/Development	–		–	–	–
Union Lists of Serials	–		–	–	–
Other (please specify)	–		–	–	–
Total Support	$248,434	$77,433	$40,000	–	$365,867

    B. Non-Financial Support Role of the State Library:

       The agency encourages libraries to consider how library
       services might be improved by interlibrary cooperation.

10. ILC COMMUNICATION DEVICES/SERVICE NETWORKS

Device/Service	State Support	Equipment (#)	Participants
WATS (outgoing-statewide)	$16,400	1	49
Teletype		4	4

11. MACHINE-READABLE DATA BASE REFERENCE SEARCHING SERVICES

   There are none.

12. INTERLIBRARY SERVICES TO SPECIAL GROUPS

   A. State library financially-supported cooperative arrangements and/or use of special services to special user groups (fiscal 1976 financial support):

SERVICES	STATE	FEDERAL	TOTAL
Service to blind and physically handicapped	$51,120	$35,096	$86,216
Service to institution-alized patrons	42,099	38,333	80,432
Service to the dis-advantaged		20,150	20,150

   B. Non-Financial Support Role of the State Library:

   Service to persons 65 and over - consultant service only.

13. PARTICIPATION IN MULTI-STATE LIBRARY NETWORKS

   A. Network: Northeast Regional Library, Corinth, MS
                              and
                          Shiloh Regional Library, Jackson, MS
      Financial Support: none
      Participation: Party to the agreement as required by law.
      Services used: State agency does not participate in services.

   B. Multi-state networks headquartered in state in which state agency has no involvement:

      There are none.

14. LEGAL BASES FOR MULTI-TYPE LIBRARY COOPERATION

   There is no enabling legislation.

15. LEGAL BARRIERS AGAINST PARTICIPATION IN MULTI-TYPE LIBRARY COOPERATION

   There are no legal barriers.

1. REPORTING AGENCY

    A. Missouri State Library
       308 East High Street
       Jefferson City, Missouri 65101
       (314) 751-4214

    B. Chief Officer: Charles O'Halloran, State Librarian

    C. Fiscal Year: 1977

2. OVERVIEW

At the present time four regional library networks exist in Missouri and three others are in the planning stage. When formed, these networks will cover the entire State. The networks are being formed under contract and each of the publicly supported libraries have statutory authorization for contractual activities. The Missouri Library Association recently adopted a networking statement which projects the organization of the State into networks, the kinds of activities that will be undertaken by present networks and possible sources for funding of the networks. At the moment the networks are funded either by federal funds through the State Library or by membership fees paid by participating libraries.

3. NUMBER OF LIBRARIES IN THE STATE

Academic:	84
Public:	155
School:	1,500
Public:	1,500
Private:	n.a.
Special:	87
Profit:	n.a.
Non-profit:	n.a.
Total	1,826 est.

4. STATE AGENCY INTERLIBRARY COOPERATION UNIT

    A. Specific ILC Unit:

       There is none.

    B. Other State Agency Offices for ILC Activities:

       Unit Name: Children's and Young Adults Services Div.
       Person in Charge: Patricia Behler, Coordinator

       Unit Name: Development of Special Library Services
       Person in Charge: Richard Miller, Coordinator

       Unit Name: Government Documents Division
       Person in Charge: Meryl Atterberry, Coordinator

(continued)

4. STATE AGENCY INTERLIBRARY COOPERATION UNIT (continued)

       Unit Name: Library Resources Division
       Person in Charge: Andrea Hawkins, Coordinator

       Unit Name: Publications Division
       Person in Charge: Madeline Matson, Coordinator

       Unit Name: Reference and Loan Services Division
       Person in Charge: Frank Pascoe, Coordinator

5. OTHER STATE-LEVEL GOVERNMENTAL ILC UNITS

       There are none.

6. OTHER STATE-LEVEL NON-GOVERNMENTAL ILC UNITS

       Name: Missouri Library Association
       Address: 403 South Sixth Street
                      Columbia, Missouri 65201
       Telephone: (314) 449-4627
       Administrator: Marilyn Lake, Executive Secretary

7. SINGLE-TYPE LIBRARY COOPERATIVES

       A. Receiving Continuing Financial Support from the State Library:

       There are none.

       B. Receiving No Continuing Financial Support from the State Library:

***   Name: Grand River Library Conference
       Address: c/o Grundy County-Jewett Norris Library
                      1331 Main Street
                      Trenton, Missouri 64683
       Telephone: (816) 359-3577
       Administrator: Catheryn Higdon, President
       Type of Libraries Served: p
       Sponsoring Body: n.a.
       Source(s) of Support: n.a.

       Name: Municipal Library Cooperative
       Address: 140 East Jefferson
                      Kirkwood, Missouri 63122
       Telephone: (314) 966-5568
       Administrator: n.a.
       Type of Libraries Served: p
       Sponsoring Body: n.a.
       Source(s) of Support: n.a.

                                    (continued)

7. SINGLE-TYPE LIBRARY COOPERATIVES (continued)

***
Name: Dogwood Library System
Address: c/o Texas County Library
                      Houston, Missouri 65483
Telephone: (417) 256-5382
Administrator: n.a.
Type of Libraries Served: p
Sponsoring Body: n.a.
Source(s) of Support: n.a.

***
Name: Higher Education Coordinating Council
                      (HECC)
Address: 4378 Lindell Blvd.
                      St. Louis, Missouri 63108
Telephone: (314) 534-2700
Administrator: Francis Gamelin, President
Type of Libraries Served: a
Sponsoring Body: n.a.
Source(s) of Support: n.a.

C. Other (Receiving occasional support from the State Library, etc.)

There are none.

8. MULTI-TYPE LIBRARY COOPERATIVES

A. Receiving Continuing Financial Support from the State Library:

There are none.

B. Receiving No Continuing Financial Support from the State Library:

***
Name: Mid-Missouri Library Network
Address: c/o Daniel Boone Regional Library
                      100 West Broadway
                      Columbia, Missouri 65201
Telephone: (314) 443-3161
Administrator: Kay Kelly
Types of Libraries Served: a, p
Sponsoring Body: n.a.
Source(s) of Support: n.a.

***
Name: Northeast Missouri Library Network
Address: c/o Northeast Missouri Library Service
                      207 West Chestnut
                      Kahoka, Missouri 63445
Telephone: (816) 727-2327
Administrator: Shannon Roy
Types of Libraries Served: a, p
Sponsoring Body: n.a.
Source(s) of Support: n.a.   (continued)

8. MULTI-TYPE LIBRARY COOPERATIVES (continued)

***

Name:	Northwest Missouri Library Network
Address:	c/o Rolling Hills Consolidated Library
	501-A North Belt Highway
	St. Joseph, Missouri 64506
Telephone:	(816) 232-5479
Administrator:	James Minges, Coordinator
Types of Libraries Served:	p, a
Sponsoring Body:	n.a.
Source(s) of Support:	Federal Funds and/or Membership Fees

***

Name:	Southwest Missouri Library Network
Address:	c/o Springfield-Greene County Library
	M.P.O. Box 737
	397 East Central
	Springfield, Missouri 65801
Telephone:	(417) 869-4621
Administrator:	Sara Parker, Coordinator
Types of Libraries Served:	p, a
Sponsoring Body:	n.a.
Source(s) of Support:	Federal Funds and/or Membership Fees

Name:	Kansas City Regional Council for Higher Education (KRCHE)
Address:	4901 Main Street, Suite 320
	Kansas City, Missouri 64112
Telephone:	(816) 361-4143
Administrator:	Dr. Lloyd J. Averill
Types of Libraries:	p, a
Sponsoring Body:	n.a.
Source(s) of Support:	n.a.

C. OTHER: (Receiving Occasional Support from State Library, etc.)

There are none.

9. INTERLIBRARY COOPERATION FUNCTIONS

A. ILC Functions Receiving Financial Support from State Library:

	State Support	Federal Support Title I	Title III	Other Support	Total Support
Interlibrary Loan	$ --	$ --	$ --	$ --	$ --
Continuing Education	--	16,565	--	--	16,565
Cooperative Acquisitions					
Cooperative Cataloging					
Cooperative Delivery	--	--	--	--	--
Cooperative Processing	--	53,700	--	--	53,700
Cooperative Reference	--	264,720	--	--	264,720

(continued)

9. INTERLIBRARY COOPERATION FUNCTIONS (continued)

	State Support	Federal Support Title I	Federal Support Title III	Other Support	Total Support
Cooperative Storage	--	--	--	--	--
Legislative Assistance	--	15,250	--	--	15,250
Planning Development	--	49,207	39,358	--	88,565
Union Lists of Serials	--	--	--	--	
Total	0	$399,442	$39,358	0	$438,800

10. ILC COMMUNICATION DEVICES/SERVICE NETWORKS

Device/Service	Support ($)	Equipment (#)	Participants
OCLC	$20,000	2 Terminals	Members of the Library Services Center

11. MACHINE-READABLE DATA BASE REFERENCE SEARCHING SERVICES

Off-Line data bases available to the Missouri State Library:

ERIC -- Through the State Department of Education

LEXIS -- Through the Missouri Supreme Court Library. LEXIS includes the US Statutes, Cases and Supreme Court Decisions plus the Statutes of six States, including Missouri. It is available on-line at the Supreme Court Library.

REGIONAL MEDICAL PROGRAM -- Through the University of Missouri-Columbia, Medical School Library. We can request Medline searches for patrons.

12. INTERLIBRARY SERVICES TO SPECIAL GROUPS

A. Services to Special User Groups:

Wolfner Library for the Blind and Physically Handicapped serves as the regional library for the blind and physically handicapped residents of Missouri. Through the mails, telephone, and local libraries, eligible users from throughout the State have access to the resources of this program.

13. PARTICIPATION IN MULTI-STATE LIBRARY NETWORKS

There are none.

14. LEGAL BASES FOR MULTI-TYPE LIBRARY COOPERATION

"70.210. DEFINITIONS.--As used in sections 70.210 to
70.320, the following terms mean:

"(1) 'Governing body', the board, body or persons in
which the powers of a municipality or political subdivision are vested;

"(2) 'Political subdivision', counties, townships, cities,
towns, villages, school, county library, city library,
city-county library, road, drainage, sewer, levee and fire
districts, soil and water conservation districts, water-
shed subdistricts, and any board of control of an art
museum.

"70.220. POLITICAL SUBDIVISIONS MAY COOPERATE WITH EACH
OTHER, WITH OTHER STATES, THE UNITED STATES OR PRIVATE
PERSONS.--Any municipality or political subdivision of
this state, as herein defined, may contract and cooperate
with any other municipality or political subdivision, or
with an elective or appointive official thereof, or with
a duly authorized agency of the United States, or of this
state, or with other states or their municipalities or
political subdivisions, or with any private person, firm,
association or corporation, for the planning, development,
construction, acquisition or operation of any public
improvement or facility, or for a common service; provided, that the subject and purposes of any such contract
or cooperative action made and entered into by such
municipality or political subdivision shall be within the
scope of the powers of such municipality or political subdivision. If such contract or cooperative action shall be
entered into between a municipality or political subdivision and an elective or appointive official of another
municipality or political subdivision, said contract or
cooperative action must be approved by the governing body
of the unit of government in which such elective or
appointive official resides."

15. LEGAL BARRIERS AGAINST PARTICIPATION IN MULTI-TYPE LIBRARY COOPERATION

There are no legal barriers.

***From time to time proposals for Library Services and Construction
Act funds for special programs have been received and granted.

1. REPORTING AGENCY

   A. Montana State Library
       930 East Lyndale
       Helena, MT 59601
       (406) 449-3004

   B. Chief Officer: Alma S. Jacobs, State Librarian

   C. Fiscal Year: 1978

2. OVERVIEW

   Six library systems - called federations in Montana - involve
   libraries in Montana's 56 counties. 79.7% of the population is
   served by libraries participating in interlibrary cooperation.
   72 of the 120 public libraries in Montana participate in the federations.

   Federations of libraries may be formed under Revised Codes of
   Montana 44-212, 1975 supp.

   Montana may enter into interstate library compacts under RCM
   44-601, 1975 supp.

3. NUMBER OF LIBRARIES IN THE STATE

   Academic   :   12
   Public   :   120
   School   :   388
      Public   :   360
      Private :   28
   Special   :   33
      Profit   :   n.a.
      Nonprofit: 33

   TOTAL   553 est.

4. STATE AGENCY INTERLIBRARY COOPERATION UNIT

   A. Unit Name   : Library Networks Program
       Person in Charge: Beth Givens, Coordinator of Library
                          Services

5. OTHER STATE-LEVEL GOVERNMENTAL ILC UNITS

   There are none.

6. OTHER STATE-LEVEL NON-GOVERNMENTAL ILC UNITS

   There are none.

7.   SINGLE-TYPE LIBRARY COOPERATIVES

     A.   Receiving Continuing Financial Support from the State Library:

          Name: Broad Valleys Federation of Libraries
          Address: Bozeman Public Library
                                35 No. Bozeman
                                Bozeman, MT 59715
          Telephone: (406) 586-2148
          Administrator: Margaret Hileman
          Type of Library Served: p
          Federal Support: $ 30,800
          State Support: 0
          Local Support $ 68,791 (est.)
          Total Support: $ 99,591 (est.)

          Name: Golden Plains Federation of Libraries
          Address: Glasgow City-County Library
                                  408 3rd Ave. So.
                                Glasgow, MT 59230
          Telephone: (406) 228-2731
          Administrator: Mary Moore
          Type of Library Served: p
          Federal Support: $ 20,000
          State Support: 0
          Local Support: $108,450
          Total Support: $128,450

          Name: Pathfinder Federation of Libraries
          Address: Great Falls Public Library
                                    2nd Ave. No. & 3rd St.
                                Great Falls, MT 59401
          Telephone: (406) 453-0349
          Administrator: Richard Gercken
          Type of Library Served: p
          Federal Support: $ 30,800
          State Support: 0
          Local Support: 513,266
          Total Support: 544,066

          Name: Sagebrush Federation of Libraries
          Address: Miles City Public Library
                                  One So. 10th St.
                                Miles City, MT 59301
          Administrator: Muriel Cooksey
          Type of Library Served: p
          Federal Support: $ 30,800
          State Support: 0
          Local Support: 95,775
          Total Support: 126,575   (continued)

7.   SINGLE-TYPE LIBRARY COOPERATIVES (continued)

          Name: South Central Federation of Libraries
          Address: Parmly Billings Library
                             510 No. Broadway
                             Billings, MT 59101
          Telephone: (406) 248-7391
          Administrator: Robert Cookingham
          Type of Library Served: p
          Federal Support: $ 30,800
          State Support: 0
          Local Support: $633,506
          Total Support: $664,306

          Name: Tamarack Federation of Libraries
          Address: City-County Library of Missoula
                             101 Adams
                             Missoula, MT 59801
          Telephone: (406) 728-5900
          Administrator: William H. Snyder
          Type of Library Served: p
          Federal Support: $ 30,800
          State Support: 0
          Local Support: 237,728
          Total Support: 268,528

     B.   RECEIVING NO CONTINUING FINANCIAL SUPPORT FROM THE STATE
          LIBRARY:

          There are none.

     C.   OTHER:

          There are none.

8.   MULTI-TYPE LIBRARY COOPERATIVES

     A.   RECEIVING CONTINUING FINANCIAL SUPPORT FROM THE STATE
          LIBRARY:

          There are none.

     B.   RECEIVING NO CONTINUING FINANCIAL SUPPORT FROM THE STATE
          LIBRARY:

          Name: Consortium of Academic and Special Li-
                               braries in Montana
          Address: University of Montana Library
                             Missoula, MT 59801
          Telephone: (406) 243-6800
          Administrator: Erling Oelz
          Types of Libraries Served: a, sp
                                                    (continued)

8. MULTI-TYPE LIBRARY COOPERATIVES (Continued)

> Sponsoring Body: Academic and Special Libraries Division
> of Montana Library Association
> Source(s) of Support: There is none.

9. INTERLIBRARY COOPERATION FUNCTIONS

> A. RECEIVING CONTINUING FINANCIAL SUPPORT FROM THE STATE
>   LIBRARY:

	State Support	Federal Support Title I	Federal Support Title III	Other Support	Total Support
Interlibrary Loan	$ 20,000	$ 8,500	$ 44,179	0	$ 72,679
Continuing Education	0	0	0	0	0
Cooperative Acquisitions	0	0	0	0	0
Cooperative Cataloging	0	0	0	0	0
Cooperative Delivery	0	0	0	0	0
Cooperative Processing	0	0	0	0	0
Cooperative Reference	0	0	0	0	0
Cooperative Storage	0	0	0	0	0
Legislative Assistance	0	0	0	0	0
Planning/Development	0	0	0	0	0
Union Lists of Serials	0	6,500	0	0	6,500
Other	0	0	0	0	0
Total Support	$ 20,000	$ 15,000	$ 44,179	0	$ 79,179

> B. NON-FINANCIAL SUPPORT ROLE OF THE STATE LIBRARY:

> There is no non-financial support role.

11. ILC COMMUNICATION DEVICES/SERVICE NETWORKS

> A. RECEIVING CONTINUING SUPPORT FROM THE STATE LIBRARY:

Device/Service	Support ($)	Equipment	Participants
Montana Information Network & Exchange	$ 13,000	Teletype Communications	8
Interlibrary Loan and Reference Network	10,000	Telephone Communications – WATS lines	8

> B. NON-FINANCIAL SUPPORT ROLE OF THE STATE LIBRARY:

> There is no non-financial support role for these services.

11. MACHINE-READABLE DATA BASE REFERENCE SEARCHING SERVICES

    There are none.

12. INTERLIBRARY SERVICES TO SPECIAL GROUPS

    A. RECEIVING CONTINUINED FINANCIAL SUPPORT FROM STATE LIBRARY:

	State	Federal	Total
Blind and Physically Handicapped	$ 72,475	$ 34,002	$ 106,477
Institutions	59,031	30,732	89,763
Special Language groups		12,000	12,000

    65 and over - partially included in No. 1

    Disadvantaged - partially included in special language groups

13. PARTICIPATION IN MULTI-STATE LIBRARY NETWORKS

    A. Extent of participation in multi-state networks:

    Network: Pacific Northwest Bibliographic Center
    Financial Support: $33,934
    Participation: a, p, sp
    Services Used: Interlibrary loan

    B. There are none.

14. LEGAL BASES FOR MULTI-TYPE LIBRARY COOPERATION

    Montana law defines library federations as a combination of
    libraries. It also defines a library network as an agree-
    ment between individual libraries or library systems, which
    may be inter-city, intra-state, or inter-state, for the
    exchange of information or to provide specific library ser-
    vices not provided in existing library federations.

15. LEGAL BARRIERS AGAINST PARTICIPATION IN MULTI-TYPE LIBRARY CO-
    OPERATION

    There are no legal barriers.

1. REPORTING AGENCY

    a. Nebraska Library Commission
       1420 P Street
       Lincoln, Nebraska 68508
       (402) 471-2045

    b. Chief Officer: John Kopischke, Director

    c. Fiscal Year: 1978

2. OVERVIEW

    Fifteen regional systems in Nebraska involve all libraries in inter-
    library cooperation. In addition, resource libraries have been
    designated to provide access to collections and/or services.
    The Regional systems are not formed under any specific statutory
    authority. Instead, the systems operate under the general enabling
    legislation cited in #14.

3. NUMBER OF LIBRARIES IN STATE

    Academic: 34
    Public: 270
    School: 718
      Public: 661
      Private: 57
    Special: 105 est.
      Profit: not available
      Nonprofit: not available

    Total: 1127 est.

4. STATE AGENCY INTERLIBRARY COOPERATION UNIT

    A. Specific ILC Unit: Reference and Information Services
       Person in Charge: Susan Kling

    B. Other ILC Units: There are none.

5. OTHER STATE-LEVEL GOVERNMENTAL ILC UNITS

    There are none.

6. OTHER STATE LEVEL NON-GOVERNMENTAL ILC UNITS

    Name: Nebraska Library Association
    Address: 1420 P Street, Lincoln, Nebraska 68503
    Telephone: (402) 471-2045
    Administrator: Marge Curtiss, President
    Activities: Promotional of library activities in Nebraska, including
                ILC

(continued)

6. OTHER STATE-LEVEL NON-GOVERNMENTAL ILC UNITS (continued)

Name: Nebraska Educational Media Association
Address: not reported
Activities: Promotional activities of school library activities in
          Nebraska

7. SINGLE-TYPE LIBRARY COOPERATIVES

A. Receiving Continuing Financial Support from the State Library:
   There are none.

B. Receiving No Continuing Financial Support from the State Library:
   Name: Educational Service Units
   Address: not reported
   Telephone: not reported
   Administrator: 19 separate units and boards
   Type of Library Served: Sch
   Sponsoring Body: State Department of Education
   Source (s) of Support: State

C. Other:
   There are none.

8. MULTI-TYPE LIBRARY COOPERATIVES

A. Receiving Continuing Financial Support from the State Library:
   Name: Central Library Network
   Address: Hastings Public Library, Hastings, Nebraska 68901
   Telephone: (402) 463-9855
   Administrator: Darlene Lyons
   Types of Libraries Served: a, p, sch, sp
   Federal Support: $22,782
   State Support: 0
   Local Support: 0
   Other Support: 0
   Total Support: $22,782

   Name: Mari Sandoz Library Network
   Address: North Platte Public Library, North Platte, Nebraska 69101
   Telephone: (308) 532-6560
   Administrator: Charlotte Ladd
   Type of Libraries Served: a, p, sch, sp
   Federal Support: $24,560
   State Support: 0
   Local Support: 0
   Other Support: 0
   Total Support: $24,560

   Name: Metropolitan Library Network
   Address: Bellevue Public Library, Bellevue, Nebraska 68005
   Telephone: (402) 291-1121
   Administrator: Violet Blumm   (continued)

212

8. MULTI-TYPE LIBRARY COOPERATIVES (continued)
    Types of Libraries Served: a, p, sch, sp
    Federal Support: $47,400
    State Support: 0
    Local Support: 0
    Other Support: 0
    Total Support: $47,400

    Name: Northern Library Network
    Address: Columbus Public Library, Columbus, Nebraska   68601
    Telephone: (402) 564-7116
    Administrator: Catherine Nore
    Type of Libraries Served: a, p, sch, sp
    Federal Support: $34,898
    State Support: 0
    Local Support: 0
    Other Support: 0
    Total Support: $34,898

    Name: Panhandle Library Network
    Address: Scottsbluff Public Library, Scottsbluff, Nebraska 69361
    Telephone: (308) 632-4424
    Administrator: Jean Howard
    Type of Libraries Served: a, p, sch, sp
    Federal Support: $30,550
    State Support: 0
    Local Support: 0
    Other Support: 0
    Total Support: $30,550

    Name: Southeastern Library Network
    Address: Beatrice Free Library, Beatrice, Nebraska 68310
    Telephone: (402) 223-3584
    Administrator: Dan DeLong
    Type of Libraries Served: a, p, sch, sp
    Federal Support: $28,338
    State Support: 0
    Local Support: 0
    Other Support: 0
    Total Support: $28,338

    B. Receiving No Continuing Financial Support from the State Library:
       There are none.

    C. Other:
       There are none.

9. INTERLIBRARY COOPERATION FUNCTIONS

	State Support	Federal Support Title I	Title III	Other Support	Total Support
A.					
Interlibrary Loan	107,500est	67,500est			175,000 est
Continuing Education					

(continued)

213

9. INTERLIBRARY COOPERATION FUNCTIONS (continued)

	State Support	Federal Support Title I	Title III	Other Support	Total Support
Cooperative Acquisitions					
Cooperative Cataloging					
Cooperative Delivery					
Cooperative Processing					
Cooperative Reference					
Cooperative Storage					
Legislative Assistance					
Planning/Development					
Union List of Serials					
Other					
Nebraska Union Catalog	24,740			40,906	65,646
Total Support	$132,240 est	67,500 est		40,906	240,646est

B. NON-FINANCIAL SUPPORT ROLE OF THE STATE LIBRARY:
There is no non-financial support role.

11. ILC COMMUNICATION DEVICES/SERVICE NETWORKS
A.

Device/Service	Support ($)	Equipment (#)	Participants
Teletype/Telephone	140,000est	20 TWX	p, a, sp
OCLC	9,000est	15	a, p, sp

B. NON-FINANCIAL SUPPORT ROLE OF THE STATE LIBRARY:
The agency assists in planning and development of the OCLC Network through the NEBASE organization.

11. MACHINE-READABLE DATA BASE REFERENCE SEARCHING SERVICES
There are none.

12. INTERLIBRARY SERVICES TO SPECIAL GROUPS

A. Services to the Blind & Physically Handicapped through the Regional and Subregional Libraries for the Blind & Physically Handicapped.
Services to the institutions through the Institutional Services Program.
Services to persons over 65, disadvantaged, special readers through special projects.

B. NON-FINANCIAL SUPPORT ROLE OF THE STATE LIBRARY:
There are none.

13. PARTICIPATION IN MULTI-STATE LIBRARY NETWORKS:

A. Network: Bibliographical Center for Research
Financial Support: not reported
Participation: Membership initiated July, 1977

(continued)

13. PARTICIPATION IN MULTI-STATE NETWORKS (continued)

    Services Used: not reported

    Network: OCLC
    Financial Support: $9,000 est
    Participation: not reported
    Services Used: cataloging and locations

  B. There are none.

14. LEGAL BASES FOR MULTI-TYPE LIBRARY COOPERATION

State legislation enabling multi-type library cooperative development: Revised Statutes of Nebraska, 51-403 "no. 5 - to be responsible
for the statewide promotion, development and coordination of library
programs and services in accord with nationally acceptable library
standards."

State legislation enabling interstate library compact:
Revised Statutes of Nebraska, 23-2204 "no. 1 - any power or powers,
privileges or authority exercised or capable of exercise by a public
agency of the state may be exercised jointly with any other public
agency of this state having such power or powers, privilege or
authority, and jointly with any public agency of any other state or
of the United States to the extent that laws of such other state or
the United States permit such joint exercise or enjoyment. Any agency
of the state government when acting jointly with any public agency
may exercise and enjoy all of the powers, privileges, and authority
conferred by Sections 23-2201 and 23-2207 upon a public agency."

State-provided statutory funding for multi type library cooperative
development: Revised Statutes of Nebraska, 23-2204 "no. 2 - any two
or more public agencies may enter into agreements with one another
for joint or cooperative action..." "no. 3 - any such agreement shall
specify the following: c) its purpose or purposes; d) the manner of
financing the joint or cooperative undertaking and of establishing
and maintaining a budget therefore."

15. LEGAL BARRIERS AGAINST PARTICIPATION IN MULTI-TYPE LIBRARY
COOPERATION
There are no legal barriers.

1. REPORTING AGENCY

    A.   Nevada State Library
           Capitol Complex
           Carson City, NV 89710
           (702) 885-5130

    B.   Chief Officer: Joseph J. Anderson, State Librarian

    C.   Fiscal Year: 1978

2. OVERVIEW

Interlibrary Cooperation in Nevada includes participation by all of public, academic, school and special libraries working in a broad organizational pattern of three regions which encompass the entire state. All 17 counties are served in this manner.

The state grant administration process has resulted in the creation of tools such as the union catalog of holdings at the state processing center, title locator indexes on microfiche, state documents catalog on microfiche, and the intermountain union list of serials. These tools have been created by the joint efforts of academic, public, and NSL librarians.

Most libraries in Nevada honor each other's library cards so that citizens may use libraries wherever they are in the State. The three regional resource centers designate interlibrary loan personnel to work on policy and procedure committees to insure smooth operation of interlibrary loan and other network-related activity. The operation of these committees is supported through the use of LSCA funds.

Chapter 378 (Nevada State Library) and Chapter 379 (Public Libraries) provide the legal basis for interlibrary loan activities.

3. NUMBER OF LIBRARIES IN THE STATE

Academic:	6
Public:	21
School:	215
Public:	209
Private:	6
Special:	31
Profit:	2
Non-profit:	29
TOTAL:	273

4. STATE AGENCY INTERLIBRARY COOPERATION UNIT

    A. Unit Name: Cooperative Services Division
        Person in Charge: Mrs. Rachael Clemison, Director

5. OTHER STATE-LEVEL GOVERNMENTAL ILC UNITS

    There are none.

6. OTHER STATE-LEVEL NON-GOVERNMENTAL ILC UNITS

    There are none.

7. SINGLE-TYPE LIBRARY COOPERATIVES

    There are none.

8. MULTI-TYPE LIBRARY COOPERATIVES

    A. Receiving Continuing Financial Support from the State Library:

        There are none.

    B. Receiving No Continuing Financial Support from the State
        Library:

        There are none.

    C. Other (Receiving Occasional Support from the State Library,
        etc.)

        There are none.

9. INTERLIBRARY COOPERATION FUNCTIONS

    A. ILC functions available throughout the state which are
        receiving continuing financial support from the State
        Library:

	State Support	Federal Support Title I	Federal Support Title III	Other Support	Total Support
Interlibrary Loan	-0-	1,700	800	-0-	2,500
Continuing Education	3,700	4,500	-0-	-0-	8,200
Cooperative Acquisitions)					
Cooperative Cataloging)					
Cooperative Processing)146,128		-0-	-0-	32,500	178,628
Cooperative Reference)					
Cooperative Delivery	-0-	169,779	-0-	-0-	169,779
Cooperative Storage	-0-	-0-	-0-	-0-	-0-
Legislative Assistance	-0-	-0-	-0-	-0-	-0-
Planning/Development	-0-	4,500	-0-	-0-	$ 4,500

(continued)

9.   INTERLIBRARY COOPERATION FUNCTIONS (continued)

	State Support	Federal Support Title I	Title III	Other Support	Total Support
Union Lists of Serials	-0-	-0-	11,000(est)	-0-	11,000
Other (please specify)	-0-	-0-	-0-	-0-	-0-
Total Support	$149,828	$180,479	$11,800	$32,500	$374,607

B. Non-Financial Support Role of the State Library:

State Library plays a planning, funding and consulting role in interlibrary loan, cooperative reference, and the media cooperative.

10.   ILC COMMUNICATION DEVICES/SERVICE NETWORKS

A. | Device/Service | Support ($) | Equipment (#) | Participants |
|---|---|---|---|
| IN-WATS | On Demand | - | Statewide |
| Telecopier | 1,440 | 2 | 2 |
| TWX | 8,380 | 4 | 4 |

B. Non-Financial Support Role of the State Library:

There is no non-financial support role for these services.

11.   MACHINE-READABLE DATA BASE REFERENCE SEARCHING SERVICES

Data Base/Vendor		Support ($)	Terminals (#)	Participants
ORBIT	SDC	1,500	1	statewide

12.   INTERLIBRARY SERVICES TO SPECIAL GROUPS
A. Financial Support Role of the State Library:
Services to the blind & physically handicapped: The Special Services Division of the State Library in cooperation with the Clark County Library District and the Utah State Library provides these services.

B. Non-Financial Support Role of the State Library:

The State Library provides personnel, facilities and equipment to Services to the Blind and Physically Handicapped.

13.   PARTICIPATION IN MULTI-STATE LIBRARY NETWORKS

A.   There are none.

B.   There are none.

14.   LEGAL BASES FOR MULTI-TYPE LIBRARY COOPERATION
State legislation enabling multi-type library   (continued)

14.   LEGAL BASES FOR MULTI-TYPE LIBRARY COOPERATION (continued)

cooperative development: NRS 378.080, paragraphs 7, 12, 14,
15, 16, 18 and NRS 378.085 (added 1973)

State legislation enabling interstate library compact: see
above.

State-provided statutory funding for multi-type library
cooperative development: Library development fund category
established in state agency budget: no formula bases; general
fund allocated based on argument for state grants of local
libraries which may include multi-type library activity.

15.   LEGAL BARRIERS AGAINST PARTICIPATION IN MULTI-TYPE LIBRARY
COOPERATION

There are no legal barriers.

1. REPORTING AGENCY

    A. New Hampshire State Library
       20 Park Street
       Concord, NH 03301
       (603) 271-2394

    B. Chief Officer: Mrs. Avis M. Duckworth, State Librarian

    C. Fiscal Year: 1978

2. OVERVIEW

    A single state system, the New Hampshire Statewide Library Development Program, involves the participating libraries in 4 geographic districts covering the entire State. 81.8 percent of the population is served by the libraries in this program. There are 185 member libraries participating of the 232 total public libraries.

    The New Hampshire Revised Statutes Annotated provides in Chapter 201-C for the statewide system of cooperative library service. RSA 201-C:13 provides for multi-type library cooperative development. RSA 201-B provides for interstate library compacts.

3. NUMBER OF LIBRARIES IN THE STATE

Academic:	26
Public:	232
School:	353
Public	312
Private	41
Special:	28
Profit	10
Non-Profit:	18
TOTAL	639 est.

4. STATE AGENCY INTERLIBRARY COOPERATION UNIT

    A. Unit Name: Division of Extension and Library Development
       Person in Charge: Mrs. Joan Blanchard, Director

    B. Unit Name: Division of Reference and Loan
       Person in Charge: Miss Stella Scheckter, Director

5. OTHER STATE-LEVEL GOVERNMENTAL ILC UNITS

    A. Agency: School Library and Educational Media Services
       Address: Division of Instruction
             Department of Education
             64 North Main Street
             Concord, NH 03301
       Cooperative activity: school and public library cooperation

6. OTHER STATE-LEVEL NON-GOVERNMENTAL ILC UNITS

    A. Organization: New Hampshire Library Council
       Address: c/o New Hampshire State Library
                20 Park Street
                Concord, NH 03301
                (603) 625-6485

       Administrator: Mrs. Helen Ogden, Chairman
       Cooperative activity: coordination of efforts and statewide programs of all library-interest organizations in the State.

7. SINGLE-TYPE LIBRARY COOPERATIVES

    A. Receiving Continuing Financial Support from the State Library:
       Name: New Hampshire Statewide Library Development Program
       Address: New Hampshire State Library, 20 Park Street, Concord,
             NH 03301
       Telephone: (603)271-2425
       Administrator: Mrs. Joan Blanchard, Director
       Type of Library Served: P
       Federal Support: $309,881
       State Support: $478,722
       Local Support: 0
       Other Support: 0
       Total Support: $788,603

    B. Receiving No Continuing Financial Support from the State Library:
       Name: New Hampshire College and University Council, Library
            Policy Committee
       Address: 2321 Elm Street, Manchester, NH 03104
       Telephone: (603)669-3432
       Administrator: Mr. Doug Lyon
       Type of Library Served: A
       Sponsoring Body: New Hampshire College and University Council
       Sources of Support: Memberships and Grant Funds

8. MULTI-TYPE LIBRARY COOPERATIVES

   A. Receiving Continuing Financial Support from the State Library:
      Name: New Hampshire Statewide Teletype Network
      Address: New Hampshire State Library, 20 Park Street, Concord,
               NH 03301
      Telephone: (603)271-2394
      Administrator: Miss Stella Scheckter
      Types of Libraries Served: a, p, sch, sp
      Federal Support: $29,680
      State Support: 0
      Local Support: 0
      Other Support: 0
      Total Support: $29,680

   B. Receiving No Continuing Financial Support from the State Library:
      Name: New Hampshire Library Council
      Address: 20 Park Street, Concord, NH 03301
      Telephone: (603)625-6485
      Administrator: Mrs. Helen Ogden
      Types of Libraries Served: a, p, sch, sp, Trustees and Friends

      Sponsoring Body: Statewide Organizations
      Source(s) of Support: Membership

   C. Other (Receiving Occasional Support from the State Library, etc)
      Name: School-Public Library Cooperation Program
      Address: New Hampshire State Library, 20 Park Street, Concord,
               NH 03301
      Telephone: (603)271-2394
      Administrator: Mrs. Joan Blanchard
      Types of Libraries Served: p, sch
      Sponsoring Bodies: N.H. Department of Education and N.H.
                         State Library
      Source(s) of Support: Federal grants

9. INTERLIBRARY COOPERATION FUNCTIONS

   A. Receiving Continuing Financial Support from the State Library:

	State Support	Federal Support Title I	Federal Support Title III	Other Support	Total Support
Interlibrary Loan	$197,886	0	$21,400	0	$219,286
Continuing Education	2,000	0	0	0	2,000

(continued)

9. INTERLIBRARY COOPERATION FUNCTIONS (continued)

	State Support	Federal Support Title I	Title III	Other Support	Total Support
Cooperative Acquisitions	0	0	0	0	0
Cooperative Cataloging	142,554	34,345	0	0	176,899
Cooperative Delivery	58,012	95,485	0	0	153,497
Cooperative Processing	0	0	0	0	0
Cooperative Reference	0	0	0	0	0
Cooperative Storage	0	0	0	0	0
Legislative Assistance	82,434	0	0	0	82,434
Planning/Development	74,770	66,076	0	0	140,846
Union Lists of Serials	0	0	5,754	0	5,754
Total Support	$557,656	195,906	27,154	0	780,716

B. NON-FINANCIAL SUPPORT ROLE OF THE STATE LIBRARY. There is no non-financial support role.

11. ILC COMMUNICATION DEVICES / SERVICE NETWORKS

A.
Device/Service	Support ($)	Equipment (#)	Participants
TWX	$21,400	14	14

B. NON-FINANCIAL SUPPORT ROLE OF THE STATE LIBRARY. There is no non-financial support role for these services.

11. MACHINE-READABLE DATA BASE REFERENCE SEARCHING SERVICES
There are none.

12. INTERLIBRARY SERVICES TO SPECIAL GROUPS

A. SERVICES
Blind and Physically Handicapped
Institutional Libraries

B. NON-FINANCIAL SUPPORT ROLE OF THE STATE LIBRARY.
Consultant Services.

13. PARTICIPATION IN MULTI-STATE LIBRARY NETWORKS

A. Name: New England Library Board
Address: 231 Capitol Avenue, Hartford, CT 06115
Telephone: (203) 525-2681
Administrator: Ms. Mary McKenzie
Financial Support: $10,100 (federal funds)   (continued)

13. PARTICIPATION IN MULTI-STATE LIBRARY NETWORKS (continued)

    A.   Network: North Country Libraries Film Cooperative
           Financial Support: $30,304.
           Participation: Maine, New Hampshire, Vermont
           Services Used: Film Service
           Network: New England Library Board
           Financial Support: $10,100.
           Participation: Six New England States
           Services Used: New England Serials Service, New England
                      Document Conservation Center, all other
                      Services.

14. LEGAL BASES FOR MULTI-TYPE LIBRARY COOPERATION

    State legislation enabling multi-type library cooperative development:
        N.H. RSA 201-C:13, 1963 and 1973.

    State legislation enabling interstate library compact:
        N.H. RSA 201-B, 1963.

15. LEGAL BARRIERS AGAINST PARTICIPATION IN MULTI-TYPE LIBRARY
    COOPERATION

    There are no legal barriers.

1. REPORTING AGENCY

    A. Division of the State Library, Archives and History
        New Jersey Department of Education
        185 West State Street
        Trenton, NJ   08625

    B. Chief Officer: David C. Palmer, Acting State Librarian

    C. Fiscal Year: 1978

2. OVERVIEW

    New Jersey has a three-level, hierarchical network which
    channels requests for information and materials from the local
    library level up to four Research Libraries. There are 323
    local public libraries, 2,184 school libraries and 80 academic
    libraries in New Jersey.

    Twenty-five local libraries, designated as Area Libraries,
    supplement local collections and provide second-level services
    to 97% of the State's residents. Only one county is without
    Area Library supplementary services.

    The library network is authorized by State statute N.J.S.
    18A:74-1 et seq. which provides State Aid funding for all
    levels of the network.

    New Jersey statutes also authorize the establishment of federa-
    tions (N.J.S. 40:9A-1 et seq.) which permits public libraries
    to engage in cooperative activities. There are three legally
    established federations in New Jersey which include 24 public
    libraries.

3. NUMBER OF LIBRARIES IN THE STATE

    Academic: 80
    Public: 323
    School: 2,184
       Public: 1,897
       Private: 287
    Special:
       Profit:) information not
       Nonprofit:)   available

    TOTAL: 2,587 est.

4. STATE AGENCY INTERLIBRARY COOPERATION UNIT

    A. Specific Unit Name: Library Development Bureau
        Person in Charge: Henry J. Michniewski, Head

    B. Other ILC Unit Name: Law and General Reference Bureau
        Person in Charge: Susan B. Roumfort, Head

5. OTHER STATE-LEVEL GOVERNMENT ILC UNITS

    There are none.

6. OTHER STATE-LEVEL NON-GOVERNMENTAL ILC UNITS

    There are none.

7. SINGLE-TYPE LIBRARY COOPERATIVES

    A. Receiving Continuing Financial Support from the State
        Library:

    Name: New Jersey State Library
    Address: 185 West State Street
                                  Trenton, NJ 08625
    Telephone: 609-292-6210
    Administrator: Ms. Susan B. Roumfort
    Type of Library   Served: p
    Federal Support: 0
    State Support: $ 64,621
    Local Support: 0
    Other Support: 0
    Total Support: $ 64,621

    Name: Newark Public Library
    Address: 5 Washington Street
                                  Newark, NJ 07101
    Telephone: 201-733-7800
    Administrator: Bernard Schein
    Type of Library   Served: p
    Federal Support: $200,000
    State Support: 148,366
    Local Support: 0
    Other Support: 0
    Total Support: $348,366

    Name: Bloomfield Public Library
    Address: 90 Broad Street
                                  Bloomfield, NJ 07003
    Telephone: 201-429-9292
    Administrator: Howard Vogt, Director
    Type of Library Served: p

(continued)

7. SINGLE-TYPE LIBRARY COOPERATIVES (continued)

    A. Receiving Continuing Financial Support from the State
       Library:

Federal Support:	$ 9,823
State Support:	54,400
Local Support:	420,240
Other Support:	0
Total Support:	$484,463

Name:	Burlington County Library
Address:	Woodlane Road
	Mount Holly, NJ 08060
Telephone:	609-267-9660
Administrator:	Mrs. Catherine Wetterling, Director
Type of Library Served:	P
Federal Support:	$ 10,614
State Support:	62,521
Local Support:	1,090,000
Other Support:	0
Total Support:	$1,163,135

Name:	Camden County Library
Address:	Laurel Road
	Voorhees, NJ 08043
Telephone:	609-772-9660
Administrator:	Mrs. Nina Ladof, Director
Type of Library Served:	P
Federal Support:	$ 12,927
State Support:	103,077
Local Support:	520,000
Other Support:	0
Total Support:	$ 636,004

Name:	Cape May County Library
Address:	Mechanic Street
	Cape May Court House, NJ 08210
Telephone:	609-465-7837
Administrator:	Mrs. Doris L. Grady, Director
Type of Library Served:	P
Federal Support:	$ 5,135
State Support:	30,314
Local Support:	444,146
Other Support:	0
Total Support:	$479,595

(continued)

7. SINGLE-TYPE LIBRARY COOPERATIVES (continued)

    A. Receiving Continuing Financial Support from the State
       Library:

Name:	Cumberland County Library
	800 East Commerce Street
	Bridgeton, NJ 08302
Telephone:	609-455-0080
Administrator:	David West, Director
Type of Library Served:	p
Federal Support:	$ 3,342
State Support:	48,429
Local Support:	367,818
Other Support:	0
Total Support:	$419,589

Name:	East Brunswick Public Library
	2 Jean Walling Civic Center Drive
	East Brunswick, NJ 08816
Telephone:	201-254-1220
Administrator:	George J. Happ, Director
Type of Library Served:	p
Federal Support:	$ 3,342
State Support:	48,429
Local Support:	540,000
Other Support:	0
Total Support:	$591,771

Name:	East Orange Public Library
	21 South Arlington Avenue
	East Orange, NJ 07018
Telephone:	201-266-5600
Administrator:	Ms. Dorothy Jones, Director
Type of Library Served:	p
Federal Support:	$ 7,929
State Support:	61,986
Local Support:	675,000
Other Support:	0
Total Support:	$744,915

(continued)

7. SINGLE-TYPE LIBRARY COOPERATIVES (continued)

    A. Receiving Continuing Financial Support from the State
       Library:

Name:	Elizabeth Public Library
Address:	11 South Broad Street
	Elizabeth, NJ 07202
Telephone:	201-354-6060
Administrator:	Mrs. Hazel Elks, Director
Type of Library Served:	p
Federal Support:	$ 1,512
State Support:	50,606
Local Support:	892,500
Other Support:	0
Total Support:	$ 944,618

Name:	Hunterdon County Library
Address:	State Highway, Route #12
	Flemington, NJ 08822
Telephone:	201-782-4218
Administrator:	Mrs. Beatrice Smith, Director
Type of Library Served:	p
Federal Support:	$ 11,060
State Support:	31,627
Local Support:	341,000
Other Support:	0
Total Support:	$ 383,687

Name:	Jersey City Public Library
Address:	472 Jersey Avenue
	Jersey City, NJ 07302
Telephone:	201-547-4500
Administrator:	Ben Grimm, Director
Type of Library Served:	P
Federal Support:	$ 14,150
State Support:	94,542
Local Support:	1,510,286
Other Support:	0
Total Support:	$1,618,978

Name:	Johnson Public Library
Address:	275 Moore Street
	Hackensack, NJ 07601
Telephone:	201-343-4169
Administrator:	John D. Shine, Director
Type of Library Served:	p
Federal Support:	$ 15,000
State Support:	98,538
Local Support:	438,900
Other Support:	n.a.
Total Support:	$552,438

(continued)

7. SINGLE-TYPE LIBRARY COOPERATIVES (continued)

    A. Receiving Continuing Financial Support from the State
       Library:

Name:	Linden Public Library
Address:	31 East Henry Street
	Linden, NJ 07036
Telephone:	201-486-3888
Administrator:	David Lance, Director
Type of Library Served:	p
Federal Support:	$ 3,629
State Support:	38,046
Local Support:	587,800
Other Support:	0
Total Support:	629,575

Name:	Monmouth County Library
Address:	25 Broad Street
	Freehold, NJ 07728
Telephone:	201-431-7220 Ext. 281
Administrator:	John Livingstone, Jr., Director
Type of Library Served:	p
Federal Support:	$ 8,580
State Support:	81,770
Local Support:	1,000,096
Other Support:	0
Total Support:	$1,090,446

Name:	Morris County Library
Address:	30 East Hanover Avenue
	Hanover Twp.
	Whippany, NJ 07981
Telephone:	201-285-6101
Administrator:	Kenneth McPherson, Director
Type of Library Served:	p
Federal Support:	$ 13,073
State Support:	71,220
Local Support:	994,000
Other Support	0
Total Support:	1,078,293

Name:	Newark Public Library
Address:	5 Washington Street
	Newark, NJ 07101
Telephone:	201-733-7800
Administrator:	Bernard Schein, Director
Type of Library Served:	p
State Support:	$ 500
Local Support:	83,745
Other Support:	2,906,838
Total Support:	2,991,083

(continued)

7. SINGLE-TYPE LIBRARY COOPERATIVES (continued)

A. Receiving Continuing Financial Support from the State Library:

Name:	Ocean County Library
Address:	15 Hooper Avenue
	Toms River, NJ 08753
Telephone:	201-439-6200
Administrator:	Joseph Garcia, Director
Type of Library Served:	p
Federal Support:	$ 5,422
State Support:	49,560
Local Support:	1,079,000
Other Support:	0
Total Support:	$1,133,982

Name:	Paterson Public Library
Address:	250 Broadway
	Paterson, NJ 07501
Telephone:	201-742-3845
Administrator:	Leo E. Fichtelberg, Director
Type of Library Served:	p
Federal Support:	$ 7,100
State Support:	62,260
Local Support:	681,174
Other Support:	0
Total Support:	$750,534

Name:	Phillipsburg Public Library
Address:	200 Frost Avenue
	Phillipsburg, NJ 08865
Telephone:	201-454-3712
Administrator:	Miss Jayne Hess, Director
Type of Library Served:	p
Federal Support:	$ 1,372
State Support:	32,176
Local Support:	192,813
Other Support:	0
Total Support:	$226,361

Name:	Plainfield Public Library
Address:	Eighth Street and Park Avenue
	Plainfield, NJ 07060
Telephone:	201-757-1111
Administrator:	Mr. L. A. Moore, Director
Type of Library Served:	p
Federal Support:	$ 6,265
State Support:	64,880
Local Support:	363,366
Other Support:	0
Total Support:	$434,511

(continued)

7. SINGLE-TYPE LIBRARY COOPERATIVES (continued)

    A. Receiving Continuing Financial Support from the State
        Library:

Name:	Ridgewood Public Library
Address:	125 North Maple Avenue
	Ridgewood, NJ 07450
Telephone:	201-652-5200
Administrator:	Robert D. Ross, Director
Type of Library Served:	p
Federal Support:	$ 9 567
State Support:	60,306
Local Support:	323,737
Other Support:	0
Total Support:	$393,610

Name:	Somerset County Library
Address:	County Administration Building
	Somerville, NJ 08876
Telephone:	201-725-4700 Ext. 234
Administrator:	Mrs. June Adams , Director
Type of Library Served:	p
Federal Support:	$ 8,803
State Support:	41,222
Local Support:	770,000
Other Support:	0
Total Support:	$820,025

Name:	Sussex County Library
Address:	Box 76 - R.D. #3
	Newton, NJ 07860
Telephone:	201-948-3660 & 201-383-2321
Administrator:	Mrs. Clare Cole, Director
Type of Library Served:	p
Federal Support:	$ 5,710
State Support:	32,637
Local Support:	488,060
Other Support:	0
Total Support:	$526,407

Name:	Trenton Public Library
Address:	120 Academy Street
	Trenton, NJ 08608
Telephone:	609-392-7188
Administrator:	Miss Veronica Cary, Director
Type of Library Served:	p
Federal Support:	$ 3,547
State Support:	64,474
Local Support:	742,073
Other Support:	0
Total Support:	$810,094

(continued)

7. SINGLE-TYPE LIBRARY COOPERATIVES (continued)

A. Receiving Continuing Financial Support from the State
    Library:

Name: Wayne Public Library
Address: 475 Valley Road
                               Wayne, NJ   07470
Telephone: 201-694-4272
Administrator: John A. Burns, Director
Type of Library Served: p
Federal Support: $ 5,685
State Support: 42,527
Local Support: 489,615
Other Support: 0
Total Support: $537,827

Name: Woodbridge Public Library
Address: George Frederick Plaza
                               Woodbridge, NJ   07095
Telephone: 201-634-4450
Administrator: Edwin P. Beckerman, Director
Type of Library Served: p
Federal Support: $ 5,312
State Support: 55,363
Local Support: 1,274,000
Other Support: 0
Total Support: $1,334,675

B. Receiving No Continuing Financial Support from the State
    Library:

Name: Mid-Bergen Federation
Address: 274 Main Street
                               Hackensack, NJ 07601
Telephone: 201-342-2584
Administrator: Mrs. Lila Cohen
Type of Library Served: p
Sponsoring Body: not reported
Source(s) of Support: Local taxes

Name: Morris-Union Federation (MUF)
Address: Berkeley Heights Public Library
                               290 Plainfield Avenue
                               Berkeley Heights, NJ   07922
Telephone: 201-464-6438
Administrator: Ms. Caren Brown
Type of Library Served: p
Sponsoring Body: not reported
Source(s) of Support: Local taxes

(continued)

7. SINGLE-TYPE LIBRARY COOPERATIVES (continued)

B. Receiving No Continuing Support from the State Library:

Name:	North Bergen Federation
Address:	30 Garber Square
	Ridgewood, NJ 07450
Telephone:	(201) 445-0848
Administrator:	Mrs. Liz Chilton
Type of Library Served:	p
Sponsoring Body:	not reported
Source of Support:	Local taxes

8. MULTI-TYPE LIBRARY COOPERATIVES

A. Receiving Continuing Financial Support from the State Library:

Name:	Princeton University
Address:	Princeton, NJ 08540
Telephone:	(609) 452-3170
Administrator:	Dr. Richard Boss
Types of Libraries Served:	a, p
Federal Support:	0
State Support:	$64,621
Local Support:	0
Total Support:	$64,621

Name:	Research Information Service
Address:	Rutgers University Libraries
	New Brunswick, NJ 08901
Telephone:	(201) 247-3854
Administrator:	Joseph C. Scorza
Types of Libraries Served:	a, p
Federal Support:	0
State Support:	$ 64,621
Local Support:	122,100
Other Support:	0
Total Support:	$186,721

B. Receiving No Continuing Financial Support from the State Library:
There are none.

C. Receiving Occasional Financial Support from the State Library:

Name:	Media Reference and Referral Center
Address:	Burlington County Library
	Woodlane Road
	Mount Holly, NJ 08060
Telephone:	609-267-9660
Administrator:	Mrs. Catherine Wetterling, Director
Type of Libraries Served:	a, p, sch
Sponsoring Body:	Burlington County Library
Source of Support:	LSCA

(continued)

8. MULTI-TYPE LIBRARY COOPERATIVES (continued)

C. Receiving Occasional Financial Support from the State
Library:

Name:	Atlantic County Cooperative Library Services
Address:	Atlantic County Library Surrogate Building Mays Landing, NJ 08330
Telephone:	609-624-2776
Administrator:	Ms. Gladys Kraus, Director
Type of Libraries Served:	a, p, sch
Sponsoring Body:	Atlantic County Library Commission
Source of Support:	LSCA (Federal)

9. INTERLIBRARY COOPERATION FUNCTIONS

A. Receiving Continuing Financial Support from the State
Library:

We have no breakdown by function. State and Federal funds
supporting interlibrary cooperation are as follows:

State Aid	$ 1,729,737
LSCA, I	414,709
LSCA III	33,425
Total	$ 2,177,871

B. Non-Financial Support Role of the State Library:

The New Jersey State Library provides non-financial support
for interlibrary cooperation through the provision of advisory
and consultative services and through participation in activities of planning organizations.

10. ILC COMMUNICATION DEVICES/SERVICE NETWORKS

A.
Device/Service	Support ($)	Equipment (#)	Participants
Teletype	15,000	5	1a,3p, 1 sch
Telephone	4,000	2	3 a, 19 p

(continued)

10. ILC COMMUNICATION DEVICES/SERVICES NETWORKS (continued)

    B. NON-FINANCIAL SUPPORT ROLE OF THE STATE LIBRARY:

       The New Jersey State Library provides non-financial support for interlibrary cooperation through the provision of advisory and consultative services and through participation in activities of planning organizations.

11. MACHINE-READABLE DATA BASE REFERENCE SEARCHING SERVICES

Data Base/Vendor	Support ($)	Terminals (#)	Participants
SDC			
Lockheed/Dialog	16,500	1	

       Terminal is located at the New Jersey State Library and backs up the statewide library network.

12. INTERLIBRARY SERVICES TO SPECIAL GROUPS
    A. There are no cooperative arrangements for special groups.

    B. Non-Financial Support Role of the State Library:

       The New Jersey State Library provides services to the handicapped through a centralized facility which is part of the State Library's operations.

13. PARTICIPATION IN MULTI-STATE LIBRARY NETWORKS

    A. Network: PALINET
       Financial Support: $26,499
       Participation: Voting member and representation on planning board.
       Services Used: Monographic Planning Mode

    B. There are no multi-state networks headquartered in NJ.

14. LEGAL BASES FOR MULTI-TYPE LIBRARY COOPERATION

    N.J.S. 18A:74-1

15. LEGAL BARRIERS AGAINST PARTICIPATION IN MULTI TYPE LIBRARY COOPERATION

    There are no legal barriers.

NEW MEXICO

1. REPORTING AGENCY

    A. The New Mexico State Library
        Post Office Box 1629
        Santa Fe, New Mexico 87503
        (505) 827-2033

    B. Chief Officer: Paul A. Agriesti, Acting State Librarian

    C. Fiscal Year: 1977

2. OVERVIEW

    New Mexico's 753 libraries participate in interlibrary activity,
    primarily in the form of interlibrary lending.

    There are no statutes enabling multi-type library cooperative
    development; nor is there state funding for such cooperative
    developments.

3. NUMBER OF LIBRARIES IN THE STATE

    Academic: 20
    Public: 68
    School: 632
        Public: 632
        Private: not available
    Special   33
        Profit: unknown
        Nonprofit: unknown

    TOTAL: 753 est.

4. STATE AGENCY INTERLIBRARY COOPERATION UNIT

    A. Specific Unit Name: Library Development
        Person in Charge: Jane Gillentine, Associate State Librarian

    B. Other Unit Name: Information Services, Resources and Systems
        Person in Charge: Sandra Esquibel, Associate State Librarian

5. OTHER STATE-LEVEL GOVERNMENTAL ILC UNITS

    There are none.

6. OTHER STATE-LEVEL NON-GOVERNMENTAL ILC UNITS

    There are none.

7. SINGLE-TYPE LIBRARY COOPERATIVES

    There are none.

8. MULTI-TYPE LIBRARY COOPERATIVES

    There are none.

9. INTERLIBRARY COOPERATIVE FUNCTIONS

	State Support	Federal Support Title I	Title III	Other Support	Total Support
Interlibrary Loan:		$27,322	$42,460		
Continuing Education:		15,088			

    (Data for blank columns unavailable. Salaries for individuals
    employed in CE and Interlibrary Loan/Cooperative activities are paid
    from state funds, not reflected here.)

10. ILC COMMUNICATION DEVICES/SERVICE NETWORKS

Device/Service	Support ($)	Equipment (#)	Participants
IN-WATS	Unavailable	1	100
TWX	$7,850	14	13

    (Salaries for individuals employed in these activities are paid from
    state funds, not reflected here.)

11. MACHINE-READABLE DATA BASE REFERENCE SEARCHING DEVICES

    There are none.

12. INTERLIBRARY SERVICES TO SPECIAL GROUPS

    There are none.

13. PARTICIPATION IN MULTI-STATE LIBRARY NETWORKS

    A. Network: SLICE/CELS
        Financial Support: $ 3,000

    B. There are no multi-state networks headquartered in New Mexico.

14. LEGAL BASES FOR MULTI-TYPE LIBRARY COOPERATION

 There is no enabling legislation.

15. LEGAL BARRIERS AGAINST PARTICIPATION IN MULTI-TYPE LIBRARY COOPERATION

 There are no legal barriers.

1. REPORTING AGENCY

    A. New York State Library
        State Education Department
        Albany, NY 12334
        Telephone: 518-474-5930

    B. Chief Officer: Joseph F. Shubert, State Librarian and
                         Assistant Commissioner for Libraries

    C. Fiscal Year: April 1 - March 31

2. OVERVIEW

All of New York State is covered by 22 public library systems whose membership includes about 700 chartered and registered public libraries. System formation is provided for under New York State Education Law, Sections 255 and 272, Commissioner's Regulations 90.3, 90.4, 90.6. Education Law 273 apportions State Aid to the systems, currently about $30 million, based on formula factors of population and square miles served, library materials expenditures, central library service, special aid to The New York Public Library Research Libraries, and local sponsor support increases. Using State and Federal aid plus local support, the systems offer their members such services as cooperative purchasing and processing of materials, expanded reference resources of the central libraries, specialized collections of audiovisual materials, systemwide interlibrary loan coordination prior to switching into the statewide network, consultative staff services, printing and public relations, etc.

Nine Reference and Research Library Resources Systems (3R's) also cover the entire State whose membership of about 450 includes the 22 public library systems, academic and research libraries, profit and non-profit special libraries, and some individual public and school libraries. 3R's systems are chartered under Education Law Section 216 and operate under Commissioner's Regulations 90.5 and 90.6. Local assistance of $828,000 comes from funds appropriated to the State Education Department and are paid to each system, as a flat grant of $92,000. The 3R's systems coordinate for their members such services as regional interlibrary loan prior to switching into the statewide network, delivery service, continuing education, cooperative acquisitions, union lists of serials and specialized materials, patent searches, etc.

The New York State Library operates NYSILL (New York State Interlibrary Loan) for all types of library users, using the library's collection as well as contracting with individual specialized resource collections in the State for interloan. The systems and resource libraries are connected to the State Library computer by teletype.

The Board of Regents of the State Education Department has proposed a bill to be introduced in the Legislature in 1978 which will encourage further cooperation among public, academic, special and school libraries in meeting the library and information needs of New York residents,
(continued)

NEW YORK

2. OVERVIEW (continued)

resulting in greater efficiency of operation and universal access to
library resources and services. The bill would (1) continue State aid
for existing public library systems, central libraries, and member libraries, and for reference and research library resources systems; (2)
provide additional incentive aid for development of school library service systems within BOCES (Boards of Cooperative Education Services);
and (3) provide incentive State aid for regional cooperation service
programs among the three types of library systems. It is estimated that
within five years this would increase existing State aid by $20 million.

3. NUMBER OF LIBRARIES IN THE STATE

Academic	231
Public	712
School	5,550 (est.)
Public	4,350 (est.)
Private	1,200 (est.)
Special	1,250 (est.)
Profit	1,000 (est.)
Non-Profit	250 (est.)
Total	7,743 (est.)

4. STATE AGENCY INTERLIBRARY COOPERATION UNIT

A. Promotion of library cooperative activites is the responsibility
of the Bureau of Regional Library Services, Robert J. Flores,
Chief, and the Bureau of Specialist Library Services, E. J. Josey,
Chief, who coordinate with operating units of the State Library.

B. Other interlibrary cooperative activities of the State Library
include NYSILL and computer and data base services which are the
responsibility of J. Van Der Veer Judd, Principal Librarian,
Technical Services.

5. OTHER STATE-LEVEL GOVERNMENTAL ILC UNITS

The following units of State Government have program responsibility
for interlibrary cooperative activities:

A. SUNY (State University of New York) Central Services
Glyn T. Evans, Director of Library Services

Twin Towers, Room 1363
99 Washington Avenue
Albany, New York 12246

B. State Education Department
Division of Arts and Humanities (Virginia Matthews, Director)
which includes the Bureau of School Libraries, (Lorre Scurrah,
Chief)
Albany, New York 12234

6. OTHER STATE-LEVEL NON-GOVERNMENTAL ILC UNITS

There are none.

7. SINGLE-TYPE LIBRARY COOPERATIVES

A. Receiving Continuing Financial Support from the State Library:

Name: Brooklyn Public Library
Address: Grand Army Plaza
         Brooklyn, New York 11238
Telephone: 212-636-3122
Administrator: Kenneth F. Duchac
Type of Library Served: p
Federal Support: $650,640   FY '76
State Support: $2,721,617   FY '76
Local Support: $12,242,574   FY '76
Other Support: $3,077,697   FY '76
Total Support: $18,692,528   FY '76

Name: Buffalo and Erie County Public Library
Address: Lafayette Square
         Buffalo, New York 14203
Telephone: 716-856-7525
Administrator: Paul M. Rooney
Type of Library Served: p
Federal Support: $36,412   FY '76
State Support: $1,276,997   FY '76
Local Support: $7,731,906   FY '76
Other Support: $202,259   FY '76
Total Support: $9,247,574   FY '76

Name: Chautauqua - Cattaraugus Library System
Address: 106 West Fifth Street
         Jamestown, New York 14701
Telephone: 716-484-7135
Administrator: Murray L. Bob
Type of Library Served: p
Federal Support: $35,773   FY '76
State Support: $423,353   FY '76
Local Support: $879,106   FY '76
Other Support: $417,687   FY '76
Total Support: $1,755,919   FY '76

Chemung-Southern Tier Library System
   Name: Steele Memorial Library of Chemung County
   Address: Lake and Church Streets
            Elmira, New York 14901
   Telephone: 607-737-2947
   Administrator: Leonard Hammer
   Type of Library Served: p

                     and   (continued)

7A. SINGLE-TYPE LIBRARY COOPERATIVES (continued)

    Name: Southern Tier Library System
    Address: Civic Center Plaza
              Corning, New York 14830
    Telephone: 607-962-3141
    Administrator: Paul Malecki
    Type of Library Served: p
    Federal Support: $51,034   FY '76
    State Support: $549,555   FY '76
    Local Support: $995,104   FY '76
    Other Support: $543,065   FY '76
    Total Support: $2,138,758   FY '76

    Name: Clinton-Essex-Franklin Library
    Address: P.O. Box 570
              Plattsburgh, New York 12901
    Telephone: 518-563-5190
    Administrator: Stanley A. Ransom
    Type of Library Served: p
    Federal Support: $26,960   FY '76
    State Support: $350,624   FY '76
    Local Support: $441,255   FY '76
    Other Support: $127,823   FY '76
    Total Support: $946,662   FY '76

    Name: Finger Lakes Library System
    Address: 314 North Cayuga Street
              Ithaca, New York 14850
    Telephone: 607-273-4074
    Administrator: William R. Weitzel
    Type of Library Served: p
    Federal Support: $7,345   FY '76
    State Support: $505,036   FY '76
    Local Support: $709,071   FY '76
    Other Support: $403,061   FY '76
    Total Support: $1,624,513   FY '76

    Name: Four County Library System
    Address: Club House Road
              Binghamton, New York 13903
    Telephone: 607-723-8236
    Administrator: Marcus A. Wright
    Type of Library Served: p
    Federal Support: $18,500   FY '76
    State Support: $604,471   FY '76
    Local Support: $1,806,973   FY '76
    Other Support: $299,885   FY '76
    Total Support: $2,729,829   FY '76

(continued)

7A. SINGLE-TYPE LIBRARY COOPERATIVES (continued)

Name: Mid-Hudson Library System
Address: 103 Market Street
          Poughkeepsie, New York 12601
Telephone: 914-471-6060
Administrator: Leon Karpel
Type of Library Served: p
Federal Support: $92,096   FY '76
State Support: $746,797   FY '76
Local Support: $1,304,089   FY '76
Other Support: $1,188,833   FY '76
Total Support: $3,331,815   FY '76

Name: Mid-York Library System
Address: 1600 Lincoln Avenue
          Utica, New York 13502
Telephone: 315-735-8328
Administrator: Alfred C. Hasemeier
Type of Library Served: p
Federal Support: $38,496   FY '76
State Support: $592,043   FY '76
Local Support: $924,097   FY '76
Other Support: $307,205   FY '76
Total Support: $1,861,841   FY '76

Name: Mohawk Valley Library Association
Address: 858 Duanesburg Road
          Schenectady, New York 12306
Telephone: 518-355-2010
Administrator: Anthony Messineo
Type of Library Served: p
Federal Support: $39,765   FY '76
State Support: $488,587   FY '76
Local Support: $1,624,915   FY '76
Other Support: $415,413   FY '76
Total Support: $2,568,680   FY '76

Name: Nassau Library System
Address: Roosevelt Field Shopping Center
          Garden City, New York 11530
Telephone: 516-741-0060
Administrator: Andrew Geddes
Type of Library Served: p
Federal Support: $114,900   FY '76
State Support: $1,548,307   FY '76
Local Support: $20,131,154   FY '76
Other Support: $1,867,239   FY '76
Total Support: $23,661,600   FY '76

(continued)

7A. SINGLE-TYPE LIBRARY COOPERATIVES (continued)

Name: New York Public Library
Address: Fifth Avenue and 42nd Street
          New York, New York 10018
Telephone: 212-790-6262
Administrator: John M. Cory
Type of Library Served: p
Federal Support: $1,423,896   FY '76
State Support: $4,202,337   FY '76
Local Support: $19,822,716   FY '76
Other Support: $13,825,874   FY '76
Total Support: $39,274,823   FY '76

Name: Nioga Library System
Address: 1425 Main Street
          Niagara Falls, New York 14305
Telephone: 716-285-1223
Administrator: Oswald H. Joerg
Type of Library Served: p
Federal Support: $58,565   FY '76
State Support: $473,690   FY '76
Local Support: $1,714,094   FY '76
Other Support: $206,040   FY '76
Total Support: $2,452,389   FY '76

Name: North Country Library System
Address: P.O. Box 192
          Watertown, New York 13601
Telephone: 315-782-5540
Administrator: Ronald L. Roberts
Type of Library Served: p
Federal Support: $16,000   FY '76
State Support: $626,756   FY '76
Local Support: $1,050,206   FY '76
Other Support: $224,726   FY '76
Total Support: $1,917,688   FY '76

Name: Onondaga Library System
Address: 327 Montgomery Street
          Syracuse, New York 13202
Telephone: 315-473-2702
Administrator: Robert P. Kinchen
Type of Library Served: p
Federal Support: $14,311   FY '76
State Support: $574,323   FY '76
Local Support: $2,558,172   FY '76
Other Support: $446,037   FY '76
Total Support: $3,592,843   FY '76

(continued)

7A. SINGLE-TYPE LIBRARY COOPERATIVES (continued)

Pioneer Library System
    Administrator: Harold S. Hacker

    Name: Monroe County Library System
    Address: 115 South Avenue
           Rochester, New York 14604
    Telephone: 716-428-7347
    Administrator: Harold S. Hacker
    Type of Library Served: p
          and
    Name: Livingston County Library System
    Name: Wyoming County Library
    Address: 303 East Main Street
           Avon, New York 14414
    Telephone: 716-226-2770
    Administrator: Walter F. Ariel
    Type of Library Served: p
          and
    Name: Ontario Cooperative Library System
    Name: Wayne County Library System
    Address: 503 West Union Street
           Newark, New York 14513
    Telephone: 315-331-2143
    Administrator: Mrs. Elizabeth Blodgett
    Type of Library Served: p
    Federal Support: $84,146   FY '76
    State Support: $1,258,998   FY '76
    Local Support: $5,865,820   FY '76
    Other Support: $1,124,930   FY '76
    Total Support: $8,333,894   FY '76

    Name: Queens Borough Public Library
    Address: 89-11 Merrick Boulevard
           Jamaica, New York 11432
    Telephone: 212-739-1900
    Administrator: Milton S. Byam
    Type of Library Served: p
    Federal Support: $316,220   FY '76
    State Support: $2,161,643   FY '76
    Local Support: $15,083,338   FY '76
    Other Support: $484,598   FY '76
    Total Support: $18,045,799   FY '76

    Name: Ramapo Catskill Library System
    Address: 619 North Street
           Middletown, New York 10940
    Telephone: 914-343-1131
    Administrator: Alfred L. Freund
    Type of Library Served: p
    Federal Support: $46,489   FY '76
    State Support: $715,458   FY '76
    Local Support: $3,610,047   FY '76   (continued)

7A. SINGLE-TYPE LIBRARY COOPERATIVES (continued)

Other Support: $797,893   FY '76
Total Support: $5,169,887   FY '76

Name: Southern Adirondack Library System
Address: 22 Whitney Place
          Saratoga Springs, New York 12866
Telephone: 518-584-7300
Administrator: Florence E. Harshe
Type of Library Served: p
Federal Support: $21,046   FY '76
State Support: $476,475   FY '76
Local Support: $554,630   FY '76
Other Support: $251,686   FY '76
Total Support: $1,303,837   FY '76

Name: Suffolk Cooperative Library System
Address: 627 N. Sunrise Service Road P.O. Box 187
          Bellport, New York 11713
Telephone: 516-286-1600
Administrator: Robert N. Sheridan
Type of Library Served: p
Federal Support: $101,524   FY '76
State Support: $1,289,607   FY '76
Local Support: $12,561,758   FY '76
Other Support: $1,702,554   FY '76
Total Support: $15,655,443   FY '76

Name: Upper Hudson Library Federation
Address: 161 Washington Avenue
          Albany, New York 12210
Telephone: 518-449-3387
Administrator: Edgar Tompkins
Type of Library Served: p
Federal Support: $252,762   FY '76
State Support: $577,336   FY '76
Local Support: $1,902,102   FY '76
Other Support: $374,012   FY '76
Total Support: $3,106,212   FY '76

Name: Westchester Library System
Address: 280 North Central Avenue
          Hartsdale, New York 10530
Telephone: 914-761-7620
Administrator: Ruth A. Weber
Type of Library Served: p
Federal Support: $101,423   FY '76
State Support: $998,470   FY '76
Local Support: $9,848,022   FY '76
Other Support: $2,006,299   FY '76
Total Support: $12,954,214   FY '76

(continued)

7.   SINGLE-TYPE LIBRARY COOPERATIVES (continued)

B. Receiving No Continuing Financial Support from the State Library:

Name: Five Associated University Libraries, Inc. (FAUL)
Address: Syracuse University Libraries
          Syracuse, New York 13210
Telephone: 315-423-2574
Administrator: Donald C. Anthony
Type of Library Served: a
Sponsoring Body: Libraries of Cornell University, University
Source(s) of Support: of Rochester, Syracuse University, SUNY at
                        Binghamton, and SUNY at Buffalo.

C.   There are none.

8.   MULTI-TYPE LIBRARY COOPERATIVES

A.   Receiving Continuing Financial Support from the State Library:

Name: Capital District Library Council for Reference and Re-
        search Resources
Address: Rensselaer Polytechnic Institute
           Troy, New York 12181
Telephone: 518-272-8834
Administrator: Charles D. Custer
Types of Libraries Served: a, p, sp, research, library systems

Federal Support: $2,500
State Support: $92,000
Local Support: 0*
Other Support: $36,533
Total Support: $131,033

Name: Central New York Library Resources Council
Address: White Branch Library
           763 Butternut Street
           Syracuse, New York 13208
Telephone: 315-478-6080
Administrator: James M. Turner, Jr.
Types of Libraries Served: a, p, sp, research, library systems

Federal Support: $17,500
State Support: $92,000
Local Support: 0*
Other Support: $9,565
Total Support: $119,065

Name: Long Island Library Resources Council, Inc.
Address: P.O. Box 31
          Bellport, New York 11713
Telephone: 516-286-2095
Administrator: David Wilder   (continued)

8A. MULTI-TYPE LIBRARY COOPERATIVES (cotni:ued)

Types of Libraries Served: a, p, sp, research, library systems

Federal Support: $3,930
State Support: $92,000
Local Support: 0*
Other Support: $22,502
Total Support: $118,432

Name: New York Metropolitan Reference and Research Library
       Agency, Inc. (METRO)
Address: 11 West 40th Street
          New York, New York 10018
Telephone: 212-695-6732
Administrator: Forrest F. Carhart, Jr.
Types of Libraries Served: a, p, sp, research, library systems

Federal Support: $3,930
State Support: $92,000
Local Support: 0*
Other Support: $64,587
Total Support: $160,517

Name: North Country Reference and Research Resources Council
Address: 73 Park Street
          Canton, New York 13617
Telephone: 315-386-4560
Administrator: Richard H. Kimball
Types of Libraries Served: a, p, sp, research, library systems

Federal Support: $5,182 (est)
State Support: $92,000
Local Support: $2,400   (est)
Other Support: $3,000   (est)
Total Support: $102,582

Name: Rochester Regional Research Library Council
Address: 50 West Main Street
          Rochester, New York 14614
Telephone: 716-232-7930
Administrator: Janet Welch
Types of Libraries Served: a, p, sp, research, library systems

Federal Support: $3,930
State Support: $92,000
Local Support: 0*
Other Support: $64,338
Total Support: $160,268

Name: South Central Research Library Council
Address: 6A Office Complex--Dewitt Building
          215 North Cayuga Street
          Ithaca, New York 14850   (continued)

8A. MULTI-TYPE LIBRARY COOPERATIVES (continued)

Telephone: 607-273-9106
Administrator: Edmond Menegaux
Types of Libraries Served: a, p, sp, research, library systems

Federal Support: $4,235
State Support: $92,000
Local Support: 0*
Other Support: $2,259
Total Support: $98,494

Name: Southeastern New York Library Resources Council
Address: 20 Academy Street
          Poughkeepsie, New York 12601
Telephone: 914-471-0625
Administrator: Jane Fulton Smith
Types of Libraries Served: a, p, sp, research, library systems

Federal Support: $18,716
State Support: $92,000
Local Support: 0*
Other Support: $9,833
Total Support: $120,549

Name: Western New York Library Resources Council
Address: Buffalo and Erie County Public Library
          Buffalo, New York 14203
Telephone: 716-852-3844
Administrator: Benjamin B. Richards II
Types of Libraries Served: a, p, sp, research, library systems

Federal Support: 0
State Support: $92,000
Local Support: 0*
Other Support: $15,859
Total Support: $107,859

* Membership fees and other support paid by local libraries is
  reported under "Other Support".

8B. Receiving No Continuing Financial Support from the State Library:

There are none.

8C. Other: There are none.

9A. INTERLIBRARY COOPERATIVE FUNCTIONS

	State Support	Federal Support Title I	Support Title III	Other Support	Total Support
Interlibrary Loan	x	x	x	x	x
Continuing Education	x	x		x	x
Cooperative Acquisitions	x	x		x	x
Cooperative Cataloging	x			x	x
Cooperative Delivery	x			x	x
Cooperative Processing	x			x	x
Cooperative Reference	x	x		x	x
Cooperative Storage				x	x
Legislative Assistance					
Planning/Development	x	x		x	x
Union Lists of Serials	x	x		x	x
Other					

Total Support FY 77	$29,848,000	$142,628	$33,140,923+
		$3,150,295	Not Available

B. NON-FINANCIAL SUPPORT ROLE OF THE STATE LIBRARY

The State Library provides Interlibrary Loan (NYSILL), Continuing Education, Cooperative Reference, and Planning and Development via staff and facilities.

10A. ILC COMMUNICATION DEVICES / SERVICE NETWORKS

Device/Service	Support ($)	Equipment (#)	Participants
Teletype and computer communication for interlibrary loan	$81,500*	37	NYSILL Participants
Watts Line (Library for Blind)	$ 3,612	1	Blind and Handicapped

* Plus Department computer time

B. NON-FINANCIAL SUPPORT ROLE OF THE STATE LIBRARY

State Library staff coordination.

11. MACHINE-READABLE DATA BASE REFERENCE SEARCHING SERVICES

The State Library financially supports the following services and makes them available for cooperative use statewide.

Data Base/Vender	Support	Terminals	Participants
BRS	$18,000 (est.)	1	Legislature and
N.Y. TIMES INFO. BANK	$ 2,500 (est.)	1	State Government
			NYSILL
MEDLARS	$25,000 (est.)	1	Participants

12. INTERLIBRARY SERVICES TO SPECIAL GROUPS

  A. Through State Aid to library systems the following groups are served:

    Blind and Visually Handicapped (NYPL)
    Physically Handicapped
    Institutionalized
    Aging
    English as second language groups
    Disadvantaged--Economically and Educationally

  B. NON-FINANCIAL SUPPORT ROLE OF THE STATE LIBRARY:

    Operates Library for Blind and Handicapped for all of New York State except Long Island and New York City.

    Staff consultants work with client organizations and systems serving these groups.

13. PARTICIPATION IN MULTI-STATE LIBRARY NETWORKS

  A. Network: OCLC
     Financial Support: $25,000
     Participation: Cooperative Cataloging
     Service Used: Cooperative Cataloging and planning for possible interface with NYSILL for interloan.

     NYSILL participates in the Council of Computerized Library Networks.

  B. There are no multi-state networks headquartered in New York State.

14. LEGAL BASES FOR MULTI-TYPE LIBRARY COOPERATION

    There is no enabling legislation at this point. See OVERVIEW, question 2.

15. LEGAL BARRIERS AGAINST PARTICIPATION IN MULTI-TYPE LIBRARY COOPERATION

    There are no legal barriers.

1. REPORTING AGENCY

    A. Department of Cultural Resources - Division of State Library
        109 East Jones Street
        Raleigh NC 27611
        (919) 733-2570

    B. Chief Officer: David N. McKay, Director/State Librarian

    C. Fiscal Year: 1976/77

2. OVERVIEW

    Interlibrary Cooperation via regional organization of public li-
    braries; centralized technical services both in the public and
    academic library sectors; and multitype cooperation in revenue
    sharing and reference, highlight North Carolina projects.

    Statutory authority for state and federal programs remains the
    same except that the 1977 State Legislature added to the General
    Statutes of North Carolina, Chapter 125-2, a paragraph which gives
    the State Library the responsibility for planning and coordinating
    interlibrary cooperation within the state as well as coordinating
    local development with regional and national programs. As a result
    of this mandate a comprehensive review of all cooperative activi-
    ties is underway which will be used as the basis for planning by
    a to-be-created Professional Advisory Committee on Interlibrary
    Cooperation.

3. NUMBER OF LIBRARIES IN THE STATE

Academic:	45
Public:	362
School:	2,230
Public:	2,005
Private:	225
Special:	78
Profit:	35
Nonprofit:	43
TOTAL:	**2,715**

4. STATE AGENCY INTERLIBRARY COOPERATION UNIT

    A. Specific Unit Within State Library Agency Responsible for Inter-
        library Cooperation:

        Unit Name: Administration Section
        Person in Charge: Alberta Smith, Consultant, Interlibrary
                            Cooperation

(continued)

4. STATE AGENCY INTERLIBRARY COOPERATION UNIT (continued)

    B. Interlibrary Cooperation Units Within Other Established Offices of the State Library Agency:

        Unit Name: Information Services Section
        Person in Charge: David Bevan, Chief

        Unit Name: Public Library Development Section
        Person in Charge: Marion Johnson, Chief

        Unit Name: Special Services Section (Blind and Physically Handicapped and Institution Services)
        Person in Charge: Charles Fox, Chief

        Unit Name: Technical Services Section
        Person in Charge: Eunice Drum, Chief

5. OTHER STATE-LEVEL GOVERNMENT ILC UNITS

    There are none.

6. OTHER STATE LEVEL NON-GOVERNMENTAL ILC UNITS

    There are none.

7. SINGLE-TYPE LIBRARY COOPERATIVES

    A. Receiving Continuing Financial Support from the State Library:

        Name: Albemarle Regional Library
        Address: Box 68, Winton, NC 27986
        Telephone: (919) 358-4521
        Administrator: Louise Boone, Director
        Type of Library Served: p
        Federal Support: $ 25,752
        State Support: 92,901
        Local Support: 83,370
        Other Support: 4,808
        Total Support: $206,831

        Name: Appalachian Regional Library
        Address: 913 C Street, North Wilkesboro, NC 28659
        Telephone: (919) 838-2818
        Administrator: Valerie Knerr, Director
        Type of Library Served: p
        Federal Support: $ 27,006
        State Support: 111,692
        Local Support: 147,745
        Other Support: 15,134
        Total Support: $301,577

(continued)

7. SINGLE-TYPE LIBRARY COOPERATIVES (continued)

Name: Avery-Mitchell-Yancey Regional Library
Address: Box 725, Spruce Pine, NC 28777
Telephone: (704) 765-4673
Administrator: William Hess, Director
Type of Library Served: p
Federal Support: $ 3,280
State Support: 65,467
Local Support: 66,059
Other Support   14,247
Total Support: $149,053

Name: B H M Regional Library
Address: 158 North Market Street, Washington, NC 27889
Telephone: (919) 946-5505
Administrator: Barbara Walker, Director
Type of Library Served: p
Federal Support: $ 5,557
State Support: 63,406
Local Support: 60,717
Other Support: 4,177
Total Support: $133,857

Name: Central N.C. Regional Library
Address: 342 South Spring Street, Burlington, NC 27215
Telephone: (919) 227-2096
Administrator: Philip Ritter, Director
Type of Library Served: p
Federal Support: $ 45,743
State Support: 119,476
Local Support: 263,037
Other Support: 32,838
Total Support: $461,094

Name: Craven-Pamlico-Carteret Regional Library
Address: 400 Johnson Street, New Bern, NC 28560
Telephone: (919) 638-2127
Administrator: Elinor Hawkins, Director
Type of Library Served: p
Federal Support: $ 8,897
State Support: 119,534
Local Support: 167,308
Other Support: 12,186
Total Support: $307,925

Name: East Albemarle Regional Library
Address: 205 East Main Street, Elizabeth City, NC 27909
Telephone: (919) 335-2511
Administrator: Anne Sanders, Director
Type of Library Served: p
Federal Support: $ 19,940
State Support: 89,736   (continued)

7. SINGLE-TYPE LIBRARY COOPERATIVES (continued)

```
Local Support:          100,368
Other Support:           13,504
Total Support:         $223,548
```

```
Name:                   Fontana Regional Library
Address:                Drawer 460, Bryson City, NC 28713
Telephone:              (704) 488-2382
Administrator:          Wayne Modlin, Director
Type of Library Served:  p
Federal Support:       $  4,178
State Support:           75,617
Local Support:           52,232
Other Support:           13,677
Total Support:         $145,704
```

```
Name:                   Gaston-Lincoln Regional Library
Address:                115 West Second Avenue, Gastonia, NC 28052
Telephone:              (704) 865-3418
Administrator:          Barbara E. Heafner, Director
Type of Library Served:  p
Federal Support:       $ 15,341
State Support:          147,718
Local Support:          542,045
Other Support:           15,493
Total Support:         $720,597
```

```
Name:                   Hyconeechee Regional Library
Address:                East Main Street, Yanceyville, NC 27379
Telephone:              (919) 694-6241
Administrator:          Lloyd Osterman, Director
Type of Library Served:  p
Federal Support:       $ 15,448
State Support:          118,496
Local Support:          113,014
Other Support:           12,041
Total Support:         $258,999
```

```
Name:                   Nantahala Regional Library
Address:                101 Blumenthal Street, Murphy, NC 28906
Telephone:              (704) 837-2025
Administrator:          Martha Palmer, Director
Type of Library Served:  p
Federal Support:       $  2,445
State Support:           65,741
Local Support:           38,167
Other Support:            4,796
Total Support:         $111,149
```

(continued)

7. SINGLE-TYPE LIBRARY COOPERATIVES (continued)

Name: Neuse Regional Library
Address: 301 North Queen Street, Kinston, NC 28501
Telephone: (919) 527-7066
Administrator: Hollis Haney, Director
Type of Library Served: p
Federal Support: $ 6,667
State Support: 107,454
Local Support: 162,375
Other Support: 8,029
Total Support: $284,525

Name: Northwestern Regional Library
Address: 111 North Front Street, Elkin, NC 28621
Telephone: (919) 835-5586
Administrator: Charles Pipes, Director
Type of Library Served: p
Federal Support: $ 18,310
State Support: 166,279
Local Support: 173,877
Other Support: 40,085
Total Support: $398,551

Name: Pettigrew Regional Library
Address: Box 786, Plymouth, NC 27962
Telephone: (919) 793-2113
Administrator: Nellie Sanders, Director
Type of Library Served: p
Federal Support: $ 20,374
State Support: 100,432
Local Support: 84,431
Other Support: 3,393
Total Support: $208,630

Name: Sandhill Regional Library
Address: 1104 East Broad Avenue, Rockingham, NC 28379
Telephone: (919) 895-9328
Administrator: William Bridgman, Director
Type of Library Served: p
Federal Support: $ 27,678
State Support: 216,435
Local Support: 236,456
Other Support: 46,632
Total Support: $527,201

B. Receiving No Continuing Financial Support from the State Library:

Name: Equipment Media Processing Center
Address: 100 S. Harrington Street, Raleigh, NC 27603
Telephone: (919) 733-7714
Administrator: Eugene Hinton   (continued)

257

7. **SINGLE-TYPE LIBRARY COOPERATIVES** (continued)

    Type of Library Served: Community Colleges
    Sponsoring Body: State Board of Education
    Source(s) of Support: State Funds

    Name: **Consortium** for Sharing Instructional Materials
    Address: Division of Educational Resources, Community
                         Colleges, Room 25, Education Building, Raleigh,
                         NC 27611
    Administrator: Joe Carter
    Types of Libraries Served: Community Colleges and Technical
                                 Institutes
    Sponsoring Body: Division of Educational Resources, Department
                       of Community Colleges
    Source(s) of Support: Department of Community Colleges

    Name: Piedmont Triad Library Council
    Address: 2120 Pinecroft Road, Greensboro, NC 27407
    Telephone: (919) 869-6092
    Administrator: Kay Anderson, Executive Secretary
    Types of Libraries Served: p   (6 systems)
    Sponsoring Body: Council of Governments and Participating Li-
                       braries
    Source(s) of Support: Council of Governments and Participating
                       Libraries

C. **Receiving Occasional Financial Support from the State Library:**

    There are none.

8. MULTI-TYPE LIBRARY COOPERATIVES

    A. Receiving Continuing Financial Support from the State Library:

        There are none.

    B. Receiving No Continuing Financial Support from the State Library:

        There are none.

    C. **Receiving Occasional Financial Support from the State Library:**

        There are none.

9. INTERLIBRARY COOPERATION FUNCTIONS

    A. Receiving Continuing Financial Support from the State Library:

(continued)

9. INTERLIBRARY COOPERATION FUNCTIONS (continued)

	State Support	Federal Support Title I	Federal Support Title III	Other Support	Total Support
Interlibrary Loan) Cooperative Reference)	$90,910		$35,973		$126,883
Cooperative Acquisition) Cooperative Cataloging) Cooperative Delivery) Cooperative Processing)	46,402				46,402
Continuing Education	30,000	12,489			42,489
Legislative Assistance	6,000				6,000
Planning/Development	45,768	23,311			69,079
Other (Film Loan Service,	90,911	93,117			184,028
Union Catalog)			27,575		27,575
Total Support	$309,991	$128,917	$63,548		$502,456

B. NON-FINANCIAL SUPPORT ROLE OF THE STATE LIBRARY :

Interlibrary Loan: Interlibrary loan requests are received at the State Library by mail or Wide Area Telephone System (WATS) from public, academic, and special libraries throughout the state. Material requests that cannot be satisfied from the State Library collection are searched in the North Carolina Union Catalog and requests are referred to relevant libraries.

Cooperative Reference: Information requests that cannot be satisfied at the local level are received at the State Library by mail or WATS line from libraries of all types across the state. The State Library staff researches the question, calling on academic library staff assistance if necessary and sends the answer to the requesting library in the shortest possible time.

Continuing Education: State Library staff assists with planning, physical arrangements, implementation and evaluation of workshops and institutes.

Planning/Development: Consultants from the State Library staff work with governmental units, library boards, citizen groups and librarians for the development and improvement of library services. They are available for consultation and assistance at all times.

Legislative Assistance: A State Library staff member is available to assist legislators and legislative researchers at all times.

Film Loan Service: In addition to circulation of films, screening programs and workshops are held for librarians.

10. ILC COMMUNICATION DEVICES / SERVICE NETWORKS

   A. State Library agency financial support of functional communica-
      tion devices and service networks among libraries within the
      state:

Device/Service	Support ($)	Equipment (#)	Participants
WATS	9,000	1	590
TWX	1,200	1	2
SOLINET	18,547	3 terminals	23
		2 printers	

   B. Non-financial support role of the State Library in the co-
      operative use of any of these devices/networks:

      There is none.

11. MACHINE-READABLE DATA BASE REFERENCE SEARCHING SERVICES

      Planned for the current fiscal year.

12. INTERLIBRARY SERVICES TO SPECIAL GROUPS

   A. Services

Services	State	Federal	Total
Blind & Physically Handicapped	$222,556	$ 26,175	$248,731
Institutionalized	63,410	53,191	116,601
Aging	(Consultant Service)	79,090	79,090
Bi-lingual	(Consultant Service)	88,000	88,000
Disadvantaged	(Consultant Service)	603,710	603,710

   B. Non-financial support role of State Library in providing the
      above services:

      Blind and Physically Handicapped: The State Library operates
      the Library for the Blind and Physically Handicapped, working
      with public libraries in cooperative ways to insure good
      service. In addition to direct service, consulting, technical
      assistance, legislative and coordination support are given.

      Institutionalized: Direct grants of State and Federal funds
      are made to establish or expand institutional library services.
      In addition consulting, planning, technical assistance, legisla-
      tive and coordination support are given.

      Aging: A consultant on the State Library staff has expertise
      and interest as well as responsibility in this area.

      Bi-lingual: Planning and coordination support are given.

(continued)

12. INTERLIBRARY SERVICES TO SPECIAL GROUPS (continued)

B. Non-financial support role of State Library in providing the above services:

Disadvantaged: Consulting, planning, technical assistance and coordination support are given. Encouragement of demonstration projects, stimulation of ideas through workshops and assistance with implementation of programs.

13. PARTICIPATION IN MULTI-STATE LIBRARY NETWORKS

Network(s):   SOLINET
Financial Support: $18,547
Participation: Member
Services Used: On-Line Cataloging
                       Interlibrary Loan Locations
                       Bibliographic Verification

14. LEGAL BASES FOR MULTI-TYPE LIBRARY COOPERATION

State legislation enabling multi-type library cooperation development.
G.S. 125-2 (4) (1973)

State legislation enabling interstate library compact.
G.S. 125-12 (1967)

State provided statutory funding for multi-type library cooperative development. G.S. 125-7

Regional Grant: Regional grants are made to legally established multi-county public libraries operating as a single administrative unit with all funds accounted for by the Regional Library as a public authority, or by one local government on behalf of all. Regional libraries must serve at least three counties or 100,000 population. The formula for the regional grant is based on per capita regional income from the local governments included in the region. As per capita local library revenues increase by 25¢, the regional allotment is increased according to a graduated scale.

15. LEGAL BARRIERS AGAINST PARTICIPATION IN MULTI-TYPE LIBRARY COOPERATION

There are none.

1. REPORTING AGENCY

A. State Library Commission
Highway 83 North
Bismarck, ND 58505
(701) 224-2492

B. Richard J. Wolfert, State Librarian

C. Fiscal Year: 1978

2. OVERVIEW

North Dakota is a one—system state. All types of libraries
(academic, technical, school, public, and special) are eligible
to participate in the North Dakota Network for Knowledge.
Citizens may tap into the Network through their local library or
directly at the State Library. Legal basis for the Network is
section 54-24-03 of the state statutes. State funding is provided for State Library participation in the Network (staff,
space, materials, communications), but all other libraries must
fund their own participation in the Network. There is no formal
agreement for Network participation. On-line access to, and/or
distribution on microfiche of a statewide union list of serials,
monographs, and A-V materials is under consideration.

3. NUMBER OF LIBRARIES IN THE STATE

Academic: 13
Public: 75
School: 623
  Public: (545)
  Private: (78)
Special: 42
  Profit: (42)
  Non-profit (0)

TOTAL: 753

4. STATE AGENCY INTERLIBRARY COOPERATION UNIT

There is no existing unit nor plans to create one.

5. OTHER STATE-LEVEL GOVERNMENT ILC UNITS

There are none.

6. OTHER STATE-LEVEL NON-GOVERNMENTAL ILC UNITS

There are none.

7. SINGLE-TYPE LIBRARY COOPERATIVES

    A. Receiving Continuing Financial Support from the State Library:

        There are none.

    B. Receiving No Continuing Financial Support from the State Library:

        Name: North Dakota Health Science Library Network
        Address: Harley E. French Medical Library
                                    University of North Dakota
                                    Grand Forks, North Dakota 58201
        Telephone: (701) 777-3993
        Administrator: Charles Bandy, Director
        Type of Library Served: Health Science
        Sponsoring Body: University of North Dakota Medical School
        Source of Support: State and federal funds

    C. Other:

        There are none.

8. MULTI-TYPE LIBRARY COOPERATIVES

    A. Receiving Continuing Financial Support from the State Library:

        Name: North Dakota Network for Knowledge
        Address: North Dakota State Library Commission
                                    Bismarck, North Dakota 58505
        Telephone: (701) 224-2492
        Administrator: Richard J. Wolfert, State Librarian
        Types of Libraries Served: a, p, sch, sp

        Federal Support: LSCA
        State Support: State appropriation
        Local Support: Local library budgets
        Other Support: None
        Total Support: No summary available. Network operates
                                    out of each library's budget. No
                                    central funding.

    B. Receiving No Continuing Financial Support from the State Library:

        There are none.

    C. Others:

        There are none.

9. INTERLIBRARY COOPERATION FUNCTIONS

A.

	State Support	Federal Support Title I	Federal Support Title III	Other Support	Total Support
Interlibrary Loan	X	X	X		
Continuing Education	X	X	X		
Cooperative Acquisitions					
Cooperative Cataloging					
Cooperative Delivery					
Cooperative Processing					
Cooperative Reference	X	X	X		
Cooperative Storage					
Legislative Assistance	X				
Planning/Development	X	X	X		
Union Lists of Serials	X	X			
Other: Union List of Books & A-V	X	X			

(Budget allocations are not available)

B. Non-Financial Support Role of the State Library:

There is no non-financial support role.

10. ILC COMMUNICATION DEVICES / SERVICE NETWORKS

A.

Device/Service	Support ($)	Equipment (#)	Participants
Teletype	10,000	16 terminals	academic & public libraries
IN-WATS	2,500	1 terminal	public libraries
WATS	?	100 terminals	academic, special, & public libraries

B. Non-Financial Support Role of the State Library:

There is no non-financial support role for these services.

11. MACHINE-READABLE DATA BASE REFERENCE SEARCHING SERVICES

There are none financed by the State Library. Such services are available in some academic libraries and via telephone from MINITEX.

12. INTERLIBRARY SERVICES TO SPECIAL GROUPS

A. Service to the blind and visually handicapped is provided to North Dakota residents eligible for this service by the South Dakota State Library under annual contract.

B. Non-Financial Support Role of the State Library:

There is none.

13. PARTICIPATION IN MULTI-STATE LIBRARY NETWORKS

    A. Network: MINITEX
       Financial Support: $30,000 annually
       Participation: Academic, special, and public libraries
       Services Used: Union List of Serials, reference, document
                       delivery, OCLC access

    B. Multi-state networks which are headquartered in your state and
       in which the state library agency has no involvement:

       There are none.

14. LEGAL BASES FOR MULTI-TYPE LIBRARY COOPERATION

    Sections 54-24-03 and 54-24-08 of state statutes. Biennial
    appropriation for State Library supports, in part, the North Dakota
    Network for Knowledge.

15. LEGAL BARRIERS AGAINST PARTICIPATION IN MULTI-TYPE LIBRARY COOPERATION

    There are no legal barriers.

1. REPORTING AGENCY

    A. The State Library of Ohio
        65 South Front Street
        Columbus OH 43215
        (614) 466-2693

    B. Chief Officer: Ira Phillips, Acting State Librarian

    C. Fiscal Year: 1978

2. OVERVIEW

    Thirteen regional systems in Ohio involve libraries in 84 of
    Ohio's 88 counties. 92.1% of the population is served by
    libraries participating in interlibrary cooperation. 238 of
    the 250 public libraries in Ohio participate.

    Regional systems may be formed under two sections of the Ohio
    Revised Code Section 3375.70-. 73 enables public libraries in
    two or more counties to form an area library service orga-
    nization (ALSO). Under Sections 3375.90-.93, four or more li-
    braries of two or more types may form a metropolitan library
    system in a metropolitan area of 250,000 or more population.
    Nine of the regional systems are operating as multicounty
    cooperatives under laws permitting libraries to contract and
    therefore are not organized under the sections cited here.
    Ohio may enter into interstate library contracts under Ohio
    Revised Code 3375.83-.85.

    Ohio Revised Code 3375.81 provides for essential service
    operations grants from state aid appropriations to operate
    ALSOs.

3. NUMBER OF LIBRARIES IN THE STATE

Academic:	122
Public:	250
School:	2,523
Public:	2,523
Private:	not available
Special:	144
Profit:	73*
Nonprofit:	71*

TOTAL:	3,039*

    *estimated

4. STATE AGENCY INTERLIBRARY COOPERATION UNIT

      A.   Specific Unit: Library Development Division
           Person in Charge: Ira Phillips, Assistant State
                              Librarian for Library Development

      B.   Other State Agency ILC Unit:

           Unit Name: Information Resources and Services
                              Division
           Person in Charge: Mrs. Catherine Mead, Assistant
                              State Librarian

5. OTHER STATE-LEVEL GOVERNMENT ILC UNITS

      There are none.

6. OTHER STATE-LEVEL NON-GOVERNMENTAL ILC UNITS

      Unit Name: Ohio Multitype Interlibrary
                         Cooperation Committee (OMICC)
      Address: 65 South Front Street
                         Columbus OH 43215
                         c/o The State Library of Ohio
      Telephone: 614-466-2693
      Administrator: Herbert F. Johnson, Chairman (Librarian of
                         Oberlin College, Oberlin 44074)
      Activites: OMICC's goal is to develop a statewide multi-
                         type interlibrary cooperation plan. OMICC is
                         composed of 15 members broadly representative
                         of libraries and organizations, including re-
                         presentatives of professional library or-
                         ganizations, the State Library Board, The
                         Board of Regents and The Ohio Department of
                         Education.

      Unit Name: Ohio Library Association
      Address: 40 South Third Street, Columbus OH 43215
      Telephone: 614-221-9057
      Administrator: A. Chapman Parsons, Executive Director
      Activities: Library Development Committee

7.   SINGLE-TYPE LIBRARY COOPERATIVES

   A.   Receiving Continuing Financial Support from the State
        Library:

        Name: Miami Valley Library Oragnization (MILO)
        Address: 215 East 3rd Street
                           Dayton OH 45402
        Telephone: 513-224-1686
        Administrator: Maria B. Overholt, Project Director
        Type of Library Served: p
        Federal Support: $105,123
        State Support: -0-
        Local Support: $ 10,108   (Calendar year 1977)
        Total Support: $115,231

        Name: Mideastern Ohio Library Organization (MOLO)
        Address: 205 East Main Street
                           Louisville OH 44641
        Telephone: 216-875-4269
        Administrator: Susan K. Schmidt, Project Director
        Type of Library Served: p
        Federal Support: $100,239
        State Support: -0-
        Local Support: $ 11,244   (Calendar year 1977)
        Total Support: $111,483

        Name: Ohio Valley Area Libraries (OVAL)
        Address: 107 W. Broadway
                           Wellston OH 45692
        Telephone: 614-384-2103
        Administrator: Maurice G. Klein, Director
        Type of Library Served: p
        Federal Support: $265,000
        State Support: $300,929
        Local Support: $ 30,520   (Calendar year 1977)
        Total Support: $596,449

(continued)

7.   SINGLE-TYPE LIBRARY COOPERATIVES (continued)

   B.   Receiving No Continuing Support from The State Library:

   Name: Consortium for Higher Education Religion
                        Studies (CHERS)
   Address: CHERS, Inc.
                        1810 Harvard Blvd.
                        Dayton OH 45406
   Telephone: 513-276-3450
   Administrator: Mrs. Edith Sotzing
   Type of Library Served: a
                                     Orientation
   Sponsoring Body: There is none.
   Source of Support: Member schools

   Name: Inter-University Library Council-Reference
                        and Interlibrary Loan Service
   Address: IULC-RAILS Office
                        The Ohio State University Library
                        1858 Neil Avenue
                        Columbus OH 43210
   Telephone: 614-422-0216
   Administrator: Mary Ellen Page
   Type of Library Served: a
   Sponsoring Body: There is none.
   Source of Support: Membership dues

   Name: Northeastern Ohio Major Academic Libraries
                        (NEOMAL)
   Address: NEOMAL Office
                        Kent State University
                        Kent OH 44242
   Telephone: 216-672-2962
   Administrator: Hyman W. Kritzer, Chairman
   Type of Library Served: a
   Sponsoring Body: There is none.
   Source of Support: Member schools

(continued)

7. SINGLE-TYPE LIBRARY COOPERATIVES (continued)

B. Receiving No Continuing Financial Support from The State
Library of Ohio:

Name: Northwest Ohio Consortium
Address: Findlay College
                   1000 North Main Street
                   Findlay OH
Telephone: 419-422-8313 Ext. 379
Administrator: Dr. Edward W. Erner
                   Chairman of Policy Council
Type of Library Served: a
Sponsoring Body: There is none.
Source of Support: Grant from Board of Regents

8. MULTITYPE LIBRARY COOPERATIVES

A. Receiving Continuing Financial Support from The State
Library of Ohio:

Name: Cleveland Area Metropolitan Library System
                   (CAMLS)
Address: 11000 Euclid Avenue, Room 309
                   Cleveland OH   44106
Telephone: 216-368-2733
Administrator: Nancy Wareham
Types of Libraries Served: a-p
Federal Support: $ 30,000
State Support: -0-
Local Support: $ 8,500   (Calendar year 1977)
Total Support: $ 38,500

Name: Central Ohio Interlibrary Network (COIN)
Address: 27 North Main Street
                   Mansfield, OH   44902
Telephone: 419-526-1337
Administrator: M. Lucille Thomson, Project Director
Types of Libraries Served: p-sch-institution
Federal Support: $113,801
State Support: -0-
Local Support: $ 13,850   (Calendar year 1977)
Total Support: $127,651

(continued)

8. MULTITYPE LIBRARY COOPERATIVES (continued)

    A. Receiving Continuing Financial Support from The State
        Library of Ohio:

        Name: INFO
        Address: Lorain Public Library
                          351 Sixth Street
                          Lorain OH 44052
        Telephone: 216-244-1192
        Administrator: Anne Kraus, Project Director
        Types of Libraries Served: a-p-sp
        Federal Support: $136,116
        State Support: -0-
        Local Support: $ 8,534   (Calendar year 1977)
        Total Support: $144,650

        Name: Greater Cincinnati Library Consortium
        Address: University of Cincinnati Library
                          Clifton Avenue
                          Cincinnati OH 45221
        Telephone: 513-475-2533
        Administrator: Cheryl Albrecht
        Types of Libraries Served: a-p-sp
        Federal Support: $ 33,000
        State Support: -0-
        Local Support: $ 17,005   (Calendar year 1977)
        Total Support: $ 50,005

        Name: Northeastern Ohio Library Association (NOLA)
        Address: 118 East Wood Street
                          Youngstown OH 44503
        Telephone: 216-746-7042
        Administrator: Mrs. Theresa Trucksis, Project Coordinator
        Types of Libraries Served: a-p-sp
        Federal Support: $ 98,280
        State Support: -0-
        Local Support: $ 10,095   (Calendar year 1977)
        Total Support: $108,375

(continued)

8. MULTITYPE LIBRARY COOPERATIVES (continued)

A. Receiving Continuing Financial Support from the State
    Library of Ohio:

Name: Northwest Library District (NORWELD)
Address: Wood County District Public Library
                    251 North Main Street
                    Bowling Green OH 43402
Telephone: 419-353-5721
Administrator: Richard Pritsky, Project Coordinator
Types of Libraries Served: a-p
Federal Support: $125,855
State Support: -0-
Local Support: $ 15,238   (Calendar year 1977)
Total Support: $141,093

Name: Southeastern Ohio Library Organization (SOLO)
Address: Regional Library Service Center
                    Route 1
                    Caldwell OH 43724
Telephone: 614-732-4817
Administrator: Raymond Mulhern, Project Coordinator
Types of Libraries Served: a-p-sch
Federal Support: $ 14,300
State Support: -0-
Local Support: $ 1,500   (Calendar year 1977)
Total Support: $ 15,800

Name: Southwestern Ohio Rural Libraries (SWORL)
Address: 95 Bourgraf Drive
                    Wilmington OH 45177
Telephone: 513-383-2503
Administrator: Mrs. Linda Harfst
Types of Libraries Served: a-p-sch
Federal Support: $152,677
State Support: -0-
Local Support: $ 9,017   (Calendar year 1977)
Total Support: $161,694

(continued)

8. MULTITYPE LIBRARY COOPERATIVES (continued)

   A. Receiving Continuing Financial Support from The State
      Library of Ohio:

      Name: Western Ohio Regional Library Development
                       System (WORLDS)
      Address: WORLDS Project Office
                       640 West Market Street
                       Lima OH 45801
      Telephone: 419-227-9370
      Administrator: Mrs. Kaye Schneider, Project Coordinator
      Types of Libraries Served: a-p-sch-sp-institution
      Federal Support: $117,676
      State Support: -0-
      Local Support: $ 10,010   (Calendar year 1977)
      Total Support: $127,686

   B. Receiving No Continuing Financial Support from The State
      Library of Ohio:

      Name: Art Research Libraries of Ohio (ARLO)
      Address: The Ohio State University Library
                       1858 Neil Avenue
                       Columbus OH 43210
      Telephone: 614-422-6184
      Administrator: Mrs. Jacqueline Sisson, Coordinator
      Types of Libraries Served: a-p-sp
      Sponsoring Body: There is none.
      Source of Support: Member libraries

      Name: Columbus Area Library and Information
                       Council (CALICO)
      Address: Battelle Memorial Institute
                       505 King Avenue
                       Columbus OH 43201
      Telephone: 614-242-6424
      Administrator: Beverly Rawles
      Types of Libraries Served: a-p-sch-sp
      Sponsoring Body: There is none.
      Source of Support: There is none.

(continued)

8. MULTITYPE LIBRARY COOPERATIVES (continued)

B. Receiving No Continuing Financial Support from The State
Library of Ohio:

Name: Committee for Library Cooperation
Address: University of Toledo Library
                   2801 Bancroft Street
                   Toledo OH 43606
Telephone: 419-537-2326
Administrator: Leslie W. Sheridan
Types of Libraries Served: a-p
Sponsoring Body: There is none.
Source of Support: There is none.

Name: Dayton-Miami Valley Library Consortium
Address: 32 North Main Street
                   Suite 1300
                   Dayton OH 45402
Telephone: 513-278-9105
Administrator: Ray Narther, Chairman
Types of Libraries Served: a-sp
Sponsoring Body: Dayton-Miami Valley Consortium of
                        Colleges and Universities
Source of Support: Membership dues

9. INTERLIBRARY COOPERATION FUNCTIONS

A. Receiving Continual Financial Support from The State Library
of Ohio:

Services	State Support	Federal	Total Support
Interlibrary Loan		$ 40,218	$ 40,218
Cooperative Acquisition			
Cooperative Cataloging	$ 14,451	$ 3,891	$ 18,342
Cooperative Processing		$ 10,500	$ 10,500
Cooperative Delivery	$ 8,000	$ 10,500	$ 18,500
Cooperative Reference	$ 10,880	$120,011	$130,891
Union Lists of Serials			
Cooperative Storage			
Continuing Education	$ 5,043	$ 30,397	$ 35,440
Planning/Development	$122,347	$262,124	$384,471
Legislative Assistance			
Public Relations	$ 9,220	$ 31,791	$ 41,011
Films/A-V	$ 4,300	$122,473	$126,773
Total Support	$174,241	$631,905	$806,146

(continued)

9. INTERLIBRARY COOPERATION FUNCTIONS (continued)

    B. NON-FINANCIAL SUPPORT ROLE OF THE STATE LIBRARY OF OHIO:

        Consultant service and planning; interlibrary loan backup
        service; coordination of teletype interlibrary loan system;
        retrospective conversion of catalogs into OCLC data bank.

10. ILC COMMUNICATION DEVICES/SERVICE NETWORKS

Device/Service	Support($)	Equipment(#)	Participants
Telephone	$ 20,715		144
Telefacsimile Communication	$ 10,200	16	13
TWX Interlibrary Loan	$ 26,428	11	11
OCLC Participation	(Supported by member fees)		
OCLC Retrospective Conversion	$550,000		8

    B. NON-FINANCIAL SUPPORT ROLE OF THE STATE LIBRARY OF OHIO:

        See 9B

11. MACHINE READABLE DATA BASE REFERENCE SEARCHING SERVICES

Data Base/Vendor	Support($)	Terminals(#)	Participants
New York Times Information Bank	$30,000	3	3-a-p-sp

12. INTERLIBRARY SERVICES TO SPECIAL GROUPS

A. Services	State Support	Federal	Total Support
Cincinnati Regional Library for Blind and Physically Handicapped	$ 86,405	$ 3,405	$ 89,810
Cleveland Regional Library for Blind and Physically Handicapped	$193,677	$ 9,208	$202,885
TOTAL	$280,082	$12,613	$292,695

    B. NON-FINANCIAL SUPPORT ROLE OF THE STATE LIBRARY OF OHIO:

        Consultant service and planning.

13. PARTICIPATION IN MULTI-STATE NETWORKS

    Name: Ohio College Library Center (OCLC)
    Address: 1125 Kinnear Road
                       Columbus, OH 43212
                       (614) 486-3661
    Financial Support: $80,000 (first time use charge and card
                       costs for State Library and 65 contract
                       libraries)
    Participation: Full member
    Services used: Cataloging, Serials, Interlibrary Loan

    Name: Kentucky, Ohio, Michigan Regional Medical
                       Library (KOMRML)
    Address: Wayne State University
                       4325 Brush
                       Detroit, MI 48202
    Telephone: (313) 577-1168
    Financial Support: 0
    Participation: a, sp
    Services used: not reported

14. LEGAL BASES FOR MULTITYPE LIBRARY COOPERATION

    American Library Laws Fourth Edition 1973
       Area Library Service Organization pages 1440-1441

    Ohio Revised Code 3375.01
       Assigns the State Library Board responsibilities for a state-
       wide program of development and coordination of library
       services.

    Ohio Revised Code 3375.70-3375.73
       Provides for formation of Area Library Service Organization
       (ALSOs) involving public libraries in two or more counties, and
       provides for governance by an ALSO Board composed of trustees
       of participating public libraries. Essential service operation
       grants are made by the State Library Board for the support of
       the ALSO. Non-public libraries may be members of an ALSO, but
       are not included in the calculation of the essential services
       grant. Grants are authorized by statute and established in
       Rules of the State Library Board.

    Ohio Revised Code 3375.83-3375.85
       Provides for Ohio entry into interstate library compacts.

    Ohio Revised Code 3375.90-3375.93
       Provides for organizing Metropolitan Library Systems (METROs)
       involving four or more libraries of two or more types in a
       metropolitan area as defined by the State Library Board of
       250,000 or more population.   (continued)

14. LEGAL BASES FOR MULTITYPE LIBRARY COOPERATION (continued)

In FY 1977 the following sums were allocated as grants by the State Library Board regional systems development and operation:

State Aid - Area Library Service Organization	$ 300,929
LSCA Title I	$1,128,828
LSCA Title III	$ 93,000
State Aid - Regional Libraries for the Blind and Physically Handicapped	$ 280,081
TOTAL	$1,802,838

15. LEGAL BARRIERS AGAINST PARTICIPATION IN MULTITYPE LIBRARY COOPERATION

The Ohio Multitype Interlibrary Cooperation Committee has prepared a statement on barriers to interlibrary cooperation in Ohio. This identifies seven major types of barriers (legal, political, financial, attitudinal, planning, lack of communication, and inadequate information). The section on legal barriers states:

"1. Legal: Better multitype interlibrary cooperation requires changes in laws and their interpretation. Ohio's legislators would be wise to update, clarify, and broaden some laws. Among these are those that deal with the establishment and operation of an Area Library Service Organization. In addition, if the state auditor and other officials interpret laws that relate to libraries inconsistently or narrowly this impedes cooperation.

Federal laws may also present legal barriers. For example, federal laws may inhibit for-profit companies or institutions from becoming members of cooperatives which are largely publicly supported. Similarly, federal Elementary and Secondary Education Act (ESEA) regulations can make it difficult for school libraries to share resources through multitype library systems. Finally, the recently enacted copyright law will affect interlibrary loan cooperation and resource sharing.

Some things viewed or cited as legal barriers may, however, be attitudinal problems. Some actions have described as prohibited by law but are found to be supported by long standing practice rather than by any law."

1. REPORTING AGENCY

    A. The Oklahoma Department of Libraries
        200 Northeast 18th Street
        Oklahoma City, Oklahoma 73105
        (405) 521-2502

    B. Chief Officer: Robert L. Clark, Jr., Director

    C. Fiscal Year: 1978

2. OVERVIEW

    The Department of Libraries has a statutory basis in inter-
    local cooperative agreements, interstate compact for library
    service and the public libraries system act. In addition,
    the Department is authorized to discharge the state's res-
    ponsibility for library service. The Oklahoma Teletype
    Interlibrary System (OTIS) provides interlibrary services
    and access to on-line data bases for each of 12 transmission
    sites, which in turn serve geographical areas assigned to
    each. Presently 30 of 77 counties are members of consolidat-
    ed multi-county library systems. The State's two major
    universities, OU and OSU have long held to an individual
    cooperative agreement sharing bibliographic records.

    Under the auspices of the Oklahoma Department of Libraries'
    Board and the LSCA Advisory Council, a Network Advisory
    Council has been established to insure that planning and
    project implementation is done within the context of the
    National plan, to survey and recommend a formal and perman-
    ent council on library networking in Oklahoma including its
    structure, governance and funding, and to advise the Depart-
    ment of Libraries on development of and policy matters aris-
    ing in the administration of networking activities. Present-
    ly, networking activities in Oklahoma are funded through the
    LSCA. The Department, along with 12 other institutions in
    Oklahoma, are members of the AMIGOS Bibliographic Council.
    Other state agency cooperative activities include continuing
    education, planning, development, and legislative assistance.

3. NUMBER OF LIBRARIES IN THE STATE

        Academic: 44
        Public: 191
        School   200
            Public   ___
            Private   ___
        Special   121
            Profit   ___
            Nonprofit   ___
        TOTAL: 556

4. STATE AGENCY INTERLIRBARY COOPERATION UNIT

    A. Specific Interlibrary Cooperation Unit

        Name: Library Resources Branch
        Person in Charge: Marian Patmon

    B. Other ILC Units: Oklahoma Teletype Interlibrary
                                  System/Oklahoma Information Lines
        Person in Charge: Mary Hardin, Head

5. OTHER STATE-LEVEL GOVERNMENTAL ILC UNITS

        Unit Name: Network Advisory Council (ad hoc)
        Chairman: Dr. James Healey
                            University of Oklahoma Library
                              School, Norman, OK 73069

    The Council is an official advisory body to the Oklahoma
    Department of Libraries and includes representation from
    all types of libraries. Project analysis, policy advice,
    planning, and recommendations for a permanent council are
    among the present activities.

6. OTHER STATE-LEVEL NON-GOVERNMENTAL ILC UNITS

    There are none.

7. SINGLE-TYPE LIBRARY COOPERATIVES

    A. Receiving Continuing Financial Support from the State Library:

        Name: Chickasaw Library System
        Address: 22 Broadlawn Village
                            Ardmore, OK 73401
        Telephone: (405) 223-3164
        Administrator: Billie M. Day, Director
        Type of Library Served: p
        Federal Support: $ 958
        State Support: 427
        Local Support: 185,576
        Other Support: 5,971
        Total Support: $192,932

        Name: Choctaw Nation Multi-County Library
                            System
        Address: 401 N. Second Street
                            McAlester, OK 74501
        Telephone: (918) 426-0456
        Administrator: Bill Strain, Director
        Type of Library Served: p
        Federal Support: not reported
        State Support: not reported
        Local Support: not reported
        Total Support: $316,746   (continued)

7. SINGLE-TYPE LIBRARY COOPERATIVES (continued)

    A. Receiving Continuing Financial Support from the State Library:

    Name: Eastern Oklahoma District Library
    Address: 801 W. Okmulgee
                                    Muskogee, OK 74401
    Telephone: (918) 683-2846
    Administrator: James Wilkerson, Director
    Type of Library Served: p
    Federal Support: not reported
    State Support: not reported
    Local Support: not reported
    Total Support: $366,866

    Name: Oklahoma County Libraries System
    Address: 131 NW Third Street
                                    Oklahoma City, OK 73102
    Telephone: (405) 235-0571
    Administrator: Lee E. Brawner, Director
    Type of Library Served: p
    Federal Support: $ 13,512   (Fiscal 1975)
    Local Support: 1,704,865
    Other Support: 129,254
    Total Support: $1,847,631

    Name: Southern Prairie Library System
    Address: 221 N. Grady
                                    Altus, OK 73521
    Telephone: (405) 477-1930
    Administrator: Rama F. Widup
    Type of Library Served: p
    Federal Support: not reported
    State Support: 2,279
    Local Support: $69,050
    Other Support: not reported
    Total Support: $79,000

    Name: Western Plains Library System
    Address: 605 Avant
                                    Clinton, OK 73601
    Telephone: (405) 323-0974
    Administrator: Dee Ann Ray, Director
    Federal Support: not reported
    State Support: $ 4,100
    Local Support: 199,991
    Other Support: not reported
    Total Support: not reported

    Name: Tulsa City-County Library
    Address: 400 Civic Center
                                    Tulsa, OK 74103
    Telephone: (918) 581-5221

(continued)

7. SINGLE-TYPE LIBRARY COOPERATIVES (continued)

   A. Receiving Continuing Financial Support from the State Library:

```
        Administrator:                Pat Woodrum, Director
        Federal Support:              not reported
        State Support:                $    23,000
        Local Support:                $ 2,423,602
        Other Support:                not reported
        Total Support:                not reported

        Name:                         Pioneer Multi-County Library
        Address:                      225 N. Webster
                                      Norman, OK  73069
        Telephone:                    (405) 321-1481
        Administrator:                William H. Lowry, Director
        Type of Library Served:       p
        Federal Support:              $ 1,185
        State Support:                not reported
        Local Support:                318,090
        Other Support:                 36, 142
        Total Support:                355,417
```

   B. Receiving No Continuing Financial Support from the State Library:

   There are none.

8. MULTI-TYPE LIBRARY COOPERATIVES

   A. Receiving Continuing Financial Support from the State Library:

   There are none.

   B. Receiving No Continuing Financial Support from the State Library:

   There are none.

9. INTERLIBRARY COOPERATION FUNCTIONS

   A. Receiving Continuing Financial Support from the State Library:

	State Support	Federal Support Title I	Federal Support Title III	Other Support	Total Support
Interlibrary Loan	$68,530	$44,736	$30,000		$143,266
Continuing Education	$10,520	$29,905			$ 40,425

(continued)

9. INTERLIBRARY COOPERATION FUNCTIONS (continued)

A. Receiving Continuing Financial Support from the State Library:

	State Support	Federal Support Title I--Title III		Other Support	Total Support
Cooperative Acquisitions	None				
Cooperative Cataloging	None				
Cooperative Delivery	None				
Cooperative Processing	None				
Cooperative Reference	131,182	20,000	5,264		156,446
Cooperative Storage	None				
Legislative Assistance	52,260				52,260
Planning/Development		156,497	8,503		165,000
Union List of Serials	None				
TOTALS	$262,492	$251,138	$43,767		$557,397

B. Non-Financial Support Role of The State Library:

Cooperative storage on informal basis as last copy library.
Cooperative delivery - Union Lists of Serials committee work.

10. ILC COMMUNICATION DEVICES/SERVICE NETWORKS

A.

Device/Service	Support ($)	Equipment (#)	Participants
WATS & TWX	$28,800	16 Teletypewriters	16 Transmission sites

B. Non-financial Support Role of the State Library:

OCLC

11. MACHINE-READABLE DATA BASE REFERENCE SEARCHING SERVICES

Data Base/Vendor	Support ($)	Terminals (#)	Participants
Lockheed)		)	OTIS Transmission sites
SDC (	$10,000	(1	State Govt.
NYT)		)	agencies

12. INTERLIBRARY SERVICES TO SPECIAL GROUPS

 A.   Grant to Library for the Blind and Physically Handicapped.
      Grants to Institutional Libraries.

 B.   Consultant services to Institutional Libraries.

13. PARTICIPATION IN MULTI-STATE LIBRARY NETWORKS

 A.   Network   AMIGOS Financial support (FY78 $36,000)
                Services (OCLC, contractual for special projects)

      Network   Southwestern Library Interstate Cooperative
                Endeavor, Financial Support (FY78 $5,000)
                Continuing Education, planning and advice
 B.   There are none.

14. LEGAL BASES FOR MULTI-TYPE LIBRARY COOPERATION

      State legislation enabling interstate library compact:
      65 O.S. Sec. 6-101.

15. LEGAL BARRIERS AGAINST PARTICIPATION IN MULTI-TYPE LIBRARY COOP-
     ERATION

      65 O.S. Sec. 3-105 (schools and institutions of higher
      learning excluded).

1. REPORTING AGENCY

    A.   Oregon State Library
           Salem, OR 97310
           (503) 378-4243

    B.   Chief Officer: Marcia Lowell, State Librarian

    C.   Fiscal Year: 1978

2. OVERVIEW

Oregon Statutes (ORS 357.400) define as local government units authorized to operate public libraries, not only cities and counties, but also school districts, community college districts and special library districts. ORS 357.410(2) states that any local government unit may "Contract with an established public library or with a private society or corporation owning and controlling a secular or nonsectarian library for the purpose of providing free use of the library for the residents of the local government unit, under such terms and conditions as may be agreed upon."

In Oregon there is currently one regional cooperative library service based on a community college district covering two counties and parts of others through contract service from the region's 17 municipal and one community college library. This is supported by a three year serial levy on real property within the district and provides all residents access to all public libraries in the district, plus interlibrary loan, books by mail and bookmobile service to rural areas, and cooperative film programs. This serves about 246,000 persons.

Six counties with a total of about 265,000 have formed a federation for interlibrary loan and continuing education. This federation has no tax base and is supported through user fees and member contributions.

Oregon Laws 1977 Chapter 261 permits the use of state aid to public libraries grant funds for establishing regional libraries.

3. NUMBER OF LIBRARIES IN THE STATE

        Academic: 47
        Public: 127
        School: 1,410 est.
           Public: 1,270
           Private: 140 est.

(continued)

3. NUMBER OF LIBRARIES IN THE STATE (continued)

>   Special: 62 est.
>   Profit: 15 est.
>   Non-Profit: 47 est.
>
>   TOTAL: 1,646 est.

4. STATE AGENCY INTERLIBRARY COOPERATION UNIT

>   A.   There is no existing unit nor plans to create one.
>   B.   Statewide and Institutional Library Development
>   Ralph Delamarter, Senior Consultant

5. OTHER STATE-LEVEL GOVERNMENTAL ILC UNITS

>   There are none.

6. OTHER STATE-LEVEL NON-GOVERNMENTAL ILC UNITS

>   Unit Name: Oregon Library Association
>   Address: Southern Oregon State College Library
>   1250 Siskiyou Blvd.
>   Ashland, Oregon   97520
>   Telephone: (503) 482-6445
>   Administrator: Richard Moore, President
>   Activity: Library Development Committee

7. SINGLE-TYPE LIBRARY COOPERATIVES

>   A.   There are none receiving continuing state library support.
>
>   B.   There are none to receive state library support.
>
>   C.   There are none which receive occasional support from the state
>   library.

8. MULTI-TYPE LIBRARY COOPERATIVES

>   A.   Receiving Continuing Support from the State Library:
>   There are none.
>
>   B.   Receiving No Continuing Support from the State Library:

>   Name: Southern Oregon Library Federation
>   Address: c/o Jackson County Library
>   Medford, OR   97501
>   Telephone: 776-7281
>   Administrator: Mrs. Ronnie Budge, President
>   Types of Libraries Served: a, p
>   Sponsoring Body: Southern Oregon Library Federation
>   Source of Support: Member assessment

(continued)

8. MULTI-TYPE LIBRARY COOPERATIVES (continued)

> Name: Chemeketa Cooperative Regional Library Service
> Address: c/o McMinnville Public Library,
>   McMinnville, OR 97128
> Telephone: 472-9371
> Administrator: Mrs. Rose Mary Caughran, Chairperson
> Types of Libraries Served: a, p
> Sponsoring Body: MidWillamette Council of Governments
> Source of Support: Real property tax (3-year serial levy)

C. Receiving Occasional Support from the State Library:

There are none.

9. INTERLIBRARY COOPERATION FUNCTIONS

A.

	State Support	Federal Support Title I	Federal Support Title II	Other Support	Total Support
Interlibrary Loan	NA	78,000	12,285		90,285*
Continuing Education		23,530			23,530
Cooperative Acquisitions		42,780			42,780
Cooperative Cataloging					
Cooperative Delivery					
Cooperative Processing					
Cooperative Reference					
Cooperative Storage					
Legislative Assistance	NA				
Planning/Development	33,478	81,923			115,401
Union List of Serials		19,000			19,000
TOTAL SUPPORT	$33,478*	$245,233	$12,285		$290,996

*   It is impossible to break out state budget contributions in these areas.

B. NON-FINANCIAL SUPPORT ROLE OF THE STATE LIBRARY:

Consultant service.

10. ILC COMMUNICATION DEVICES/SERVICE NETWORKS

Device/Service	Support $	Equipment #	Participants
In-WATS	$8,500		185 public libraries
Telephone Credit Cards	4,500		185 public libraries

B. There is no non-financial support for these services.

11. MACHINE-READABLE DATA BASE REFERENCE SEARCHING SERVICES

Data Base/Vendor	Support $	Terminals #	Participants
Lockheed	$2,070+	1	Statewide

12. INTERLIBRARY SERVICES TO SPECIAL GROUPS

A. Services to Special Groups Provided Through Cooperative
    Arrangements: There are none.

B. Non-Financial Support Role of the State Library: There is
    none.

13. PARTICIPATION IN MULTI-STATE LIBRARY NETWORKS

A. Network: Western Council of State Librarians
    Financial Support: $3,000
    Participation: Member
    Services Used: Continuing Education Planning

B. There are none.

14. LEGAL BASES FOR MULTI-TYPE LIBRARY COOPERATION

American Library Laws   p.1522-1525, 1532, 1534

15. LEGAL BARRIERS AGAINST PARTICIPATION IN MULTI-TYPE LIBRARY
     COOPERATION

There are none.

1. REPORTING AGENCY

A. Pennsylvania Department of Education
State Library of Pennsylvania
PO Box 1601
Harrisburg, PA 17126
(717) 787-2646

B. Chief Officer: Ernest E. Doerschuk, Jr., State Librarian

C. Fiscal Year: 1978

2. OVERVIEW

Under provisions of The Library Code, twenty-seven public libraries
have been designated as District Library Centers; District Library
Centers provide supplementary library services to local public libraries within their districts, coordinate the services of those
libraries which by contract become part of the district library center system, and provide consultant assistance to local libraries and
to local governments or communities which seek to establish libraries.
The entire state is included in the twenty-seven districts. State
aid funds are paid to the district library centers for district services, in addition to the state aid which they receive as local
public libraries. Standards for district library centers have been
developed by the State Library, and approved by the Adivsory Council
on Library Development.

There is no legislation authorizing multi-type cooperative systems,
and no state funding. Pennsylvania libraries have actively joined
in multi-type library activities, as subsequent parts of this report
will show.

3. NUMBER OF LIBRARIES IN THE STATE

Academic:	223
Public:	380
School:	3,317+
Public:	3,317 (actual figure not available; this is number
Private:	Unknown of buildings)
Special:	376+
Profit:	Breakdown between profit and non-profit not made
Non-profit:	Breakdown between profit and non-profit not made
Total:	4,296+

4. STATE AGENCY INTERLIBRARY COOPERATION UNIT

A. Unit name: Bureau of Library Development
Person in Charge: David R. Hoffman, Coordinator,
Interlibrary Cooperation

(continued)

4. STATE AGENCY INTERLIBRARY COOPERATION (continued)

B. Unit name: General Library Bureau
   Person in Charge: Mrs. Mirjana Tolmachev, Coordinator
                       User Services

5. OTHER STATE-LEVEL GOVERNMENTAL ILC UNITS

   There are none.

6. OTHER STATE-LEVEL NON-GOVERNMENTAL ILC UNITS

   Unit Name: Council of Pennsylvania Library Networks
   Address: c/o State Library of Pennsylvania
                       Box 1601
                       Harrisburg, PA   17126
   Telephone: (717) 787-8007
   Administrator: There is none; the State Librarian acts as
                       chairman of the Council
   Activities: The Council of Pennsylvania Library Networks
                       is an informal group with representatives from
                       thirteen organizations or state-wide programs
                       which meets periodically to (a) share infor-
                       mation among network representatives, (b)
                       identify, produce, or distribute information
                       about cooperative activities, (c) sponsor or
                       participate in programs or conferences, (d)
                       undertake when appropriate joint planning
                       among cooperative groups, and (e) advise the
                       State Librarian on matters concerning the State
                       Library's role in library cooperation.

7. SINGLE-TYPE LIBRARY COOPERATIVES

   A. Receiving Continuing Financial Support from the State Library:

      Name: Aliquippa District Library Center
                         (B. F. Jones Memorial Library)
      Address: 633 Franklin Avenue
                         Aliquippa, PA   15001
      Telephone: (412) 375-7174
      Administrator: Frank E. Virostek, Coordinator
      Type of Library Served: p
      Federal Support: $9,711*
      State Support: $52,831
      Local Support: -0-
      Other Support: -0-
      Total Support: $62,542

      Name: Allentown District Library Center
                         (Allentown Public Library)
      Address: 914 Hamilton Mall
                         Allentown, PA   18101   (continued)

289

7. SINGLE-TYPE LIBRARY COOPERATIVES (continued)

```
Telephone:          (215) 434-4894
Administrator:      Kathryn Stephanoff, Director
Type of Library Served:  p
Federal Support:    $15,112*
State Support:      $71,083
Local Support:      -0-
Other Support:      -0-
Total Support:      $86,195


Name:               Altoona District Library Center
                    (Altoona Area Public Library)
Address:            1600 Fifth Avenue
                    Altoona, PA  16602
Telephone:          (814) 946-0417
Administrator:      Patricia J. Connell, Director
Type of Library Served:  p
Federal Support:    $13,369*
State Support:      $54,436
Local Support:      -0-
Other Support:      -0-
Total Support:      $67,805


Name:               Bellefonte District Library Center
                    (Centre County Library)
Address:            200 North Allegheny Street
                    Bellefonte, PA  16823
Telephone:          (814) 355-1516
Administrator:      Gary D. Wolfe, Coordinator of District Services
Type of Library Served:  p
Federal Support:    $35,708*
State Support:      $56,543
Local Support:      -0-
Other Support:      -0-
Total Support:      $92,251


Name:               Bethlehem District Library Center
                    (Bethlehem Public Library)
Address:            11 West Church Street
                    Bethlehem, PA  18018
Telephone:          (215) 867-3761
Administrator:      Jack M. Berk, Director
Type of Library Served:  p
Federal Support:    $13,656*
State Support:      $37,488
Local Support:      -0-
Other Support:      -0-
Total Support:      $51,144


Name:               Chambersburg District Library Center
                    (Conococheague District Library)
```

(continued)

7. SINGLE-TYPE LIBRARY COOPERATIVES (continued)

Address: 102 North Main Street
Chambersburg, PA 17201
Telephone: (717) 263-1054
Administrator: Richard T. Ezell, Director
Type of Library Served: p
Federal Support: $20,491*
State Support: $31,828
Local Support: -0-
Other Support: -0-
Total Support: $52,319

Name: Clarion District Library Association
(Clarion Free Library)
Address: Ross Memorial Building
P.O. Box 325
Clarion, PA 16214
Telephone: (814) 226-6340
Administrator: Allan Gray, Coordinator of District Services
Type of Library Served: p
Federal Support: $6,500*
State Support: $39,993
Local Support: -0-
Other Support: -0-
Total Support: $46,493

Name: Doylestown District Library Center
(Bucks County Free Library)
Address: 50 North Main Street
Doylestown, PA 18901
Telephone: (215) 348-9081
Administrator: Harry S. Weeks, Director
Type of Library Served: p
Federal Support: $13,625*
State Support: $109,769
Local Support: -0-
Other Support: -0-
Total Support: $123,394

Name: Easton District Library Center
(Easton Area Public Library)
Address: Sixth and Church Streets
Easton, PA 18042
Telephone: (215) 258-2917
Administrator: Quentin de Streel, Director
Type of Library Served: p
Federal Support: $15,112*
State Support: $34,654
Local Support: -0-
Other Support: -0-
Total Support: $49,766 (continued)

7. SINGLE-TYPE LIBRARY COOPERATIVES (continued)

      Name: Erie District Library Center
                               (Erie City and County Library)
      Address: P.O. Box 1631
                               Erie, PA   16501

      Telephone: (814) 452-2333
      Administrator: Kenneth G. Sivulich, Executive Director
      Type of Library Served: p
      Federal Support: $14,313*
      State Support: $86,479
      Local Support: -0-
      Other Support: -0-
      Total Support: $100,792

      Name: Harrisburg District Library Center
                               (Dauphin County Library)
      Address: Front and Walnut Streets
                               Harrisburg, PA   17101
      Telephone: (717) 234-4961
      Administrator: Harry R. Courtright, Driector
      Type of Library Served: p
      Federal Support: $16,325*
      State Support: $126,882
      Local Support: -0-
      Other Support: -0-
      Total Support: $143,207

      Name: Johnstown District Library Center
                               (Cambria County Library System)
      Address: 248 Main Street
                               Johnstown, PA   15901
      Telephone: (814) 536-5131
      Administrator: Robert N. Costa, Director
      Type of Library Served: p
      Federal Support: $11,658*
      State Support: $86,322
      Local Support: -0-
      Other Support: -0-
      Total Support: $97,980

      Name: Lancaster District Library Center
                               (Lancaster County Library)
      Address: 125 North Duke Street
                               Lancaster, PA   17602
      Telephone: (717) 394-2651
      Administrator: Robert N. Case, Director
      Type of Library Served: p
      Federal Support: $19,964*
      State Support: $81,307
      Local Support: -0-
      Other Support: -0-
      Total Support: $101,271   (continued)

7. SINGLE-TYPE LIBRARY COOPERATIVES (continued)

Name: Monessen District Library Center
                   (Monessen Public Library)
Address: 326 Donner Avenue
                   Monessen, PA 15062
Telephone: (412) 684-4750
Administrator: Frank K. Shaffer, Director
Type of Library Served: p
Federal Support: $9,534*
State Support: $64,956
Local Support: -0-
Other Support: -0-
Total Support: $74,490

Name: New Castle District Library Center
                   (New Castle Public Library)
Address: 106 East North Street
                   New Castle, PA 16101
Telephone: (412) 658-6659
Administrator: Helen M. Roux, Director
Type of Library Served: p
Federal Support: $11,245 *
State Support: $110,658
Local Support: -0-
Other Support: -0-
Total Support: $121,903

Name: Norristown District Library Center
                   (Montgomery County-Norristown Public Library)
Address: Swede and Elm Streets
                   Norristown, PA 19401
Telephone: (215) 277-3355
Administrator: Mrs. Pearl Frankenfield, Director
Type of Library Served: p
Federal Support: $27,242*
State Support: $160,616
Local Support: -0-
Other Support: -0-
Total Support: $187,858

Name: Philadelphia District Library Center
                   (Free Library of Philadelphia)
Address: Logan Square
                   Philadelphia, PA 19103
Telephone: (215) 686-5300
Administrator: Keith Doms, Director
Type of Library Served: p
Federal Support: $23,603*
State Support: $638,761
Local Support: -0-
Other Support: -0-   (continued)

7. SINGLE-TYPE LIBRARY COOPERATIVES (continued)

    Total Support: $662,364

    Name: Pittsburgh District Library Center
                              (Carnegie Library of Pittsburgh)
    Address: 4400 Forbes Avenue
                              Pittsburgh, PA 15213
    Telephone: (412) 622-3100
    Administrator: Anthony A. Martin, Director
    Type of Library Served: p
    Federal Support: $15,788*
    State Support: $480,304
    Local Support: -0-
    Other Support: -0-
    Total Support: $496,092

    Name: Pottsville District Center
                              (Pottsville Free Public Library)
    Address: Third and Market Streets
                              Pottsville, PA 17901
    Telephone: (717) 622-8880
    Administrator: Malcolm Hill, Director
    Type of Library Served: p
    Federal Support: $20,491*
    State Support: $50,792
    Local Support: -0-
    Other Support: -0-
    Total Support: $71,283

    Name: Reading District Library Center
                              (Reading Public Library)
    Address: Fifth and Franklin Streets
                              Reading, PA 19602
    Telephone: (215) 374-4548
    Administrator: Edmond J. Doherty, Director
    Type of Library Served: p
    Federal Support: $16,325*
    State Support: $75,291
    Local Support: -0-
    Other Support: -0-
    Total Support: $91,616

    Name: Scranton District Library Center
                              (Scranton Public Library)
    Address: Washington Avenue and Vine Street
                              Scranton, PA 18503
    Telephone: (717) 961-2451
    Administrator: Sumner F. White, Director
    Type of Library Served: p
    Federal Support: $16,132*
    State Support: $81,242

(continued)

7. SINGLE-TYPE LIBRARY COOPERATIVES (continued)

Local Support: -0-
Other Support: -0-
Total Support: $97,374

Name: Warren District Library Center
                    (Warren Library Association)
Address: P.O. Box 489
                    Warren, PA 16365
Telephone: (814) 723-4650
Administrator: Ann Lesser, Director
Type of Library Served: p
Federal Support: $11,186*
State Support: $37,347
Local Support: -0-
Other Support: -0-
Total Support: $48,533

Name: Washington District Library Center
                    (Citizens Library)
Address: 55 South College Street
                    Washington, PA 15301
Telephone: (412) 222-2400
Administrator: Mrs. Louise H. Stuart, Director
Type of Library Served: p
Federal Support: $9,298*
State Support: $55,426
Local Support: -0-
Other Support: -0-
Total Support: $64,724

Name: West Chester District Library Center
                    (Chester County Public Library)
Address: 235 West Market Street
                    West Chester, PA 19380
Telephone: (215) 696-8960
Administrator: Robert O. Sondrol, Director
Type of Library Served: p
Federal Support: $18,144*
State Support: $71,608
Local Support: -0-
Other Support: -0-
Total Support: $89,752

Name: Wilkes-Barre District Library Center
                    (Osterhout Free Library)
Address: 71 South Franklin Street
                    Wilkes-Barre, PA 18701
Telephone: (717) 823-0156
Administrator: Joan Costello, Director
Type of Library Served: p

(continued)

7. SINGLE-TYPE LIBRARY COOPERATIVE (continued)

    Federal Support: $21,201
    State Support: $88,003
    Local Support: -0-
    Other Support: -0-
    Total Support: $109,204

    Name: Williamsport District Library Center
                  (James V. Brown Library)
    Address: 19 East Fourth Street
                  Williamsport, PA 17701
    Telephone: (717) 326-0536
    Administrator: Robert C. Machinski, Director
    Type of Library Served: p
    Federal Support: $12,686*
    State Support: $114,158
    Local Support: -0-
    Other Support: -0-
    Total Support: $126,844

    Name: York District Library Center
                  (Martin Memorial Library)
    Address: 159 East Market Street
                  York, PA 17401
    Telephone: (717) 843-3978
    Administrator: Marycatherine Weaver, Director
    Type of Library Served: p
    Federal Support: $15,551*
    State Support: $83,882
    Local Support: -0-
    Other Support: -0-
    Total Support: $99,433

  *District Library Center programs as such are supported with
   state funds in the amount of 25¢ per capita for population in
   the district. Federal funds may be granted on a project basis
   but are not assured continuing funds.

B. Receiving No Continuing Financial Support from the State Library:

    Name: ABC 16mm Film Consortium
    Address: See District Library Centers in Altoona,
                  Bellefonte, Johnstown
    Telephone: See above
    Administrator: See District Library Centers above
    Type of Library Served: p
    Sponsoring Body: See above
    Source(s) of Support: DLC funds and local budgets

    Name: ABE Tri-District
    Address: See District Library Centers in Allentown,

(continued)

7. SINGLE-TYPE LIBRARY COOPERATIVES (continued)

B. Receiving No Continuing Financial Support from the State Library:

```
                              Bethlehem, Easton
      Telephone:              See above
      Administrator:          See District Library Centers above
      Type of Library Served:  p
      Sponsoring Body:        See above
      Source(s) of Support:   DLC funds


      Name:                   Central Pennsylvania Consortium
      Address:                c/o Gettysburg College
                              Gettysburg, PA   17325
      Telephone:              (717) 334-3131
      Administrator:          Arden K. Smith, Director
      Type of Library Served:  a
      Source(s) of Support:   Uniform fee paid by members


      Name:                   Council of Pennsylvania State College and
                              University Library Directors
      Address:                c/o Robert S. Bravard
                              Stevenson Library
                              Lock Haven State College
                              Lock Haven, PA   17745
      Telephone:              (717) 748-5351
      Administrator:          Organization has no staff
      Type of Library Served:  a
      Sponsoring Body:        N/A
      Source(s) of Support:   Organization has no budget


      Name:                   District Library Center Administrators
                              Organization
      Address:                c/o Jack M. Berk
                              Bethlehem Public Library
                              11 West Church Street
                              Bethlehem, PA   18018
      Telephone:              (215) 867-3761
      Administrator:          Organization has no staff
      Type of Library Served:  p
      Sponsoring Body:        N/A
      Source(s) of Support:   Organization has no budget.


      Name:                   Erie Medical Librarians Group
                              c/o St. Vincent Health Center Library
                              232 West 25th Street
                              Erie, PA   16512
      Telephone:              (814) 459-4000
      Administrator:          Organization has no staff
      Type of Library Served:  sp
      Sponsoring Body:        N/A
      Source(s) of Support:   Organization has no budget


      Name:                   Health Information Library Network of North-
```
(continued)

7B.   SINGLE-TYPE LIBRARY COOPERATIVES (continued)

                        eastern Pennsylvania
        Address: c/o Medical Library
                        Veterans' Administration Hospital
                        Wilkes-Barre, Pa 18711
        Telephone: (717)824-3521
        Administrator: Organization has no staff
        Type of Library Served: sp
        Sponsoring Body: Northeastern Pennsylvania Bibliographic
                        Center
        Source(s) of Support: Uniform fee paid by member libraries

        Name: Lancaster, York, Conococheague Film Consor-
                        tium
        Address: c/o Martin Memorial Library
                        159 East Market Street
                        York, PA 17401
        Telephone: (717) 843-3978
        Administrator: Organization has no staff
        Type of Library Served: p
        Sponsoring Body: District Library Centers in Lancaster, York,
                        and Chambersburg
        Source(s) of Support: DLC funds

        Name: Lehigh Valley Area Health Education Center
                        Health Sciences Libraries Consortium
        Address: Room 2422 EP
                        1627 Chew Street
                        Allentown, PA 18102
        Telephone: (215) 821-2435
        Administrator: Karen Weston, Library Coordinator
        Type of Library Served: sp
        Sponsoring Body: Lehigh Valley Area Health Education Center
        Source(s) of Support: Donated services

        Name: Lehigh Valley Association of Independent
                        College Libraries
        Address: 87 West Church Street
                        Bethlehem, PA 18018
        Telephone: (215) 691-6131
        Administrator: Dr. Frank T. Conlon, LVAIC Coordinator
        Type of Library Served: a
        Sponsoring Body: Lehigh Valley Association of Independent
                        Colleges
        Source(s) of Support: College funds

        Name: Pittsburgh-East Hospital Library Cooperative
        Address: c/o Medical Library
                        St. Margaret Memorial Hospital
                        265 East 46th Street
                        Pittsburgh, PA 15201
                                        (continued)

7B. SINGLE-TYPE LIBRARY COOPERATIVES (continued)

  B. Receiving No Continuing Financial Support from the State Library:

    Telephone: (412) 622-7120
    Type of Library Served: sp
    Sponsoring Body: N/A
    Source(s) of Support: Hospitals' funds

    Name: Somerset County Medical Library Consortium
    Address: c/o Somerset State Hospital Library
                  Box 631
                  Somerset, PA 15501
    Telephone: (814) 445-6501
    Administrator: Organization has no staff
    Type of Library Served: sp
    Sponsoring Body: N/A
    Source(s) of Support: Hospitals' funds

    Name: Tri-County Film Cooperative
    Address: See District Library Centers in Doylestown,
                  Norristown, West Chester
    Telephone: See above
    Administrator: Organization has no staff
    Type of Library Served: p
    Sponsoring Body: See above
    Source(s) of Support: DLC funds

    Name: Tri-State College Library Cooperative
    Address: c/o Gertrude Kistler Memorial Library
                  Rosemont College
                  Rosemont, PA 19010
    Telephone: (215) 525-0796
    Administrator: Mrs. Sylva Baker, Executive Secretary
    Type of Library Served: a
    Sponsoring Body: N/A
    Source(s) of Support: Membership dues

    Name: Western Pennsylvania Public Library 16mm Film
                  Cooperative
    Address: See District Library Centers in Aliquippa,
                  Clarion, Erie, New Castle, Warren
    Telephone: See above
    Administrator: Organization has no staff
    Type of Library Served: p
    Sponsoring Body: See above
    Source(s) of Support: DLC funds

8. MULTI-TYPE LIBRARY COOPERATIVES

  A. Receiving Continuing Financial Support from the State Library:

    Name: Regional Library Resource Center Program
                                            (continued)

8. MULTI-TYPE LIBRARY COOPERATIVES (continued)

    Address: c/o State Library of Pennsylvania
                             PO Box 1601
                             Harrisburg, PA 17126
    Telephone: (717) 787-2646
    Administrator: Ernest E. Doerschuk, Jr., State Librarian
    Type of Library Served: a, p*
    Federal Support: -0-
    State Support: $400,000
    Local Support: -0-
    Other Support: -0-
    Total Support: $400,000

*Users of this state-supported services are public libraries, al-
though one of the resource center libraries is an academic
library

B. Receiving No Continuing Financial Support from the State Library:

    Name: Associated College Libraries of Central Penn-
                             sylvania
    Address: c/o Virginia Christopher, ACLCP Secretary
                             Elizabethtown College Library
                             Elizabethtown, PA 17022
    Telephone: (717) 367-1151
    Administrator: Organization has no staff
    Type of Library Served: a, p
    Sponsoring Body: N/A
    Source(s) of Support: Uniform fee paid by member libraries

    Name: Mid-Eastern Regional Medical Library Service
    Address: c/o College of Physicians of Philadelphia
                             19 South 22nd Street
                             Philadelphia, PA 19103
    Telephone: (215) 561-6050
    Administrator: June H. Fulton, Director, MERMLS
    Type of Library Served: a, p, sp
    Sponsoring Body: College of Physicians of Philadelphia
    Source(s) of Support: Federal contract funds through NLM

    Name: Northeastern Pennsylvania Bibliographic Center
    Address: D. Leonard Corgan Library
                             King's College
                             14 West Jackson Street
                             Wilkes-Barre, PA 18711
    Telephone: (717) 824-9931
    Administrator: Mary Barrett, Director
    Type of Library Served: a, p, sp
    Sponsoring Body: N/A
    Source(s) of Support: Uniform fee paid by members libraries

(continued)

8. MULTI-TYPE LIBRARY COOPERATIVES (continued)

Name: Northwest Interlibrary Cooperative of Pennsyl-
                         vania
Address: c/o Behrend College Library
                         Pennsylvania State University
                         Station Road
                         Erie, PA 16510
Telephone: (814) 898-1511, ext. 273
Administrator: Organization has no staff
Type of Library Served: a, p, sp
Sponsoring Body: N/A
Source(s) of Support: Organization has no budget

Name: PALINET and Union Library Catalogue of Pennsyl-
                         vania
Address: 3420 Walnut Street
                         Philadelphia, PA 19174
Telephone: (215) 382-7031
Administrator: Robert C. Stewart, Executive Director
Type of Library Served: a, p, sp
Sponsoring Body: N/A
Source(s) of Support: Fees paid by member libraries

Name: Pittsburgh Regional Library Center
Address: Chatham College
                         Pittsburgh, PA 15232
Telephone: (412) 441-6409
Administrator: Stephen B. Folts, Executive Director
Type of Library Served: a, p, sp
Sponsoring Body: N/A
Source(s) of Support: Fees paid by member libraries

Name: School Delivery Service
Address: c/o Lancaster-Lebanon Intermediate Unit 13
                         1110 Enterprise Road
                         East Petersburg, PA 17520
Telephone: (717) 569-7331
Administrator: William L. Counts, Jr., Assistant Executive
                         Director, Programs
Type of Library Served: p, sch
Sponsoring Body: Intermediate Unit 13 and Lancaster County
                         Library
Source(s) of Support: County Library and IU funds

Name: Susquehanna Library Cooperative
Address: c/o Ellen Clarke Bertrand Library
                         Bucknell University
                         Lewisburg, PA 17837
Telephone: (717) 524-3056
Administrator: Organization has no staff
Type of Library Served: a, p, sp

(continued)

8. MULTI-TYPE LIBRARY COOPERATIVES (continued)

        Sponsoring Body: N/A
        Source(s) of Support: Uniform fee paid by member libraries

        Name: Tri-County Library Consortium
        Address: c/o New Castle District Library Center
                                106 East North Street
                                New Castle, PA 16101
        Telephone: (814) 658-6659
        Administrator: Organization has no staff
        Type of Library Served: a, p, sch, sp
        Sponsoring Body: New Castle District Library Center
        Source(s) of Support: Organization has no budget

        Name: West Metropolitan Health Information and
                                Library Consortium
        Address: 15th & Upland Avenue
                                Upland, Chester, PA   19013
        Telephone: (215) 874-6853
        Administrator: (position vacant)
        Type of Library Served: a, p, sp
        Source(s) of Support: Fees paid by member libraries and grant
                                support from NLM

C. Other (Receiving Occasional Support from the State Library):

        Name: Interlibrary Delivery Service of Pennsylvania
        Address: c/o Dauphin County Library System
                                Front and Walnut Streets
                                Harrisburg, PA 17101
        Telephone: (717) 234-4961
        Administrator: David Reynolds, Coordinator
        Type of Library Served: a, p, sp
        Sponsoring Body: N/A
        Source(s) of Support: Uniform fee paid by member libraries,
                                supplemented by occasional LSCA grants
                                from State Library

9. INTERLIBRARY COOPERATION FUNCTIONS

    A. Receiving Continuing Financial Support from the State Library

	State Support	Federal Support Title I	Title III	Other Support	Total Support
Interlibrary Loan	*				*
Continuing Education	*				*
Cooperative Acquisitions	*				*
Cooperative Cataloging	*				*
Cooperative Delivery	*				*
Cooperative Processing	*				*

(continued)

9. INTERLIBRARY COOPERATION FUNCTIONS (continued)

Cooperative Reference	*	*
Cooperative Storage	*	*
Legislative Assistance		
Planning/Development	*	*
Union Lists of Serials	*	*
Other		

Total support	$3,377,575	$3,377,575

*All of these functions are carried out to some extent by one or more of the state-funded district library centers or the regional library resource centers, but a breakdown of costs by object is not available. Federal funds may be used to support any of these functions on a project basis, but no continuing federal funding is used for these services.

B. NON-FINANCIAL SUPPORT ROLE OF THE STATE LIBRARY:

Consultant assistance from the Bureau of Library Development to libraries of all kinds wishing to participate in or initiate cooperative programs with libraries of the same or other types.

10. ILC COMMUNICATION DEVICES/SERVICE NETWORKS

A.
Device/Service	Support ($)	Equipment (#)	Participants
Telephone	No		
Teletype	No*	38	38
Telefacsimile	No		
On-line computer terminals (OCLC)	$231,962**	25	25 - p

*No state support; over the past ten years, however, LSCA funds have been used to purchase 38 TWX machines for public and academic libraries
**Support from LSCA funds; OCLC use will be fully funded with local funds after FY 78.

B. NON-FINANCIAL SUPPORT ROLE OF THE STATE LIBRARY:

Consultant assistance from the Bureau of Library Development to libraries of all kinds wishing to acquire or use specialized communication systems

11. MACHINE-READABLE DATA BASE REFERENCE SEARCHING SERVICES

There were none receiving state support in 1977.

12. INTERLIBRARY SERVICES TO SPECIAL GROUPS

    A. Services   State Support   State Support*

       Services to blind and physically
       handicapped, under contract with
       Free Library of Philadelphia and
       Carnegie Library of Pittsburgh $858,000*

       *This is the only program of services to special groups re-
       ceiving continuing funding from the State Library; LSCA funds
       are used on a project basis to augment this service and also
       to assist in programs of services to the institutionalized, aged,
       special language groups, and disadvantaged persons.

    B. NON-FINANCIAL SUPPORT ROLE OF THE STATE LIBRARY:

       Consultant service from the Bureau of Library Development is
       available to libraries, institutions, and organizations in
       planning and coordinating cooperative activities for special
       groups.

13. PARTICIPATION IN MULTI-STATE LIBRARY NETWORKS

    A. Networks in which the state holds membership:

       Network: PALINET and Union Library Catalogue of
                            Pennsylvania
       Financial Support: Membership fee
       Participation: Member
       Services Used: OCLC system for cataloging and interlibrary
                            loan location

       Network: Center for Research Libraries
       Financial Support: Membership fee
       Participation: Member
       Services Used: Interlibrary loan and deposit of materials

    B. Networks headquartered in Pennsylvania in which the state li-
       brary agency does not hold membership:

       Network: Pittsburgh Regional Library Center (PRLC)
       Address: Chatham College
                            Pittsburgh, PA 15232
       Administrator: Stephen B. Foltz, Executive Director
       Financial Support: Membership fees, grants
       Area Served: Pennsylvania (western), West Virginia

14. LEGAL BASES FOR MULTI-TYPE LIBRARY COOPERATION

Only Section 201 (17) of the Library Code as amended, which authorizes the State Library to "receive funds allocated to the State for library purposes by the Federal government or by private agencies and to administer such funds in library maintenance, improvement or extension programs consistent with Federal and State library objectives."

15. LEGAL BARRIERS AGAINST PARTICIPATION IN MULTI-TYPE LIBRARY COOPERATION

There are no legal barriers.

RHODE ISLAND

1. REPORTING AGENCY

    A. R.I. Department of State Library Services
        95 Davis Street, Providence, R.I. 02908
        401-277-2726

    B. Chief Officer: Jewel Drickamer, Director

    C. Fiscal Year: 1978

2. OVERVIEW

    Since 1968 Rhode Island has had a statewide library network.
    In 1977 all but two towns are included. The state is covered
    by five Interrelated Library Systems which serve the entire
    population and work toward the coordination of all types of
    libraries.

    Section 29-6-1 of Rhode Island law (Chapter 3.1) states it to
    be the policy of this state to coordinate on a cooperative
    basis the resources of academic, free public, school and
    special libraries. Sections 29-6-7, 29-6-7.1, 29-6-8, and
    29-6-9 authorize the designation and funding of the libraries
    serving the network. Two academic libraries were newly
    designated to serve as Special Research Centers in fiscal 1978.
    Interlibrary loan and library development are the two chief
    cooperative activities.

3. NUMBER OF LIBRARIES IN THE STATE

Academic:	13
Public:	48
School:	492
Public:	379
Private:	113
Special:	84
Profit:	30
Non-profit:	54
Total	637

4. STATE AGENCY INTERLIBRARY COOPERATION UNIT

    A. Unit Name: Division of Planning and Development
        Person in Charge: Beverly A. Jones, Chief

    B. There are none.

5. OTHER STATE-LEVEL GOVERNMENTAL ILC UNITS

    There are none.

6. OTHER STATE-LEVEL NON-GOVERNMENTAL ILC UNITS

> Organization: Consortium of Rhode Island Academic and Research
> Libraries
> Address: Bryant College Library
> John Mowry Road, Smithfield, R.I. 02917
> Administrator: John P. Hannon, Director
> Telephone: 401-231-1200
> Cooperative activity: Coordinates the activities of this type
> of research library - no formal
> organization

7. SINGLE-TYPE LIBRARY COOPERATIVES

> A. Receiving Continuing Financial Support from the State
> Library:

> There are none.

> B. Receiving No Continuing Financial Support from the State
> Library:

> Name: Woonasquaget A-V Cooperative
> North Providence Union Free
> Library
> Address: 8 George Street, North Providence,
> R.I. 02911
> Telephone: 401-231-5300
> Administrator: Mary Ellen Hardiman, Librarian
> Type of Library Served: P
> Sponsoring Body: cooperating libraries
> Source (s) of Support: cooperating libraries

> C. Other:

> There are none.

8. MULTI-TYPE LIBRARY COOPERATIVES

> A. Receiving Continuing Financial Support from the State
> Library:

> Name: Rhode Island Interrelated Library
> Network
> Address: 95 Davis Street, Providence, R.I.
> 02908
> Telephone: 401-277-2726
> Administrator: Jewel Drickamer, Director
> Types of Libraries Served: a, p, sch, sp
> Federal Support: $151,005
> State Support: $296,557
> Local Support: -0-

(continued)

8. MULTI-TYPE LIBRARY COOPERATIVES (continued)

> A. Other Support: -0-
> Total Support: $447,562

Name:	Rhode Island Library Film Cooperative
Address:	600 Sandy Lane, Warwick, R.I. 02886
Telephone:	401-739-2278
Administrator:	Richard W. Robbins, Director
Types of Libraries Served:	a, p, sch, sp
Federal Support:	-0-
State Support:	$30,000
Local Support:	*
Other Support:	$12,775
Total Support:	*

> *Participating public libraries pay an assessment of 2½ cents per capita minimum, others pay a flat fee. Total amount of support varies from year to year.

> B. Receiving No Continuing Financial Support from the State Library:

> There are none.

> C. Other:

> There are none.

9. INTERLIBRARY COOPERATION FUNCTIONS

> A. Receiving Continuing Financial Support from the State Library:

	State Support	Federal Support Title I	Title III	Other Support	Total Support
Interlibrary Loan	X	X	X	The Depart-	
Continuing Education	X	X		ment's budget	
Cooperative Acquisitions	none	none	none	is a meld of	
Cooperative Cataloging	none	none	none	state and	
Cooperative Delivery	X	X	X	federal funds	
Cooperative Processing	none	none	none	and amounts	
Cooperative Reference	X	X	X	for individ-	
Cooperative Storage	none	none	none	ual activities	
Legislative Assistance	none	none	none	separately	
Planning/Development	X	X	X	cannot be	
Union Lists of Serials	none	none	none	broken out.	
Other (please specify)				Total $703,485 est.	

9. INTERLIBRARY COOPERATION FUNCTIONS (continued)

    B. Non-financial Support Role of the State Library:

        There is no non-financial support role.

10. ILC COMMUNICATION DEVICES / SERVICE NETWORKS

    A.

DEVICE/SERVICE	SUPPORT ($)	EQUIPMENT (#)	PARTICIPANTS
Teletype	$10,000	9	9
Telex		1	

    B. Non-financial Support Role of the State Library:

        There is no non-financial support role for
        these services.

11. MACHINE-READABLE DATA BASE REFERENCE SEARCHING SERVICES

    There are none.

12. INTERLIBRARY SERVICE TO SPECIAL GROUPS

    A.

SERVICES	STATE	FEDERAL	TOTAL
*Regional Library for the Blind and Physically Handicapped	$36,153	$38,649	$74,802
Institutional Library Services	$73,525	$42,447	$115,972

    *This is done totally within the Department, but
    cooperating with public and private agencies.

    B. Non-financial Support Role of the State Library:

    The Regional Library for the Blind and Physically
    Handicapped participates in statewide, regional and
    national planning, gives technical assistance to individ-
    uals and groups, does consulting, and aids in cooperative
    activities.

    Institutional Library Services participates in
    statewide, regional and national planning, gives
    technical assistance to individuals and groups, does
    consulting, and aids in cooperative activities.

13. PARTICIPATION IN MULTI-STATE LIBRARY NETWORKS

    A. Network: New England Library Board (NELB)
        Financial Support: $10,000
        Participation: full membership
        Services Used: all, including the New England Document
                          Conservation Center and the New England
                          Serials Service

        Network: New England Library Information Network
        Financial Support: $10,823   (NELINET)
        Participation: full membership
        Services Used: all, including on-line access to OCLC

    B. No multi-state networks are headquartered in Rhode Island.

14. LEGAL BASES FOR MULTI-TYPE LIBRARY COOPERATION

    State legislation enabling multi-type library cooperative
development; library cooperatives: <u>American Library Laws</u>,
p. 1587: Rhode Island General Laws: 29-6-5. Cooperative
library services. Any city or town may enter into an
agreement with another city or town, or more than one other, to
establish or maintain free library service, or one or more
aspects thereof....

    Interrelated library systems. <u>American Library Laws</u>, p. 1588:
Rhode Island General Laws: 29-6-7. Interrelated Library
systems; grants-in-aid. - In order for the department of state
library services to coordinate on a cooperative basis library
resources throughout the state, to provide improved library
services, the department is authorized to establish five (5)
interrelated library systems....

    State legislation enabling multi-type library cooperative
development: Principal public library. <u>American Library Laws</u>,
p. 1589: Rhode Island General Laws: 29-6-8. Principal public
library. - The department of state library services is hereby
authorized to designate the Providence public library as the
"principal public library" in the state....

    Special research centers. <u>American Library Laws</u>, p. 1590:
Rhode Island General Laws: 29-6-9. The department of state
library services is hereby authorized to designate certain
other libraries, such as those at Brown University, the
University of Rhode Island and Rhode Island College, as
"special research centers"....

    State legislation enabling interstate library compact: Inter-
state library compact. <u>American Library Laws</u>, p. 1591: Rhode
Island General Laws: 29-5-1. Compact. - The interstate
library compact is hereby enacted into law and entered into by

14. LEGAL BASES FOR MULTI-TYPE LIBRARY COOPERATION (continued)

this state with all states legally joining therein....

State-provided statutory funding for multi-type library cooperative development: Interrelated library systems; grant-in-aid. American Library Laws, p. 1589: Rhode Island General Laws: 29-6-7. Each Regional library center so designated hereunder by the Department shall be eligible for an annual grant-in-aid (in addition to any other grants-in-aid under the provisions of this chapter) of thirty thousand dollars ($30,000) base grant plus twenty-five (25¢) per capita of the population of the cities and towns served by it (other than the city or town where same is located) based on the latest decennial census by the United States census bureau....

Principal public library. American Library Laws, p. 1590: Rhode Island General Laws: 29-6-8. - such principal public library shall be eligible for an annual grant-in-aid in addition to any other grants-in-aid under this chapter of not less than one hundred thousand dollars ($100,000)....

Special research centers. American Library Laws, p. 1590: Rhode Island General Laws: 29-6-9. A special research center shall be eligible for an annual grant-in-aid in an amount to be determined by the director of state library services....

15. LEGAL BARRIERS AGAINST PARTICIPATION IN MULTI-TYPE LIBRARY COOPERATION

Director of state library services - Duties. American Library Laws, p. 1582-1583: Rhode Island General Laws: 29-3.1-7. par. (6). To make rules and regulations under which state or federal funds, which may now or hereafter be appropriated to further library development or use within the state, shall be granted to cities or towns or other agencies for improved library service....

1. REPORTING AGENCY

   A. South Carolina State Library
       1500 Senate Street
       P.O. Box 11469
       Columbia, SC 29211
       (803) 758-3181

   B. Chief Officer: Estellene P. Walker, Librarian

   C. Fiscal Year: not reported

2. OVERVIEW

   The South Carolina State Library has the responsibility for
   creating and improving public and institutional library service
   throughout the state, for reference and research service to
   state government and state government agencies; for providing
   library service to the visually and physically handicapped; for
   the supervision of public library building construction in the
   state; for reference and interloan service; and for consultant
   service to public libraries and to state institutions.

3. NUMBER OF LIBRARIES IN THE STATE

   Academic: 49
   Public: 39
   School: 1,086
     Public   1,086
     Private   n.a.
   Special: 81
     Profit   n.a.
     Non-Profit   n.a.
   Institutional 30

   Total   1,285

4. STATE AGENCY INTERLIBRARY COOPERATION UNIT

   A. Specific Unit Responsible for ILC Activities:

       Unit Name: Field Services
       Person in Charge: Margie E. Herron, Director of Field
                               Services

   B. Other Units Responsible for ILC Activities:

       Unit Name: Readers' Services
       Supervisor: Lea Walsh, Interlibrary Loan
                               Librarian

5. OTHER STATE-LEVEL GOVERNMENTAL ILC UNITS

   Not reported.

6. OTHER STATE-LEVEL NON-GOVERNMENTAL ILC UNITS

   Not reported.

7. SINGLE-TYPE COOPERATIVES

   A. Receiving Continuing Financial Support from the State Library:

Name:	Area Reference Resource Centers
Address:	Florence
	Greenville
	Charleston
Federal Support:	$92,000
State Support:	not reported
Local Support:	not reported
Other Support:	not reported
Total Support:	$102,000

8. MULTITYPE LIBRARY COOPERATIVES

   A. Receiving Continuing Financial Support from the State Library:
   There are none.

   B. Receiving No Continuing Financial Support from the State LIbrary:
   There are none.

   B. Receiving Occasional Financial Support from the State Library:
   There are none.

9. INTERLIBRARY COOPERATION FUNCTIONS

   A. Receiving Continuing Financial Support from the State LIbrary:

   Not reported.

   B. Non-Financial Support Role of the State Library:
   Not reported.

10. ILC COMMUNICATION DEVICES / SERVICE NETWORKS
    Not reported.

11. MACHINE-READABLE DATA BASE REFERENCE SEARCHING SERVICES
    Not reported.

12. INTERLIBRARY SERVICES TO SPECIAL GROUPS
    Not reported.

13. PARTICIPATION IN MULTI-STATE LIBRARY NETWORKS

    Not reported.

14. LEGAL BASES FOR MULTI-TYPE LIBRARY COOPERATION

    Not reported.

15. LEGAL BARRIERS AGAINST PARTICIPATION IN MULTI-TYPE LIBRARY
    COOPERATION

    There are no legal barriers.

1.   REPORTING AGENCY

    A.   South Dakota State Library
         State Library Building
         Pierre, South Dakota   57501
         (605) 224-3131
         TWX   910 668-2222

    B.   Chief Officer: Herschel V. Anderson, State Librarian

    C.   Fiscal Year: 1978

2.   OVERVIEW

    The libraries of South Dakota are organized into one single
    multitype system. The system is informal rather than being a
    formal one with contracts, acronyms, etc. It is based upon the
    mutual dependence of each library in the state upon all the
    others with each maintaining its independence. This system is
    made possible through the statutes governing the South Dakota
    State Library Commission that require it to promote inter-
    library cooperation among and between the state's libraries and
    to provide instate, and access to out-of-state, networks for
    all types of libraries. There are a union catalog of the
    holdings of major libraries, a union list of serials, In-WATS
    and teletype communications systems, and a multi-state biblio-
    graphical center that provides central access and cost reduc-
    tions to machine readable data base reference services for all
    libraries, a location service, and coordinated multi-state
    planning, training, and installation of service network access
    for OCLC and BALLOTS. The State Library assumes many of these
    costs for all libraries and serves as a switching center for
    requests received from school, public, governmental, and small
    academic libraries.

3.   NUMBER OF LIBRARIES IN THE STATE

         Academic: 21
         Public: 128
         School: 305
            Public: 201
            Private: 104
         Special: 38(est.)
            Profit: 4(est.)
            Non-Profit: 34(est.)

         TOTAL: 492(est.)

4.   STATE AGENCY INTERLIBRARY COOPERATION UNIT

    A.   Unit Name: Interlibrary Cooperative Services
         Person in Charge: Thomas E. Taylor

(continued)

4. STATE AGENCY INTERLIBRARY COOPERATION UNIT (continued)

   B.   Other State Agency Units with ILC Responsibilities:

   Unit Name: Documents Service (State Depository Sys.)
   Person in Charge: Robert J. Newby

   Unit Name: Technical Services (State Central
                           Discard Center)
   Person in Charge: Rebecca L. Bell

   Unit Name: Audiovisual Services (Central Film
                           Distribution Center)
   Person in Charge: Ann E. Eichinger

   Unit Name: Reference Services (Research Assistance)
   Person in Charge: Mary J. Frasier

   Unit Name: Consulting Services (Planning and Con-
                           tinuing Education)
   Person in Charge: Dorothy M. Liegl

   Unit Name: Handicapped Services (Multi-State
                           Handicapped Services)
   Person in Charge: John J. Vincent

5. OTHER STATE-LEVEL GOVERNMENTAL ILC UNITS

   There are none.

6. OTHER STATE-LEVEL NON-GOVERNMENTAL ILC UNITS

   There are none.

7. SINGLE-TYPE LIBRARY COOPERATIVES

   A.   Receiving Continuing Financial Support from the State
        Library:

        Name: Colleges of Mid-America
        Address: Sioux Falls College, Norman B. Mears Library,
                    1501 South Prairie Avenue, Sioux Falls, S.D.
                    57101
        Telephone: (605) 336-2850
        Administrator: Jane Kolbe, Librarian
        Type of Library Served: Small sectarian academic in
                                    South Dakota and Northwestern
                                    Iowa
        Federal Support: $2,500   LSCA Title III (TWX Grant)
        State Support: Multi-state bibliographical center
                           services, payment of all access and
                           transaction fees for machine readable
                           data base reference searches, payment of
                           all location services, payment of access
                           fees to network services. None of these
                           costs separated specifically for these

7.　SINGLE-TYPE LIBRARY COOPERATIVES (continued)

    A.　Receiving Continuing Financial Support from the State
        Library (continued):

        State Support: five academic institutions.
        Local Support: Unknown.
        Other Support: Unknown.
        Total Support: Cannot be ascertained.

    B.　Receiving No Continuing Financial Support from the State
        Library:

        There are none.

    C.　Other:

        There are none.

8.　MULTI-TYPE LIBRARY COOPERATIVES

    A.　Receiving Continuing Financial Support from the State
        Library:

        There are none.

    B.　Receiving No Continuing Financial Support from the State
        Library:

        Name:　SHARE (Document Distribution System)
        Address:　I.D. Weeks Library, University of South Dakota
                Vermillion, S.D.　57069
        Telephone:　(605)　677-5371
        Administrator:　Bob Carmack, Librarian
        Types of Libraries Served:　a, sp
        Sponsoring Body:　South Dakota Board of Regents
        Source of Support:　State funds

        Name:　Sturgis/Meade County Cooperative
        Address:　Sturgis Public Library, Sturgis, S.D.　57785
        Telephone:　(605) 347-2740
        Administrator:　Carol A. Davis, Librarian
        Types of Libraries Served:　p, sch
        Federal Support:　None (Started as LSCA demonstration 1972)
        Local Support:　$54,000
        Other Support:　None
        Total Support:　$54,000

    C.　Other:

        There are none.

9. INTERLIBRARY COOPERATION FUNCTIONS

   A. Receiving Continuing Financial Support from the State
      Library:

	State Support	Federal Support		Other Support	Total Support
		Title I	Title III		
Interlibrary Loan	$45,581	$	$34,000	$	$79,581
Continuing Education	12,494	6,701			19,195
Union List of Serials	5,000				5,000
Union Catalog	9,461				9,461
Multi-State Center	7,200				7,200
Research Data Bases	72,971				72,971
Locations				9,829	9,829
Planning/Development	10,000				10,000
Documents System	16,870				16,870
Discard Center	2,385				2,385
Film Library	68,465	40,600			109,065
Total Support	$250,427	$47,301	$43,829	$ 0	$341,557

   B. Non-Financial Support Role of the State Library:

      The South Dakota State Library continuously monitors and
      coordinates all cooperative projects within the state and
      offers advice, planning assistance, legal guidance through
      elected state officials, and multi-state planning
      expertise.

10. ILC COMMUNICATION DEVICES / SERVICE NETWORKS

    A. State Library Financial Support:

Device/Service	Support ($)	Equipment (#)	Participants
In-WATS Telephone	$17,000		492
Teletype	37,000	13	13
On-Line Computer Terminals (OCLC)	7,200*	4	6
Dial Access	*		
Computer Terminals (Lockheed, SDC,etc.)		2	2

   * The State Library pays access to network privileges with these
     funds which in turn allow the libraries concerned to access central
     multi-state training, expertise, transmission costs at lower rates
     and computer time at group rates.

(continued)

10. ILC COMMUNICATION DEVICES / SERVICE NETWORK (continued)

    B. Non-Financial Support Role of the State Library:

    The South Dakota State Library continuously monitors and coordin-
    ates all cooperative projects within the state.

11. MACHINE READABLE DATA BASE REFERENCE SEARCHING SERVICES

    The South Dakota State Library supports the cooperative use of all
    available machine-readable data bases provided by the Bibliograph-
    ical Center for Research, Rocky Mountain Region, Inc., and by the
    National Medical LIbrary. These include Lockheed, SDC, Information
    Bank, BRS, and MEDLINE. It pays some $70,000 for central access and
    searching for all libraries in South Dakota through the Biblio-
    graphical Center for Research and pays computer time for those
    libraries wishing their own internal search capability (2 libraries)
    It forwards and pays searching costs for all MEDLINE searches for
    citizens and libraries outside the medical school community to the
    University of South Dakota Lommen Health Sciences Library.

12. INTERLIBRARY SERVICES TO SPECIAL GROUPS

    Central Library Service to all Handicapped Citizens
    Central Film Library Services to all types of libraries
    Institutional Services to ten institutions serving the aged, the
        incarcerated, and the mentally or physically handicapped.
    Books by mail services to Indian Reservation areas.

13. PARTICIPATION IN MULTI-STATE LIBRARY NETWORKS

    A. State Library Memberships in Multi-State Networks:

       Network: Bibliographical Center for Research, Rocky-Mountain
                  Region, Inc., Denver, Colorado.
       Financial Support: $90,000
       Participation: Colorado, Iowa, Kansas, Nebraska, South
                        Dakota, Utah, and Wyoming
       Services Used: Location services, training and planning,
                        access to research data bases, OCLC and
                        BALLOTS.

       Network: Western Council of State Libraries, c/o Nevada
                  State Library
       Financial Support: $3,000
       Participation: Alaska, Arizona, California, Colorado, Idaho,
                        Iowa, Montana, Nebraska, Nevada, Oregon,
                        South Dakota, Utah, Washington, and Wyoming.
       Services Used: Continuing Education, Staff Development, and
                        Multi-state planning for Resource Sharing

13. PARTICPATION IN MULTI-STATE LIBRARY NETWORKS

    A. State Library Memberships in Multi-State Networks:

        Network: South Dakota/North Dakota Library for the
                     Handicapped
        Financial Support: $72,815
        Participation: North Dakota, South Dakota
        Services Used: All Handicapped Services

        Network: Western Braille Service, Utah State Library
        Financial Support: $2,000
        Participation: All western states from the Dakotas and
                     Colorado west excepting California and
                     Hawaii
        Services Used: Braille access

    B. Multi-state networks headquartered in South Dakota:

        South Dakota/North Dakota Library for the Handicapped
        South Dakota State Library
        State Library Building
        Pierre, South Dakota 57501

14. LEGAL BASE FOR MULTI-TYPE LIBRARY COOPERATION

The South Dakota State Library Commission may cooperate on a multi-type basis under the following sections of the South Dakota Codified Laws: SDCL 14-1-40(3) and (4); 14-1-44(2), (4), (5), (6) and (7); 14-1-46; 14-1-48; 14-1-49; 14-1-51; 14-1-59(4); and 14-1-60(1) and (2). The Commission also may utilize an Interstate Library Compact as designated in SDCL Chapter 14-7.

15. LEGAL BARRIERS AGAINST PARTICIPATION IN MULTI-TYPE LIBRARY COOPERATION:

There are no legal barriers.

1. REPORTING AGENCY

    A. Tennessee State Library and Archives
        403 Seventh Avenue, North
        Nashville, TN 37219
        (165) 741-2451

    B. Chief Officer: Katheryn C. Culbertson, State Librarian and
                        Archivist

    C. Fiscal Year: 1977

2. OVERVIEW

    Sixteen regional systems in Tennessee involve the 95 counties in the
    State. 100% of the population is served by libraries participating
    in interlibrary cooperation.

    State legislation enabling multi-type library cooperative develop-
    ment: Tennessee Code Annotated, S. 10-104. Function number four
    is the encouragement of library development within the state...to
    enter into local, regional or interstate contracts with competent
    agencies in the furtherance of library services.

    State legislation enabling interstate library compact: Tennessee
    Code Annotated, 1971 Suppl. S.10-701 to 10-706. Provide for library
    services which transcend governmental boundaries; authorizes co-
    operation and sharing among localities, states and others in provid-
    ing joint or cooperative library services in areas where it is the
    most effective way of providing adequate and efficient service.

3. NUMBER OF LIBRARIES IN THE STATE

Academic:	63
Public:	179
School:	1,863
Public:	1,741
Private:	122
Special:	39
Profit:	20
Non-profit:	19
TOTAL:	2,144

4. STATE AGENCY INTERLIBRARY COOPERATION UNIT

    A. Unit Name: State Library
        Person in Charge: Kendall Cram, Director
        Activities: Interlibrary loan; Cooperative ac-
                              quisitions with Joint Universities

                                              (continued)

4. STATE AGENCY INTERLIBRARY COOPERATION UNIT (continued)

    A. Activities: Libraries, Public Library of Nashville and Davidson County and other area libraries in designated subject areas.

    B. Unit Name: Public Libraries Section
       Person in Charge: Olivia K. Young, Director

5. OTHER STATE-LEVEL GOVERNMENTAL ILC UNITS

    There are none.

6. OTHER STATE-LEVEL NON-GOVERNMENTAL ILC UNITS

    Unit Name: Tennessee Higher Education Commission
    Address: 908 Andrew Jackson State Office Building
                      Nashville, TN 37219
    Telephone: (615) 741-2418
    Administrator: Dr. Wayne Brown, Director
    Activities: Sponsored a library survey

    Unit Name: Tennessee Library Association
    Address: P. O. Box 12085
                      Nashville, TN 37212
    Telephone: (615) 297-8316
    Administrator: Mrs. Betty Nance, Executive Director
    Activities: Recommendation of statewide interlibrary loan code; Support of Southeastern States Cooperative Library Survey.

7. SINGLE-TYPE LIBRARY COOPERATIVES

    A. Receiving Continuing Financial Support from the State Library:

    Name: Chattanooga Public Library
    Address: 1001 Broad Street
                      Chattanooga, TN 37402
    Telephone: (615) 757-5312
    Administrator: Mrs. Kathryn Arnold
    Type of Library Served: P
    Federal Support: $25,000
    State Support: $35,000
    Local Support: N/A
    Other Support: N/A
    Total Support: $60,000

    Name: Knoxville-Knox County Public Library
    Address: 500 West Church Ave.
                      Knoxville, TN 37902
    Telephone: (615) 523-0781

(continued)

7. SINGLE-TYPE LIBRARY COOPERATIVES (continued)

    A. Receiving Continuing Financial Support from the State Library:

    Administrator: Miss Lucile Deaderick
    Type of Library Served: P
    Federal Support: $25,000
    State Support: $35,000
    Local Support: N/A
    Other Support: N/A
    Total Support: $60,000

    Name: Memphis Public Library & Information Center
    Address: 1850 Peabody Ave.
                                Memphis, TN 38104
    Telephone: (901) 528-2950
    Administrator: C. Lamar Wallis
    Type of Library Served: P
    Federal Support: $25,000
    State Support: $35,000
    Local Support: N/A
    Other Support: N/A
    Total Support: $60,000

    Name: Public Library of Nashville and Davidson
                                County, 8th and Union, Nashville, TN 37203
    Telephone: (615) 244-4700
    Administrator: D. Marshall Stewart
    Type of Library Served: P
    Federal Support: $25,000
    State Support: $35,000
    Local Support: N/A
    Other Support: N/A
    Total Support: $60,000

    B. Receiving No Continuing Financial Support from the State
        Library:

    Name: Joint Universities Libraries
    Address: 21st Avenue, South
                                Nashville, TN 37203
    Telephone: (615) 322-2835
    Administrator: Frank P. Grisham, Director
    Type of Library Served: a
    Sponsoring Body: Joint Universities Libraries Board of
                                Trust (members from Peabody, Scarritt
                                and Vanderbilt Boards of Trust)
    Source(s) of Support: J.U.L. budget - Joint Universities

(continued)

7. SINGLE-TYPE LIBRARY COOPERATIVES (continued)

    B. Receiving No Continuing Financial Support from the State Library:

Name:	Southern College - University Union: Library Group
Address:	Vanderbilt University, Dr. Tivis Nelson, Off. 21st Ave., South Nashville, TN 37203
Telephone:	(615) 322-2508
Administrator:	None of library group
Type of Library Served:	a
Sponsoring Body:	Members of participating colleges
Source(s) of Support:	Participating Colleges

Name:	Mid-Appalachia College, Council, Inc.
Address:	510 Shelby St. - P. O. Box 391 Bristol, TN 37620
Telephone:	(615) 968-1187
Administrator:	Dr. Jack Snider
Type of Library Served:	a
Sponsoring Body:	None
Source(s) of Support:	Colleges involved

Name:	Bristol, Tennessee-Virginia Public Library
Address:	Bristol, VA 37620
Telephone:	(703) 669-9444
Administrator:	Willie Nelms
Type of Library Served:	p
Sponsoring Body:	Board of Trustees with members from both cities.
Source(s) of Support:	Bristol, Tennessee and Bristol, Virginia jointly fund the main library operation on the basis of one-half each.

Name:	University of Tennessee Health Sciences Library
Address:	800 Madison Avenue Memphis, TN 38163
Telephone:	(901) 528-5638
Administrator:	Jess Martin, Director
Type of Library Served:	a
Sponsoring Body:	University of Tennessee
Source(s) of Support:	Library budget - administered by Director of Health Sciences Library

Name:	Shiloh Regional Library-Corinth Regional Library Compact
Address:	Hamilton Hills Shopping Center Jackson, TN 38301
Telephone:	(901) 668-0710

(continued)

7. SINGLE-TYPE LIBRARY COOPERATIVES (continued)

    B. Receiving No Continuing Financial Support from the State Library:

Administrator:	Mrs. Anne Thurmond, Director
Type of Library Served:	p
Sponsoring Body:	Shiloh Regional Library and Northeast Regional Library
Source(s) of Support:	Shiloh Regional Library, Jackson, TN and the Northeast Regional Library, Corinth, Miss., place books from Shiloh in the Mississippi towns of Corinth, Luka and Ripley in return for library services to residents of Shiloh Region.

8. MULTI-TYPE LIBRARY COOPERATIVES

    A. Receiving Continuing Financial Support from the State Library:

Name:	Tennessee Union Catalog
Address:	Joint University Libraries
	Twenty-first Avenue, South
	Nashville, TN 37203
Administrator:	Mrs. Florence Greenwood, Director
Types of Libraries Served:	a, p, sp
Federal Support:	0
State Support:	$35,536
Local Support:	0
Other Support:	0
Total Support:	$35,536

    B. Receiving No Continuing Financial Support from the State Library:

Name:	Memphis Library Council
Address:	Memphis Theological Seminary
Administrator:	Richard Magrill - Chairman (Changes Annually)
Types of Libraries Served:	a, p, sch, sp
Sponsoring Body:	None
Source(s) of Support:	No source of support - no dues
Name:	Memphis & Shelby County Public Library & Information Center- Shelby State Community College
Address:	Shelby State Community College Memphis, TN
Administrator:	Dr. Jess H. Parrish, President
Types of Libraries Served:	a, p

(continued)

8. MULTI-TYPE LIBRARY COOPERATIVES (continued)

   B. Receiving No Continuing Financial Support from the State Library:

Sponsoring Body:	Shelby State Community College
Source(s) of Support:	Library budget for Shelby S.C.C. is drawn upon by Memphis Public to operate the Shelby S.C.C. Library - contractual agreement

Name:	Oak Ridge - University of Tennessee Union Catalog
Address:	Oak Ridge Public Library
	Oak Ridge, TN 37830
Administrator:	Mrs. Connie Battle, Director
Types of Libraries Served:	Any library - a, p, sch, sp

Sponsoring Body:	University of Tennessee Library
Source(s) of Support:	Printed list of serials available in U. T. Library - supplied to Oak Ridge at no cost.

   C. Other (Receiving Occasional Support from the State Library Etc.):

   There is none.

9. INTERLIBRARY COOPERATION FUNCTIONS

   A. Receiving Continuing Support from the State Library:

	STATE SUPPORT	FEDERAL SUPPORT	TOTAL SUPPORT
INTERLIBRARY LOAN	Cannot break out	Cannout break out	
CONTINUING EDUCATION	None	None	
COOPERATIVE ACQUISITIONS	None	None	
COOPERATIVE CATALOGING	None	None	
COOPERATIVE DELIVERY	None	None	
COOPERATIVE PROCESSING	None	None	
COOPERATIVE REFERENCE	$35,536	Cannot break out	$35,536
COOPERATIVE STORAGE	None	None	
LEGISLATIVE ASSISTANCE	None	None	
PLANNING/DEVELOPMENT	Cannot break out		
UNION LISTS OF SERIALS	None	None	
OTHER			

   B. Non-financial support role of the State Library:

   Consulting, planning and coordinating

10. ILC COMMUNICATION DEVICES/SERVICE NETWORKS

   A.   Receiving Continuing Financial Support from the State Library:

DEVICE/SERVICE	SUPPORT	EQUIPMENT	PARTICIPANTS
TWX	Cannot break out	4	See # 7
WATS (In & Out)	Cannot break out	4 installa-tions	See # 7

   B.   There is no non-financial support role for these services.

11.   MACHINE-READABLE DATA BASE REFERENCE SEARCHING SERVICES

   There are none.

12.   INTERLIBRARY SERVICES TO SPECIAL GROUPS

   A.   There are none.

   B.   There are none.

13.   PARTICIPATION MULTI-STATE LIBRARY NETWORKS

   A.   There are none.

   B.   There are none.

14.   LEGAL BASES FOR MULTI-TYPE LIBRARY COOPERATION

   There is no enabling legislation.

15.   LEGAL BARRIERS AGAINST PARTICIPATION IN MULTITYPE LIBRARY
   COOPERATION

   There are none.

1. REPORTING AGENCY

    A.   Texas State Library
        P.O. Box 12927/Capitol Station
        Austin, Texas   78711
        (512) 475-2116

    B.   Dorman H. Winfrey
        Director and Librarian

    C.   Fiscal Year: 1977

2. OVERVIEW

    Interlibrary Cooperation is evolving around non-profit consortia such as the AMIGOS Bibliographic Council with 49 or more Texas members and the Council of Research and Academic Libraries (CORAL). These organizations exist as legally independent of the governmental structure of the state. State legislation enables the formation of non-profit cooperatives, and the formation of governmental cooperatives is authorized under the Interlocal Cooperation Act, Article 4413 (32c). The Southwestern Library Association's Continuing Education for Library Staffs (CELS) Project represents a slightly different approach. Funding for AMIGOS and CELS are provided through contracts for service with individual libraries or with the State on behalf of other libraries. There is no state legislation authorizing an interstate library compact or statutory funding of multi-type library cooperatives.

3. NUMBER OF LIBRARIES IN THE STATE

    Academic: 149
    Public: 381
    School: 2,997 (approx.)
        Public: 2,997 (approx.)
        Private: not available
    Special: 670
        Profit: not available
        Non-Profit: not available

    Total: 4,197 est.

4. STATE AGENCY INTERLIBRARY COOPERATION UNIT

    A.   Library Development Division
        Raymond Hitt, Director

    B.   Network Development Department
        Al Quinn, Manager

5. OTHER STATE-LEVEL GOVERNMENTAL ILC UNITS

        Unit name: Texas Education Agency
        Address: 201 East 11th Street
                     Austin, Texas   78711
        Telephone: (512) 475-2407

        Unit name: Coordinating Board, Texas College
                     and University System
        Address: 11th Floor
                     LBJ State Office Building
                     Austin, Texas   78711
        Telephone: (512) 475-4361

6. OTHER STATE-LEVEL NON-GOVERNMENTAL ILC UNITS

        There are none.

7. SINGLE-TYPE LIBRARY COOPERATIVES

        A.   Receiving Continuing Financial Support from the
              State Library:

              Name: Big Country Library System
              Address: Abilene Public Library
                            202 Cedar Street
                            Abilene, Texas   79601
              Telephone: (915) 673-2311
              Administrator: Ms. Alice Specht, Coordinator
              Type of Library Served: p
              Federal Support: $ 84,579
              State Support: 96,035
              Local Support: -0-
              Other Support: -0-
              Total Support: $180,614

              Name: Texas Panhandle Library System
              Address: Amarillo Public Library
                            Box 2171
                            Amarillo, Texas   79105
              Telephone: (806) 372-4211
              Administrator: Ms. Ann Ousley, Coordinator
               Type of Library Served: p
              Federal Support: $ 85,955
               State Support: 97,599
              Local Support: -0-
              Other Support: -0-
              Total Support: $183,554

              Name: Central Texas Library System
              Address: Austin Public Library
                            Box 2287
                            Austin, Texas   78767 (continued)

7.   SINGLE-TYPE LIBRARY COOPERATIVES (continued)

```
                    Telephone:      (512) 474-5355
                    Administrator: Ms. Biruta Kearl, Coordinator
                    Type of Library Served:  p
                    Federal Support:    $157,960
                    State Support:       179,356
                    Local Support:         -0-
                    Other Support:         -0-
                    Total Support:      $337,316


                    Name:           South Texas Library System
                    Address:        La Retama Public Library
                                    505 North Mesquite
                                    Corpus Christi, Texas    78401
                    Telephone:      (512) 882-6502
                    Administrator: Ms. Beverley G. Van Camp,
                                    Coordinator
                    Type of Library Served:  p
                    Federal Support:    $158,373
                    State Support:       179,825
                    Local Support:         -0-
                    Other Support:         -0-
                    Total Support:      $338,198


                    Name:           Northeast Texas Library System
                    Address:        Dallas Public Library
                                    1954 Commerce
                                    Dallas, Texas    75201
                    Telephone:      (214) 651-9266
                    Administrator: Ms. Elizabeth Crabb
                    Type of Library Served: p
                    Federal Support:    $328,816
                    State Support:       373,354
                    Local Support:         -0-
                    Other Support:         -0-
                    Total Support:      $702,170


                    Name:           Texas Trans Pecos Library System
                    Address:        El Paso Public Library
                                    501 North Oregon
                                    El Paso, Texas    79901
                    Telephone:      (915) 543-3810
                    Administrator: Ms. Marilyn Hinshaw, Coordinator
                    Type of Library Served: p
                    Federal Support:    $ 96,970
                    State Support:       110,104
                    Local Support:         -0-
                    Other Support:         -0-
                    Total Support:      $207,074
```

(continued)

7.   SINGLE-TYPE LIBRARY COOPERATIVES (continued)

Name: North Texas Library System
Address: Fort Worth Public Library
                 Ninth and Throckmorton
                 Fort Worth, Texas   76102
Telephone: (817) 335-6073
Administrator: William Duncan, Coordinator
Type of Library Served: p
Federal Support: $180,263
State Support: 204,681
Local Support: -0-
Other Support: -0-
Total Support: $384,944

Name: Houston Area Library System
Address: Houston Public Library
                 500 McKinney
                 Houston, Texas   77002
Telephone: (713) 222-4704
Administrator: Ms. Cynthia Corbin, Coordinator
Type of Library Served: p
Federal Support: $420,921
State Support: 477,935
Local Support: -0-
Other Support: -0-
Total Support: $898,856

Name: West Texas Library System
Address: George and Helen Mahon Library
                 Ninth and Avenue L
                 Lubbock, Texas   79401
Telephone: (806) 762-5442
Administrator: Steve Cottrell, Coordinator
Type of Library Served: p
Federal Support: $124,918
State Support: 141,838
Local Support: -0-
Other Support: -0-
Total Support: $266,756

Name: San Antonio Major Resource System
Address: San Antonio Public Library
                 203 South St. Mary's Street
                 San Antonio, Texas   78205
Telephone: (512) 223-5538
Administrator: Ms. Judy Lytle, Coordinator
Type of Library Served: p
Federal Support: $196,922
State Support: 223,596
Local Support: -0-
Other Support: -0-
Total Support: $420,518   (continued)

7.   SINGLE-TYPE LIBRARY COOPERATIVES (continued)

        B.   Receiving No Continuing Financial Support from
           the State Library:

Name: Coastal Bend Health Sciences
                    Library Consortium
Address: Memorial Medical Center
                    2606 Hospital Boulevard
                    Corpus Christi, Texas   78405
Telephone: (512) 854-4511, ext. 278
Administrator: Dorothy Williams
Type of Library Served: medical
Sponsoring Body: Not Available
Source of Support: Not Available

Name: South Central Regional Medical
                    Library Program (TALON)
Address: University of Texas Health Science
                    Center Library
                    5323 Harry Hines Boulevard
                    Dallas, Texas   75207
Telephone: (214) 688-2626
Administrator: Donald Hendricks
Type of Library Served: medical
Sponsoring Body: Not Available
Source of Support: Not Available

Name: North Central Texas Film
                    Cooperative (PLANT)
Address: 900 Civic Center Drive
                    Richardson, Texas   75080
Telephone: (214) 276-5178
Administrator: Lowell Lindsey
Type of Library Served: p
Sponsoring Body: Not Available
Source of Support: Not Available

Name: Southwest Academic Library
                    Consortium (SWALC)
Address: University of Texas at El Paso
                    Library
                    El Paso, Texas   79968
Telephone: (915) 747-5684
Administrator: Fred W. Hanes
Type of Library Served: a
Sponsoring Body: Not Available
Source of Support: Not Available

Name: Multi-County Library Association
Address: Butt-Holdsworth Memorial Library
                    505 Water Street
                    Kerrville, Texas   78028 (continued)

7.   SINGLE-TYPE LIBRARY COOPERATIVES (continued)

Telephone: (512) 257-8422
Administrator: Evelyn Jaeggli
Type of Library Served: p
Sponsoring Body: Not Available
Source of Support: Membership Fees

Name: Tarrant Regional Library
                  Association (TRLA)
Address: Keller Public Library
                  P.O. Box 464
                  Keller, Texas   76248
Telephone: (817) 431-9011
Administrator: Mrs. Doris Foster
Type of Library Served: p
Sponsoring Body: Not Available
Source of Support: Not Available

Name: State Agency Libraries of Texas
                  (SALT)
Address: Texas State Library
                  P.O. Box 12927/Capitol Station
                  Austin, Texas   78711
Telephone: (512) 475-4356
Administrator: Barbara Duke (Consultant)
Type of Library Served: sp
Sponsoring Body: Texas State Library
Source of Support: In-Kind Contributions

C.   Other:

There are none.

8.   MULTI-TYPE LIBRARY COOPERATIVES

A.   Receiving Continuing Financial Support from the
     State Library:

There are none.

B.   Receiving No Continuing Financial Support from
     the State Library:

Name: Regional Information and Communi-
                  cation Exchange (RICE)
Address: Rice University
                  Fondren Library
                  6100 Main Street
                  Houston, Texas   77001
Telephone: (713) 528-3553
Administrator: Betty Jo Dollar
                          (continued)

333

8.   MULTI-TYPE LIBRARY COOPERATIVES (continued)

> Types of Libraries Served: a, sp
> Sponsoring Body: Rice University
> Source of Support: Membership fees
>
> Name: The Texas List
> Address: Wilson Publishing Company
>   1939 West Gray
>   Houston, Texas   77019
> Telephone: (512) 476-5015
> Administrator: Lois Bebout
> Types of Libraries Served: a, p, sp, state
>
> Sponsoring Body: Private
> Source of Support: Sale of the Texas List
>
> Name: Del Norte Biosciences Library
>   Consortium
> Address: 1101 North Campbell
>   El Paso, Texas   79901
> Telephone: (915) 544-1880
> Administrator: Esperanza Moreno
> Types of Libraries Served: a, p, sp
>
> Source of Support: Membership Fees
>
> Name: Industrial Information Services
> Address: Southern Methodist University
>   Science Information Center,
>   Room 119
>   Dallas, Texas   75222
> Telephone: (214) 747-5684
> Administrator: Devertt D. Bickston
> Types of Libraries Served: a, sp
> Source of Support: Membership fees
>
> Name: Dallas Area Media Project (DAMP)
> Address: 5323 Harry Hines Boulevard
>   Dallas, Texas   75235
> Telephone: (214) 688-2005
> Administrator: Mary M. Rydesky
> Types of Libraries Served: a, sp
> Source of Support: Membership fees

C.   Receiving Occasional Support from the State
      Library:

> Name: AMIGOS Bibliographic Council
> Address: 11300 North Central Expressway
>   Suite 321
>   Dallas, Texas   75243

(continued)

8.   MULTI-TYPE LIBRARY COOPERATIVES (continued)

                    Telephone: (214) 750-6130
                    Administrator: James Kennedy
                    Types of Libraries Served: a, p, sch, sp

                    Source of Support: State grants, private grants,
                        membership fees, payment for products

                    Name: Texas Information Exchange (TIE)
                    Address: The General Libraries, MAI 2108
                                    The University of Texas at Austin
                                    Austin, Texas   78712
                    Telephone: (512) 471-3811
                    Administrator: Gary Menges
                    Types of Libraries Served: a, p, Texas State
                                    Library
                    Source of Support: Membership fees

                    Name: Council of Research and Academic
                                    Libraries (CORAL)
                    Address: Texas Lutheran College Library
                                    Seguin, Texas   78155
                    Telephone: (512) 658-0222
                    Administrator: Warren Lussky
                    Types of Libraries Served: a, p, sp, Federal
                                    Government, Medical, Foreign
                                    Institutions

9.   INTERLIBRARY COOPERATION FUNCTIONS

        A.   Receiving Continuing Financial Support from
             the State Library:

	State Support	Federal Support Title I	Federal Support Title III	Other Support	Total Support
Interlibrary Loan	107,975	557,335	-0-	-0-	665,310
Continuing Education	118,760	-0-	19,800	-0-	138,560
Cooperative Acquisitions	-0-	-0-	-0-	-0-	-0-
Cooperative Cataloging	15,000	477,203	-0-	-0-	492,203
Cooperative Delivery	-0-	-0-	-0-	-0-	-0-
Cooperative Processing	-0-	-0-	-0-	-0-	-0-
Cooperative Reference	-0-	-0-	-0-	-0-	-0-
Cooperative Storage	-0-	-0-	-0-	-0-	-0-
Legislative Assistance	-0-	-0-	-0-	-0-	-0-
Planning/Development	97,969	-0-	-0-	23,736	121,705
Union Lists of Serials	-0-	-0-	-0-	-0-	-0-
Other					
Total Support	339,704	1,034,538	19,800	23,736	1,417,778

(continued)

9.   INTERLIBRARY COOPERATION FUNCTIONS (continued)

  B.   Non-Financial Support Role of the State Library:

    There is no non-financial support role.

10.   ILC COMMUNICATION DEVICES / SERVICE NETWORKS

  A.   Supported by the State Library:

Device/Service	Support ($)	Equipment (#)	Participants
Teletypes	42,064	11	10
Telephone	40,095	17	10
OCLC Terminals	(Planned)*	28*	10*

  B.   Non-Financial Support Role of the State Library:

    There is no non-financial support role for these services.

11.   MACHINE-READABLE DATA BASE REFERENCE SEARCHING SERVICES

There are none.

12.   INTERLIBRARY SERVICES TO SPECIAL GROUPS

  A.   A State Library Consultant for library services to the institutionalized is provided.

    The State Library Agency supports centralized library services for the blind and physically handicapped.

  B.   Non-Financial Support Role of the State Library:

    There are none.

13.   PARTICIPATION IN MULTI-STATE LIBRARY NETWORKS

  A.   Network: AMIGOS Bibliographic Council
    Financial Support: State ($15,000), and
                        Federal ($477,203)
    Participation: Contractual Services
    Services Used: Cataloging and Card Production

    Network: Southwestern Library Association's
              Continuing Education for Library Staffs
              Project (CELS)
    Financial Support: State ($19,800)
    Participation: Contractual Services
    Services Used: Consulting Services in Continu-
                    ing Education   (continued)

13.   PARTICIPATION IN MULTI-STATE LIBRARY NETWORKS (continued)

    B.   There are none.

14.   LEGAL BASES FOR MULTI-TYPE LIBRARY COOPERATION

"The governing body of a major resource center and
the Commission may enter into contracts and agreements
with the governing bodies of other libraries, including but not limited to other public libraries, school
libraries and media centers, academic libraries,
technical information and research libraries, or
systems of such libraries, to provide specialized
resources and services to the major resource system in
effecting the purposes of this Act." (Library Systems
Act, Vernon's Annotated Civil Statutes, Article 5446a,
61st Legislature, Regular Session.)

Formation of non-profit cooperations and governmental
cooperatives are authorized under the Interlocal
Cooperation Act, Article 4413 (32c).

15.   LEGAL BARRIERS AGAINST PARTICIPATION IN MULTI-TYPE LIBRARY
COOPERATION

There are no legal barriers.

1. REPORTING AGENCY

    A.   Utah State Library Commission
          2150 South 300 West, Suite 16
          Salt Lake City, Utah   84115
          (801) 533-5875

    B.   Chief Officer: Russell L. Davis, Director

    C.   Fiscal Year: 1978

2. OVERVIEW

    All libraries in Utah engage in interlibrary cooperation under
    the auspices of the State Library. The State Library coordin-
    ates an interlibrary loan and reference service network cover-
    ing the entire state. A film circuit provides audio-visual
    materials to public libraries. The State Library also directs
    a program for the location, distribution and name authority
    control for state documents. A centralized acquisitions,
    cataloging and processing service currently serves over 400
    public and school libraries. In cooperation with the Library
    of Congress, the State Library acts as a Multi-State Center
    supplying braille materials and catalogs, tapes, and equipment
    to regional libraries in the west serving the blind and physi-
    cally handicapped.

    Future plans include the development of a COM union list for
    the state through data captured from OCLC and BALLOTS. All
    major academic libraries and over 400 public, school and spe-
    cial libraries will be included.

    Interlibrary cooperative activities are authorized under the
    Utah Code, Title 37, Chapter 4-4. Funding is administered by
    the Utah State Library Commission from state and federal monies.

3. NUMBER OF LIBRARIES IN THE STATE

          Academic: 11
          Public: 51
          School: 577
             Public: 542
             Private: 35
          Special: 35
             Profit: 25 est.
             Nonprofit: 10 est.

          TOTAL: 674 est.

4. STATE AGENCY INTERLIBRARY COOPERATION UNIT
          A.   There is no existing unit nor plans to create one.

                                                    (continued)

338

4. STATE AGENCY INTERLIBRARY COOPERATION UNIT (continued)

    B.   All professional staff members are assigned responsibility for interlibrary cooperation activities. However, the following are directly responsible within their divisions:

          Unit Name: Technical Services Division
          Person in Charge: Amy Owen, Director

          Unit Name: Reference Division
          Person in Charge: David Allred, Director

          Unit Name: Multi-State Center
          Person in Charge: Gerald Buttars, Director

          Unit Name: Extension Division
          Person in Charge: Paul Buttars, Director

5. OTHER STATE-LEVEL GOVERNMENT ILC UNITS

    There are none.

6. OTHER STATE-LEVEL NON-GOVERNMENTAL ILC UNITS

    There are none.

7. SINGLE-TYPE LIBRARY COOPERATIVES

    A.   Receiving Continuing Financial Support from the State Library:

    There are none.

    B.   Receiving No Continuing Financial Support from the State Library:

    Name: Utah College Library Council (UCLC)
    Address: University and 2nd South, Provo, UT 84602
    Telephone: (801) 374-1211 Ext. 3210
    Administrator: David Thomas, Librarian BYU College of
                    Law
    Type of Library Served: a

    Sponsoring Body: All Utah Colleges and Universities
    Source(s) of Support: Membership Dues

    Name: Urban Public Library Council
    Address: 2150 South 300 West, Salt Lake City, UT 84115
    Telephone: (801) 533-5875
    Administrator: Russel L. Davis, Director State Library

(continued)

7. SINGLE -TYPE LIBRARY COOPERATIVES   (continued)

    B. Receiving No Continuing Financial Support from the State Library:

        Type of Library Served: p (all urban public libraries in Utah)
        Sponsoring Body: All Urban Public libraries in Utah
        Source(s) of Support: Membership Dues

    C. Other:

        There are none.

8. MULTI-TYPE LIBRARY COOPERATIVES

    A. Receiving Continuing Financial Support from the State Library:

        There are none.

    B. Receiving No Continuing Financial Support from the State Library:

        There are none.

    C. Other:

        There are none.

9. INTERLIBRARY COOPERATION FUNCTIONS

    A. Receiving Continuing Financial Support from State Library:

	State Support	Federal Support Title I	Title III	Other Support	Total Support
Cooperative Acquisitions					
Cooperative Cataloging	289,700	14,428	45,662	0	349,790
Cooperative Processing					
Interlibrary Loan					
Legislative Assistance	50,200	191,200	0	0	241,400
Cooperative Reference					
Cooperative Audio-Visual	95,405	0	0	2,000	97,405
Multi-State Center				69,000	69,000
Blind & Physic. Handic.	133,600	93,300	0	101,600	328,500
Cooperative Bookmobile	478,700	111,900	0	343,800	934,400
Institutional Services	0	30,000	0	0	30,000
Total Support	$1,047,605	440,828	45,662	516,400	$2,050,495

(continued)

9. INTERLIBRARY COOPERATION FUNCTIONS (continued)

    B. Non-Financial Support Role of the State Library

    There is none.

10. ILC COMMUNICATION DEVICES / SERVICE NETWORKS

    A. Receiving Continuing Support from the State Library:

Device/Service	Support ($)	Equipment (#)	Participants
WATS	17,690	3	Entire State
Teletype	500	1	Entire State
Telefacsimile Communications	0	1	Entire State
On-Line Computer Terminals		3	Entire State

    B. Non-Financial Role of the State Library:

    There is none.

11. MACHINE-READABLE DATA BASE REFERENCE SEARCHING SERVICES

Date Base/Vendor	Support ($)	Terminals (#)	Participants
Metro	18,466	5	Entire State
BCR	9,000	9	Entire State
Biblio	42,969	3	Entire State
Inter-Loan	2,000	1	Entire State

12. INTERLIBRARY SERVICES TO SPECIAL GROUPS

    A. List services to special user groups that are provided through cooperative arrangements within the state:

    There are none.

    B. Non-Financial Role of the State Library:
    There is none.

13. PARTICIPATION IN MULTI-STATE LIBRARY NETWORKS

    A. Network(s): Rocky Mountain Bibliographical Center for Research (BCR)
    Financial Support: 7,200

(continued)

13.   PARTICIPATION IN MULTI-STATE LIBRARY NETWORKS (continued)

        A.   Participation: Entire State
            Services Used: Utah has a contract with BCR for total
                       participation in their interloan activ-
                       ities.

            Network(s):   Western Council of State Libraries
            Financial Support: 3,000
            Participation: Entire State
            Services Used: Cooperative sharing of Resource and
                       Staff Development

            Network(s):   Multi-State Center
            Financial Support: 0
            Participation: 15 Western States
            Services Used: Supplying of Braille materials, cata-
                       logs, tapes, and equipment for servic-
                       ing the blind and physically handicap-
                       ped.

        B.   There are no multi-state networks headquartered in
            Utah.

14.   LEGAL BASES FOR MULTI-TYPE LIBRARY COOPERATION

        "Library Laws of Utah" - 1963
        37-3-10
        Authority is given to Boards, agencies and political sub-
        divisions to cooperate, merge or consolidate.
        37-4-4
        State Library Commission powers and duties require that:
        The State Library Commission shall promote and develop
        library services throughout the state in cooperation with
        other agencies where practical; shall promote the establish-
        ment of district & regional or multi-county libraries as
        conditions require; shall serve as the agency of the state
        for the administration of any state or federal funds; shall
        aid and provide general advisory assistance in the develop-
        ment of statewide school library service; shall give assis-
        tance, advice and counsel to all tax supported libraries
        and to all communities or persons proposing to establish
        libraries and may conduct courses and institutes on the
        approved methods of operation, selection of books, or other
        activities necessary to the proper administration
        of a library.

15.   LEGAL BARRIERS AGAINST PARTICIPATION IN MULTI-TYPE LIBRARY
      COOPERATION

        There are no legal barriers.

1. REPORTING AGENCY

    A. Vermont Department of Libraries
        Montpelier, Vermont 05602
        (802) 828-3265

    B. Chief Officer: Patricia E. Klinck, State Librarian

    C. Fiscal Year: 1977

2. OVERVIEW

    There is no specific enabling legislation covering intrastate inter-
    library cooperation in Vermont and no specific provision for
    funding. Vermont may enter into interstate library agreements under
    22 VSA 21-44. However, the absence of restrictive legislation has
    allowed the state to develop an efficient working Resource Sharing
    Network in which all libraries in Vermont participate, regardless
    of type, both as lenders and consumers.

    Activities include adding cards (locations) to the Vermont Union
    Catalog from all types of libraries, maintenance of the VUC, pro-
    viding materials or access to materials via the Vermont Interlibrary
    Loan Network and maintenance of the DOL-UVM Access Office.

3. NUMBER OF LIBRARIES IN THE STATE

Academic:	26
Public:	223
School	not available
Public:	not available
Private:	not available
Special:	64
Profit:	unable to break out
Non-Profit:	unable to break out
Total	313 est.

4. STATE AGENCY INTERLIBRARY COOPERATION UNIT

    A. Unit Name: Reference Services Unit
        Person in Charge: Fred Lerner, Reference Services Librarian

    B. Unit Name: Library User Services Division
        Person in Charge: Mrs. Dorothy B. Allen, Director of Library
                                      User Services

5. OTHER STATE-LEVEL GOVERNMENTAL UNITS

    There are none.

6. OTHER STATE-LEVEL NON-GOVERNMENTAL ILC UNITS

    Unit Name: Vermont Library Association

(continued)

6. OTHER STATE-LEVEL NON-GOVERNMENTAL ILC UNITS (continued)

Address: Box 803, Burlington, Vermont 05401
Telephone: (802) 893-4794
Executive Secretary: Ann Rugerio
Activities: Annual VLA/VLTA/VEMA conference, continuing
                      education, revising interlibrary loan code.

Unit Name: Vermont Library Trustees Association
Address: c/o Mrs. Harriett Manning Harris, Box 12,
             Barton, Vermont 05822
Telephone: (802) 525-6528
Activities: Annual VLA/VLTA/VEMA conference, continuing
             education.

Unit Name: Vermont Educational Media Association
President: John Hilliard, 2 Brierbrook Lane, Springfield,
             Vermont 05156
Activities: Annual VLA/VLTA/VEMA conference, sharing of
             a-v resources, regional meetings to share
             ideas and materials, publish newsletter.

7. SINGLE-TYPE LIBRARY COOPERATIVES

   A. Receiving Continuing Financial Support from the State Library:

      There are none.

   B. Receiving No Continuing Financial Support from the State
      Library:

      There are none.

   C. Receiving Occasional Financial Support from the State Library:

      Name: Hartland Public Libraries
      Address: Box 137, Hartland, Vermont 05048
      Telephone: (802) 436-2473
      Administrator: Mrs. Ellen Yahn
      Type of Libraries Served: p
      Sponsoring Body: Town of Hartland
      Sources of Support: Town taxes, revenue sharing, misc. income

      Name: Jericho-Underhill Library Cooperative
      Address: Underhill, Vermont 05489
      Telephone: (802) 899-4962
      Coordinator: Mrs. Mary B. Fell
      Type of Libraries Served: p
      Sponsoring Body: Towns of Jericho and Underhill
      Sources of Support: Town tax appropriations, miscellaneous
                               income

(continued)

7C. SINGLE-TYPE LIBRARY COOPERATIVES (continued)

> Name: Hartford Cooperating Libraries
> Address: Quechee Library Association, Quechee, Vermont
>   05059
> Telephone: (802) 295-3546
> Coordinator: Mrs. Pauline Cole
> Type of Libraries Served: p
> Sponsoring Body: Town of Hartford
> Sources of Support: Town tax appropriations,
>   miscellaneous income

8. MULTI-TYPE LIBRARY COOPERATIVES

A. Receiving Continuing Financial Support from the State Library:

> Name: Department of Libraries Regional Library
>   System
> Address: Montpelier, Vermont   05602
> Telephone: (802) 828-3261
> Administrator: Kent Gray, Assistant State Librarian
> Types of Libraries Served: a, p, sch, sp
> Federal Support: $213,249
> State Support: 65,504
> Local Support: 0
> Other Support: 0
> Total Support: $278,753

> Name: Vermont Resource Sharing System
> Address: Vermont Department of Libraries, Montpelier,
>   Vermont 05602
> Telephone: (802) 828-3261
> Administrator: Sally B. Roberts
> Types of Libraries Served: p, sch, a, sp, state agencies
> Federal support: $33,577
> State Support: $58,145
> Local Support: unknown
> Other Support: unknown
> Total Support: unknown

B. Receiving No Continuing Financial Support From the State Library:

> Name: Thetford Library Federation, Inc.
> Address: Thetford, Vermont   05074
> Telephone: (802) 785-4361
> President: William Slade
> Types of Libraries Served: p, sch, hist
> Sponsoring Body: Town of Thetford
> Sources of Support: Tax appropriations, revenue sharing,
>   miscellaneous income

> Name: Fairfax Community Library
> Address: Box 165, Fairfax, Vermont 05454   (continued)

8. B. MULTI-TYPE LIBRARY COOPERATIVES (continued)

       Telephone: (802) 849-6878
       Administrator: Mrs. Marnie Kneeland
       Types of Libraries Served: p, sch, hist
       Sponsoring Body: Town of Fairfax
       Sources of Support: Tax appropriations, revenue sharing,
                                   miscellaneous income

       Name: Wolcott Community Library
       Address: c/o Wolcott School, Wolcott, Vermont   05680
       Telephone: (802) 888-2401
       Administrator: Mrs. Betty Martin
       Types of Libraries Served: p, sch
       Sponsoring Body: Town of Wolcott
       Sources of Support: Tax appropriations, revenue sharing

   C. Receiving Occasional Financial Support From the State Library:

       Those library cooperatives listed in B above.

9. INTERLIBRARY COOPERATION FUNCTIONS

   A.

	State Support	Federal Support Title I	Title III	Other Support	Total Support
Interlibrary Loan		unable to break out			
Continuing Education		unable to break out			
Cooperative Acquisitions		unable to break out			
Cooperative Cataloging		$8370			
Cooperative Delivery	$7777	$4054			
Cooperative Processing		unable to break out			
Cooperative Reference		unable to break out			
Cooperative Storage	0	0	0	0	0
Legislative Assistance		unable to break out			
Planning/Development		unable to break out			
Union List of Serials		unable to break out			
Other					
Total Support		cannot be determined			

   B. Non-Financial Support Role of the State Library:

       The above activities are carried out by the state library agency.
       The state library agency also assists in the development and
       improvement of other cooperative activities by providing
       consultant, planning, technical, and coordinative assistance.

10. ILC COMMUNICATION DEVICES / SERVICE NETWORKS

    A.

Device/Service	Support ($)	Equipment (#)	Participants
Teletype	unable to break out	12	12
Telephone (outgoing WATS, accept collect calls)		NA	236

    B. Non-Financial Support Role of the State Library:

    There is no non-financial support role for these services.

11. MACHINE-READABLE DATA BASE REFERENCE SEARCHING SERVICES

The state library agency through the UVM-DOL Access Office has access to the data bases used by that institution. Charges are on use-time only. FY78 budget $1000.

12. INTERLIBRARY SERVICES TO SPECIAL GROUPS

    A. Regional Library for the Blind and Physically Handicapped; library materials and equipment for the institutionalized; books-by-mail service for disadvantaged, isolated, those over 65; circulating French-language collection; foundation collection; library science collection.

    B. Non-Financial Support Role of the State Library:

    Department of Libraries administers programs, provides equipment and materials, consultant service, planning, technical assistance, coordinative assistance.

13. PARTICIPATION IN MULTI-STATE LIBRARY NETWORKS

    A. Network: North Country Libraries Film Co-op
       Financial Support: Unable to break out
       Participation: Maine, New Hampshire, Vermont
       Services Used: Select, cooperatively purchase, and rotate blocks of films among the three states, have previewing sessions to determine purchase of films for co-op, co-op has a coordinator hired by the three states.

       Network: New England Library Board
       Financial Support: $6300 and travel expenses for meetings
       Participation: Maine, New Hampshire, Massachusetts, Connecticut, Rhode Island, Vermont
       Services Used: New England Serials Service, New England Documents Conservation Center, New York Times

(continued)

13. PARTICIPATION IN MULTI-STATE LIBRARY NETWORKS (continued)

    Information Bank, Personnel Cooperative
    Interchange.

    Network: New Hampshire Centralized Card Service
    Financial Support: $8370
    Participation: New Hampshire, Maine, Vermont (all public
                           libraries in Vermont meeting Vermont
                           Standards for Public Libraries)
    Services Used: Catalog cards for materials published in a
                           specific time frame.

    B. There are no multi-state networks headquartered in Vermont.

14. LEGAL BASES FOR MULTI-TYPE LIBRARY COOPERATION

    There is no enabling legislation.

15. LEGAL BARRIERS AGAINST PARTICIPATION IN MULTI-TYPE LIBRARY COOPERA-
    TION

    There are no legal barriers.

1. REPORTING AGENCY

   A. Virginia State Library
       11th and Capitol Streets
       Richmond, Virginia 23219
       (804) 786-2332

   B. Chief Officer: Donald Haynes, State Librarian

   C. Fiscal Year: 1977 (Items 9 and 10 are FY 1976 data)

2. OVERVIEW

   The State Library works closely with the Library Advisory Committee of the State Council of Higher Education and the Library Development and Cooperative Programs Committees of the Virginia Library Association concerning planning for cooperative
   activities among all types of Virginia libraries. During the
   past year a statewide interlibrary loan referral center has
   been established at the State Library. Studies are underway
   concerning the coordination of a statewide collections development policy and the establishment of a central storage
   facility to house serials files which have research value but
   are in low demand. In addition, the State Library is planning to establish a regional automated circulation system
   which, hopefully, when perfected, will be suitable as a proto-
   type for other areas and lead eventually to statewide communication among all regions.

   State legislation enabling multitype library cooperative development is found in the Code of Virginia, Title 42.1-9,
   which establishes the authority of the State Library to "enter
   into contracts---for the purpose of providing cooperative library service."

   State-provided statutory funding for multi-type library cooperative development is found in the Code of Virginia, Title
   42.1-57, which empowers the Library Board of Virginia "to ac-
   cept grants of federal funds for libraries and to allocate such
   funds to libraries under any plan approved by the Board and the
   appropriate federal authorities."

   The standard interstate library compact, in use nationally,
   also is included in the Code of Virginia, Title 42.1-75.

3. NUMBER OF LIBRARIES IN THE STATE

   Academic: 87
   Public: 88
   School: 1,804
       Public: na
       Private: na

(continued)

3. NUMBER OF LIBRARIES IN THE STATE (continued)

              Special: 139
              Profit: 48
              Non-Profit: 70
              Institutional: 25*

      TOTAL: 2,118   *(4 non-profit special are duplicated
                                        in institutional category because of
                                        their dual role as professional
                                        and patient libraries.)

4. STATE AGENCY INTERLIBRARY COOPERATION UNIT

    A.   Unit Name: General Library Branch, Interlibrary
                                Loan Center
        Person in Charge: Jean Bear, Head, General Library Branch

    B.   Unit Name: Office of Library Cooperation
        Person in Charge: Suzanne Shook, Cooperative Programs
                                Librarian

5. OTHER STATE-LEVEL GOVERNMENT ILC UNITS

    A.   Unit Name: Bureau of School Libraries and Teach-
                                ing Materials, State Department of
                                Education
        Address: 616 East Main Street
                                Richmond, Virginia 23219
        Telephone: (804) 786-7705
        Administrator: Mrs. Mary Stuart Mason, Supervisor of
                                School Libraries and Textbooks
        Activities: Although this bureau provides guidance
                                and administers funding in support of
                                school library programs throughout Vir-
                                ginia, regional cooperative activities
                                are carried on locally within school
                                divisions. These will be mentioned
                                under the single-type library coopera-
                                tives category.

    B.   Unit Name: State Council of Higher Education for
                                Virginia
                                Library Advisory Committee
        Address: 700 Fidelity Building
                                Ninth and Main Streets
                                Richmond, Virginia 23219
        Telephone: (804) 786-3051
        Administrator: John Molnar, Library Planning Coordi-
                                nator
        Activities: This committee studies and recommends
                                procedures for expanding and improv-
                                ing library resources and services in
                                                  (continued)

5. OTHER STATE-LEVEL GOVERNMENTAL ILC UNITS (continued)

higher education in the state, including the establishment and operation of special projects, the development of experimental activities, and the development of financial support and staffing guidelines.

Continuing operating costs are shared by the State Council and participating institutions; occasional staff support and funding for special projects are provided by the State Council.

Committee membership includes library directors of all state-supported 4-year institutions of higher education, selected representatives from the Virfinia Community College System, privately-supported 4-year institutions of higher education, and special libraries and the State Librarian in an ex officio capacity.

During 1977 the State Council for Higher Education published the Virginia Plan for Academic Library Cooperation, a document including recommendations for cooperative ventures which would affect the quality of service provided by all types of libraries in Virginia.

6. OTHER STATE-LEVEL NON-GOVERNMENTAL ILC UNITS

Unit Name: Virginia Library Association
Address: P. O. Box 12445
                Richmond, Virginia 23241
Telephone: (804) 332-5161, extension 127
Administrator: Eugene T. Fischer, Executive Secretary
                (Director, Campbell County Public
                Library, Rustburg)
Activities: This association, specifically through the study and recommendations of its Library Development and its Cooperative Programs Committees, provides support and input for cooperative activities involving all types of libraries. The VLA ad hoc Continuing Education Committee works closely with the LSCA Title III Continuing Education Committee of the State Library

(continued)

351

6.   OTHER STATE-LEVEL NON-GOVERNMENTAL ILC UNITS (continued)

in coordinating efforts toward ful-
filling the continuing education
needs of Virginia librarians.

7.   SINGLE-TYPE LIBRARY COOPERATIVES

A.   Receiving Continuing Financial Support from the State
Library:

There are none.

B.   Receiving No Continuing Financial Support from the State
Library:

Name: Richmond Area Library Directors
Address: Virginia State Library
                      11th and Capitol Streets
                      Richmond, Virginia 23219
Telephone: (804) 786-2321
Administrator: William R. Chamberlain, Public Library
                      Consultant, Virginia State Library
Type of Library Served: p
Sponsoring Body: There is none.
Source(s) of Support: Local funding and possibly grants
                       administered by the State Library.

Name: Tidewater Area Library Directors
Address: Portsmouth Public Library, Churchland
                      Branch
                      3215 Academy Avenue
                      Portsmouth, Virginia 23703
Telephone: (804) 484-5584
Administrator: W. A. Brown, III, Secretary
Type of Library Served: p
Sponsoring Body: There is none.
Source(s) of Support: Local funding and possibly grants
                       administered by the State Library.

Name: Richmond Area Research Library Direc-
                      tors
Address: 11th and Capitol Streets
                      Richmond, Virginia 23219
Telephone: (804) 786-2303
Administrator: Miss Jean T. Bear, Head, General Li-
                      brary Branch, State Library, and
                      chairman of the group
Type of Library Served: a
Sponsoring Body: There is none.
Source(s) of Support: Group is eligible to apply to the
                       State Library, the Council of

(continued)

7.   SINGLE-TYPE LIBRARY COOPERATIVES (continued)

                              Higher Education, and other approp-
                              riate agencies for grant money.

Name: Richmond Area Film Library Cooperative
Address: Learning Resources Center
                   Boatwright Memorial Library
                   University of Richmond, Virginia 23173
Telephone: (804) 285-6314
Administrator: Mr. Terry Goldman, Director of Learn-
                   ing Resources Center and chairman
Type of Library Served: a
Sponsoring Body: There is none.
Source(s) of Support: Group is eligible to apply to the
                        State Library and other appropri-
                        ate agencies for grant money.

Name: Richmond Theological Center
Address: Union Theological Seminary Library
                   3401 Brook Road
                   Richmond, Virginia 23227
Telephone: (804) 355-0671
Administrator: Dr. John B. Trotti
Type of Library Served: a
Sponsoring Body: Union Theological Seminary
Sources(s) of Support: Through a prorata contractual
                         arrangement, the Presbyterian
                         School of Education and the Vir-
                         ginia Union University School of
                         Theology share the resources of
                         the Union Theological Seminary
                         Library.

Name: Shenandoah Valley Independent College
                   Library Cooperative
Address: Bridgewater College
                   Bridgewater, Virginia 22812
Telephone: (804) 828-2501, Ext. 334
Administrator: Mr. Orland Wages, Bridgewater College
                   Librarian
Type of Library Served: a
Sponsoring Body: The member libraries of Bridgewater,
                   Eastern Mennonite, and Mary Baldwin
                   Colleges
Source(s) of Support: The organization is eligible to
                        apply to the appropriate
                        agencies for grant money.

Name: Library Affairs Committee
Address: University Center in Virginia
                   1518 Willow Lawn Drive, Suite # 102
                   Richmond, VA 23226   (continued)

353

7.   SINGLE-TYPE LIBRARY COOPERATIVES (continued)

Telephone: (804) 282-3372
Administrator: Dr. Kenneth Erfft, Director
Type of Library Served: a
Sponsoring Body: The 23 private and state-supported
                      Virginia colleges and libraries who
                      are center members.
Source(s) of Support: Funding comes via a contractual
                      arrangement with members; in ad-
                      dition the center is eligible to
                      apply to the appropriate agen-
                      cies for grant money.

Name: Cooperative College Library Center,
                      Inc.
Address: 159 Forrest Avenue, N.E., Suite #602
                      Atlanta, Georgia 30303
Telephone: (404) 659-6886
Administrator: Mr. Hillis Davis, Director
Type of Library Served: a
Sponsoring Body: The 29 member institutions, includ-
                      ing from Virginia, Virginia State
                      College in Petersburg and Virginia
                      Union University in Richmond.
Source(s) of Support: In addition to contractual ar-
                      rangements among the member in-
                      stitutions, the Center is eligi-
                      ble to apply for grants from ap-
                      propriate agencies and founda-
                      tions and has received, in the
                      past, both federal funding and
                      grants from the Carnegie Cor-
                      poration and the Danforth
                      Foundation.

Name: Tri-College Center of Virginia, Li-
                      brary Consortium
Address: Lynchburg College Library
                      Lynchburg, Virginia 24501
Telephone: (804) 845-9071
Administrator: Mrs. Mary Scudder, Lynchburg College
                      Librarian and contact person for
                      Cooperative
Type of Library Served: a
Sponsoring Body: The three private college member in-
                      stitutions, Sweet Briar, Lynchburg,
                      and Randolph-Macon Woman's Colleges
Source(s) of Funding: The consortium is eligible to
                      apply to appropriate agencies
                      for grant money.

                                      (continued)

354

7.　SINGLE-TYPE LIBRARY COOPERATIVES (continued)

　　　　　Name:　　　　　　　　Dileniwisco Media Center
　　　　　Address:　　　　　　 1032 Virginia Avenue
　　　　　　　　　　　　　　　 Norton, Virginia 24273
　　　　　Telephone:　　　　　 (703) 679-2180
　　　　　Administrator:　　　 Mr. Ronald Lawson
　　　　　Type of Library Served:　sch
　　　　　Sponsoring Body:　　 The school systems of the member ju-
　　　　　　　　　　　　　　　 risdictions, Dickenson, Lee, Scott,
　　　　　　　　　　　　　　　 and Wise counties and the City of
　　　　　　　　　　　　　　　 Norton.
　　　　　Source(s) of Funding:　 State and federal funding ad-
　　　　　　　　　　　　　　　 ministered by the State Depart-
　　　　　　　　　　　　　　　 ment of Education

　　　　　Name:　　　　　　　　Eastern Virginia Medline Consortium
　　　　　Address:　　　　　　 Post Office Box 1980
　　　　　　　　　　　　　　　 Norfolk, Virginia 23501
　　　　　Telephone:　　　　　 (804) 446-5644
　　　　　Administrator:　　　 Mrs. Suad Jones, Readers' Services
　　　　　　　　　　　　　　　 Librarian, Eastern Virginia Medical
　　　　　　　　　　　　　　　 School Library
　　　　　Type of Library Served:　This is a single-type library
　　　　　　　　　　　　　　　 cooperative by organization
　　　　　　　　　　　　　　　 including Eastern Virginia Medi-
　　　　　　　　　　　　　　　 cal School Library, Portsmouth
　　　　　　　　　　　　　　　 Medical Center and the Kecough-
　　　　　　　　　　　　　　　 tan Veterans' Administration
　　　　　　　　　　　　　　　 Hospital at Hampton, but its
　　　　　　　　　　　　　　　 services are available to all
　　　　　　　　　　　　　　　 types of libraries.
　　　　　Sponsoring Body:　　 National Library of Medicine
　　　　　Source(s) of Support:　 Institutional budgets of parti-
　　　　　　　　　　　　　　　 cipants

　　C.　　Receiving Support from the State Council of Higher Edu-
　　　　　cation:

　　　　　Name:　　　　　　　　Capitol Consortium for Continuing
　　　　　　　　　　　　　　　 Higher Education, Librarians' Net-
　　　　　　　　　　　　　　　 working Committee
　　　　　Address:　　　　　　 Virginia Commonwealth University
　　　　　　　　　　　　　　　 301 West Franklin Street
　　　　　　　　　　　　　　　 Richmond, Virginia 23284
　　　　　Telephone:　　　　　 (804) 770-8561
　　　　　Administrator:　　　 Dr. Roland J. Scott
　　　　　Type of Library Served:　a
　　　　　Sponsoring Body:　　 State Council of Higher Education
　　　　　Source(s) of Support:　 State grants administered by
　　　　　　　　　　　　　　　 the Council of Higher Educa-
　　　　　　　　　　　　　　　 tion
　　　　　　　　　　　　　　　　　　　　　　　 (continued)

7. SINGLE-TYPE LIBRARY COOPERATIVES (continued)

Name: Valley of Virginia Consortium for
                        Continuing Higher Education, Libra-
                        rians' Networking Committee
Address: James Madison University
                        Harrisonburg, Virginia 22801
Telephone: (703) 433-6112
Administrator: Dr. Grant Rush
Type of Library Served: a
Sponsoring Body: State Council of Higher Education
                        for Virginia
Source(s) of Support: State grants administered by
                        the Council of Higher Educa-
                        tion

Name: Western Regional Consortium for
                        Continuing Higher Education, Libra-
                        rians' Networking Committee
Address: Virginia Polytechnic Institute and
                        State University
                        Blacksburg, Virginia 24061
Telephone: (703) 951-5631
Administrator: Dr. Edward G. Simpson, Jr.
Type of Library Served: a
Sponsoring Body: State Council of Higher Education
                        for Virginia
Source(s) of Funding: State grants administered by
                        the Council of Higher Educa-
                        tion

Name: Tidewater Consortium for Continuing
                        Higher Education, Librarians' Net-
                        working Committee
Address: Virginia Associated Research Campus
                        12070 Jefferson Avenue
                        Newport News, Virginia 23606
Telephone: (804) 877-9231
Administrator: Mr. Lawrence Dotalo
Type of Library Served: a
Sponsoring Body: State Council of Higher Education
                        for Virginia
Source(s) of Funding: State grants administered by
                        the Council of Higher Educa-
                        tion

Name: Central Virginia Consortium for
                        Continuing Higher Education, Libra-
                        rians' Networking Committee
Address: Post Office Box 3697
                        Charlottesville, Virginia 22903
Telephone: (804) 924-7153
(continued)

7.   SINGLE-TYPE LIBRARY COOPERATIVES (continued)

        Administrator: Dr. Howard Bryant (acting)
        Type of Library Served: a
        Sponsoring Body: State Council of Higher Education
                      for Virginia
        Source(s) of Funding: State grants administered by
                      the Council of Higher Educa-
                      tion

        Name: Consortium for Continuing Higher
                      Education in Northern Virginia,
                      Librarians' Networking Committee
        Address: 4210 Roberts Road
                      Fairfax, Virginia 22030
        Telephone: (703) 323-2155
        Administrator: Mr. Dean Brundage
        Type of Library Served: a
        Sponsoring Body: State Council of Higher Education
                      for Virginia
        Source(s) of Funding: State grants administered by
                      the Council of Higher Educa-
                      tion

8.   MULTI-TYPE LIBRARY COOPERATIVES

    A.   Receiving Continuing Financial Support from the State
        Library:

        Name: Metropolitan Washington Council of
                      Governments, Library Council
        Address: 1225 Connecticut Avenue, N.W.
                      Washington, D. C. 20036
        Telephone: (202) 223-0800
        Administrator: Mrs. Barbara Robinson, Chief of
                      Library Programs
        Types of Libraries Served: a, p, sp, sch
        Federal support: Contract is set up by calendar year.
        State support: Contract is set up by calendar year.
        Total support: $18,000.00 (Virginia's share for
                      calendar year 1977)

    B.   Receiving No Continuing Financial Support from the
        State Library:

        Name: Lynchburg Area Library Cooperative
        Address: Sweet Briar College library
                      Sweet Briar, Virginia 24595
        Telephone: (804) 381-5541
        Administrator: Mr. Henry James, Jr., Chairman
        Types of Libraries Served: a, p, sp
        Sponsoring Body: 14 member libraries   (continued)

8.   MULTI-TYPE LIBRARY COOPERATIVES (continued)

Source(s) of Support: The cooperative is eligible to apply for grant money administered by the State Library and other appropriate agencies or foundations.

Name: Roanoke Valley Library Association
Address: The Library
                         Hollins College
                         Hollins, Virginia 24020
Telephone: (703) 362-6591
Administrator: Richard E. Kirkwood, Hollins College Librarian and Association chairman
Type of Libraries Served: a, p, sp
Sponsoring Body: 13 member libraries
Source(s) of Support: The Association is eligible to apply for grant money administered by the State Library and other appropriate agencies or foundations.

Name: Planning District III Consortium of Libraries
Address: Kelly Library
                         Emory and Henry College
                         Emory, Virginia 24327
Telephone: (703) 944-3114
Administrator: Mr. L. S. Strohl, III, Emory and Henry College Librarian and Consortium Chairman
Types of Libraries Served: a, p, sp, institutional
Sponsoring Body: 10 member libraries
Source(s) of Support: The Consortium is eligible to apply for grant money administered by the State Library and other appropriate agencies or foundations.

C.   Receiving Occasional Support from the State Library:

These are listed under item B as explained in the Source(s) of Support category.

9.   INTERLIBRARY COOPERATION FUNCTIONS

A.   Receiving Continuing Financial Support from the State Library:

(continued)

9. INTERLIBRARY COOPERATION FUNCTIONS (continued)

	State Support	Federal Support Title I	Federal Support Title III	Other Support	Total Support
*Interlibrary Loan	(not possible to provide breakdown of figures)				
**Continuing Education(1)	$160.00	$30,473.00	$2,099.00	-	$32,732.00
Cooperative Acquisitions					
Cooperative Cataloging					
Cooperative Delivery					
Cooperative Processing					
Cooperative Reference					
Cooperative Storage					
Legislative Assistance					
Planning/Development	(not possible to provide breakdown of figures)				
Union List of Serials					
**Regional Projects involving multitype cooperatives and also including the Piedmont Books by Mail Program.	49,861.00	9,248.00	30,455.00		89,564.00
TOTAL SUPPORT:	$50,021.00	39,721.00	32,554.00		$122,296.00

*The State Library has worked in close cooperation with the Council of Higher Education involving statewide planning for programs such as co-ordinated collection development, centralized storage facilities for in-frequently used serials, updating the Virginia Union List of Serials, and, in fact, has established, as recommended, a statewide interli-brary loan referral center as an extension of the service currently provided under the auspices of the General Library Branch and as a part of the Virginia Interlibrary Communications (VIC) System.

(1) A continuing education advisory committee, representing a cross section of the Virginia library community, plays a major role in plan-ning and coordinating seminars sponsored with the use of cooperative funding. An effort is made to avoid duplication and to offer programs of a broad interest or topics that are not being presented by other groups within the state; a close working relationship is maintained with the Virginia Library Association ad hoc Continuing Education Committee.

**Figures for fiscal year 1976

B. Non-Financial Support Role of the State Library:

In providing consulting services and encouragement to li-brarians throughout the state engaging in interlibrary cooperation the State Library offers assistance in ad-dition to grant administration.

10. ILC COMMUNICATION DEVICES/SERVICE NETWORKS

(continued)

10.　ILC COMMUNICATION DEVICES/SERVICE NETWORKS (continued)

A.

DEVICE/SERVICE	SUPPORT($)	EQUIPMENT	PARTICIPANTS
InWATS line	*	-	All Virginia libraries
Teletype machines (both a part of Virginia Inter-library Communications System)	*	-	17 research libraries directly (all libraries indirectly through State Library Inter-library Loan Center)

*Fiscal year 1976 total figure for both was $32,244.00

B.　Non-Financial Support Role of the State Library:

Continuing effort is made to publicize the availability of these services with interlibrary loan workshops throughout the state being conducted as needed.

11.　MACHINE-READABLE DATA BASE REFERENCE SEARCHING SERVICES

There are none receiving direct financial support from the State Library at this time.

12.　INTERLIBRARY SERVICES TO SPECIAL GROUPS

A.　The State Library has financially-supported cooperative arrangements for consultant services to the Library for the Blind and Visually Handicapped which operates under the State Commission for the Visually Handicapped; to state institutions for library service to residents and to other libraries providing services for the physically handicapped.

The Virginia Medical Information System (VAMIS) is a statewide biomedical library service available to all health practitioners in the Commonwealth. The libraries at the University of Virginia Medical Center and the Medical College of Virginia at Virginia Commonwealth University offer extension services to those in the health professions not affiliated with the medical schools. This cooperative project began in 1970 with funds from the Virginia Regional Medical Program. The State of Virginia now supports the program.

Reference questions are answered when submitted by mail or telephone. Both medical center librarians have terminals for searching the health science literature. If an item is not owned by either of the VAMIS service cen-

(continued)

12.　INTERLIBRARY SERVICES TO SPECIAL GROUPS (continued)

> ters, the request is forwarded to the National Library
> of Medicine.
>
> The <u>Virginia Union List of Biomedical Serials</u>, a listing
> of journals owned by contributing libraries throughout
> the Commonwealth, is distributed free of charge to local
> libraries in Virginia.

>> B.　Non-Financial Support Role of the State Library:
>>
>> There is none.

13.　PARTICIPATION IN MULTI-STATE LIBRARY NETWORKS

>> A.　Network:　Southeastern Library Network (SOLINET)

Financial Support:	Total figures not available.
Participation:	State Library contributes cataloging information to data base. 18 Virginia academic libraries also are members.
Services Used:	Cataloging; purchase of archives tapes for libraries in the state.

>> B.　There are no multi-state networks with headquarters
>> in Virginia.

14.　LEGAL BASIS FOR MULTI-TYPE LIBRARY COOPERATION:

> This information is included in Item #2, Overview.

15.　LEGAL BARRIERS AGAINST PARTICIPATION IN MULTI-TYPE LIBRARY COOPERA-
TION:

> There are none.

1. REPORTING AGENCY

    A.   Washington State Library
        Olympia, WA 98504
        (206) 753-5592

    B.   Chief Officer: Roderick G. Swartz, State Librarian

    C.   Fiscal Year: 1977

2. OVERVIEW

    The Washington Library Network is composed of four components tying libraries together in cooperative services. The components are: interlibrary systems, reference/referral, telecommunications, and computer systems. Enabling legislation passed in 1975 allowed the State Library Commission to establish rules and regulations governing the network development. Multi-type library activities are being encouraged within each of the seven library service areas. While state funds have provided development monies, operational funds for full participation of all types of libraries remains a long-range goal.

3. NUMBER OF LIBRARIES IN THE STATE

    Academic: 49
    Public: 77
    School: 2,206
       Public: 1,970 est.
       Private: 236 est.
    Special: 168
       Profit: 30
       Nonprofit: 138

    TOTAL: 2,500 est.

4. STATE AGENCY INTERLIBRARY COOPERATION UNIT

    A. Unit Name: Consultant Services Division
       Person in Charge: (vacant) Chief, Consultant Services

    B. Unit Name: Washington Library Network
       Person in Charge: Raymond DeBuse, Associate Director of Network

       Unit Name: Information Services Division
       Person in Charge: Gene Bismuti, Chief

       Unit Name: Documents Distribution Center
       Person in Charge: Ann Bregent, Documents Librarian

5. OTHER STATE-LEVEL GOVERNMENT ILC UNITS

Unit Name: Data Processing Authority
Address: 2604 – 12 Court SW
              Olympia, WA 98504
Activities: Under RCW 43.105 the Data Processing Author-
              ity is responsible for development and main-
              tenance of a coordinated statewide plan for
              data processing and data communications sys-
              tem. Under RCW 43.105 has joint responsibi-
              lity with State Library Commission to devel-
              op schedule of network fees and other data
              processing related activities.

Unit Name: WLN Executive Council
Address: Washington State Library
              Olympia, WA 98504
Activities: Responsible for governance structure of the
              Washington Library Network. Composed of
              eleven members representative of all types
              of libraries, it advises the State Library
              Commission concerning policies and opera-
              tions of the network.

Unit Name: WLN Representative Assembly
Address: Washington State Library
              Olympia, WA 98504

Activities: A broad-based, multi-type library assembly
              responsible to support the cooperative
              activities of WLN. Composed of approxi-
              mately sixty persons, it is chaired by the
              Chairperson of the Executive Council.

6. OTHER STATE-LEVEL NON-GOVERNMENTAL ILC UNITS

There are none.

7. SINGLE-TYPE LIBRARY COOPERATIVES

A. Receiving Continuing Financial Support from the State
    Library:

There are none.

B. Receiving No Continuing Financial Support from the State
    Library:
    Name: King County Library System
    Address: 300 – 8th Avenue North
              Seattle, WA 98109

(continued)

7.   SINGLE-TYPE LIBRARY COOPERATIVES (continued)

      B.   Receiving No Continuing Financial Support from the State
            Library:
            Name: Kitsap Regional Library
            Address: 312 North Callow
                         Bremerton, WA 98310

            Name: Timberland Regional Library
            Address: 1006 Sleater-Kinney S.E.
                         Lacey, WA 98503

            Name: Sno-Isle Regional Library
            Address: P.O. Box 148
                         Marysville, WA 98270

            Name: Pierce County Library
            Address: 2356 Tacoma Avenue South
                         Tacoma, WA 98402

            Type: Public
            Activity: In order to provide more convenient access to
                         library materials and services, a cooperative
                         use agreement between five library districts
                         representing ten counties adopted the policy
                         that any resident within the service area of one
                         of the libraries may use the services of all
                         five libraries.

      C.   Receives Administrative and Operational Support from the
            State Library:
            Name: Washington Library Film Circuit
            Address: Washington State Library
                         Olympia, WA 98504
            Administrator: Jane Wolcott
            Type: Public
            Activity: Provides cooperative 16mm film service for its
                         members. Present member systems are:
                             Timberland Regional Library (5)
                             Auburn Public (1)
                             King County Library System (5)
                             Everett Public (1)
                             Kitsap Regional Library (2)
                             Longview Public (2)
                             Mid-Columbia Regional Library (1)
                             North Olympic Library System (1)
                             Richland Public (1)
                             Seattle Public (1)
                             Sno-Isle Regional Library (4)
                             Spokane County (1)
                             Spokane Public (1)
                             Tacoma Public (2)
                                                         (continued)

7.   SINGLE-TYPE LIBRARY COOPERATIVES (continued)

   C.   Receives Administrative and Operational Support from the
        State Library :
        Activity: (continued)
                        Walla Walla Public (1)
                        Whatcom County (1)
                        Bellingham Public (1)
                        Whitman County (1)
                        Yakima Valley Regional Library (2)

                 Total population served 2,537,720. Percentage
                 served 75.51% figured from 1976 Annual Statisti-
                 cal Bulletin. Per packet membership is $1,725.00.

8.   MULTI-TYPE LIBRARY COOPERATIVES

   A.   Receiving Continuing Financial Support from the State
        Library:

        There are none.

   B.   Formally-organized multi-type library cooperative organiza-
        tions receiving no continuing financial assistance from the
        state library agency:
        Name: Spokane Inland Empire Libraries (SPIEL)
        Type: p, a, sch. sp

        Name: Cassette Tape Cooperative
        Address: c/o Don Lee
                     Educational Service District #111
                     5601 - 6th Avenue
                     Tacoma, WA 98406
        Administrator: Don Lee
        Type: The Evergreen State College   a
                     Seattle   sch
                     Tumwater   sch
                     Grand Staff Library at Ft. Lewis   sp
                     Bellingham   p
                     Camas   p
                     Everett   p
                     Ft. Vancouver   p
                     Kelso   p
                     Longview   p
                     Pierce County   p
                     Puyallup   p
                     Tacoma   p
                     Whatcom County   p
                     Educational Service Districts
                     104, 109, 111, 112, 114   sch
        Activity: Duplication of tapes are upon request from mem-
                   ber library. Masters (3472) were purchased with
                                                       (continued)

365

8. MULTI-TYPE LIBRARY COOPERATIVES (continued)

    B. Formally-organized multi-type library cooperative organiza-
        tions receiving no continuing financial assistance from the
        state library agency:
        Activity: (continued)
                    copyright privileges. In 1975 approximately
                    15,000 tapes were duplicated at $1.25 per tape.
                    Examples of subjects represented are: dramatized
                    literature and history; biographies; authors dis-
                    cussing books; interviews with prominent person-
                    alities; lectures on ecology, music, science.

    C. Receiving Administrative and Grant Support from the State
        Library:
        Name: Central Library Service Area
        Address: Washington State Library
                    Olympia, WA 98504
        Chairperson: Mary Lou McGalliard
        Types of Libraries Served:
                    Public   9
                    Academic   4
                    K-12   4
                    Special   1
        Sponsoring Body: Washington State Library Commission
        Sources of Support: Administration and operational from
                             Washington State Library

        Name: King County Library Service Area
        Address: Washington State Library
                    Olympia, WA 98504
        Chairperson: Erma Jean Morgan
        Types of Libraries Served:
                    Public   4
                    Academic   11
                    K-12   5
                    Special   13
        Sponsoring Body: Washington State Library Commission
        Sources of Support: Administration and operational from
                             Washington State Library

        Name: Northeast Library Service Area
        Address: Washington State Library
                    Olympia, WA 98504
        Chairperson: June Perrin
        Types of Libraries Served:
                    Public   18
                    Academic   7
                    K-12   13
                    Special   3
        Sponsoring Body: Washington State Library Commission

(continued)

8. MULTI-TYPE LIBRARY COOPERATIVES (continued)

> C. Receiving Administrative and Grant Support from the State
>   Library: (continued)
>   Sources of Support: Administration and operational from
>   Washington State Library. Grant in
>   amount of $19,725 (FY 1978) will pro-
>   vide delivery services among academic
>   and public libraries in Spokane area
>   and will link with delivery services
>   in Pullman, Washington/Moscow, Idaho
>   area.
>
>   Name: Northwest Library Service Area
>   Address: Washington State Library
>   Olympia, WA 98504
>   Chairperson: Gertrude Eichelsdoerfer
>   Types of Libraries Served:
>   Public   12
>   Academic   5
>   K-12   6
>   Special   2
>   Sponsoring Body: Washington State Library Commission
>   Sources of Support: Administration and operational from
>   Washington State Library. Grant in
>   amount of $18,960 (FY 1978) will fund
>   a coordinator whose responsibilities
>   will be the identification of re-
>   sources, development of communication
>   linkages, and implementation of train-
>   ing sessions for the personnel of the
>   multi-type libraries.
>
>   Name: Southeast Library Service Area
>   Address: Washington State Library
>   Olympia, WA 98504
>   Chairperson: Byrdean Vickery
>   Types of Libraries Served:
>   Public   9
>   Academic   4
>   K-12   13
>   Special   3
>   Sponsoring Body: Washington State Library Commission
>   Sources of Support: Adminisration and operational from
>   Washington State Library. Grant in
>   amount of $27,400 (FY 1978) will fund
>   a coordinator whose responsibilities
>   will be the identification of re-
>   sources and implementation of skill
>   sessions for personnel of the multi-
>   type libraries.

(continued)

8. MULTI-TYPE LIBRARY COOPERATIVES (continued)

    C. Receiving Administrative and Grant Support from the State
        Library: (continued)
        Name: Southwest Library Service Area
        Address: Washington State Library
                    Olympia, WA 98504
        Chairperson: Irene Conable
        Types of Libraries Served:
                    Public   8
                    Academic   2
                    K-12   5
                    Special   5
        Sponsoring Body: Washington State Library Commission
        Sources of Support: Administration and Operational from
                              Washington State Library. Grant in
                              amount of $31,150 (FY 1978) will allow
                              sharing of resources to expand refer-
                              ence/referral services and utilization
                              of delivery services among libraries
                              of all types in those counties border-
                              ing Columbia River between Oregon and
                              Washington.

        Name: West Library Service Area
        Address: Washington State Library
                    Olympia, WA 98504
        Chairperson: Marile Creager, Co-Chairperson
                       Frank Kilham, Co-Chairperson
        Types of Libraries Served:
                    Public   10
                    Academic   12
                    K-12   10
                    Special   4
        Sponsoring Body: Washington State Library Commission
        Sources of Support: Administrative and Operational from
                              Washington State Library. Grant in
                              amount of $50,681 (FY 1978) will test
                              a multi-type library approach to pro-
                              vide services in a county without
                              countywide library service, using
                              existing school facilities as commu-
                              nity outlets.

9. INTERLIBRARY COOPERATION FUNCTIONS (FY 1977)

	State Support	Federal Support Title I	Federal Support Title IV	Other Support	Total Support
A.					
Interlibrary Loan					
PNBC		$95,458	$47,642		$143,100
Resource Sharing		60,500			60,500

(continued)

9. INTERLIBRARY COOPERATION FUNCTIONS (continued)

A. (continued)	State Support	Federal Support Title I	Federal Support Title IV	Other Support	Total Support
Cooperative Cataloging (no separate figures available)					
Continuing Education (WICHE)		$22,444			$22,444
Planning/Development (WSACL)		75,625			75,625
Total Support		$254,027	$47,642		$301,669

B. Non-Financial Support Role for the State Library:
   Consultant Services
   Interlibrary Loan backup
   Reference/Referral
   Cataloging Support

10. ILC COMMUNICATION DEVICES/SERVICE NETWORKS

A.

	Support ($)	Equipment (#)	Participants
State Controlled Area Network (telephone service)	$38,205.12	NA	36
In-Wats Reference Line to Washington State Library	1,200.00	NA	NR

B. Non-financial Support Role for the State Library:

   Consultant service concerning telecommunications, computer equipment, etc.

11. MACHINE-READABLE DATA BASE REFERENCE SEARCHING SERVICES

Data Base/Vendor	Support ($)	Equipment (#)	Participants
SDC	$5,000	3	3
Lockheed			
InfoBank			

12. INTERLIBRARY SERVICES TO SPECIAL GROUPS

Services	State	Federal LSCA	Federal Other Sources	Total
Washington Regional Library for Blind and Physically Handicapped	$207,000	$25,220	$127,500	$359,720
Institutional Library Services	408,007	13,912		421,919

13. PARTICIPATION IN MULTI-STATE LIBRARY NETWORKS

    A. Networks: Pacific Northwest Bibliographic Center
        Financial Support: $143,100.00
        Participation: Serve on Board of Directors
        Services Used: All

    B. There are none.

14. LEGAL BASES FOR MULTI-TYPE LIBRARY COOPERATION

    State legislation enabling multi-type library cooperative development:
        Chapter 31, Laws of 1975-76, 2nd Extraordinary Session. (Senate Bill 3094 - Establishing the Washington Library Network and placing responsibility for Network with the Washington State Library Commission.)

    State legislation enabling interstate library compact:
        Interstate Library Compact, RCW 27.18.010 - 27.18.050

    State-provided statutory funding for multi-type library cooperative development:
        There is none.

15. LEGAL BARRIERS AGAINST PARTICIPATION IN MULTITYPE LIBRARY COOPERATION

    No known legal barriers, except for Constitutional prohibition for state funding of private church-related colleges, and institutional interpretations of law which often inhibits cooperative activities.

1. REPORTING AGENCY

   a. West Virginia Library Commission
      Science & Cultural Center
      Charleston, West Virginia 25305
      304-348-2041

   b. Frederic J. Glazer, Director

   c. Fiscal Year: 1977

2. OVERVIEW

   The interlibrary loan network in West Virginia is sponsored and
   supported by the state agency. Thirteen public libraries are
   designated as regional or service center libraries. Requests
   from other libraries in the region are channeled through these
   centers either to the appropriate locations or the Library Comm.
   Requests are made either via teletype (10 college/university
   libraries; 2 regional) or WATS line. All libraries in the state
   are capable of initiating requests.
   In October of 1976 the West Virginia Union Catalog, maintained by
   the Library Commission, was converted to microfiche. The 348
   fiche produced contain a catalog representing an estimated
   3,000,000 volumes. The microform edition is supplemented every
   two months by cumulated updates in microfiche form distributed by
   the Library Commission. The purpose of creating the microfiche
   edition of the West Virginia Union Catalog is to provide libraries
   with a copy of the catalog and thus to facilitate interlibrary
   borrowing.
   Thrity-seven copies of the "Catfiche" were distributed to the
   libraries most active in interlibrary borrowing. The subsequent
   bi-monthly cumulations have been distributed to the same libraries.
   The Commission had hoped to purchase and distribute more free
   copies of the basic union catalog to more libraries, but funds
   limited this plan. Presently 59 libraries are contributing
   holdings to the catalog which forms the basis for all interlibrary
   loans in the state.

3. NUMBER OF LIBRARIES IN THE STATE
   Academic: 25
   Public: 123
   School: 1,370
      Public: 1,370
      Private: Not Available
   Special: 74
      Profit: 27
      Non-Profit: 47

   Total: 1,592 est.

371

4. STATE AGENCY INTERLIBRARY COOPERATION UNIT

    A. Specific Unit Responsible for ILC Activities:

       There is no existing unit nor plans to create one.

    B. Other Units with ILC Responsibilities:

       Unit Name: West Virginia Union Catalog and Interlibrary Loan Network
       Person in Charge: Judith Prosser, Librarian III

5. OTHER STATE-LEVEL GOVERNMENTAL ILC UNITS

       There are none.

6. OTHER STATE-LEVEL NON-GOVERNMENTAL ILC UNITS

       There are none.

7. SINGLE-TYPE LIBRARY COOPERATIVES

    A. Receiving Continuing Financial Support from the State Library:

       There are none.

    B. Receiving No Continuing Financial Support from the State Library:

       There are none.

    C. Receiving Occasional Financial Support from the State Library:

       There are none.

8. MULTI-TYPE LIBRARY COOPERATIVES

    A. Receiving Continuing Financial Support from the State Library:

       There are none.

    B. Receiving No Continuing Financial Support from the State Library:

       There are none.

    C. Receiving Occasional Financial Support from the State Library:

       There are none.

9.   INTERLIBRARY COOPERATION FUNCTIONS

A. Receiving Continuing Financial Support from the State Library:

	State Support	Federal Support		Other Support	Total Support
		Title I	Title III		
Interlibrary Loan	$125,561		$50,115		$175,676
Continuing Education		18,000			18,000
Cooperative Acquisitions					
Cooperative Cataloging					
Cooperative Delivery					
Cooperative Processing					
Cooperative Reference					
Cooperative Storage					
Legislative Assistance					
Planning/Development					
Union Lists of Serials					
Other (please specify					
Total Support	$125,561	$18,000	$50,115		$193,676

B. Non-Financial Support Role of the State Library:

There is none.

10.   ILC COMMUNICATION DEVICES /SERVICE NETWORKS

A. | Device/Service | Support ($) | Equipment (#) | Participants |
|---|---|---|---|
| TWX | $9,000 | 13 | 13 |
| Code A Phone (WATS) | 8,400 | Statewide | 198 |

B.   NON-FINANCIAL SUPPORT ROLE OF THE STATE LIBRARY :
There is no non-financial support role for these services.

11.   MACHINE-READABLE DATA BASE REFERENCE SEARCHING SERVICES

Date Base/ Vendor	Support ($)	Terminals (#)	Participants
Lockheed, SDC, Information Bank	$18,000	1	Statewide

12.   INTERLIBRARY SERVICES TO SPECIAL GROUPS

A.   Blind & Physically Handicapped-West Virginia Library Commission
Institutions-West Virginia Library Commission

B.   NON-FINANCIAL SUPPORT ROLE OF THE STATE LIBRARY:
There is none.

13. PARTICIPATION IN MULTI-STATE LIBRARY NETWORKS

   A. Network: Pittsburgh Regional Library Center
      Financial Support: not reported
      Participation: Informal cooperation
      Services Used: OCLC

14. LEGAL BASES FOR MULTI-TYPE LIBRARY COOPERATION

   West Virginia Statutes 10.1A.1. Interstate Compact authorizes
   cooperation and sharing with respect to those types of library
   facilities and services which can be more economically
   or efficiently developed and maintained on a cooperative basis.

15. LEGAL BARRIERS AGAINST PARTICIPATION IN MULTI-TYPE LIBRARY
   COOPERATION

   There are no legal barriers.

1. REPORTING AGENCY

    A. Division for Library Services
        Department of Public Instruction
        126 Langdon Street
        Madison, Wisconsin 53702
        (608)266-2205

    B. Chief Officer: W. Lyle Eberhart, Administrator

    C. Fiscal Year: 1978

2. OVERVIEW

    A Task Force on Interlibrary Cooperation and Resource Sharing was
    initiated in July 1975. It completed its work at the end of June
    1976 and produced a report, Interlibrary Cooperation: A Wisconsin
    Plan. Among the major recommendations of the Task Force were:
    1) that a statewide Council on Library Development and Networking,
    interconnected with a Professional Advisory Committee, be es-
    tablished to serve as the major coordinating agency for cooperative
    planning of those projects having statewide impact; and 2) that
    area multitype organizations be established to foster cooperation
    and resource sharing at that level among librarians from all types
    of libraries. These organizations were to be statutorily recog-
    nized and able to receive state funding.

    The 1977-79 State Biennial Budget contains a provision for a
    Legislative Council study. The Legislative Council is to study
    and submit to the Legislature by November 15, 1978, recommen-
    dations concerning public library systems, the Division for
    Library Services, and the relationship of the Reference and Loan
    Library to other library service in the state. Although the
    precise areas to be studied have not been determined, it is
    expected that major concerns for state-level and area-level co-
    operation and resource sharing will be addressed.

    Wisconsin has 12 public library systems covering 47 of the state's
    72 counties and serving 68% of the state's population. There are
    four legally incorporated intertype library councils in the state.
    A great deal of Task Force discussion focused on alliance be-
    tween public library systems and proposed area multitype organ-
    izations, although there was not concensus on the roles and
    responsibilities of the two organizations. Public Library systems
    are statutorily mandated to participate in cooperative activities.
    The existing councils do not have statutory recognition or funding.

3. NUMBER OF LIBRARIES IN THE STATE

    Academic: 75
    Public: 340
    School: 2,438

(continued)

3. NUMBER OF LIBRARIES IN THE STATE (continued)

        Public: 1,704
        Private: 734
    Special: Total: 389
      Profit: Unknown
      Nonprofit: Unknown

      TOTAL: 3,242

4. STATE AGENCY INTERLIBRARY COOPERATION UNIT

    A. Unit Name: Bureau of Public and Cooperative Library Services
        Person in Charge: Kathleen Imhoff, Director
                         Margaret Branson, Intertype Library Services Consultant
    B. Unit Name: Bureau for Reference and Loan Services
        Person in Charge: Peter Hamon, Director
    C. Unit Name: Bureau for School Library Media Programs
        Person in Charge: Dianne Williams, Director

5. OTHER STATE-LEVEL GOVERNMENTAL ILC UNITS

        Unit Name: Council on Library Development
        Address: c/o Division for Library Services
                          126 Langdon Street
                          Madison, Wisconsin 53702
        Activities: Has statutory responsibility to advise the state superintendent with regard to the general policies and activities of the state's programs for library development and interlibrary cooperation.

6. OTHER STATE-LEVEL NON-GOVERNMENTAL ILC UNITS

        Unit Name: Council of Wisconsin Librarians (COWL)
        Address: 728 State Street
                           Madison, Wisconsin 53706
        Telephone: (608) 263-4962
        Administrator: James P. Bishop, Chairperson (Director, Carthage College Library, Kenosha, Wisconsin 53140)
        Activities: COWL has established two major state network services: Wisconsin Interlibrary Loan Service, WILS, which provides direct access for the state's academic libraries and indirect access by contract for the clientele served by the Division for Library Services', Reference and Loan Library to the holdings of the University of Wisconsin-Madison Libraries; and the
                                          (continued)

6. OTHER STATE-LEVEL NON-GOVERNMENTAL ILC UNITS (continued)

> Wisconsin Library Consortium (WLC), which provides Wisconsin libraries of all types access to the services of the Ohio College Library Center. Membership on COWL includes public, school, academic and special library representation.

7. SINGLE-TYPE LIBRARY COOPERATIVES

A. Receiving Continuing Support from the State Library:

Name: La Crosse Area Library System
Address: 800 Main Street
                       La Crosse, Wisconsin 54601
Telephone: (608) 784-3151
Administrator: James W. White
Type of Library Served: p
Federal Support: $ 7,000
State Support: $128,753
Local Support: $ 44,760
Other Support: -0-
Total Support: $180,513

Name: Calumet-Manitowoc Counties Library System
Address: 808 Hamilton Street
                       Manitowoc, Wisconsin 54220
Telephone: (414) 682-6861
Administrator: Barbara Kelly
Type of Library Served: p
Federal Support: $ 22,060
State Support: $ 73,535
Local Support $ 94,820
Other Support: -0-
Total Support $190,415

Name: Mid-Wisconsin Federated Library System
Address: 32 Sheboygan Street
                       Fond du Lac, Wisconsin 54935
Telephone: (414) 921-3670
Administrator: Eugene G. McLane
Type of Library Served: p
Federal Support: $ 16,000
State Support: $125,526
Local Support: -0-
Other Support: -0-
Total Support: $141,526

Name: Milwaukee County Federated Library System
Address: 814 W. Wisconsin Avenue
                       Milwaukee, Wisconsin 53233
Telephone: (414) 278-3020

(continued)

7. SINGLE-TYPE LIBRARY COOPERATIVES (continued)

Administrator: Henry Bates, Jr.
Type of Library Served: p
Federal Support: -0-
State Support: $806,069
Local Support: -0-
Other Support: -0-
Total Support: $806,069

Name: Nicolet Federated Library System
Address: 515 Pine Street
                     Green Bay, Wisconsin 54301
Telephone: (414) 497-3443
Administrator: Ron Gorsegnor
Type of Library Served: p
Federal Support: -0-
State Support: $259,482
Local Support: -0-
Other Support: -0-
Total Support: $259,482

Name: Northwest Wisconsin Library System
Address: 502 Second Street West
                     Ashland, Wisconsin 54806
Telephone: (715) 682-8027
Administrator: William Sloggy
Type of Library Served: p
Federal Support: $ 20,000
State Support: $180,470
Local Support: $ 76,152
Other Support: -0-
Total Support: $276,622

Name: Outagamie-Waupaca Counties Federated
                     Library System
Address: 121 S. Oneida Street
                     Appleton, Wisconsin 54911
Telephone: (414) 734-8873
Administrator: Richard Krumwiede
Type of Library Served: p
Federal Support: $ 22,846
State Support: $104,358
Local Support: -0-
Other Support: -0-
Total Support: $127,204

Name: Rock County Library System
Address: 316 S. Main Street
                     Janesville, Wisconsin 53545
Telephone: (608) 756-1890
Administrator: Janice S. Farley
Type of Library Served: p
Federal Support: $ 20,000

(continued)

7. SINGLE-TYPE LIBRARY COOPERATIVES (continued)

State Support: $ 87,085
Local Support: $ 46,000
Other Support: -0-
Total Support: $153,085

Name: South Central Library System
Address: 201 West Mifflin Street
                      Madison, Wisconsin 53703
Telephone: (608) 266-4181
Administrator: Roger Pearson
Type of Library Served: p
Federal Support: $ 36,600
State Support: $295,271
Local Support: -0-
Other Support: -0-
Total Support: $331,871

Name: Southwest Wisconsin Library System
Address: 1775 Fourth Street
                      Fennimore, Wisconsin 53809
Telephone: (608) 822-3393
Administrator: Serena Nelson
Type of Library Served: p
Federal Support: -0-
State Support: $111,767
Local Support: $ 65,695
Other Support: -0-
Total Support: $177,462

Name: Winnefox Federated Library System
Address: 106 Washington Avenue
                      Oshkosh, Wisconsin 54901
Telephone: (414) 424-0473
Administrator: Leonard Archer
Type of Library Served: p
Federal Support: -0-
State Support: $126,040
Local Support: -0-
Other Support: -0-
Total Support: $126,040

Name: Wisconsin Valley Library Service
Address: 400 First Street
                      Wausau, Wisconsin 54401
Telephone: (715) 845-7214
Administrator: Wayne Bassett
Type of Library Served: p
Federal Support: $ 45,858
State Support: $361,591
Local Support: $ 35,270
Other Support: -0-
Total Support: $442,719

(continued)

7. SINGLE-TYPE LIBRARY COOPERATIVES (continued)

      Name: Wisconsin Interlibrary Loan Service
                                  (WILS)
      Address: 728 State Street
                                    Madison, Wisconsin 53706
      Telephone: (608) 263-4962
      Administrator: Nancy Marshall
      Type of Library Served: a; (p, sch, sp indirectly served
                                    through resource contact with Division
                                    for Library Services)
      Federal Support: $ 3,918
      State Support: $ 75,000
      Local Support: $ 89,109
      Other Support: -0-
      Total Support: $168,027

   B. Receiving No Continuing Financial Support From the State
      Library:

      There are none.

8. MULTITYPE LIBRARY COOPERATIVES

   A. Receiving Continuing Financial Support from the State Library:

      There are none.

   B. Receiving No Continuing Financial Support from the State
      Library:

      There are none.

   C. Other (Receiving Occasional Support from the State Library):

      Name: Madison Area Library Council
      Address: 201 W. Mifflin Street
                                    Madison, Wisconsin 53703
      Telephone: (608) 238-5612
      Administrator: Ann Clark
      Types of Libraries Served: a, p, sch, sp
      Sponsoring Body: None
      Source(s) of Support: Local, state (through system), federal

      Name: Library Council of Metropolitan
                                    Milwaukee
      Address: 814 W. Wisconsin Avenue
                                  Milwaukee, Wisconsin 53233
      Telephone: (414) 271-8470
      Administrator: Mary Cronin
      Types of Libraries Served: a, p, sch, sp
      Sponsoring Body: None
      Source(s) of Support: Local, federal   (continued)

8. MULTITYPE LIBRARY COOPERATIVES (continued)

Name: Northeast Wisconsin Intertype Libraries
Address: c/o University of Wisconsin-Green Bay
                          110 S. University Circle Drive
                          Green Bay, Wisconsin 54302
Telephone: (414) 465-2383
Administrator: Kurt Rothe
Types of Libraries Served: a, p, sch, sp
Sponsoring Body: None
Source(s) of Support: local, federal

Name: Tri-County Library Council
Address: c/o University of Wisconsin-Parkside
                          Wood Road
                          Kenosha, Wisconsin 53141
Telephone: (414) 553-2617
Administrator: Mary Alice Seemeyer
Types of Libraries Served: a, p, sch, sp
Sponsoring Body: None
Source(s) of Support: local, federal

9. INTERLIBRARY COOPERATION FUNCTIONS

   A. Receiving Continuing Financial Support from the State Library:

	State Support	Federal Support Title I	Federal Support Title III	Other Support	Total Support
Interlibrary Loan	157,000				157,000
Continuing Education					
Cooperative Acquisitions					
Cooperative Cataloging					
Cooperative Delivery					
Cooperative Processing					
Cooperative Reference					
Cooperative Storage					
Legislative Assistance					
Planning/Development			50,109		50,109
Union Lists of Serials					
Other (please specify)					
Total Support	$157,000		$50,109		$207,109

   B. Non-Financial Support Role of the State Library Agency:

   State consultants work with organizations representing all
   types of libraries in planning and implementing cooperative
   projects.

11. ILC COMMUNICATION DEVICES/SERVICE NETWORKS

    A. RECEIVING CONTINUING FINANCIAL SUPPORT FROM THE STATE
       LIBRARY: (Continued)

II. ILC COMMUNICATION DEVICES/SERVICES NETWORKS (continued)

Device/Service	Support ($)	Equipment (#)	Participants
TWX and TWP	$19,000	12	13

B. NON-FINANCIAL SUPPORT ROLE OF THE STATE LIBRARY:

There is no non-financial support role for these services.

C. MACHINE-READABLE DATA BASE REFERENCE SEARCHING SERVICES:

Data Base/Vendor	Support ($)	Terminals (#)	Participants
ERIC, BRS, SDC, Lockheed	$1,000 (contract)	3	3,200

12. INTERLIBRARY SERVICES TO SPECIAL GROUPS

A. The state library agency has a contract with Milwaukee Public Library to serve as the Wisconsin Regional Library for the Blind and Physically Handicapped.

B. NON-FINANCIAL SUPPORT ROLE OF THE STATE LIBRARY:

State consultants work with state institutions. One public library consultant has responsibility for service to special users.

13. PARTICIPATION IN MULTI-STATE LIBRARY NETWORKS

A. Network: Midwest Region Library Network (MIDLNET)
Financial Support: $10,000 initial membership to October, 1978
Participation: Administrator is Board member, Executive committee member, President, 1976-77
Services Used: Participation in planning, supervision, work-shops.

14. LEGAL BASES FOR MULTITYPE LIBRARY COOPERATION

There is a lack of legislation to support specific network structures.

15. LEGAL BARRIERS AGAINST PARTICIPATION IN MULTITYPE LIBRARY COOPERATION

It is questionable whether nonpublic schools and special libraries in the private sector may benefit from cooperative services paid for from public tax funds.

1. REPORTING AGENCY

    A. Wyoming State Library
        Supreme Court and State Library Building
        Cheyenne, WY 82002

    B. Chief Officer: William H. Williams, State Librarian

    C. Fiscal Year: 1977

2. OVERVIEW

    Efforts in interlibrary cooperation within the State of Wyoming stem
    mainly through programs that have been initiated and supported by the
    State Library. They include the entire state, made up of 23 counties
    and their county library systems. The Wyoming State Library is em-
    powered under Wyoming Statute 9-207.3, "for the responsibility of the
    extension and development of library services throughout the state".
    There are no regional cooperatives, although plans are being formu-
    lated to possibly implement regional systems in the future. The
    main programs of cooperation are in the fields of continuing educa-
    tion, interlibrary loan and reference, union list of state holdings,
    and telephone and teletype communications network.

3. NUMBER OF LIBRARIES IN THE STATE

    Academic: 8
    Public: 80
    School: 308
        Public: 300 est.
        Private: 8 est.
    Special: 11
        Profit: not available
        Non-profit: 11 est.

    TOTAL: 407 est.

4. STATE AGENCY INTERLIBRARY COOPERATION UNIT

    A. Unit Name: Library Development Section
        Person in Charge: Ms. Kathleen Darcy, Library Development
                           Officer
    B. There is no person charged with interlibrary cooperation activi-
        ties.

5. OTHER STATE-LEVEL GOVERNMENTAL ILC UNITS

        There are none.

6. OTHER STATE-LEVEL NON-GOVERNMENTAL ILC UNITS

        There are none.

7. SINGLE-TYPE LIBRARY COOPERATIVES

    A. Receiving Continuing Financial Support from the State Library:

    There are none.

    B. Receiving No Continuing Financial Support from the State Library:

    There are none.

8. MULTI-TYPE LIBRARY COOPERATIVES

    A. Receiving Continuing Financial Support from the State Library:

    There are none.

    B. Receiving No Continuing Financial Support from the State Library:

    There are none.

9. INTERLIBRARY COOPERATION FUNCTIONS

		State support	Federal	Total Support
1.	Interlibrary Loan	$34,800	$42,000	$ 76,800
2.	Cooperative Acquisition	18,400	20,000	38,400
3.	Cooperative Cataloging			*
4.	Cooperative Processing			*
5.	Cooperative Delivery	0	0	0
6.	Cooperative Reference	16,000	5,071	21,071
7.	Unions Lists of Serials	1,150	2,450	3,600
8.	Cooperative Storage	0	0	0
9.	Continuing Education	10,500	12,500	23,000
10.	Planning/Development	0	10,000	10,000
11.	Legislative Assistance	0	0	0
12.	Other	0	0	0
	TOTAL SUPPORT	$80,850	$92,021	$172,871

    * (3 & 4). The State Library furnishes cataloging and proces-
sing for state institutions and state agencies. There is no
cooperative program for local level libraries.

10. ILC COMMUNICATION DEVICES/SERVICE NETWORKS

    A.
Device/Service	Support	Equipment	Participants
Telephone credit card	$14,000		All Wyoming Libraries
TWX	2,000	2	All Wyoming Libraries

(continued)

11. MACHINE-READABLE DATA BASE REFERENCE SEARCHING SERVICES

Data base/vendor	Support	Terminals	Participants
Metro/Bibliographical Center for Research	$7,200	0	0

12. INTERLIBRARY SERVICES TO SPECIAL GROUPS

A. Services

Services	State support	Federal	Total Support
Access to IBM, Talking Books, Braille through Utah Regional Library for the Blind	0	$ 2,500	$ 2,500
Large Print Materials	0	10,000	10,000
Textbooks for Visually Handicapped	0	1,000	1,000
Special equipment for Physically Handicapped	0	7,000	7,000
Library materials for the Institutionalized	0	16,000	16,000

B. Non-Financial Support Role of the State Library:

Consulting services to local and institutional libraries.

13. PARTICIPATION IN MULTI-STATE NETWORKS

Network: Bibliographical Center for Research, Inc. (BCR).
Financial Support: $16,500.
Participation: Interloan for all Wyoming Libraries.
Services Used: Metro.

14. LEGAL BASES FOR MULTI-TYPE LIBRARY COOPERATION

There is no enabling legislation.

15. LEGAL BARRIERS AGAINST PARTICIPATION IN MULTITYPE LIBRARY COOPERATION

There are no legal barriers.

385

1. REPORTING AGENCY

> A.   Department of Education
> Public Library Service
> Teniente César González St.
> Urb. Industrial Tres Monjitas
> Hato Rey, Puerto Rico   00919

> B.   Chief Officer: Mr. Carlos Chardón
> Secretary of Education
> Commonwealth of Puerto Rico

> C.   Fiscal Year: 1977

2. OVERVIEW

The only project funded with Title III of LSCA FY 73 and 74 consists of the reproduction of the card catalog of the Puerto Rican Collection of the University of Puerto Rico Library, Rio Piedras Campus, and its availability to the public through five public libraries scattered around the island. It also involves the reproduction and distribution to participating public libraries of the catalog cards that are continuously being added to the Puerto Rican Collection.

The Puerto Rican Collection of the University of Puerto Rico is a non-circulating research collection of works on all subjects written by Puerto Ricans or relating to Puerto Ricans, including those living abroad. Its holdings consist of books, periodicals, newspapers, government publications, magnetic tapes, microfilms, posters, maps, engravings, documents, and a collection of pamphlets and vertical file materials. It is the largest such collection in the world.

The card catalog of this collection was reproduced for the benefit of the general public which had no access to these materials which were used exclusively by students and faculty of the University of Puerto Rico, Rio Piedras Campus.

After the card catalog has been placed in the participating libraries, the Public Library files a petition with the University Library. In return, the latter sends the Public Library a microfilm which the user reads with a micro-reader printer. After it is used, the microfilm is returned to the University Library.

3. NUMBER OF LIBRARIES IN THE STATE

(continued)

3. NUMBER OF LIBRARIES IN THE STATE   (continued)

Academic:	15
Public:	60
School:	699
Public:	618
Private:	81
Special:	11
TOTAL	785

4. STATE AGENCY INTERLIBRARY COOPERATION UNIT

    A.   Unit name: Public Library Service

    B.   Person in charge of
           interlibrary cooperation
           activities: Miss Olga L. Hernández,
                                        Librarian V

5. OTHER STATE-LEVEL GOVERNMENTAL ILC UNITS

    There are none.

6. OTHER STATE-LEVEL NON-GOVERNMENTAL ILC UNITS

    There are none.

7. SINGLE-TYPE LIBRARY COOPERATIVES

    There are none.

8. MULTI-TYPE LIBRARY COOPERATIVES

    There are none.

9. INTERLIBRARY COOPERATION FUNCTIONS

    A.   There are none.

    B.   Non-Financial Support Role of the State Library :

        There is no non-financial support role for
        these services.

11. ILC COMMUNICATION DEVICES / SERVICE NETWORKS

    A.   There is no financial support role for these devices.

    B.   There is no non-financial support role for these services.

11. MACHINE-READABLE DATA BASE REFERENCE SEARCHING SERVICES

    There are none.

12. INTERLIBRARY SERVICES TO SPECIAL GROUPS

    A.   There are none.

    B.   Non-financial Support Role of State Library

    There are none.

13. PARTICIPATION IN MULTI-STATE LIBRARY NETWORKS

    A.   There are none.

    B.   There are none.

14. LEGAL BASES FOR MULTI-TYPE LIBRARY COOPERATION

    There is no enabling legislation.

15. LEGAL BARRIERS AGAINST PARTICIPATION IN MULTI-TYPE LIBRARY COOPERATION

    There are no legal barriers.

TRUST TERRITORY
OF THE PACIFIC ISLANDS

1.   REPORTING AGENCY

A.   Department of Education
Trust Territory Headquarters
Saipan, Mariana Islands 96950

B.   Chief Officer: Daniel J. Peacock, Supervisor of Library
Services

C.   Fiscal Year: 1977

2.   OVERVIEW

Although interlibrary cooperation is practiced in the Trust
Territory, there is, as yet, no statutory enablement. The
funding of interlibrary cooperative projects has been provided by the Library Services and Construction Act, Title III.
These funds have been used to produce regional bibliographies
which, when the total region has been covered, will serve us
in the manner of a printed union catalog.

The "state" agency performs a variety of tasks such as acquisitions on behalf of all public libraries and, to a lesser
extent, all school libraries. Although the manner in which
this is done cannot be said to fall neatly within the context
of this survey, it can be said that these things are done within the spirit of library cooperation.

3.   NUMBER OF LIBRARIES IN THE STATE

Academic: 2
Public :   5
School :   45
    Public: 30
    Private: 15
Special :   27 est.
    Profit: 0
    Nonprofit: 27 est.

TOTAL   : 79 est.

4.   STATE AGENCY INTERLIBRARY COOPERATION UNIT

A.   There is no specific ILC unit.

B.   There are no other units with ILC responsibilities.

5.   OTHER STATE-LEVEL GOVERNMENTAL ILC UNITS

There are none.

6.   OTHER STATE-LEVEL NON-GOVERNMENTAL ILC UNITS

There are none.

7. SINGLE-TYPE LIBRARY COOPERATIVES

   A. Receiving Continuing Financial Support from the State Library:
      There are none.

   B. Receiving No Continuing Financial Support from the State Library:
      There are none.

   C. Receiving Occasional Financial Support from the State Library:
      There are none.

8. MULTITYPE LIBRARY COOPERATIVES

   A. Receiving Continuing Financial Support from the State Library:
      There are none.

   B. Receiving No Continuing Financial Support from the State Library:
      There are none.

   C. Receiving Occasional Financial Support from the State Library:
      There are none.

9. INTERLIBRARY COOPERATION FUNCTIONS

   A and B.   There are none.

10. ILC COMMUNICATION DEVICES / SERVICE NETWORKS

    A and B.   There are none.

11. MACHINE-READABLE DATA BASE REFERENCE SEARCHING SERVICES

    There are none.

12. INTERLIBRARY SERVICES TO SPECIAL GROUPS

    A and B.   There are none.

13. PARTICIPATION IN MULTI-STATE LIBRARY NETWORKS

    A.   There is no participation in multi-state networks.

    B.   There are no multi-state networks headquartered in the Territory.

14. LEGAL BASES FOR MULTI-TYPE LIBRARY COOPERATION

    There are none.

15. LEGAL BARRIERS AGAINST PARTICIPATION IN MULTI-TYPE LIBRARY
    COOPERATION

    There are none.

VIRGIN ISLANDS OF THE UNITED STATES

1. REPORTING AGENCY

    A. Bureau of Libraries, Museums, and Archaeological Services
        Department of Conservation and Cultural Affairs
        Virgin Islands of the United States
        P. O. Box 390
        St. Thomas, V.I.   00801
        (809)   774-0630

    B. Dr. Henry C. Chang, Director (Territorial Librarian)

    C. Fiscal Year: 1977

2. OVERVIEW

    The Bureau, which administers the five public library branches
    on three islands in the Territory, provides administrative ser-
    vices, including Research, Development and Systems, and central-
    ized technical processing for these libraries, serving the entire
    Territorial population and visitors.   Through a grant from the
    U.S. Office of Education, demonstration projects for the produc-
    tion of union lists and expansion of interlibrary loan activity
    have involved school, public, academic and special libraries.
    Plans for a multi-service network for all types of libraries in
    the Territory are being developed, primarily by Bureau staff with
    input from local and Puerto Rican librarians.   The following
    projects are in the research or planning stage: centralized A-V
    services, centralized ordering and processing, union catalogs of
    books, staff training workshops, and access to machine-readable
    data base searching services.   Through membership in the Associ-
    ation of Caribbean University and Research Libraries, the Bureau
    will act as a focal point in the exchange of government documents
    and other publications of the Region.

    There is no statutory authority for general development of inter-
    type library cooperatives.   Title 3, Virgin Islands Code, Section
    883, establishes depository libraries and requires the Territorial
    Librarian to collect and distribute local government publications
    to designated public and academic libraries within the Territory.
    Bureau staff will catalog this material for all depositories.

    Cooperative activities are funded by both Federal (U.S.O.E. grant,
    VISTA workers, LSCA Title III) and local revenues.

3. NUMBER OF LIBRARIES IN THE STATE

        Academic: 4
        Public: 5
        School: 48
            Public: 34
            Non-Public: 14

(continued)

3. NUMBER OF LIBRARIES IN THE STATE (continued)

Special: 8
   Profit: 0
   Non-Profit   8

TOTAL: 65

4. STATE INTERLIBRARY COOPERATION UNIT

A. The V.I. Demonstration Library Network project is in the planning and demonstration phase and is not at this time part of the organizational structure. As the network develops, a separate office may be set up within the Bureau, or the network may be established as a separate entity.

B. Unit Name: Research and Development Office
   Supervisor: Dr. Henry C. Chang, Director

5. OTHER STATE-LEVEL GOVERNMENT ILC UNITS

Unit Name: Bureau of Library Services and Instructional Materials (BLSIM)
Address: V.I. Department of Education
              P. O. Box 630
              St. Thomas, V.I. 00801
Administrator: Mrs. Fiolina Mills, Acting Director

Cooperative activities: Acquires, maintains and delivers audio-visual materials and equipment for the public and non-public schools in the Virgin Islands. Supplies community agencies with educational films. Administers the following Federal programs: ESEA, Titles II and IV, and NDEA, Title III. Provides in-service training and workshops for school media personnel. Maintains a resource center of professional materials for all V.I. teachers. Director serves on advisory board of V.I. Demonstration Library Network Project.

6. OTHER STATE-LEVEL NON-GOVERNMENTAL ILC UNITS

A. Unit Name: Library
    Address: College of the Virgin Islands
                St. Thomas, V.I. 00801
    Administrator: Mr. Ernest Wagner, Librarian

Cooperative activities: Developed union list of periodicals for the two college libraries and affiliated institues. The format and college entries for this list form the basis of the expanded list to be published for the V.I. Demonstration Library Network. Librarian serves on Network's Advisory Board.

(continued)

6. OTHER STATE-LEVEL NON-GOVERNMENTAL ILC UNITS   (continued)

    B. Unit Name: St. Croix Library Association
        Address: P.O.Box 6760
                    Sunny Isles, Christiansted
                    St. Croix, U.S.V.I.   00820
                    Mrs. Sylvania Golphin, President

    C. Unit Name: St. Thomas/St. John Library Association
        Address: P.O.Box 4515
                    St. Thomas, U.S.V.I.   00801
                    c/o Ms. Rose Bergamini, President

Meetings include discussions of common problems by academic, public and school librarians and media specialists.

7. SINGLE-TYPE LIBRARY COOPERATIVES

There are none.

8. MULTI-TYPE LIBRARY COOPERATIVES

There are none.

9. INTERLIBRARY COOPERATIVE FUNCTIONS

    A. Receiving Continuing Financial Support from the State Library Agency:

The following activities were supported from undifferentiated and matching local funds and by LSCA Title III ($12,000); some were supported in part by a federal research and demonstration grant ($29,500).

      Interlibrary loan
      Cooperative delivery
      Cooperative processing
      Cooperative reference
      Union list of periodicals
      Union list of 16mm motion pictures
      Planning/Development
      Outreach services
      Publications series, including bimonthly Newsletter
      Children's TV series
      Directory of libraries

    B. Non-financial support role of the state library:

Sponsor of successful proposal for research and demonstration grant which has permitted increased cooperative activity during report year and planning for future developments; contributor of staff and facilities for cooperative activities.

393

10. ILC COMMUNICATION DEVICES/SERVICE NETWORK

   A. Receiving Continuing Financial Support from the State Library:

Service	Support ($)	Equipment (#)	Participants
Telefacsimile	None during report year- to be tested fiscal 1978	Xerox Tele- copier 400	2 Public Library branches; Bureau

   B. Non-financial support role includes staff for planning and evaluation.

11. MACHINE READABLE DATA BASE REFERENCE SEARCHING SERVICES

   There are none.

12. INTERLIBRARY SERVICES TO SPECIAL GROUPS

   Blind and physically handicapped (Regional Library)
   Outreach to prisoners
   Outreach to elderly
   Juvenile services

13. PARTICIPATION IN MULTI-STATE LIBRARY NETWORKS

   A. Memberships

Organization:	Association of Caribbean University and Research Libraries (ACURIL)
Financial support:	Membership fees $150
Participation:	Regional distribution center for exchange of government documents and other publications with Caribbean libraries Indexing of local periodicals for project in English-speaking Caribbean.

   B. There are no multi-state networks headquartered in the Territory.

14. LEGAL BASES FOR MULTI-TYPE LIBRARY COOPERATION

   The only enabling legislation, passed within the report year, relates to the collection, indexing, and deposit of V.I. Government documents (Title 3, V.I. Code, Sec. 883). Other library Cooperative legislation is under review.

15. LEGAL BARRIERS AGAINST PARTICIPATION IN MULTI-TYPE LIBRARY COOPERATION

   There are no legal barriers.

APPENDICES

ASSOCIATION OF STATE LIBRARY AGENCIES

AMERICAN LIBRARY ASSOCIATION

50 EAST HURON STREET · CHICAGO, ILLINOIS 60611 · (312) 944-6780

August 24, 1977

Dear State Librarian:

In 1976, a subcommittee of the ASLA Interlibrary Cooperation Committee conducted a survey of interlibrary cooperation activities in which the fifty state library agencies were involved. Using the results of this survey, to which all fifty states responded, the subcommittee compiled the 1976 <u>ASLA Report on Interlibrary Cooperation</u>. One free copy was distributed to each state agency and territory which cooperated in the project. Additional copies were sold and the first edition is now almost out of print.

The 1976 <u>ASLA Report on Interlibrary Cooperation</u> was well received and has become an invaluable reference tool. In the dynamic field of interlibrary cooperation, however, such a report must be revised frequently to claim continuing usefulness. Accordingly, the ASLA Interlibrary Cooperation Committee has again appointed a subcommittee to produce a 1978 Report on Interlibrary Cooperation, with a target date for distribution of January 1978.

The attached questionnaire differs in several ways from the 1976 one, as described in the <u>Instructions for Completing the Questionnaire</u>. The differences result from suggestions the ASLA Office and subcommittee members have received from users of the Report. An index and several appendices will be included in the 1978 Report. In order to make the second edition even more useful than the first, we invite your cooperation in completing the attached questionnaire as fully as possible and in meeting the deadlines which have been set for the Report.

The deadline for receipt of your entry in camera-ready form is Sept. 23, 1977. We are committed to including entries from all fifty states and the territories. Since we are changing the size of the published report and since we had quite a lot of editing and re-typing to handle in 1976, we ask that you follow the <u>Instructions for Completing the Questionnaire</u> and the <u>Instructions for Use of ASLA Masters</u> carefully, to minimize the work required for subcommittee members who are volunteering their time and effort to make this new edition possible.

The new questionnaire has been pre-tested in three states and suggestions from those states have been incorporated. If you have questions, please call Beth Hamilton (312) 828-0928 (except between August 31 and September 14) or Lyle Eberhart (608) 266-2205. And please, return your questionnaire to Beth Hamilton by September 23. The questionnaire has been approved by the COSLA Questionnaire Screening Committee.

(continued)

Thank you for helping to make the <u>1978 ASLA Report on Interlibrary Cooperation</u> possible.

Sincerely,
The ASLA Subcommittee to Produce the 1978 Report

Richard G. Akeroyd, Jr.
William T. DeJohn
W. Lyle Eberhart
Ruth J. Patrick
Mary R. Power
Donald B. Simpson
Beth A. Hamilton, Chair

APPENDIX I

SURVEY INSTRUMENT

INSTRUCTIONS FOR COMPLETING THE QUESTIONNAIRE

1. Changes in the 1978 Questionnaire: The 1978 questionnaire is changed
   from that used in 1976, in the following ways:

   a) All answers will be numbered and all, including "There are none."
       will be part of the published entry.

   b) Question 2 requests a background statement of the state's interli-
       brary cooperation (ILC) activities in narrative form. This should
       be LIMITED to ten sentences which give such information as the
       statutory basis for activities and funding (or the absence thereof),
       the extent of geographical coverage in the state (for example, is
       the entire state divided into multi-county systems?), the scope of
       ILC activities, and plans for major new developments.

   c) In Questions 7 and 8, additional data is requested on each coopera-
       tive organization - full address, telephone number, key staff,
       sponsoring organization (if known).

   d) In Questions 2 and 7 through 13, if exact dollar figures are not
       known and estimates are used, please follow the dollar amount by
       "est." to denote estimates.

   e) In Questions 6 through 10, in reporting types of libraries, use
       abbreviations: a= academic; p= public; sch= school; sp= special.

   f) An index of subjects, organizations, and names will be a new fea-
       ture and will include data requested in 1c above.

   g) For Question 14, please describe state laws in short narrative form
       or by citing American Library Laws, rather than citing state stat-
       utes in full.

   h) Several new appendices will be included. One will be on multi-
       state networks, covering those identified in the 1976 survey.
       Data will be given for AMIGOS, BALLOTS, BCR, MIDLNET, NELB,
       NELINET, OCLC, PALINET, PNBC, PRLC, SLICE, SOLINET.

2. DEADLINES: August 24, 1977 Questionnaires mailed to state libraries.
                September 23, 1977 Responses due at ALA headquarters.
                November 2, 1977 Editing completed; camera copy to printer.
                January 4, 1978 Distribution of the Report.

3. CONTENT AND FORMAT

   a) Use fiscal 1977 data throughout the response; if you cannot; iden-
       tify the time period covered.

   b) Assume that "federal support" means only federal funds disbursed
       through the state agency. When it is possible to present separate
       Title I and Title III amounts for Questions 7 through 13, please
       do so.

   c) Complete all questions, even when the answer is "There are none."
       Repeat subject headings which are in italics in the questionnaire

399

SURVEY INSTRUMENT

3. CONTENT AND FORMAT (continued)

in the final camera copy.

d) Please follow the format outlined in the enclosed <u>Instructions for Use of ASLA Masters</u>. Samples of a few completed pages are enclosed.

e) Use the ASLA Masters sent with this questionnaire. Note: The blue lines will not show on the printed copy.

f) Please number your pages from 1 to whatever at point D. Also number each answer following the numbering on the questionnaire.

g) Please <u>do not fold</u> camera copy but mail it in a manila folder, first class.

4. <u>DEFINITIONS</u>

a) Academic library consortia: organized as separate entities with the goal of improving library service for participating libraries of which more than half are academic libraries which are administratively independent of one another.

b) Formal organization: one which has statutory basis or is legally incorporated, with constitution and bylaws, a governing unit, and a formal budget which is spent to fulfill the objectives and goals of its member units.

c) Interlibrary Cooperation (ILC): joint activities among two or more libraries of the same or different types which are beyond the scope of traditional interlibrary loan activities as defined by the ALA Interlibrary Loan Code.

d) Multitype Cooperative: a formal organization to allow for sharing resources, personnel, facilities, and/or programs among libraries having different legal bases and being of different types.

e) Network: formal cooperative structures which cross jurisdictional, institutional, and often political boundaries to join, in a common enterprise, several types of libraries, library systems, and/or other library agencies.

f) Single-type Cooperative: a group of libraries of the same type working together to achieve common goals (for example, a public library system).

SURVEY INSTRUMENT

INSTRUCTIONS FOR USE OF ASLA MASTERS

1. Use an electric typewriter, preferably IBM Selectric Prestige Elite #72 (or equivalent 12-pitch) using a carbon ribbon.

2. Type state name on each page. Use top line (A), typing in the name in capital letters and centered.

3. Begin typing text at point (B). Type within the margins indicated.

4. Last line of text on the page should end at point (C).

5. Type in page number at point (D). Center page number in the area shown. Begin your entry with page 1.

6. Vertical center line will help you center the State name and page number.

7. Diagrams and charts should fit into the text area between lines (B) and (C).

8. Use the same spacing and indentations as used in the Sample Entry.

9. Please type to point (C) on each page; if continuing an answer to the next page, please use "continued" where you stop and repeat the item number with "continued" on the following page (See Sample Entry).

APPENDIX I

THE 1978 ASLA REPORT ON INTERLIBRARY COOPERATION

<u>QUESTIONNAIRE</u>

Note: Please repeat exact wording in your camera copy of any headings
which appear *in italics* in this questionnaire.

1. *REPORTING AGENCY*

a. Give the name, mailing address, and telephone number of the
state library agency.

b. Give the name and title of the chief officer.

c. *Fiscal year:*

2. *OVERVIEW*

Please describe briefly the status of interlibrary cooperation
(ILC) activities in your state, listing in narrative form the
statutory enablement and funding (or absence of either), the
extent of geographic coverage in the state, the scope of ILC
activities, and any plans for major new developments.

3. *NUMBER OF LIBRARIES IN THE STATE*

Academic: _____
Public: _____
School: _____
*   Public:*   _____
*   Private:*   _____
Special: _____
*   Profit:*   _____
*   Non-profit:* _____

Total: _____

4. *STATE AGENCY INTERLIBRARY COOPERATION UNIT*

A. List the name and person in charge of any SPECIFIC unit within
the organizational framework of your agency (e.g., division,
office, bureau, or person) for which the sole responsibility
is the promotion of library cooperative activities.

<u>or</u>
If there is no existing unit, describe any plans to create one.

<u>or</u>
If there is no existing unit, nor any plans to create one,
please state that *There is no existing unit nor plans to create
one.*

(continued)

402

(Continued from last page)

> B. Within any of the other established office of the state library
> agency (e.g., Public Services Division, Interlibrary Loan, etc.)
> is there a person charged with interlibrary cooperation activ-
> ities? If so, please cite unit name and title of supervisor.

5. *OTHER STATE-LEVEL GOVERNMENTAL ILC UNITS*

Are there other governmental units at the state level which have
statutory responsibility for ILC activities? If so, give agency
name and address and description of the activities. If not, please
state that *There are none.*

6. *OTHER STATE-LEVEL NON-GOVERNMENTAL ILC UNITS*

Are there any other formal organizations at the state level which
have responsibility for ILC activities? If so, give organization
name, address, telephone number, administrator, and a description
of activities, including types of libraries involved. If none,
state *There are none.*

7. *SINGLE-TYPE LIBRARY COOPERATIVES* (Please provide separate listings
for all formally-organized single-type (one type of library only)
cooperatives which are:

A. *Receiving Continuing Financial Support from the State Library:*
    Name:
    Address:
    Telephone:
    Administrator:
    Type of Library Served:
    Federal Support:
    State Support:
    Local Support:
    Other Support:
    Total Support:

B. *Receiving No Continuing Financial Support from the State Library:*
    Name:
    Address:
    Telephone:
    Administrator:
    Type of Library Served:
    Sponsoring Body:
    Source(s) of Support:

C. *Other* (Use your own heading, e.g., *Receiving Occasional Support..,*
    etc.)
    Name:
    Address:
    Telephone:
    Administrator:

(continued)

(Continued from last page)

> *Type of Library Served:*
> *Sponsoring Body:*
> *Source(s) of Support:*

8. *MULTI-TYPE LIBRARY COOPERATIVES* (Please provide separate listings for all formally-organized multi-type (two or more library types) cooperatives which are:
   A. *Receiving Continuing Financial Support from the State Library:*
      Name:
      Address:
      Telephone:
      Administrator:
      Types of Libraries Served:
      Federal Support:
      State Support:
      Local Support:
      Other Support:
      Total Support:

   B. *Receiving No Continuing Financial Support from the State Library:*

      Name:
      Address:
      Telephone:
      Administrator:
      Types of Libraries Served:
      Sponsoring Body:
      Source(s) of Support:

   C. *Other (Receiving Occasional Support from the State Library, etc.)*
      Name:
      Address:
      Telephone:
      Administrator:
      Types of Libraries Served:
      Sponsoring Body:
      Source(s) of Support:

9. *INTERLIBRARY COOPERATION FUNCTIONS*

   A. Complete the matrix for ILC functions available throughout the state which are *Receiving Continuing Financial Support from the State Library:*

State Support	*Federal Support*		*Other Support*	*Total Support*
	Title I	*Title III*		

(continued)

(Continued from last page)

Interlibrary Loan
Continuing Education
Cooperative Acquisitions
Cooperative Cataloging
Cooperative Delivery
Cooperative Processing
Cooperative Reference
Cooperative Storage
Legislative Assistance
Planning/Development
Union Lists of Serials
Other (please specify)

Total Support

B. Describe any *NON-FINANCIAL SUPPORT ROLE OF THE STATE LIBRARY*
    for the above functions. If none, state *There is no non-
    financial support role.*

10. *ILC COMMUNICATION DEVICES / SERVICE NETWORKS*

A. Does the state library agency financially support the coopera-
    tive use of any of the following communications devices and
    service networks among libraries within the state: telephone
    (e.g., WATS, credit cards), teletype, telefacsimile communi-
    cations, on-line computer terminals (e.g., OCLC, BALLOTS), and
    other devices. If so, provide type of device/network support
    dollars, number of pieces of installed equipment, and number
    and types of participants.

    Device/Service   Support ($)   Equipment (#)   Participants

B. Describe any *NON-FINANCIAL SUPPORT ROLE OF THE STATE LIBRARY*
    in the cooperative use of any of these devices/networks. If
    none, please state *There is no non-financial support role for
    these services.*

11. *MACHINE-READABLE DATA BASE REFERENCE SEARCHING SERVICES*

Does the state library agency financially support the cooperative
use of any machine-readable reference searching services. If so,
give name of the data base (e.g., ERIC, MEDLINE, INFORMATION BANK)
or vendors (e.g., BRS, SDC, Lockheed), support dollars, number of
terminals installed, number and type of participating libraries.
If none, please state *There are none.*

Date Base / Vendor   Support ($)   Terminals (#)   Participants

(continued)

(Continued from last page)

12. *INTERLIBRARY SERVICES TO SPECIAL GROUPS*

    A.   List services to special user groups that are provided through cooperative arrangements within the state (e.g., to the blind and visually handicapped, to the physically handicapped, to the institutionalized, to persons over 65, to special language groups, to the disadvantaged, etc.) If none, please state *There are none.*

    B.   Describe any *NON-FINANCIAL SUPPORT ROLE OF THE STATE LIBRARY* in providing the above services. If none, please state *There are none.*

13. *PARTICIPATION IN MULTI-STATE LIBRARY NETWORKS*

    A.   Please complete the form below for multi-state networks in which your state library agency holds memberships, indicate the extent of financial and other involvements, and list network services used. If none, please state *There are none.*

        Network(s):
        Financial Support:
        Participation:
        Services Used:

    B.   Please list multi-state networks which are headquartered in your state and in which the state library agency has no involvement.

14. *LEGAL BASES FOR MULTI-TYPE LIBRARY COOPERATION*

Provide a narrative statement on enabling legislation and funding appropriations which support cooperation between more than one type of library. OR, provide citations to <u>American Library Laws</u> and its supplements. If no legislation exists, please state *There is no enabling legislation.*

15. *LEGAL BARRIERS AGAINST PARTICIPATION IN MULTI-TYPE LIBRARY COOPERATION*

Describe any legal barriers which prohibit or limit participation in state-supported multi-type library cooperation activities for any type of library. If none, state *There are no legal barriers.*

****

(continued)

(Continued from last page)

THANK YOU!

Please send your camera-ready, originally-typed, unfolded entry to

Mrs. Beth A. Hamilton
Illinois Regional Library Council
425 North Michigan Avenue, Suite 1366
Chicago, IL 60611

MULTI-STATE LIBRARY NETWORKS [1]

AMIGOS

AMIGOS Bibliographic Council
11300 North Central Expressway
Suite 321
Dallas, TX 75243
(214) 750-6130
James H. Kennedy, Executive Director

BALLOTS

(Bibliographic Automation of Large Library Operations
Using a Time-Sharing System)
BALLOTS Center
Encina Commons, Stanford University
Stanford, CA 94305
(415) 497-0650
Ed Sharo, Acting Director

BCR

Bibliographical Center for Research
Rocky Mountain Region, Inc.
245 Columbine, Suite 212
Denver, CO 80206
(303) 388-9261
Donald B. Simpson, Executive Director

CCLS

Cooperative College Library Center, Inc.
159 Forrest Avenue, N.E. Suite 602
Atlanta, GA 30303
(404) 659-6886
Hillis D. Davis, Director

CLENE

Continuing Library Education Network and Exchange
620 Michigan Avenue, N.E.
Washington, DC 20064
(202) 635-5085
Elizabeth W. Stone, Executive Director

FEDLINK

Federal Library Committee
Library of Congress
Navy Yard Annex, Room 400
Washington, DC 20540
(202) 426-6055
James P. Riley, Executive Director

(continued)

APPENDIX II

MULTI-STATE LIBRARY NETWORKS

MIDLNET
>   Midwest Region Library Network
>   c/o University of Wisconsin-Green Bay
>   2420 Nicolet Drive
>   Green Bay, WI 54302
>   (414) 465-2750
>   T. John Metz, Executive Director

MINITEX
>   Minnesota Interlibrary Telecommunications Exchange
>   c/o 30 Wilson Library
>   University of Minnesota
>   Minneapolis, MN 55455
>   (612) 376-3925
>   Alice E. Wilcox, Director

NELB
>   New England Library Board
>   231 Capitol Avenue
>   Hartford, CT 06115
>   (203) 525-2681
>   Mary A. McKenzie, Executive Director

NELINET
>   New England Library Information Network
>   40 Gime Street
>   Wellesley, MA 02181
>   (617) 235-8021
>   John Linford, Director

OCLC
>   Ohio College Library Center
>   1125 Kinnear Road
>   Columbus, OH 43212
>   (614) 486-3661
>   Frederick Kilgour, Executive Director

PALINET
>   Pennsylvania Area Library Network
>   3420 Walnut Street
>   Philadelphia, PA 19174
>   (215) 382-7031
>   Robert C. Stewart, Executive Director

(continued)

MULTI-STATE LIBRARY NETWORKS

<u>PNBC</u>
>Pacific Northwest Bibliographic Center
>c/o University of Washington
>Suzzallo Library
>Seattle, WA 98195
>(206) 543-1878
>William T. DeJohn, Director

<u>RLG</u>
>Research Libraries Group
>45 South Main Street
>Branford, CT 06405
>(203) 481-0369
>James E. Skipper, President

<u>SOLINET</u>
>Southeastern Library Network
>Suite 410
>615 Peachtree Street, N.E.
>Atlanta, GA 30308
>(404) 875-0745
>Charles H. Stevens, Director

---

[1]Criteria used to determine inclusion eligibility:

a. The organization's regular operations and/or services are carried out across state lines, involving <u>three or more</u> states.

b. The organization and/or its members engage in cooperative library activities which are beyond the scope of the traditional interlibrary loan activities as set forth in the American Library Association interlibrary loan code.

c. The organization's members are primarily or exclusively libraries.

d. The organization was organized for the mutual benefit of those libraries participating (i.e., not merely selling library services for a profit-making corporation).

NUMBERS OF LIBRARIES BY STATE AND BY TYPE

| State | Academic | Public | School | | Special | | Total |
			Public	Private	Profit	Non-Profit	Reported
AL	56	176	1,312	293	80*	44*	1,961*
AK	13	85	149	8	5	33	293
AZ	22	131	650	86	134	13	1,036
AR	35	40	825--------+		35*--------+		935*
CA	161	175	4,000*	300*	400*	75*	5,111*
CO	48	113	181	nav	185*--------+		527*
CT	53	204	850*	118*	350*--------+		1,575*
DE	11	24	nav	nav	32*--------+		67*
FL	112	149	1,982	1,150	41	152	3,586
GA	82	309	1,767	nav	54*	89*	2,301*
HI	22	1[1]	226	85*	8*	77*	419*
ID	10	120	377	26	3	9	545
IL	141	572	4,001	nav	122*	194*	5,030*
IN	57	239	2,149--------+		37	23*	2,505*
IA	65	500	1,794	225*	38*	30	2,652*
KS	48	304	1,600	nav	95*--------+		2,047*
KY	49	112	1,166	140	25	51	1,543
LA	32	64	1,316	nav	11	54	1,477*
ME	22	238	353--------+		50*--------+		663*
MD	48	24	24	nav	125	140	361
MA	116	384	1,882--------+		350--------+		2,732
MI	97	359	3,375*	350*	64*	46*	4,291*
MN	71	143	1,509*	475*	65*	35*	2,298*
MS	46	44	621	nav	28--------+		739*
MO	84	155	1,500	nav	87--------+		1,826*
MT	12	120	360	28	nav	33	553*
NE	34	270	661	57	105*--------+		1,127*
NV	6	21	209	6	2	29	273
NH	26	232	312	41	10	18	639
NJ	80	323	1,897	287	nav	nav	2,587*
NM	20	68	632	nav	33--------+		753*
NY	231	712	4,350*	1,200*	1,000*	250*	7,743*
NC	45	362	2,005	225	35	43	2,715
ND	13	75	545	78	42	0	753
OH	122	250	2,523	nav	73*	71*	3,039*
OK	44	191	200--------+		121--------+		556
OR	47	127	1,270	140*	15*	47*	1,646*
PA	223	380	3,317*	nav	376*--------+		4,296*
RI	13	48	379	113	30	54	637
SC	49	39	1,086	nav	111--------+		1,285

(continued)

NUMBERS OF LIBRARIES BY STATE AND BY TYPE

(continued)

State	Academic	Public	School Public	School Private	Special Profit	Special Non-Profit	Total Reported
SD	21	128	201	104	4*	34*	492*
TN	63	179	1,741	122	20	19	2,144
TX	149	381	2,997*	nav	670--------+		4,197*
UT	11	51	542	35	25*	10*	674*
VT	26	223	nav	nav	64--------+		313*
VA	87	88	1,804--------+		69	70	2,118
WA	49	77	1,970*	236*	30	138	2,500*
WV	25	123	1,370	nav	27	47	1,592*
WI	75	340	1,704	734	389--------+		3,242
WY	8	80	300*	8*	nav	11*	407*

TOTAL   2,980   9,553   65,984*   6,670*   5,675* 1,939*   92,801*
REPORTED

*	Estimated
--------+	Reported Together
nav	Not Available

[1] One system with 44 branches

STATE LIBRARY AGENCY INTERLIBRARY COOPERATION UNITS

State	Unit Exists?	Specific Unit Name	# Other St. Lib. Units	#St-Level Govt. Units
AL	yes	Library Development Division	0	0
AK	no	--------------------------	9	1
AZ	no	--------------------------	1	2
AR	yes	Library Development	1	1
CA	no	--------------------------	1	0
CO	yes	Library Development Services	1	0
CT	no	--------------------------	5	0
DE	yes	Delaware Rapid ILL and Ref. Ser.	0	0
FL	yes	Bureau of Library Development	1	0
GA	no	--------------------------	2	0
HI	yes	Research and Evaluation Services	0	0
ID	no	--------------------------	all staff	0
IL	yes	Library Development Group	4	2
IN	yes	Extension Division	0	0
IA	yes	Office of Interlibrary Cooperation	0	1
KS	yes	Interlibrary Coop, Res. Shar., Dev.	0	0
KY	yes	Interlibrary Cooperation	0	0
LA	yes	Library Development Division	4	0
ME	yes	Library Development Services	0	0
MD	no	--------------------------	1	0
MA	yes	LSCA Project Director	2	0
MI	yes	College and University Program	0	0
MN	yes	Entire agency functions in ILC	–	2
MS	yes	Library Development Division	1	0
MO	no	--------------------------	6	0
MT	yes	Library Networks Program	0	0
NE	yes	Reference and Information Services	0	0
NV	yes	Cooperative Services Division	0	0
NH	yes	Div. of Extension and Lib. Develop.	1	1
NJ	yes	Library Development Bureau	1	0
NM	yes	Library Development	1	0
NY	yes	Bureaus: Reg. Libs; Specialist LS	1	2
NC	yes	Administration: Interlib. Coop.	4	0
ND	no	--------------------------	0	0
OH	yes	Library Development Division	1	0
OK	yes	Library Resources Branch	1	1
OR	no	--------------------------	1	0
PA	yes	Bureau of Library Development	1	0
RI	yes	Div. Planning and Development	0	0
SC	yes	Field Services	1	n.r.
SD	yes	Interlibrary Cooperative Services	6	0
TN	yes	State Library Director	1	0
TX	yes	Library Development Division	1	2
UT	no	--------------------------	4	0
VT	yes	Reference Services Unit	1	1
VA	yes	General Library Branch, ILL Center	1	2
WA	yes	Consultant Services Section	3	3
WV	no	--------------------------	1	0
WI	yes	Bur. of Public/Cooperative Lib. Ser.	2	1
WY	yes	Library Development Section	0	0

NUMBER AND SOURCE OF SUPPORT OF COOPERATIVES BY STATE[1]

State	Multitypes (#) SS	Other	Academic	Public	School	Special	Single Total
AL	0	(1)	0	20	0	0	20
AK	0	0	0	0	0	0	0
AZ	1	0	(1)	13	0	0	14
AR	0	(1)	(2)	17	0	0	19
CA	0	(2)	0	20	0	0	20
CO	7	0	0	0	0	0	0
CT	0	(5)	(3)	(3)	0	(4)	10
DE	0	(1)	0	0	0	0	0
FL	1	(2)	0	9	0	0	9
GA	0	(10)	(4)	46	0	0	50
HI	0	0	0	1	0	0	1
ID	6	0	0	0	0	2	2
IL	19	(1)	(8)	(1)	0	(5)	14
IN	0	(10)	0	1+(1)	0	0	2
IA	1	(4)	(6)	7	0	0	13
KS	7	(3)	0	0	0	0	0
KY	0	(6)	(2)	0	0	0	2
LA	0	(3)	(6)	0	0	(1)	7
ME	1	0	0	0	0	0	0
MD	1	0	0	3+(1)	0	0	4
MA	0	(12)	(1)	1	0	(3)	5
MI	2	(3)	(3)	26+(2)	22	(4)	57
MN	1	(3)	(2)	13	0	(7)	22
MS	0	0	0	16	0	0	16
MO	0	(5)	(1)	(3)	0	0	4
MT	0	(1)	0	(6)	0	0	6
NE	0	(6)	0	0	19	0	19
NV	0	0	0	0	0	0	0
NH	2	(5)	1	1	0	0	2
NJ	2	(2)	0	27+(3)	0	0	30
NM	0	0	0	0	0	0	0
NY	9	0	(1)	25	0	0	26
NC	0	0	(2)	15+(1)	0	0	18
ND	1	0	0	0	0	(1)	1
OH	0	(13)	(4)	1 +(2)	0	0	7
OK	0	0	0	8	0	0	8
OR	0	(2)	0	0	0	0	0
PA	1	(11)	(4)	27+(6)	0	(5)	42
RI	2	0	0	(1)	0	0	1
SC	0	0	0	4?	0	0	4
SD	0	(2)	6	0	0	0	6
TN	1	(3)	(4)	4+(2)	0	0	10
TX	0	(8)	(1)	10+(3)	0	(3)	17
UT	0	0	(1)	(1)	0	0	2
VT	2	(3)	0	(3)	0	0	3
VA	1	(3)	6+(7)	(2)	(1)	(1)	17
WA	2	(6)	0	(5)	0	0	5
WV	0	0	0	0	0	0	0
WI	4	0	1	12	0	0	13
WY	0	0	0	0	0	0	0

[1]SS denotes multitype cooperatives supported by state, not federal, funds;
numbers in ( ) are cooperatives not funded with state funds

STATE LIBRARY PARTICIPATION IN MULTISTATE LIBRARY NETWORKS

State	Multistate Network in which membership is held	Multistate network services used
Alabama	SOLINET	
Alaska	PNBC, WCSL , Washington LN	ILL; Ref; Cat; C.E.; Con
Arizona	None	
Arkansas	AMIGOS, CLENE, SLICE/CELS	Cat; C.E.
California	BALLOTS	Cat; Reference
Colorado	BCR	Cat; Reference; ILL
Connecticut	NELB, NELINET	Coop. Serials, cons; OCLC
Delaware	None	
Florida	SOLINET, CLENE	OCLC, Cont. Education
Georgia	SERMLP, SOLINET, CCLC	ILL; Ref; OCLC
Hawaii	None	
Idaho	PNBC, West. Cncl. State Libs.	ILL; Ref; Cont. Education
Illinois	OCLC, CRL, MHSLN, CLENE	Not reported
Indiana	OCLC through INCOLSA	Cat; ILL
Iowa	BCR	OCLC; Data Base Services
Kansas	BCR	OCLC; Data Base Services
Kentucky	SOLINET	Biblio info; cat; ILL
Louisiana	SLICE/CELS	Humanities Project; C.E.
Maine	NELB; North Ctry. Film Coop.	Serials Ser; Document Cons.
Maryland	None	
Massachusetts	NELB; NELINET; NERMLS	Not reported
Michigan	MIDLNET	Cataloging
Minnesota	MIDLNET; MINITEX	Data Base Ser; ILL; Deliv.
Mississippi	None	
Missouri	None	
Montana	PNBC	ILL
Nebraska	BCR; OCLC	Cataloging, ILL
Nevada	None	
New Hampshire	NELB; North Ctry. Film Coop.	Serials; Doc. Cons; Films
New Jersey	PALINET	Monographic Planning
New Mexico	SLICE/CELS	Cont. Education
New York	OCLC	Coop. Cataloging
North Carolina	SOLINET	Cat; ILL info; biblio ver.
North Dakota	MINITEX	ILL; Doc. Delivery
Ohio	OCLC	Cat; Serials; ILL
Oklahoma	AMIGOS, SLICE/CELS	OCLC; Cont. Education
Oregon	Western Cncl. State Libs.	Cont. Education
Pennsylvania	PALINET; CRL	OCLC; ILL; Mat. Deposit
Rhode Island	NELB; NELINET	Serials; Conservation; OCLC
South Carolina	SOLINET	Not reported
South Dakota	BCR, WCSL; SD/ND-Handicapped	Data Base Ser; ILL; OCLC
Tennessee	None	
Texas	AMIGOS; SLICE/CELS	Cataloging; Cont. Education
Utah	BCR; West. Cncl. State Libs.	ILL; Cont. Education
Vermont	NELB; North Ctry Film Coop; NHCS	Serials, Docs; Film;Cat.
Virginia	SOLINET	Cataloging
Washington	PNBC	All PNBC services
West Virginia	PRLC	Informal participation
Wisconsin	MIDLNET	All MIDLNET services
Wyoming	BCR	ILL; Data Base Service